WITHDRAWN

Dependent States

DEPENDENT STATES

The Child's Part in Nineteenth-Century
American Culture

Karen Sánchez-Eppler

The University of Chicago Press
Chicago and London

Karen Sánchez-Eppler is professor of American studies and English at Amherst College.

The University of Chicago Press, Chicago 60637
The University of Chicago Press, Ltd., London
© 2005 by The University of Chicago
All rights reserved. Published 2005
Printed in the United States of America

14 13 12 11 10 09 08 07 06 05   1 2 3 4 5

ISBN: 0-226-73459-5 (cloth)

Library of Congress Cataloging-in-Publication Data

Sánchez-Eppler, Karen.
    Dependent states : the child's part in nineteenth-century American culture / by Karen Sánchez-Eppler.
        p.   cm.
    Includes bibliographical references and index.
    ISBN 0-226-73459-5 (alk. paper)
    1. Children—United States—History—19th century. 2. Children—United States—Social conditions—19th century. 3. Socialization—United States—History—19th century. 4. Children—Books and reading—United States—History—19th century. 5. Childrens literature, American—History and criticism. 6. United States—Social conditions—19th century. I. Title.

HQ792.U56S26 2005
305.23'0973'09034—dc22   2004027423

To my parents
Klaus and Joyce Eppler
who have always known how to pay attention to children
and to my children
Elías and Alma
who have taught me new ways to see

CONTENTS

ACKNOWLEDGMENTS

This book is about dependency. Studying childhood fed my skepticism about adult claims to autonomy; but I have always known that the greatest pleasures of this work come from collaboration. In the many years it took for these initially disparate essays to coalesce into a book, a wonderful array of friends and family supported me.

My colleagues at Amherst and the surrounding colleges provided inspiration in the daily ways that really count. What a boon to work on this interdisciplinary project among scholars so willing to share what they know. This book owes much to Michèle Barale, David Blight, Myrna Breitbart, Anston Bosman, Cathy Ciepiela, Carol Clark, Jeffrey Ferguson, Jan Dizard, Robert Gooding-Williams, Allen Guttmann, Deborah Gewertz, Jay Grossman, Patrick Johnson, Gordie Levin, Marisa Parham, Kathy Peiss, Emily Todd, Martha Umphrey, and Elizabeth Young. Teaching with Kristin Bumiller helped me understand the connections between my scholarship and the contemporary politics of the family; Rhonda Cobham-Sander read drafts and always asked the illuminating question; Frank Couvares gave me a temperance book from his family's attic; Judy Frank, my most clear-sighted ally, shared her passionate grip on what matters in a sentence or a life; Barry O'Connell pushed me to assert the stakes of this project; Andy Parker read drafts with rigorous generosity and invariably knew just what I should read whenever I was stuck; and Marni Sandweiss shared my love of archival burrowing—

her own scrupulous scholarship set the standard for this nonhistorian. The kernels of this book sprouted in an Amherst College class where we first noticed the odd childhood dynamics of temperance fiction; Michael Elliott and Dara Rossman were there. Karen Graves, Susan Raymond-Fic, and Julie Howland have taken care of many onerous details with much skill and warmth, and Julie proofread the manuscript with her perfectionist's eye.

The Northeast Nineteenth-Century American Women Writers Study Group has made an intellectual home—for me and for this project—unlike anything else I have known in academia. I thank all the participants in these sessions for many hours of remarkable conversation, and especially Robin Bernstein, Lois Brown, Anna Mae Duane, Ellen Gruber Garvey, Joan Hedrick, Carolyn Karcher, Mary Loeffelholz, Franny Nudelman, Carla Peterson, Jean Pfaelzer, Sarah Robbins, Shirley Samuels, and Sandra Zagavell. The Five College Childhood Studies Faculty Seminar has only been in existence for two years, but its collegiality and sense of a burgeoning interdisciplinary field provided a forum for finishing this book. I am particularly grateful to Rachel Conrad, Susan Ethredge, and L. Brown Kennedy.

There are other scholars who have been companions in this work. Priscilla Wald was on an American Studies Association panel with me when this project began and evaluated the manuscript at the end—a happy token of parallel lives. Laura Wexler taught me to look at photographs and modeled intellectual integrity and emotional generosity. June Howard gave me encouragement and shared her pleasure in the sentimental. P. Gabrielle Foreman talked with me about power, race, and desire. Amy Kaplan and I found ourselves writing about domesticity and imperialism—same time, same café—and it was Amy who insisted that I explore child death. Meredith McGill immersed me in the History of the Book, argued with me about Hawthorne, and created writing groups when we all needed one and no one else had the energy. I have seldom spent time with Pat Crain and Gillian Brown, but I have felt much buoyed by watching their childhood projects unfold. I am honored by the unusual care, sharp insight, and pungent prose with which Pat Crain reviewed this manuscript—as I revised I couldn't keep myself from borrowing an occasional verb. Gillian Brown died this fall; she has been for me an inspiration and mentor. This book is an homage to all her rigorous questions "in the name of the child."

The materials at the heart of this book, quirky ephemera, still exist only because of good libraries and librarians. I am grateful for all the help I received from the Amherst College Library (especially Margaret Groesbeck and Daria D'Arienzo), the George Eastman House, the Huntington Library, the New York Historical Society, the New York Public Library, the Library of Congress, the Massachusetts Historical Society, the Smith College Library, and the Sophia Smith Collection. At the American Antiquarian Society, throughout a decade of sporadic visits, the knowledgeable staff remembered my interests and put what I needed in my hands: special thanks to Joanne Chaison, Dennis Laurie, Caroline Sloat, Thomas Knoles, and Laura Wasowicz. I also thank these collections for permission to cite from manuscript sources. Amherst College photographer Frank Ward made fine photographs from nineteenth-century books in my collection.

Time and support for this project were provided by an Amherst Senior Sabbatical Fellowship, a fellowship from the National Endowment for the Humanities, and a Fulbright at the University of Malaga in Spain, where I owe a particular debt of thanks for the gracious hosting of Basia Oziebo. Amherst College also generously facilitated this project through a series of Faculty Research Awards.

Alan Thomas, my editor and a model of patience and encouragement, held his faith and interest in *Dependent States* over many years. Randolph Petilos and Monica Holliday have overseen the publication process with firmness and warmth, and Evan Young has edited these pages with a light and graceful hand.

My thinking about childhood evolved in the company of the many families who have raised their children alongside mine. Things learned about kids and about books with Aaron and Robin Hayden, Amy Henry and Robert Wilfong, and Shoshana Sokoloff and Jeff Rubin weave through these pages, as does the teacherly wisdom and playfulness of Jen Lindstrom. The remarkable community of Northampton Friends Meeting (Quaker) provided a spiritual ground and a place of quiet in a too busy life.

In writing about children and families one's own stands always, of course, as the place to begin. Conscious of the precariousness of childhood, I dedicate *Dependent States* to my parents, Klaus and Joyce Eppler, with gratitude for the strong and continuing support that has held me all my life. Amy Eppler-Epstein, my sister and always the best of playmates and thought-mates, inspires me with her own work combating homelessness and with her ways of making a family. During the decade it has taken me to write this book, my children have grown into their graceful and perceptive teens. I dedicate this book to them as well: Elías and Alma Sánchez-Eppler fed this project with the wonder, vulnerability, and strength of their remarkable young lives. Tending and gazing at their childhoods is my greatest joy. Benigno Sánchez-Eppler remains my companion in all this—the sea, as we have said for twenty years now, in which I swim.

INTRODUCTION

The Child's Part in the Making of American Culture

> [Nov.] 7th
> It snowed hard all day. We began to study geography this
> evening. Mama played on the guitar and we marched around
> the table.
>
> Nov. 9th
> Nothing in particular happened a most beautiful day.
> —Diary of Mary Ware Allen, from the collection of the Ameri-
> can Antiquarian Society

Mary Ware Allen writes in her diary with a careful, rounded
hand. The year is 1827. Mary, eight years old, keeps account
of these days because some grown-up thought that she
should. Adult goals and expectations discerned something
of value in these habits of attention and introspection, this
practice in writing and making order. While Mary's diary
hones these skills, it also provides her with a space in which
to give her own shape to days largely ordered by an adult's
sense of what is important. Weather, lessons, family, play are
all listed in these pages with an equanimity that has no reason to rank or distinguish, or to provide any causal connections. Is a day most beautiful because the weather is fine—
for journal entries should mention the weather—or is it most
beautiful because nothing particular happened, the splendor
of the ordinary? Thus in these pages Mary Allen gives what,

since the early nineteenth century, adults have increasingly sought in children: a sense of immanence and innocence, more immediate than rational.
Pedagogical goals may have prompted this writing, but it is undoubtedly the
cherishing of these childish words and perceptions that has caused them to
be preserved these 170 years. The project of fitting a child for the adult world
and the celebration of childhood as a distinct and special stage meet in these
pages: socialization and idealization intertwine.

Walt Whitman sees in this double attitude toward childhood, at once
ideal and in need of training, a model for the reciprocity of identity: the child
"becomes part" of the objects of the world as that world "becomes part" of
the child.

> There was a child went forth every day,
> And the first object he looked upon and received with wonder or pity or
>   love or dread, that object he became,
> And that object became part of him for the day or a certain part of the
>   day . . . or for many years or stretching cycles of years.
>
> The early lilacs became part of this child,
> And grass and white and red morning glories, and white and red clover,
>   and the song of the phoebe-bird. . . .[1]

Whitman's poem seeks a timeless universality—"stretching cycles of years"—
that, while enmeshing the child in the things of the world, refuses all historical specificity. But this idea of the child as transparent is itself a Romantic invention, a very particular historical understanding of what childhood means
and how it functions in the social world, locating this poem in a specific cultural moment just as early lilacs and white and red morning glories suggest
the specifics of season and region.

In *Dependent States* I am concerned with dependency as an issue both
of personal agency and of national or institutional relationships. This book
explores the particular history of how children and childhood "became part"
of nineteenth-century American culture, and what such "becoming part" entailed for individual children and for social structures and cultural norms.
Children appear in my study in three distinct but interrelated ways:

---

1. Walt Whitman, "There Was a Child Went Forth," *Leaves of Grass* (1855), in *Walt Whitman Poetry and Prose* (New York: The Library of America, 1996), 138. See also the revised version of this poem from the 1891 edition, 491–93.

- They are objects of socialization: taught to conform to social expectations by child-rearing experts, by parents, by schools, and by didactic stories.
- They are forces of socialization: ideas about childhood and the innocent figure of the child evoked in a wide range of cultural and political discourses in attempts to reform, direct, or influence the nation.
- They are children: individuals inhabiting and negotiating these often conflicting roles as best they can.

Thus, this book treats children and childhood as part of cultural studies—significant and varied participants in the making of social meaning. The question of the kind of attention we give to children is not just historical; it remains present and pressing now in a nation that constantly trumpets its love of and concern for children, as it cynically deploys the "poster child" to secure allegiance to any and all political agendas, and yet consistently fails to support the daily needs of children, underfunding schools, dismantling welfare programs, refusing to grant children's voices an assured role in the institutions that most directly impact their lives, and generally disregarding the rampant juvenilization of poverty. The disjunction between the rhetorical power of childhood and its lived precariousness remains as glaring and dangerous in the twenty-first century as it was in the nineteenth. These are issues of social agency and care—of what it means to live in a state of dependency—and they prompt us to think about how the wielding of children's charms might actually support the meeting of children's needs. It is my hope that learning to see childhood's complex part in American culture can help enable such redress.

Children are rarely recognized as cultural presences in this way. While childhood frequently grounds accounts of individual identity—the root of psychic life—it remains a largely unexamined and under-theorized aspect of national life. Following Philippe Ariés's monumental *Centuries of Childhood*, the last three decades have produced discrete historical studies that provide richly detailed accounts of the lives of American children, although the social history of children remains far scantier than that of virtually any other demographic group. Historical and cultural studies have tended to discount childhood as a significant site of analysis because children are primarily seen as passive receptors of culture. The predominant accounts of children's culture depict it as conservative and derivative, casting childhood as the repository of older cultural forms relinquished by adults. Children thus function as the scavengers and inheritors of an eviscerated culture, turning proverbs into nursery rhymes, making the fashion dolls designed for women into playthings, or, as with Louisa May Alcott's *Little Women,* preserving as childhood reading forms of domestic fiction more widely read a generation before.[2] Childhood is not only culturally, but also legally and biologically understood as a period of dependency, and hence it is easy to dismiss children as historical actors. The very belief in children's "specialness"—how as vulnerable, innocent, ignorant beings they require adult protection and training—thus marks childhood as culturally irrelevant.

For most scholars changes in the status of children are of note for what they indicate about shifts in social priorities—that is, about changes in the desires and experiences of adults. "Children did not initiate these changes," Mary Lynn Stevens Heininger writes as an introduction to the ways that childhood did change during the nineteenth and early twentieth centuries. "Rather the transformations occurred as a result of major shifts in almost every aspect of adult lives."[3] Thus, much of the most insightful work on children has seen childhood essentially as a discourse among adults. "It will not be an issue here," Jacqueline Rose writes in her study of *Peter Pan,* "of what the child wants, but of what the adult desires—desires in the very act of construing the child as the object of its speech."[4] As Virginia Blum recognizes, this is true even of those cultural forms, like psychoanalysis or literature, that seem most to value childhood as a source of insight and meaning, so that "the study of the child . . . becomes a perpetual re-enactment of the suppression of the actual child in favor of adult imperatives."[5] Children matter then not as selves, but as stages in the process of making an adult identity—as if childhood could only be meaningful in retrospect. Such suppressions are not only epistemological but material. Most of what we can know about nineteenth-century childhoods comes through objects produced by adults: school and

2. On nursery rhymes see Iona Opie and Peter Opie, eds., *The Oxford Dictionary of Nursery Rhymes* (New York: Oxford University Press, 1951). On dolls see Karin Calvert, *Children in the House: The Material Culture of Early Childhood 1600–1900* (Boston: Northeastern University Press, 1992), 50. Richard H. Brodhead's account of *Little Women* as "a kind of miracle of preservation, perpetuating the conventions of the previous generation's domestic fiction with a freedom from modification rare in any tradition," places writing for children within the array of increasingly differentiated postbellum literary marketplaces. Brodhead, "Starting Out in the 1860s: Alcott, Authorship and the Postbellum Literary Field," in *Cultures of Letters: Scenes of Reading and Writing in Nineteenth-Century America* (Chicago: University of Chicago Press, 1993), 89.

3. Mary Lynn Stevens Heininger, "Children, Childhood and Change in America, 1820–1920," in *A Century of Childhood: 1820–1920* (Rochester, N.Y.: The Margaret Woodbury Strong Museum), 1.

4. Jacqueline Rose, "Introduction," in *The Case of Peter Pan: The Impossibility of Children's Fiction* (London: Macmillan, 1984), 2.

5. Virginia L. Blum, *Hide and Seek: The Child between Psychoanalysis and Fiction* (Urbana: University of Illinois Press, 1995), 5.

other institutional records, child-rearing manuals, fiction, photographs, cloth-ing, furniture, even toys. There are now library collections of "children's lit-erature," things written for a child audience. But there are as yet no archives of children's writing, and most documents penned by children are scattered, often unmarked, within collections of family or institutional papers. All of which is to say that the questions of power that characterize children's social place vex the study of childhood as well. "If politics is ultimately about the distribution of power then the power imbalance between children and adults remains at heart a profoundly political matter," writes Henry Jenkins.[6] The study of childhood is inevitably enmeshed in this politics—all accounts of childhood are structured by the impossibility of ever fully separating children from adult desires and control. Still, the last few years have begun to see the formation of children's studies as a field of inquiry, with disparate work done in anthropology, education, history, literature, medicine, philosophy, popu-lar culture, psychology, and sociology pulled together in a number of thick and provocative new anthologies.[7]

The histories that we do have of American childhood tell of the gradual and uneven transformation of cultural attitudes toward children, which in-creasingly cast children as distinct from adults, their specialness valued in emotional rather than economic terms. Thus at the beginning of the nine-teenth century almost all children participated in some version of family-

6. Henry Jenkins, "Introduction: Childhood Innocence and Other Modern Myths," in his *The Children's Culture Reader* (New York: New York University Press, 1998), 31.

7. Peter Pufall and Richard Unsworth, eds., *Rethinking Childhood* (New Brunswick, N.J.: Rutgers University Press, 2004); Caroline Levander and Carol Singly, eds., *The American Child: A Cultural Studies Reader* (New Brunswick, N.J.: Rutgers University Press, 2003). Paula S. Fass and Mary Ann Mason, eds., *Childhood and America* (New York: New York University Press, 2000); Jenkins, ed., *Children's Culture Reader;* Nancy Scheper-Hughes and Carolyn Sargent, eds., *Small Wars: The Cultural Politics of Childhood* (Berkeley: University of California Press, 1998); Karín Lesnik-Oberstein, *Children in Culture: Approaches to Childhood* (New York: St. Martin's Press, 1998). Sharon Stephens, ed., *Children and the Politics of Culture* (Princeton, N.J.: Princeton University Press, 1995); Elliott West and Paula Petrik, eds., *Small Worlds: Chil-dren and Adolescents in America, 1850–1950* (Lawrence: University of Kansas Press, 1992). In a similar synthesizing, field-making move, the volumes in *Twayne's History of American Child-hood Series* provide a cogent and comprehensive overview of historical studies on childhood. For volumes that address the nineteenth century see Jacqueline S. Reinier, *From Virtue to Char-acter: American Childhood 1775–1850* (New York: Twayne Publishers, 1996); Priscilla Ferguson Clement, *Growing Pains: Children in the Industrial Age, 1850–1890* (New York: Twayne Publish-ers, 1997); Selma Cantor Berrol, *Growing Up American: Immigrant Children in America Then and Now* (New York: Twayne Publishers, 1995); Gail Schmunk Murray, *American Children's Lit-erature and the Construction of Childhood* (New York: Twayne Publishers, 1998); and Leroy Ashby, *Endangered Children: Dependency, Neglect and Abuse in America* (New York: Twayne Publishers, 1997). "The Society for the History of Children and Youth" was founded in the sum-mer of 2001, another important marker of the institutionalization of childhood studies.

supporting labor, while by the beginning of the twentieth, states had begun to pass child-labor laws and to view children working not as normative but as abusive. Gradually losing their economic importance, children came to be understood as primarily engaged in emotional work: requiring and express-ing the family's idealized capacity for love and joy. Thus as the family came to be recognized as the principal moral and social organizing unit of the na-tion, these claims largely rested on the shifting status of childhood. Child-hood—valued for love, not labor—demonstrates the nature of this new mode of social organization even more clearly than changes in the status of women, for whom love, after all, was seen as a kind of work. Along with these changes in the family's use of its children came changes in the understand-ing of the character of childhood. Calvinist conceptions of "infant depravity" and the inherent sinfulness of children, Lockean conceptions of childhood as a "blank slate" upon which parental authority must write, Romantic visions of the child as natural and as innocent as nature vied and mingled with each other. Each set of presumptions prompted different disciplinary norms: from the physical pain of the rod to the sense of shame produced by maternal dis-appointment and withdrawal of love. Assumptions about the most appropri-ate stories to tell to children varied with these changes in perspective, didac-ticism giving way to humor and fantasy. So too, these various understandings of childhood presumed different parental roles, whether to prepare children for adult worries and responsibilities or to protect and cherish them in a freer world of imagination and play.

Philippe Ariés's account of the invention of childhood as a social category reveals it to be an idea constructed by historical forces in response to more general cultural needs; thus he shows the specific utility of the idea of the child as different from adults in sanctioning the learned classes (now needed to train the young) and privatizing the family (now needed to protect the in-nocent).[8] Accounts of the shifting definitions of childhood in America show how the middle-class family constituted itself around the raising of children.[9] So too children as consumers and as commodities have been recognized as powerful forces in the economy of mass production and popular culture.[10]

---

8. Philippe Ariés, *Centuries of Childhood: A Social History of Family Life,* trans. Robert Baldick (New York: Alfred A. Knopf, 1962).

9. Mary Ryan, *Cradle of the Middle Class: The Family in Oneida County, New York, 1790–1865* (New York: Cambridge University Press, 1981).

10. Gary Cross, in *Kids' Stuff: Toys and the Changing World of American Childhood* (Cam-bridge: Harvard University Press, 1997), focuses on twentieth-century marketing to children in ways that are mindful of, if somewhat idealistic about, the nineteenth-century origins of these practices. Most of this scholarship has explored contemporary child consumers. For particularly

Similarly, ideas about children's specialness and separateness coincide with the growth of governmental power and visibility, suggesting that the welfare of children served to inform and justify the expansion of the state, creating agencies and institutions, and granting to them a new capacity to intervene in daily domestic life. Such an account sees children less as the object of control than as a rationale for it.[11] In all of these cases, to evoke the child and the needs of the child becomes a source of self-validation and power. James Kincaid calls childhood "a wonderfully hollow category, able to be filled up with anyone's overflowing emotions."[12] He is primarily concerned with erotic emotion, with the ways in which the figure of the innocent child is used to express and contain adult sexuality. But as with Whitman's "There Was a Child Went Forth," such hollowness and transparency cast the child as available to be filled with anything and everything. So Henry Jenkins writes of the "semiotically adhesive child" effectively evoked in the interest of widely divergent political agendas.[13] "If the child, and stories about the child," Adam Phillips concludes, "have become our most convincing essentialism, it is perhaps because children are as their parents always say, impossible. They want more than they can have," thus serving to express desire itself.[14] Such conjuring of childhood innocence and avidity has done little to protect or fulfill actual children; "the cherished myth of child-centeredness," as Nancy Scheper-Hughes and Carolyn Sargent call it, "conceals the extent to which adult centeredness

compelling examples see Ellen Seiter, *Sold Separately: Children and Parents in Consumer Cultures* (New Brunswick, N.J.: Rutgers University Press, 1993), on the familial power dynamics and distinct children's culture that are sparked by toy and entertainment industries; and Lynn Spigel, "Television and the Family Circle: The Popular Reception of a New Medium," in *Logics of Television: Essays in Cultural Criticism,* ed. Patricia Mellencamp (Bloomington: Indiana University Press, 1990), which discusses why families with children were the first to purchase television sets.

11. Jacques Donzelot, *The Policing of Families,* trans. Robert Hurley (Baltimore: Johns Hopkins University Press, 1997). I would concur, however, with Linda Gordon's caution that such agendas were rarely self-conscious sources for social intervention: "child-saving" agencies were "not merely a mask for intervention whose 'real' purposes were other—such as labor discipline. The child protectors were primarily motivated to rescue children from cruelty. However their own [Protestant, middle-class] values and anxieties made that cruelty more visible and disturbing than it once had been." Gordon, *Heroes of Their Own Lives: The Politics and History of Family Violence, Boston 1880–1960* (New York: Viking, 1988), 30.

12. James R. Kincaid, *Child-Loving: The Erotic Child and Victorian Culture* (New York: Routledge, 1992), 12.

13. Henry Jenkins, "Introduction: Childhood Innocence and Other Modern Myths," in *Children's Culture Reader,* 15. Jenkins describes, for example, how both the Democratic and Republican presidential conventions of 1996 wielded the child as a political icon.

14. Adam Phillips, *The Beast in the Nursery* (New York: Pantheon Books, 1998), 155. See Patricia Crain's reading of this passage as a measure of the impossibilities of what adults want from childhood, in "Childhood as Spectacle," *American Literary History* 11 (fall 1999): 553.

has displaced children" and the prevalence, both historically and now, of neglect and abuse.[15]

These large-scale cultural transitions in the meaning of childhood do not
have clear temporal boundaries, and in the negotiation of these new understandings there is much variation on the basis of class, region, gender, and
race. Indeed, in many ways ideas about childhood articulated these differences of status: childhood schooling and leisure serve as prime markers of
middle-class identity, of differences between boys and girls even within the
same family, of the transition from an agricultural to an urban/industrial
economy, and of racial inequality. Moreover, the rate at which rhetoric and
ideals change differs from that for behavior. Throughout the nineteenth century, while sentimental images of childhood as a time of delight, imagination,
and love quickly proliferated, the role of children's labor in the household
economy and the reliance on corporal punishment diminished far more
slowly—even for the white, urban middle class. Changes in the meaning and
experience of childhood are thus, in Mary Poovey's useful phrase, an "uneven development" both because ideology and behavior progress at different
rates and because during periods of cultural transition beliefs and practices
themselves prove variable, even contradictory.[16] Such unevenness is particularly characteristic of the history of childhood, because parents inevitably
draw—in repetition or reaction—on their own experiences as children and
hence on earlier models of child-rearing. I am interested in such unevenness
in advantages and development because I believe that it is in this flux, in the
back-and-forth of change with all its inequities, rather than in any coherent,
teleological trajectory, that culture is lived and that meaning inheres.

In an attempt to acknowledge and encompass this flux, *Dependent States*
stretches from the 1820s through the 1870s, from the beginnings of specialty
publications for children to the first institutionalizations of childhood as a
distinct life stage in mandatory schooling and child-labor laws; organized not
chronologically but thematically, each section moves back and forth through
these decades of definitional change. The three-part structure of this study
spins outward as well from book, to family, to nation, destabilizing the traditional binaries that would see the nineteenth-century home as a "separate
sphere." This is because another significant unevenness in the cultural meaning of childhood derives from how the rearing of children proves a primary

15. Nancy Scheper-Hughes and Carolyn Sargent, "Introduction: The Cultural Politics of
Childhood," in *Small Wars*, 10.

16. Mary Poovey, *Uneven Developments: The Ideological Work of Gender in Mid-Victorian
England* (Chicago: University of Chicago Press, 1988).

site of interaction between public standards and private life. Each chapter offers a case study grounded in highly particular materials (diaries, letters, poems, school compositions, and newspapers produced by children, imaginative and didactic fiction written for or about children, photographs of children, objects used by children, data and reports from institutions that treat children) that enable me to trace the complex interactions between children and the public sphere of political, social, religious, and economic change. The age limits of childhood remained flexible and variable as well. Howard Chudacoff argues that age only became a meaningful form of classification at the end of the nineteenth century, and he locates the earliest sites of systematic age-consciousness as the introduction of age-groupings in graded common schools during the 1850s and the opening of the first U.S. pediatric hospitals during the same decade.[17] Thus for the nineteenth century, childhood is better understood as a status or idea associated with innocence and dependency than as a specific developmental or biological period. The seventeen-year-old Charles Wiggin, invalid son of a wealthy merchant ship owner, living in his parents' home, where he seems to have spent most of his time learning magic tricks and printing out stories on his novelty parlor press, is in many ways far more a "child" than Mary Anne C., who began selling matches on the streets of New York at the age of eight.[18] My study of childhood reflects this age latitude, ranging from infancy through adolescence, treating childhood not as a specific period of years but as a set of social conditions.

I begin with children's initiation into literacy, since here the process by which the lived experience of children is transmuted into a discourse of childhood appears most self-evident and self-conscious. Childhood primers present lessons in reading and writing as forces of socialization, a means of teaching morals and forming character, far more than as a set of specific skills. While literacy claims to change the behavior of children, over the century childhood is increasingly praised for embodying what is best about the literary—imaginative freedom. In part one I explore the tension between fiction's association of childhood with imagination and the confining tropes of literacy primers, discovering in children's own diary writing a remarkable conflation of these apparently antithetical understandings of writing, as liberating ideals and punitive practices merge in a single childish sentence.

17. Howard P. Chudacoff, *How Old Are You? Age Consciousness in American Culture* (Princeton, N.J.: Princeton University Press, 1989), 29.
18. Charles H. Wiggin's Diary for 1859–1860 is in the collection of the American Antiquarian Society. Mary Anne C.'s letters are printed in the *Fourth Annual Report on the Children's Aid Society* (New York, 1857), 42–43.

As I have outlined above, throughout the nineteenth century the cultural functions of childhood were increasingly understood in emotional and imaginative terms, and any individual or historical agency attributed to children was based on this emotional power. Thus the transition from punishment to love that manifests itself in this tension over the nature of childhood literacy underlies the nineteenth-century reconfiguration of the structures and role of family life in general. If children were social actors they acted through affective ties; it was as innocent victims, by loving and being loved, by their religious faith, or their faith in fantasy, that they could reform the nation. Children can simultaneously and seamlessly function as both objects and subjects of social control, since in their state of dependency it is precisely what they lack that makes them rhetorically efficacious. Part two, "The Child and the Making of Home," details these tensions in two exemplary instances of how childhood vulnerability bolsters family life: stories of abusive parents and images of children's death. In the first I explore how the love of children inside the family might serve as a mode of social control through analysis of a frequent motif of temperance fiction in which children are imagined as capable of reforming their drunken fathers. In these formulaic stories the hollowness of innocence and vulnerability grants to childhood extraordinary rhetorical powers of conversion. Such images do little, of course, to assist any actual child. Thus the very potency of the discourses that surround childhood may ultimately prove blinding, masking children's experience. In these ways historical and cultural attention to childhood may indeed perpetuate historical and cultural inattention to children.

In *Dependent States,* I hope to find instead a method that will analyze and illuminate the ties between the powerful discourses of childhood and the lives—sometimes competent, sometimes vulnerable—of individual children. This is not simply a relation of paradox and opposition. My study of child death, and particularly of postmortem photographs of children, in the second chapter of this section shows how the loss of a son or daughter may endow commodities with sentimental meaning, the individual faces in these photographs personalizing a more general account of how childhood serves to legitimate institutional structures by infusing them with affect. Here the emotional charge of individual familial relations, a general discourse of cherished children, and a new technology bolster each other, working together to make the figure of the child such a potent force in the cultural and economic structures of the nation. This move from the family to the marketplace continues in part three, where I find that the letters written to the Children's Aid Society by New York street children reveal how these children adapted the prevalent philanthropic and literary images of "newsboys," "match-girls," and "urchins" for their own, often quite different purposes. Here the discourse of childhood becomes one of the survival tools available to individual children. In the final chapter of part 3 I look at how these domestic images play in the construction of an American empire. My reading of Sunday School stories about missionary work finds the image of angelic American children evangelizing the world paired with the conversion of these same children through stories about "little heathens." In these children's double roles all difference between agents and objects of missionary action collapses.

The tension in these chapters between depicting childhood as a rhetoric for the articulation of social norms, and recognizing children as particular persons affected and often betrayed by those very norms is ultimately discernable as a tension inherent in America's attitude toward childhood. Recourse to the imagery of childhood usually masks the institutional and structural forces at work—the evocation of childhood making proscriptions appear "natural." Studying the double role of children as subjects and objects of socialization therefore reveals how structural and institutional power is enacted in individual lives. Thus, as Carolyn Steedman notes of the child acrobat Mignon, children offer a "personification" of cultural concerns—lavishing a beguiling face and affect on more abstract or institutional forces.[19] The trope of personification is a useful model for thinking about the cultural expression children provide, because it focuses so precisely on the slippage between what is and what is not a person. The relation between childhood as a discourse and children as persons has proven so entangled because American society has so frequently employed children to give personal, emotional expression to social and institutional structures.

For adults the appeal and power of childhood appear predominantly sentimental. One goal of *Dependent States* is to revisit questions about the role of sentimentality in American political and cultural life that have dominated recent feminist analysis of the nineteenth century, including my own, and to ask what happens to these understandings if we approach them by way of children and childhood, if we see this new emotional order not only as a function of gender divisions (these too a mix of behavior and ideals), but as a product of and a response to ideas about childhood and the acts of children. I am thus interested in how focusing on childhood may supplement and reconfigure feminist analysis and methodologies. In many ways the study of children and childhood is an outgrowth of feminist work and concern, and much of the previous cultural attention to children occurred within studies

---

19. Carolyn Steedman, *Strange Dislocations: Childhood and the Idea of Human Interiority, 1780–1930* (Cambridge: Harvard University Press, 1995), 18.

of women's lives and analyses of the mythologies of motherhood. Earlier waves of feminist scholarship elaborated patterns of dismissal in the treatment of women, "hidden from history," that are comparable to the erasure of children as subjects for cultural study. The reclamation of women as subjects of inquiry has, of course, radically changed the methodology of historical and cultural studies, altering at the most fundamental level the nature of the field, the way knowledge is organized, and what counts as meaningful concerns. In these terms the study of childhood is itself in its infancy. Yet I believe that it may ultimately prove to have similarly large effects.

The focus on children as subjects of cultural analysis does not simply replicate feminist expansions of the field. Inchoate, children are often presented as not yet fully human, so that the figure of the child demarcates the boundaries of personhood, a limiting case for agency, voice, or enfranchisement. Hence for people who are not male, or white, or American, or considered sufficiently sane or sufficiently rich, exclusion from civil rights has often been implemented through analogies to the child.[20] For these disenfranchised groups claims to agency have entailed the severing of this link, the demonstration of all of the ways that they are not children. Children, however, cannot separate themselves from the logic of infantilization. To see children as part must also entail wrestling with the ways that they are "partial." Recent "Child Rights" campaigns have modeled themselves on other civil rights movements, but it has become clear even to participants in these efforts that such equations are fundamentally misguided, since one of the rights of children should be the right of dependency, the right to care, protection, and guidance.[21] Conversely, the political potency of the figure of the child derives from vulnerability and preciousness, and garners no political agency. Thus one of the transformations wrought by the study of childhood is the reevalu-

20. Diana Fuss, ed., *Human, All Too Human* (New York: Routledge, 1996), presents children as "borderlanders," "a contested limitcase" in the mapping of the human (pp. 3, 5). Anna Mae Duane, in *Suffering Childhood in Early America: Race, Nation and the Disciplined Body* (PhD. dissertation, Fordham University, 2004), undertakes an extended exploration of the commonplace equation of child and other in colonial America, assessing the implications of such analogies for both sides and for the production of interiority.

21. The 1989 *United Nations Convention on the Rights of the Child* (Geneva: United Nations, 1989) compiles the defining documents for all subsequent discourse around children's rights; its preamble draws on earlier United Nations declarations to note that "childhood is entitled to special care and assistance," "the child by reason of his physical and mental immaturity, needs special safeguards and care," et cetera. For a compendium of international examples demonstrating the utility and limits of rights discourse for addressing children's needs see Jude Fernando, ed., *Children's Rights* (Thousand Oaks, Calif.: Sage, 2001). For an impassioned argument for preserving legal distinctions between children and adults see Laura Purdy, *In Their Best Interest? The Case against Equal Rights for Children* (Ithaca, N.Y.: Cornell University Press, 1992).

ation of conceptions of autonomy, power, and agency as goals of political inclusion. Considering children as historical actors entails coming to terms with this status of the partial subject. As critics of the contemporary state have noted, independence may generally be overrated as a desideratum of civic society; interdependence or partial independence may be far more accurate terms for understanding civic life.[22] Recognizing childhood as part of cultural studies presses us to examine what it might mean to claim voice, agency, or rights for a figure who is not, cannot, and indeed should not be fully autonomous. Children's dependent state embodies a mode of identity, of relation to family, institution, or nation, that may indeed offer a more accurate and productive model for social interaction than the ideal autonomous individual of liberalism's rights discourse ever has.

Attention to childhood promises to reorganize knowledge in more structural ways as well, since childhood's status as a category of identity remains so fluid. Studies of nineteenth-century domesticity and sentimentality have increasingly resisted static binary explanations—separate-spheres ideology giving way to an understanding of the home as deeply implicated in market forces, of sentimentality as having an economic, public, and political as well as a personal and emotional efficacy. So too scholars have recognized that these social and political forms are not erected simply along gender lines— there were many culturally important "sentimental men."[23] Nevertheless, the binary oppositions of male/female or market/home continue to haunt this scholarship. Age offers an interesting corrective as a way of approaching cultural analysis, because unlike gender, or race, or even class, age is inherently transitional. We may know that none of these other categories are absolute, but they still retain some experiential boundedness. Childhood, in contrast, is a status defined by its mutability—a stage inevitably passed through. This may be one of the reasons it has proven so easy to dismiss childhood as a place of cultural meaning, to view childhood teleologically in terms of the goal of adulthood rather than as significant in itself. But it is this very changeability that makes age such a useful addition to the terms of social understanding.

22. On the problems with the traditional understandings of dependence and independence see Nancy Fraser and Linda Gordon, "A Genealogy of Dependency: Tracing a Keyword of the U.S. Welfare State," *Signs* 19 (1994): 309–36.

23. See for example Gillian Brown, *Domestic Individualism: Imagining Self in Nineteenth-Century America* (Berkeley: University of California Press, 1990); Lora Romero, *Home Fronts: Domesticity and Its Critics in the Antebellum United States* (Durham, N.C.: Duke University Press, 1997); the *No More Separate Spheres!* special issue of *American Literature*, ed. Cathy N. Davidson (September 1998); and Mary Chapman and Glenn Hendler, eds., *Sentimental Men: Masculinity and the Politics of Affect in American Culture* (Berkeley: University of California Press, 1999).

The opposition between young and old is different because however alien children may seem, young will become old, and old once was young.

The transitoriness of childhood is part of what gives it such emotional force. For adults, childhood is not only teleological, pointing toward unknown futures, but also archeological and nostalgic, recovering a lost past. As a site of cultural meaning childhood thus fluctuates between past and future, expressing desire. Even for the child, the fact that childhood is lived does not prevent it from being idealized, a thing of imagination and memory. "You're nostalgic for childhood whilst it's happening to you," Carolyn Steedman observes, and for children, too, childhood can be an object of desire.[24] Ten-year-old Harriet Appleton wrote a poem in her blank book that richly encapsulates the complexities of a child's relation to childhood—its desirability and its transience:

> "To a Picture of My Mother"
>
> Oh my Mother my fond mother!
> How kind she looks at me!
> With a smile upon her curling lip
> And the babe upon her knee
>
> I would I were as innocent
> As playful and as mild
> As beautiful and charming
> As that darling little child
>
> There's no tear upon thy rosy cheek
> No frown upon thy brow
> I would that thou could'st stem the world
> As free from care as now
>   (H. Appleton)[25]

This poem presents itself as an appreciation of the mother, but the assurance of the first lines that the fondness and kindness of the mother are directed at "me" dissolves into a recognition that it is the babe who actually occupies the mother's lap and who displays the qualities that would elicit such love. While

24. Carolyn Kay Steedman, *Landscape for a Good Woman: A Story of Two Lives* (New Brunswick, N.J.: Rutgers University Press, 1987), 146.

25. Harriet Appleton, blank book containing sketches, poems, and stories dated 1852, in the Curtis Family Papers collection of the Massachusetts Historical Society.

this poem allows Harriet to voice nostalgia and envy for the lost position of "darling little child," it also gives her authority over such babes. In the second stanza Harriet's "I would" posits the desire to return to the innocence of babyhood; but she addresses the third stanza to the baby, and there the "I would" sounds distinctly maternal, expressing both a wish to protect and a hint that the tears, frowns, and cares of growing up are unavoidable. The title claims that this poem is written "To a Picture of My Mother," raising the possibility that this could be an old picture, and hence that the baby in it could be Harriet herself. As she shuttles between the wish to be baby and the desire to be mother Harriet encapsulates the dilemma of childhood—how it proves a period of both remarkable freedom and inherent powerlessness, something to be yearned for and to escape—the precarious power of the partial subject. Indeed, for an adult reader the ten-year-old Harriet's nostalgia for babyhood can easily become itself a mark of childhood's allure. That even children should be charmed by the idea of the child is yet another of childhood's charms. Such circles of desire are implicated in the difficulties of disentangling the experiences of children from the discourses of childhood. I believe childhood may prove one of the most lucid places for understanding the relation between individual identity and cultural discourses in general precisely because of these entanglements. As the real and imagined site of becoming human, of entry into the social world, childhood is the time during which we must each first discover how we are and are not "part."

The ideal child who goes forth in Whitman's poem does not remain an abstraction; he is startlingly individuated by an act of violence. Thus, the collision in my own work between ideas about childhood and the lives of children is staged in this poem as well. After the long list of things in the natural and social world that have "become part" of the child, Whitman lists "His own parents . . . they and of them became part of him," providing a benign and stereotypical image of "the mother at home" and then,

> The father, strong, selfsufficient, manly, mean, angered, unjust,
> The blow, the quick loud word, the tight bargain, the crafty lure,
> > The family usages, the language, the company, the furniture . . .
> > the yearning and swelling heart,
> > Affection that will not be gainsayed. . . . The sense of what is real
> > . . . the thought if after all it should prove unreal,
> The doubts of daytime and the doubts of nighttime . . . the curious
> > whether and how,
> Whether that which appears so is so. . . . Or is it all flashes and specks?
> > > > > > > > > > > > > > (138–139)

As "the blow" fractures any complacent vision of the relation between child and world, marking the child as no longer generic, it raises questions about the "real" and "unreal," "the curious whether and how." The world no longer appears simply to be absorbed; the relation of self to world that seems so easy at the poem's beginning has become a site of anxiety and uncertainty. Whitman's poem is a speculation in epistemology, an account of how and if one knows what is real, and of how such questions form the self. But it situates those issues of knowledge and identity in the slap of hand on flesh, the smack of the individual against the ideal. In making these questions about "a child," Whitman recognizes childhood as a primary site for working out the individuation of self and what the relation between the individual and cultural structures might be. Mary Ware Allen's diary, with which I began, mirrors and reverses these procedures; it seems so emphatically individual and immediate, all "family usages" and "furniture" and its own precise and idiosyncratic "language." A social historian could learn much from even this brief passage about the use of guitars in middle-class households, or the intergenerational and noncommercial nature of play (traits that would be largely eroded fifty years later), or the impact of the weather on household activities, or the age at which a girl might study geography, or the place of such study in the structure of the family's day. But her diary also invites us to imagine other perspectives, to attempt to understand the sense of self and world that would distinguish these incidents, that would think that what mattered in a day was the march around a table. To recognize children and childhood as part of cultural studies is to mark as a site of cultural meaning and importance what has otherwise seemed either sentimentally loaded or sweetly irrelevant. It is not to pretend that children are fully independent actors, unhampered by the constraints of adult regulation and desire; but neither is it to see children as incapable of defining their own terms and grounds of power and meaning. I find, in Mary Ware Allen's diary, a source not only of information but of methodology, a model for recognizing value and a capacity for asserting social meaning in the lives of children: "Nothing in particular happened a most beautiful day."

PART ONE

Childhood Fictions:
Imagining Literacy and Literature

....

CHAPTER ONE

The Writing of Childhood

Childhood Reading from Primers to Novels

"It is your duty to learn to read and you must do it, if it is hard," Rollo's father explains to his young son. Rollo had hoped to be amused by a book with pictures in it, and has found instead that the book on his father's lap holds only letters and that "learning to read is hard work." The mixture of warmth and discipline with which Rollo is initiated into reading by his father, and with which thousands of mid-nineteenth-century American children were initiated into reading by Jacob Abbott's influential series of *Rollo* books, underscores the responsibility and intimacy of these lessons.[1] For most middle-class American children, gaining admission into the strictures and possibilities of letters stood—and still stands—as a principal task of childhood. Jacob Abbott recognizes that his insistence on the "hard work" of literacy runs counter to the hopes of his young readers, and even to

An earlier version of portions of this chapter appeared in Richard H. Millington, ed., *The Cambridge Companion to Nathaniel Hawthorne.* Reprinted with the permission of Cambridge University Press.

1. Jacob Abbott, *Rollo Learning to Read* (1835; reprinted Boston: Phillips Sampson and Co., 1855), 12, 10. The Rollo series begins, interestingly enough, with books about the initiation into language and literacy. *Rollo Learning to Read* is the second in the series. *Rollo Learning to Talk* (also 1835) was the first. These were followed quickly by *Rollo at Work, Rollo at Play, Rollo at School,* and ultimately nearly sixty more little volumes in the Rollo and Franconia series.

the assumptions of their parents: "If Rollo had begun to learn to read, expecting to find it play, he would have been disappointed and discouraged a great deal sooner," Abbott writes in explanation of his pedagogical approach (15). Such reasoning, and the book as a whole, presumes that ultimately reading will prove a source of delight. *Peter Parley's Primer,* published the same year, lures children to read with pictures of play (fig. 1.1). The tension in such pedagogy—recognizing both play and labor in children and in books—attests to the ambivalence of cultural transition. Abbott's warning serves too as a useful gloss on the hard cultural work accomplished through the literary initiations of childhood. To contemporary scholars, literature and children may seem to offer similarly suspicious sites for historical analysis; both may appear too much engaged in imagination and play to provide a serious vantage onto cultural knowledge. These presumptions about reading and about childhood are the product of a single cultural moment: it was during the middle decades of the nineteenth century that the American book market came to be dominated by fiction, and that the concept of childhood became associated

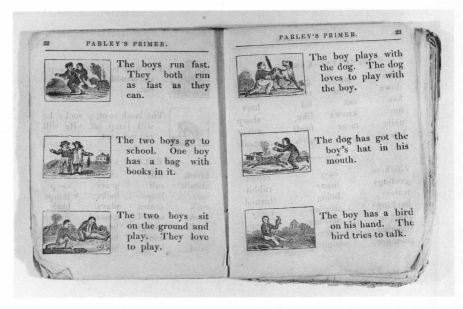

Fig. 1.1. Despite the lack of visual evidence, the Primer insists that the boy of the second passage has books in his bag, but such efforts to insert school and books into this reading lesson are overwhelmed by all the images and verses that affirm how much boys, and dogs, "love to play." [Samuel Goodrich], *Peter Parley's Primer* (Philadelphia: Henry Anners, 1835), 22–23. Courtesy of Amherst College Archives and Special Collections.

with fantasy and fun. I will argue that such changes in attitudes toward fiction and toward children are not merely simultaneous—diverse escapist responses to the same social stresses—but are profoundly implicated in each other.

This chapter explores the intimate bonds between children and literature through the conjunction of three modes of writing childhood: child-rearing manuals and school primers that proscribe, correct, and moralize the relation of children to the written word; children's own diary writing, which bears the marks of such lessons, as well as suggesting in more individual terms what initiation into literacy entails; and fiction written for or about children that demonstrates the import of children's books and ideas of childhood in the shaping of the American literary marketplace as a whole. I will focus my discussion of fiction on two mid-century authors who anchor their radically different literary careers in the relation between childhood and writing: Harriet Wilson, whose novelistic account of northern racism testifies to the new appeal of fiction as a mechanism for social change, and who uses the figure of the child as an access to individual and political agency; and Nathaniel Hawthorne, whose "American Romance" epitomizes new claims for the aesthetic prestige of fiction, and for whom children provide a significant subject and audience. In the heterogeneity of this terrain I wish to emphasize the reciprocal relations between children and books—how childhood was shaped by the academic, moral, and imaginative charge of literacy instruction, and in turn how ideas about childhood marked the emerging American literary canon.

The concept of "literacy," a coherent system that includes both reading and writing, only developed near the end of this period. It is itself an American invention, the earliest noted use being a claim in the 1883 *New England Journal of Education* that "Massachusetts is the first state in the Union in literacy."[2] Thus to explore the relations between children's reading, children's writing, and the rising prestige of fiction during the early and mid-nineteenth century is to enter a terrain in which all the pieces remain in flux. With state commitments to public education so unevenly dispersed, and with the tasks of learning to read and write still carrying different valences in terms of social

---

2. *New England Journal of Education* 17 (1883): 54. "Literacy" contrasts with "literate," a far older term of high cultural connotations; the familiarity with letters and literature it implies conjures the learned, not the schoolboy. Indeed literacy seems to have been derived as a back-formation from "illiteracy," a word for an ignorance of letters and general lack of education that has been in use since the 1660s. See the *Oxford English Dictionary* entries for these words and Raymond Williams's entry for "Literature" in *Keywords: A Vocabulary of Culture and Society* (New York: Oxford University Press, 1976), where he explains that this term was coined "to express the achievement and possession of what were increasingly seen as general and necessary skills." I will continue, anachronistically, to employ the term "literacy" as a way of demarking a system that was actively being formed during this period.

status, the links between reading and writing that we now take for granted were in the process of being forged. I suspect it is precisely because literacy was not yet fully a system, just as childhood did not carry a single stable meaning, that the kind of interrelations this chapter traces proved possible.

The standard accounts of the rising stature of the novel in the United States and of the history of juvenile publishing tend to present this relation in oppositional rather than reciprocal terms.[3] In these accounts the idea of reading as a source of play and delight chafes against pedagogical modes that emphasize studious diligence and ethical constraints. Literature and literacy seem very different things. The earliest American books intended for child readers were primers. From *The New England Primer* to Noah Webster's *American Spelling Book* they treated reading as a form of virtue. Even as the content of that virtue shifted from spiritual to republican concerns, the moral insistence of these pedagogical texts continued to inform ideas about childhood and reading well into the nineteenth century.[4] As we have seen with *Peter Parley,* there were some playful aspects to these primers; moreover, by the mid-1700s British story and "nonsense" books were being promoted by

3. Sarah Robbins offers a useful corrective to this tendency, as she traces the rise of a genre that was simultaneously literary and pedagogical: the plots of the "domestic literary narratives" she studies center on maternal lessons in reading and writing. See Robbins, *Managing Literacy, Mothering America: Women's Narratives on Reading and Writing in the Nineteenth Century* (Pittsburgh: University of Pittsburgh Press, 2004).

4. An advertisement list includes the *New England Primer* as early as 1683; further evidence suggests that Benjamin Harris had printed an edition of the *Primer* in 1690, but the earliest extant copies were printed by S. Kneeland and T. Green in 1727. While the precise origins of the *Primer* remain unknown, its reign as the dominant text for literacy instruction in the Colonial period and Early Republic stretched a good 150 years. See Paul Leicester Ford, ed., *The New England Primer: A History of Its Origin and Development* (New York: Dodd, Mead, 1897); and Gillian Avery, "Origins of the *New England Primer,*" *Proceeding of the American Antiquarian Society* 113 (1999): 33–61. Patricia Crain's *The Story of A: The Alphabetization of America from* The New England Primer *to* The Scarlet Letter (Palo Alto, Calif.: Stanford University Press, 2000), 38–52, gives a brilliant account of the ways in which the *Primer*'s image-alphabet combines scripture with more festive and commercial motifs from bawdy proverbs to tavern signs, demonstrating that the *Primer* is as firmly grounded in the pragmatic values of print shop and marketplace as in the moral sureties of religious orthodoxy, and hence illuminating the eruption of play in even this earliest of American children's books.

Noah Webster's *The American Spelling Book* (Boston: Thomas and Andrews, 1798), together with his dictionaries, presented literacy as an essential guarantor of the new nation: "a good system of education should be the first article in the code of political regulations," he explained in his essay "On the Education of Youth in America," in *Essays on Education in the Early Republic,* ed. Frederick Rudolph (Cambridge: Harvard University Press, 1965), 64. For a helpful account of uses and reception of Webster's Spellers see E. Jennifer Monaghan, *A Common Heritage: Noah Webster's Blue-Back Speller* (Hamden, Conn.: Archon Books, 1983).

Murray's *American Children's Literature* provides a succinct summary of these pedagogical trends, and the continuities as well as differences in the shift from Puritanism to patriotism as the grounds of literacy instruction.

American booksellers. Still, significant quantities of imaginative literature for children only began to be produced in the United States after the War of 1812, and it was only in the 1820s that stories for children developed what Gillian Avery terms a discernibly "American style."[5] What was most American about them, indeed, was their pedagogical moral seriousness and their focus on self-consciously American virtues—honesty, industry, independence, and piety. It is easy to trace through these school primers and juvenile stories the malleability of ideas of virtue and the competing claims of faith, patriotism, and economic success—yet the sense of reading as a tool and sign of the good remained remarkably consistent. Ronald Zboray blames the "nationalistic-moralistic emphasis of reading instruction" and the generally punitive and boring schoolhouse regime, with its birch rods, public humiliations, and obsessive drilling of dull facts, for largely squelching "students' relish for reading."[6] Certainly any aesthetic or intellectual pleasures of reading appear in schoolbooks tightly shackled to ethical and patriotic lessons.[7] But beyond this, primers insist that a child's relation to books stands in itself as the surest marker of virtue: "Good boys will use their books with care," Webster's *Spelling Book* advises; "Let me see your new book. . . . You must keep it clean," warns *Sanders's Pictorial Primer. The United States School Primer* ties care for books to material success: "This boy loves his book. He will be wise

---

5. Gillian Avery, *Behold the Child: American Children and Their Books 1621–1922* (Baltimore: Johns Hopkins University Press, 1994), 2. See also Avery's account of how the London publisher John Newbery's line of children's "play-things" were marketed and pirated in America as early as the 1740s (40).

6. Ronald Zboray, in *A Fictive People: Antebellum Economic Development and the Reading Public* (New York: Oxford University Press, 1993), argues both that the common school was the largest force in the expansion of the reading public and that it largely undermined the desire to read (96–104, quoted passages, 103). For an argument that measures the psychic and personal rather than the literary results of these strictures see Barbara Finkelstein, "Reading, Writing, and the Acquisition of Identity in the United States," in *Regulated Children / Liberated Children: Education in Psychohistorical Perspective* (New York: Psycho-history Press, 1979). See Lee Soltow and Edward Stevens, *The Rise of Literacy and the Common School in the United States: A Socioeconomic Analysis to 1870* (Chicago: University of Chicago Press, 1981), for a grim but compelling account of educational inequality by social class and the oppressive effects of the Common School's association of literacy and education with moral and social worth. Sunday schools were another prominent and moralizing source of reading instruction, and until quite late in the century Sunday school libraries would prove for many nineteenth-century American communities the most reliable, and often the only, source of books intended for young readers. See Anne M. Boylan, *Sunday School: The Formation of an American Institution, 1790–1880* (New Haven, Conn.: Yale University Press, 1988).

7. Ruth Miller Elson's chapter, "Schoolbooks and 'Culture,'" provides a wonderful summary of the anti-intellectualism of American school books and their clear preference for "useful knowledge," including the valuing of moral content over style. In *Guardians of Tradition: American Schoolbooks of the Nineteenth Century* (Lincoln: University of Nebraska Press, 1964).

and rich in all the good things of this world."[8] In 1864 T. H. Fowler of Aga-
wam, Massachusetts, marked the passages he had been assigned as exercises in parsing in his copy of the *Class Book of Prose and Poetry*.[9] The subject matter of the *Class Book* is diverse, but the sentences Fowler was asked
to divide into grammatical components reflect little of this variety. They almost all refer to the moral lessons offered by schooling and literacy themselves: "Industry is not only the means of improvement, but also the foundation of pleasure," "the good instructor teaches in his life, and proves his
words by his actions." Thus even as late as the1860s and at a quite advanced
level of literacy instruction, the sense of reading as source and sign of personal virtue persists. This understanding of the moral content of reading even
crosses the rigid boundary of race. The *Memoir of James Jackson*, rare in that
it describes the schooling of an African-American child in 1830s Boston, similarly links goodness and the desire to read; it is "because he was so good a
boy, and so anxious to begin school" that James is permitted to enter primary
school at the young age of four "before he had learned all his letters."[10] The
anxiety of reading for an African-American child undoubtedly has roots in
the outlawing of slave literacy, and the violence that met the schooling of free
blacks in the North as well as in the South. Susan Paul, James's teacher and
the author of this memoir, uses the word "anxious" three times in two short
paragraphs in her effort to describe James's desire to learn to read.[11] Present-

8. Noah Webster, *The Elementary Spelling Book* (New York: G. F. Cooledge and Brother,
1829), 37; Charles W. Sanders, *Sanders's Pictorial Primer* (New York: Ivison, Phinney and Co.,
1860), 24; *United States School Primer* (New York: G. F. Cooledge and Brother, 1839), 16.

9. Truman Rickard and Hiram Orcutt, *Class Book of Prose and Poetry: Consisting of Selections from the Best English and American Authors Designed as Exercises in Parsing; for the use
of Common Schools and Academies* (Boston: Roberts S. Davis & Co., 1863), 29, 54. .

I purchased Fowler's copy of the *Class Book* at a used bookstore in South Brookfield, Massachusetts. Fowler was in the advanced stages of his education in reading and writing (he could
parse), demonstrating that the moral strictures of literacy instruction were not limited to the
teaching of young children, just as the late date of this volume suggests how long this pedagogical model endured. In their analyses of data from Ohio teachers, who had been asked in 1853 to
record which of their students could read and write, Soltow and Stevens conclude that "enrollment in the subject of grammar was decisive in determining whether or not children were
judged to be literate." Soltow and Stevens, *The Rise of Literacy*, 4–5.

10. Susan Paul, *Memoir of James Jackson, the attentive and obedient scholar, who died in
Boston, October 31, 1833, aged six years and eleven months* (1835), ed. Lois Brown (Cambridge:
Harvard University Press, 2000), 73.

11. Lois Brown recounts the history of African-American schooling and attitudes toward
black literacy in her splendid introduction to the *Memoir*, and she ties this history to Paul's emphasis on how "anxious" James is to learn (see 21–24, and 40–50, especially page 42). Susan M.
Ryan's chapter, "Pedagogies of Emancipation," in *The Grammar of Good Intentions: Race and the
Antebellum Culture of Benevolence* (Ithaca, N.Y.: Cornell University Press, 2003), 109–42, offers a
good account of the contradictory attitudes toward black schooling in literature and in practice.

ing him as a good boy and a devoted, anxious student, Paul adopts the mainstream lessons of school's virtue for the radical cause of racial equality. What is striking about reading the *Memoir of James Jackson* in the context of other school texts is the extent of its conformity, despite racial difference: for a mid-nineteenth-century American child to read is to be "good," and such goodness is always anxious.

Since American children's books remained decidedly dour and didactic long after the literary market for adults had embraced the novel as the most desirable and best-selling literary form, children appear in literary history less as embodiments of the imagination than as brakes on the heady run toward the fictional.[12] Cathy Davidson's powerful account of America's beleaguered but enthusiastic turn to the novel does not pay particular heed to writing for children, or to the place of childhood in this cultural transformation, but many of the critical voices she cites do evoke children in their fight against the novel: "Parents take care to feed their children with wholesome diet; and yet how unconcerned about the provision for the mind."[13] Throughout the nineteenth century concern about the moral content of fiction and the dangerous excitement of the fictional form were generally expressed in terms of the risks such writing poses to the "vulnerable innocence" of "young" readers.[14] Even Lydia Maria Child, who edited one of the nation's first and most

12. Histories of children's literature tend to look teleologically toward the fictional and imaginative as a goal that American writing for children proved notably slow in achieving. See Avery, *Behold the Child*, 57–72 and 123–52 for discussions of American resistance to fantasy stories and the few works of whimsy produced anyway. Murray, *American Children's Literature;* Anne Scott MacLeod, *American Childhood: Essays on Children's Literature of the Nineteenth and Twentieth Centuries* (Athens, Ga.: University of Georgia Press, 1994); and, combining the Anglo-American traditions, Peter Hunt, *An Introduction to Children's Literature* (New York: Oxford University Press, 1994), all trace a similar trajectory.

13. Cathy N. Davidson, *Revolution and the Word: The Rise of the Novel in America* (New York: Oxford University Press, 1986), quoting the Reverend Enos Hitchcock, 47.

14. Nina Baym, *Novels, Readers and Reviewers: Responses to Fiction in Antebellum America* (Ithaca, N.Y.: Cornell University Press, 1984), 181. Baym structures her argument around the specific vulnerabilities of gender; recognizing the review as a form of cultural surveillance, she explores how "assessments of the novel still invoke the intention to suppress, or direct, or improve, the female reader" (194). Yet it is clear from the many reviews she cites that it is *young* women—or as one reviewer put it, "youthful or excitable minds" (191)—who are seen as most at risk from novel reading.

Similarly, Michael Denning's account of the efforts to control working-class leisure through the stigmatization of dime novels inevitably culminates in genteel anxieties about "their effects on young people" like the "boy murderer" Jesse Pomeroy. *Mechanic Accents: Dime Novels and Working Class Culture in America* (London: Verso, 1987), 49; quoting J. P. Quincy, U.S. Bureau of Education, *Public Libraries in the United States of America: Their History, Condition, and Management* (Washington, D.C.: Government Printing Office, 1876). Cultural surveillance of class and gender are thus expressed through the figure of the child reader.

successful juvenile literary magazines, and who included in *The Mother's Book* not just general advice on childhood reading but eleven pages of age-graded and annotated reading lists composed almost entirely of stories and poems, still feared that "it has a bad effect to encourage an early love for works of fiction." She introduces her lists with a caution against "children's forming the habit of reading nothing but *stories,* which are, in fact, *little novels.*"[15] Jacob Abbott appears similarly defensive: "It is not wrong for me to make up a little story to amuse you, if I do not try to deceive you by it," he has Rollo's father explain reassuringly in a chapter pedagogically titled "Fictitious Stories."[16] Since "the pure mind of a child loves truth," the Association for the Improvement of Juvenile Books averred, fiction would inevitably prove corrupting, provoking "evil tendencies."[17] The sight of a young child playing with a Bible incites the Calvinist pastor John S. C. Abbott (Jacob's older and grimmer brother) to a lecture on parental authority that should prevent such blasphemy, but the choice of this particular wrongdoing suggests as well the great temptation and delight even in the holiest of books and intimates that such "forbidden amusement" might be allied to the play of childhood.[18] The child stands as a kind of model reader, the strongest exemplar of how reading might shape identity and character, precisely because children are viewed as least able to evaluate or resist fiction's allures. We can thus see the genre of children's literature that developed in the United States during the 1820s as an effort to protect children from the novels that provided the shared recreational reading of children and their parents throughout the century.[19] General cultural anxieties about fiction are tied in deep and tenacious

15. Lydia Maria Child, *The Mother's Book* (Boston: Carter and Hendee, 1831), 86–87. All subsequent citations will be given parenthetically.

16. Jacob Abbott, *Rollo Learning to Read,* 97. Having taught this phrase, Abbott employs it as a subtitle in other chapters to ensure that he does not deceive his young readers into believing, for example, that rabbits can talk—"Bunny, a Fictitious Story" (111).

17. Association for the Improvement of Juvenile Books, *First Reading Lessons for Children* (Philadelphia: Grigg and Elliot, 1830), v.

18. John S. C. Abbott, *The Mother at Home* (1833; reprint Sterling, Va.: G A M Publishers, 1989), 12–13.

19. William J. Gilmore, *Reading Becomes a Necessity of Life: Material Cultural Life in Rural New England, 1780–1835* (Knoxville: University of Tennessee Press, 1989), in his detailed account of the growth in book ownership in New Windsor, Connecticut, describes both how school readers become part of family libraries (220) and the extent to which children read or were read to from adult books and newspapers (117). Murray notes the quantities of "adult" fiction read by children throughout the nineteenth century (53). Anne Scott MacLeod's essay "Children, Adults, and Reading at the Turn of the Century" demonstrates that the practice of family reading continued through the century's end; her list of the most popular books contains mostly mid-nineteenth-century and mostly British authors, and a mix of more sophisticated and more

ways to concerns about childhood; these intense efforts to separate child from story ultimately testify to the interconnectedness of the two. A young reader is a "pure unsullied sheet . . . ready to receive any impression that may be made upon it," and in this familiar Lockean conceit of the impressionable child, worries about the relation between child and book go so far as to cast the child as a book, as pages awaiting the press.[20]

This sense of the intense tie between child and book pervades literacy instruction. "My Book and Heart shall never part," chimes the *New England Primer's* verse-alphabet, and while a few of these couplets directly address the child reader (as in B's "Thy Life to Mend / This Book Attend"), only this couplet presents itself as actually voiced by the child [figs. 1.2 and 1.3]. Ventriloquizing its young readers, the rhyme requires that they speak their attachment to books. Over a century later in *The School Boy; or a Guide for Youth to Truth and Duty* John Abbott strives to convince his young readers that school-work offers a reliable measure of identity: a boy whose writing-book is all "blots and scrawls" not only "looks dull and stupid" himself but is without inner worth, "ashamed to look anyone frankly in the face."[21] *Sanders's Second Reader* describes modes of practicing penmanship that multiply errors, warning that a child who

> looked only at his own writing . . . kept copying his own faults, and made more
> beside; so that every line down the page was much worse than the one before
> it. . . . So there are some boys who never try to improve in their conduct; but
> they seem to copy their own faults day after day, and so, really grow worse—
> more careless, more idle, more selfish, or more wilful.[22]

Such accounts present training in reading and writing not just as academic skills, or even as a metaphor of moral improvement, but as an essential element in the molding of each child's character. The causal chain of "so's" grounds faults of conduct and morals as a failure in copying. Carefully fol-

accessible works: Dickens, Thackeray, Stevenson, the Brontës, Alcott, Hawthorne, Cooper (116). U. C. Knoepflmacher's study of mid-nineteenth-century English fantasy writing suggests a similar blending of adult and child readers: *Ventures into Childland: Victorians, Fairy Tales, and Femininity* (Chicago: University of Chicago Press, 1998), xiii.

20. Rensselaer Bentley, *Pictorial Primer* (New York: Cooledge, 1842), 5.

21. John S. C. Abbott, *The School Boy; or a Guide for Youth to Truth and Duty* (Boston: Crocker and Brewster, 1839), 19, 17, 14.

22. Charles W. Sanders, *Sanders's Second Reader* (New York: Ivison, Phinney and Co., 1853), 34.

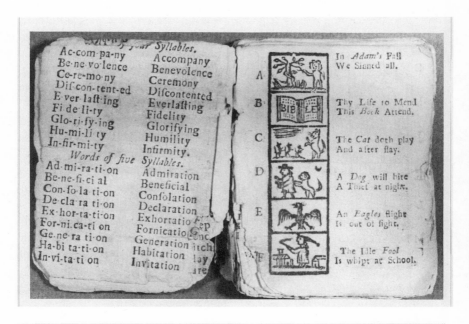

Figs. 1.2 and 1.3. *The New England Primer, Enlarged for more easy attaining the true reading of English. To which is added, the Assembly of Divines catechism*, A–F and G–S (Boston: S. Kneeland and T. Green, 1727). Copyright © American Antiquarian Society.

lowing the model in his exercise book, Eli Lee Harrison fills a page with the injunction "Follow the examples of the good and wise."[23] Even as the figure of the vulnerable and receptive "young reader" served literary reviewers and social commentators as a useful tool for policing the marketplace for fiction, this same sense of children's intimate bond to books prompted educators to present learning to read and write as acts of moral formation.[24] The perceived links between children and books were called upon to contain and discipline what was thought wayward in both.

In this shared waywardness of mischief and fantasy we can catch the glimmer of an alternative possibility that the liaison between childhood and literature might prove not confining but liberating, inviting and enabling play. Not until well into the second half of the century—long after fiction had claimed popular precedence and even artistic respectability, and the few remaining moral qualms had come to seem old-fashioned and hollow worries—would childhood begin to be associated with imagination and children's books begin to encourage fantasy. Yet children are implicated in this new appetite for fiction all along. The record-setting bestsellers of the 1850s contained an unprecedented and diverse crop of child heroines: not only the piety and suffering of Ellen Montgomery, Gerty, or Little Eva, but also Eva's sunbeam dances, Gerty's passion, and the naughty play of Topsy or Capitola the Mad-Cap.[25] As Hawthorne's Pearl and Wilson's Frado demonstrate, children became important in the understanding and forging of fiction, even in books that largely presented themselves as dissenting from the dominant tropes of the domestic novel. Thus children appear in fiction as repositories of feeling and fantasy, decades before their own relation to books is articulated in such terms. The novel's lurch into respectability rests, in part, on its capacity to incorporate the very children who were being warned away from its dangerous pages.

23. Eli Lee Harrison's copybook from the 1850s is in the private collection of Pat Pfliegler; facsimile pages are available at www.merrycoz.org/lee/Lee.HTML.

24. The relations between fiction and child-rearing are even more convoluted since parenting advice books often took a fictional form. The two best studies of these manuals are Mary Ryan's *The Empire of the Mother: American Writing about Domesticity, 1830–1860* (New York: Harrington Park Press, 1985), and Bernard Wishy's *The Child and the Republic: The Dawn of American Child Nurture* (Philadelphia: University of Pennsylvania Press, 1968). The seamless ease with which both these studies pass without comment between advice books and novels is itself testimony to these linkages. Recent work like Kathleen McHugh's *American Domesticity: From How-To Manual to Hollywood Melodrama* (New York: Oxford University Press, 1999) suggests how much the traditions of domestic manuals have continued to influence fictional forms.

25. Ellen Montgomery is the heroine of the first American novel to sell over a million copies, Susan Warner's *The Wide, Wide World* (1850); Eva and Topsy are from *Uncle Tom's Cabin* (1851); Gerty is from Maria Cummins's *The Lamplighter* (1854); and Capitola is the heroine of E.D.E.N. Southworth's *The Hidden Hand* (1859).

When, in 1872, Jacob Abbott wrote his final child-rearing manual, he went so far as to suggest not only that fictitiousness might prove "not wrong," as Rollo's father put it, but even that play and imagination could actually serve as disciplinary tools to produce order and truth. In *Gentle Measures in the Management of the Young; or,* as the long subtitle explains, *The Principles on which a Firm Parental Authority may be Established and Maintained, without Violence or Anger, and the Right Development of the Moral and Mental Capacities be Promoted by Methods in Harmony with the Structure and the Characteristics of the Juvenile Mind,* Abbott insists that the secret of parental authority rests upon the right relation to storytelling.[26] By then the "juvenile mind" had come to be seen as having "structures and characteristics" of its own. Abbott recognized these precisely as the traits of impressionability and imaginative excitability that had caused so many to worry about the effect of fiction on the young, and the gentle measures Abbott advises rely on these traits through an emphasis on make-believe and the telling of stories. The capacity to invent tales or to engage in imaginary conversations with errant balls or misbehaving dolls is an "easy and inexhaustible resource" for parents, Abbott explains, and is of "immense practical value": "there is literally no end to the modes by which persons having the charge of young children can avail themselves of their vivid imaginative powers to inculcate moral lessons or influence their conduct" (201, 204, 211). Thus when Louisa lies about having eaten an apple, recapitulating the culture's foundational narrative of disobedience and deceit, her mother corrects her with a bedtime story.[27] Her tale of two children who tell the truth about eating apples is a fiction. Even within the fictional world of this imaginary mother the only examples of apple-eating are stories of disobedience and lies: Adam and Eve lied about their apples as Louisa did about hers. Yet shamed by this tale, Louisa promises "Mama, I am determined never to tell you another wrong story as long as I live" (24). Abbott presents such tales not as deceptive and dangerous falsehoods, "wrong stories," but as the ideal in parenting and in narrative—a fiction that creates a commitment to truth. *Gentle Measures* contends that for

---

26. Jacob Abbott, *Gentle Measures in the Management of the Young* (New York: Harper and Brothers, 1872). Subsequent citations will be given parenthetically. For a rich discussion of this manual's transitional role in a more scientific understanding of child development, see Wishy, *The Child and the Republic,* 94–104.

27. John Abbott had presented a case markedly similar to Louisa's in his child-rearing manual *The Child at Home; or the Principles of Filial Duty Familiarly Illustrated* (New York: American Tract Society, 1833), where a girl who denies having eaten green apples is physically proved a liar through the punitive and revelatory powers of a "nauseous emetic." The difference in their advice demonstrates how much had changed in attitudes toward juvenile discipline over these forty years, as well as the differences in temperament between these two brothers.

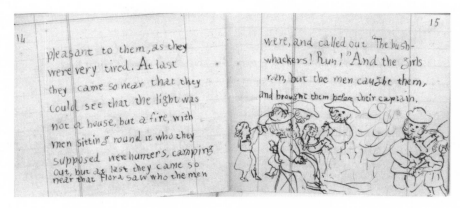

Fig. 1.4. *Flora Hamilton, or the Blackberry Party,* made by Ellen Day Hale as part of the Hale children's "Charlieshope Library" of tiny homemade books. This particular volume, probably produced in 1866, tells of the encounter between a party of Union girls and some Confederate soldiers. The library as a whole covers a wide range of genres, including many fantasy or fairy tales. The Hale children are well aware of publishing conventions, carefully denoting their publishing house on this two-inch page. Hale Family Papers. Courtesy of the Sophia Smith Collection, Smith College.

children the true and untrue blend, that childhood is in important ways suffused by imaginings, and that despite the "obligation to speak the truth" and the "inviolable sacredness . . . [of the] spoken word" (223 and 226), childhood, language, pleasure, and maybe even virtue, are intimately bound up with what is not strictly factual. Thus the links between childhood and the fictive that had figured earlier in the century as an anxious tug-of-war (books disciplining children, fears for the young reader censoring books) gradually come to be reimagined as mutually validating. As an 1866 review of "Children's Books of the Year" evenhandedly asserts, "A child is as much injured by being debarred his proper rations of fancy as of fact,—of fact as of fancy."[28] When the children of the Hale family and their friends began to create their own library of tiny homemade books they moved seamlessly between "true stories," historical fiction, and fairy tales (fig. 1.4).

"The child is always something of a poet," John Greenleaf Whittier could write in 1873, as if this assessment of "the child's creative faculty of imagination" were self-evident.[29] The acceptance, even celebration, of the imagi-

28. "Children's Books of the Year," *North American Review* 102 (January 1866): 237.

29. John Greenleaf Whittier, "Preface," in *Child Life in Prose* (Boston: James R. Osgood and Co., 1874), v. Interestingly, this question of whether or not children are "natural poets" remains very much in force in contemporary pedagogical debates; for a nice overview see Myra Cohen Livingston, *The Child as Poet: Myth or Reality?* (Boston: Horn Book Inc., 1984).

nation at stake in such comments reconceives children's imperfect or unfin-
ished socialization as a mark of freedom and a source of power. In these
terms children no longer need books to teach them virtue; instead their very
lack of conventional understanding makes them already poetry. John Bull, in
an introduction to a privately printed volume of poems written by his young
daughter, stresses Lucy's playfulness rather than her piety; clearly afraid
that anyone stumbling upon this book might think his daughter "morbid" or
"precocious," he explains that "she said that 'The Resurrection Hymn' was
composed while swinging on a clothes line" (fig. 1.5). Lucy's poem "Poetry
Everywhere" similarly came to her, he reports, while sledding:[30]

> Poetry, poetry everywhere;
> You breathe it in the summer air,
> You see it in the green wild woods
> It nestles in the first spring buds.
>
> You find it in the primrose rare,
> 'Tis in the apple blossom fair,
> It smiles in the maidens and youths,
> You taste it in the apple-juice!
>
> 'Tis poetry, poetry, everywhere—
> It nestles in the violets fair,
> It peeps out of the first spring grass—
> Things without poetry are very scarce.

The conventional link between poetry and youth proves so strong for Lucy
that she transforms the snow of her January inspiration into spring. Children's writing is engaged in learning conventions of form and content, and
Lucy is extraordinarily prolific and polished in this work; she clearly strives

---

30. Lucy Catlin Bull, *A Child's Poems from October to October, 1870–1871* (Hartford, Conn.:
Case, Lockwood and Brainard, 1872), "Poetry is Everywhere," 25. In his Preface to the volume
John Bull asserts that "in a word, she is neither morbid nor precocious" (ii). He discusses
Lucy's composition of the poems "Poetry is Everywhere" and "The Resurrection Hymn" on iv.
The hymn itself is religiously and stylistically conservative, with no hint of the clothesline:

> Come ye saints that do rejoice
> In the blessed Savior's name
> Enter into heavenly joys
> And his peaceful kingdom claim,
> Far beyond the crystal river,
> There is peace and joy forever. (66–67)

Fig. 1.5. With its dreamy background and faraway gaze, this image of child-poet Lucy Bull holding a book presents literacy as an ethereal and imaginative quality. Books were standard props of American portraiture, but it is only in the postbellum period that they became signs not of sobriety but of fancy. Frontispiece, Lucy Catlin Bull, *A Child's Poems from October to October, 1870–1871* (Hartford, Conn.: Case, Lockwood and Brainard, 1872). Copyright © American Antiquarian Society.

to write serious, grown-up poems. Still "youth" is responsible for what is best about this poem—the forced rhyme and real enthusiasm of "apple-juice!" To value this line above the "first spring buds" and "primrose rare" locates the poetic in an imaginative freedom and unconventionality associated with childhood, even though it is clear that Lucy's own sense of the poetic would emphasize conformity to literary tradition. Children's initiation into literacy exemplifies the split nature of both childhood and literature. The sense of children as inadequate and dependent, needing to be taught, disciplined, and formed, alternates with the idealization of that formlessness as truth, freedom, art. Dependence and illusion appear in D. W. Winnicott's psychological observations as the primary conditions of childhood. His account of children's uses of "transitional objects" and play in general to produce a middle space of contingent freedom between the imaginary and the real describes a mode of negotiating dependency that appears richly consonant with the processes of creativity and compliance that permeate literacy training. In noting the increasing porosity between ideas of childhood and ideas of fiction during this period, I would go further, to suggest that Winnicott's concept of the transitional object—"a resting-place . . . in the perpetual human task of keeping inner and outer reality separate yet interrelated"—depicts not only an individual psychic project but also a generalized cultural need, and one that the celebration of fiction and the idealization of childhood both strive to fulfill.[31]

The Lessons of Children's Diaries

In children's own writing, the complex interrelations I have sketched between childhood literacy and the valuing of fiction permeate every page. But in this practice the larger historical trajectory appears subsumed within the daily contradictions of these children's relation to their literacy, both the play it enables and its "hard work." The diaries I draw upon here represent a very

---

31. D. W. Winnicott, "Transitional Objects and Transitional Phenomena," reprinted in *Playing and Reality* (New York: Routledge, 1989), 1–26, quotation from page 2. Winnicott is himself clear that the "intermediate area of experience" produced through the young child's use of transitional objects "is retained in the intense experiencing that belongs to the arts and to religion and to imaginative living, and to creative scientific work" (14). See Adam Phillips, *Winnicott* (Harvard University Press, 1988), for a fine account of Winnicott's thinking here that emphasizes the sense of reciprocity and continuity he brings to the psychological processes of childhood differentiation: "the use of Transitional Phenomena was not for Winnicott, as it was for Freud, a process of cumulative disillusionment, it was not a growing capacity for mourning, but a growing capacity to tolerate the continual and increasingly sophisticated illusionment–disillusionment–re-illusionment process throughout the life-cycle" (121).

slim demographic slice of nineteenth-century American childhood. All of these children come from affluent and highly literate homes in New York and New England. Their families valued these children's writing enough to encourage this activity and to preserve the product. Diary keeping was not a general part of literacy instruction in nineteenth-century America—most children practiced their writing largely through more mechanical, less personal tasks.[32] These diaries should thus be seen as offering best instances, childhood literacy at its most personal, empowered, and liberating. The diaries I explore range from the late 1820s to the late 1860s, but to my surprise the attitudes toward writing they reveal do not square easily with the historical pattern I have traced above with the children of the 1820s stressing literacy's moral lessons and those who write later in the century probing its imaginative possibilities. Instead, virtually all of these children fluctuate in their writing between presenting literacy as a discipline and finding in the act of writing an invitation to imagine and play. If writing still largely figures in these journals as something to worry about, a measure for reckoning moral and pedagogical worth, it is not only that. The glee, anxiety, and drudgery of writing collide on these pages, attesting to the contradictions in social attitudes toward both literacy and childhood.

As for the basic mechanics of writing, penmanship, children's diaries are far easier to read than most nineteenth-century manuscripts. Engaged in the process of learning to write, lessons that traditionally consisted of repetitively tracing the letters of a standard school hand, young writers may be hesitant or uneven in forming their letters, but they are usually far more careful and the shapes of their letters more standard than are those of more individual-

32. Bronson Alcott at the Temple Street School, Thoreau with his students in Concord, and Margaret Fuller at the Green Street School all famously required their students to keep diaries, but these schools were sites of radical educational experimentation, and student comments in the diaries that survive as well as Elizabeth Peabody's defense of the practice at Temple Street all suggest how unusual these expectations for self-exploration were within the context of literacy training. See Elizabeth Peabody, *Record of a School: Exemplifying the General Principles of Spiritual Culture* (Boston: J. Munroe, 1835); Daniel Shealy, "Margaret Fuller and her 'Maiden': Evelina Metcalf's 1838 School Journal" and Paula Kopacz, "The School Journal of Hannah (Anna) Gale" (both kept for Fuller's class), in *Studies in the American Renaissance*, ed. Joel Myerson (Charlottesville: University Press of Virginia, 1996); and the diary Edmund Quincy Sewall kept while being taught by John and Henry David Thoreau in 1840, in the collection of the American Antiquarian Society. Harriet Appleton's school compositions, preserved in the Curtis Family Papers collection of the Massachusetts Historical Society, includes a diary kept as a school assignment for November 12–28, 1855, but unlike the more introspective diaries urged by Alcott, Fuller, and the Thoreau brothers, this diary is specifically objective and informative rather than personal, since Harriet has been assigned to record one interesting piece of information learned each day.

ized adult hands.[33] The diaries reveal the children's clear pride in their signatures and authorship, and a sense of the space for self-invention afforded
by writing. Louisa Jane Trumbull, whose family called her Jenny, begins her
first diary at age seven by writing, with high seriousness, "Born October 12th
1822, Louisa Jane Trumbull" on the top of the first page; on page 19, now
ten, she tries writing her full name as if on a printed sign, all capitals with
each letter painstakingly made of dots, but gives up at the "r" of Trumbull. Eli
Harrison adds various versions of his name on many pages of his copybook,
personalizing these routine lessons. Thirteen-year-old "Sam" Bigelow, still
enough of a boy to fill his diary with snowball fights, ball games, traps for
bobolinks, and spats with siblings, decorates the covers of the inexpensive
paper-bound blank-books he employs for his journal with an array of signatures: "Samuel A. Bigelow," "Master Samuel A. Bigelow," or the quite elab-
orately penned "Hon. S. Augustus B." It is with a somewhat more serious
sense of impersonating futures that sixteen-year-old Greely Stevenson Curtis,
still at school, practices writing his name "Mr. G. S. Curtis" "Boston" "New
York" "The Bank" scattered in a far more elegant hand than his usual writing down an otherwise blank page.[34] Writing serves these young people as a
tool for conjuring more adult selves.

These youthful self-namings reveal the power and pleasure of writing,
but the obvious laboriousness of their hands betrays the extent to which writing is for most of these children a still-developing skill. They recognize the
acquisition of these skills as boon and responsibility. Mary Ware Allen, at
eight, revels in her own grown-up prowess and the noteworthiness of literacy, as she records as the only event of a day that her little sister "Lucy said
all her letters."[35] These children's relation to their journals and to writing

33. See Meredith McGill, "The Duplicity of the Pen," in *Language Machines: Technologies of Literacy and Cultural Production,* ed. Jeffrey Masten, Peter Stallybrass, and Nancy Vickers (New York: Routledge, 1997), for a discussion of the production of individuality through the copying of a standardized hand. Thomas Augst, in his rich and insightful study of the literary practices of young men pursuing work as clerks, notes both the clear consistency of their cleri-cal hands and the way that upon becoming successful professionals or businessmen they may allow these studied hands to degenerate into more individual and illegible scrawls. Augst, *The Clerk's Tale: Young Men and Moral Life in Nineteenth-Century America* (Chicago: University of Chicago Press, 2003), 80.

34. Louisa Jane Trumbull's diaries from 1829 through 1837 are in the Trumbull Family Pa-pers collection of the American Antiquarian Society. The diaries of Samuel A. Bigelow from 1851 and 1852 are in the "Bigelow" collection of the Massachusetts Historical Society. Greely Stevenson Curtis's diaries for 1846 and 1847 are in the Curtis Family Papers collection of the Massachusetts Historical Society; these signatures come on the page after the entry for Feb-ruary 24, 1847.

35. Allen, November 19, 1827.

itself is one of the most frequent topics of their daily entries. In these comments they often sound like literacy primers, presenting their journals as opportunities to practice and improve their skills in penmanship and composition. Lucy Bull's somewhat satiric poem "Mabel's Good Behavior" allies penmanship with the patterned copying of other virtues:

> Very neat was her handwriting;
>   She could write as well as Lou—
> Never quarreling, never fighting,
>   Mabel is the pattern for you.
>   (24)

The act of writing remains self-conscious for children, and their obvious effort to learn to write makes the expectations and significance attached to literacy visible in ways that they would never be in more practiced hands.

These pages sport not only plenty of the "blots and scrawls" that John Abbott portrayed as moral blemishes in *The School Boy,* but also many passages in which children criticize, apologize for, and try to justify splattered ink and poor handwriting. "While I was writing yesterdays Journal John tripped over the ink box and spilled the ink," Sam Bigelow explains below a splotch. That he feels the need to offer such an excuse reflects the fact that blots are punishable offences at school; "I had to stay into recess for my writing, I got a blot on my book," Sam complains a few weeks later. Still Sam comes to recognize the practice in writing offered by his journal as less punitive and perfectionist than other forums. On the first pages of his first journal he writes with great care, "I began my journal to day it is rather cloudey to-day this morning," and his early pages are full of corrections that strive for an improved style. But by the end of 1851, Sam's first year of journal writing, his penmanship has become less careful and he will go for pages making no corrections at all, certainly nothing of the stylistic nicety that would change a repetitive "today" for a fresh "this morning." He recognizes his journal as a pedagogical tool, conjoined to schoolroom rigors, but it is also evidently a somewhat freer space where lapses do not bar him from recess and where the constant requirements of self-correction are not quite so heavy.[36] Grenville Norcross keeps a diary each year from his seventh birthday through his sixteenth. At some point he copies over the smudged pencil journal he kept the year he was eight, correcting mistakes and adding explanatory footnotes. Occasionally he notes how he has fixed his grammar, recording how the passage

---

36. Bigelow, entries for April 26, May 9, and January 6, 1851.

read "originally," at the bottom of the page. Preserving his youthful errors even as he corrects them, Grenville reveals the layered nature of his relation to literacy acquisition—allowing him to appear in this journal as both novice and master.[37]

In a kaleidoscope of literacy lessons, Jenny Trumbull copied a school composition "On Letter Writing" into her journal as a means of preserving it "that I may have it to read at some future time," noting with pride that "this is the first composition which I ever wrote." Jenny's use of her journal to keep things that matter to her, that a school composition matters in this way, that in it she should write about writing, all reflect her sense of the importance of writing as a sort of receptacle and measure of self. In her composition writing well is presented as a mark of propriety and gentility, a sign of class more than of ethics.

> Before you write a sentence examine it to see that there is nothing improper or vulgar in it. To write a letter with negligence without proper stops crooked lines and great flourishes is inelegant. When a letter is written thus the common apology is "you must excuse the writing. I have a very bad pen." or "I am in a great hurry."

Later that year, amidst a splattering of ink, Jenny would take recourse to these very excuses:

> I never knew such awful horr'd pens as these sticks but I am in hopes that the rest of this page in fact the rest of this book will look better and be written as wel if not better than the best that is written in this book or this journal which is in fact a book.

The question of the status of her writing—if she writes in a blank book does that make this journal a book?—highlights Jenny's intent to create a lasting record of herself, and hence the desire for her writing to "look better" does find in these appearances both a bookmaker's pride and a kind of moral force. A later entry produced in Jenny's very best handwriting elaborates her sense of journal-writing as a mechanism of moral examination:

> Another week has passed away and another evening devoted to writing in my journal has come round it seems proper that I should view my conduct of the

37. Grenville H. Norcross, Diary, see for example January 17, 1862, where "the way we did it*" is annotated at the bottom of the page "*originally done." Norcross diaries for 1860–1876 are in the collection of the American Antiquarian Society.

past week and to form some good resolutions for the preceding. Have I improved any? Am I a better child? If so I have not lived in vain.[38]

In the extreme meticulousness of this page, Jenny's care in writing well is an important part of the answer she provides to the questions concerning self-improvement. Jenny undoubtedly intends larger ethical concerns than good penmanship when she reviews her week's conduct; still, just as the practice of journal-keeping invites these rituals of introspection and seems the "proper" use of these pages, the ideological linking of literacy with virtue makes it all but impossible to assess oneself a "better child" on a blotted page (figs. 1.6 and 1.7).

These children's commitment to literacy is thus hedged round with anxieties, with questions of moral and social worth. This double bind is particularly evident in their accounts of schooling, where children's assertions of the importance of their studies are frequently juxtaposed with largely discouraged accounts of their experiences with the process. "School will begin Monday, Oh dear!" Jenny Trumbull writes. "I am sure that I don't want to go to school to learn Geography and History!" Her exclamations suggest perhaps some excitement as well as worry. Grenville Norcross spends August at the beach, where his diary records that amongst his many holiday amusements he "Played school," but once school actually begins in September he has little to say about it beyond the fact that he "went."[39] Nowhere does an idealized sense of school's value collide more painfully with its daily grind than in the little notebook kept by William Henry Potter during his school year at an academy in Colchester, Connecticut, in 1836.

> The sun rose this morning upon the finest ~~morning~~ the vernal season has yet disbursed and reminded me that today were to ᵇᵉ thrown open the portals of our academic halls—today were we to commence a new term xxxxx today to meet old friends and see new faces xxxxx today to draw our study chairs nearer the tables and our minds nearer our books.

Potter labels the cover of his little book "Pursuits," and the pages that follow this celebration of minds drawn nearer to books provides a detailed timetable of his school assignments, and of the hours he dedicates—or plans to dedicate—to studying them. The gap between his opening passage, which seeks to cast his school experience within the elegant periods of the Latin rhetoric

38. Trumbull, February 12, November undated 1833, and February 22, 1834.
39. Trumbull, November 8, 1829; Grenville H. Norcross, August 14, 1861.

was own hand — I never knows such dutiful hands fends These pretty bad - I am in hopes that the rest of this page in fact the rest of this book will look better and be written as well if not better than the but that is written in this book on this journal which is in fact a book I must stop for the present as written I have otherwise en- joyments." — "Poor Johnny Vanderbroeker" - - "There is Lucy'

§ 2
"Worcester. Saturday evening. February 22d 1834. Another week has passed away and another evening devoted to writing in my journal has come round - it seems fit and proper that I should review my conduct of the past week and to form some good resolutions for the preceding - Have I improved any; Am I a better child? If so I have not lived in vain. If not I have offended my Maker and Preserver - May the next week be passed more profitably and may it be daily preparing my= self to meet the great and universal Judge at the last day before the Judgement seat of Christ. May my conduct on this earth be such that I can meet death with composure and with pleasure - My

he would be learning in Colchester, contrasts painfully with the anxiety that pervades his lists of assignments: "Rose @ 6—(2 hours too late)" he begins one day's entry; "if I get to studying by 5 or ¼ 5 in the morning I will proceed thus," starts another.[40] William is serious about his schooling, and his sense of its importance informs the care he takes in organizing his days. He evidently sees this diary as a tool for improving his academic performance; the diary itself is very much part of his education, even as it records the difficulty of mastery, how he feels always behind his and his teachers' expectations.

Twelve-year-old Louis Pope Gratacap balances his aversion to school with a dutiful sense of its future worth.

> I got up this morning feeling very miserable because it was so near Monday when I would have to go to school . . . getting up at the outlandish time of six o'clock for 6 ½ months through Rain, and Snow, and Hail, it was perfectly abominable but then I remembered that I was now laying the foundation to my future studies, I am now preparing my brain so that in after years I may be perhaps a learned man.

Louis's sense of schooling as "the foundation to my future" echoes endless advice-books and primers, and like William's elaborate opening, the language for celebrating school recites school's lessons. The topic of school seems to demand that the emphatic personality of "outlandish" and "abominable," the parodic/heroic excess of "Rain, Snow, and Hail," be replaced with pious clichés. Louis "remembered" this phrase, as children might recall the *New England Primer's* similar ventriloquy "My Book and Heart shall never part," and in accepting this lesson he records a kind of conversion, the past tense of his complaints giving way to the present affirmation of "I am now." It is impossible to be sure of the tone of Louis's capitulation, there may be an ironic edge to this sudden remembering of school's value, but in any case, go he must, and the next few weeks of entries display real pleasure in his learning as well as accounts of school's dullness and injustice.[41] Lilian Brinstool's use of her 1871 *Union Speller* sides more emphatically with pleasure. She practiced her penmanship by copying between the lines in her own

40. William Henry Potter, Diary, opening passage May 19, 1836, entries for September 30 and December 18, 1836, in the collection of the New York Public Library.

41. Louis Pope Gratacap, Diary, January 2, 1863, in the collection of the New York Public Library. On January 13 he expresses surprise and pride in having made "quite a respectable" map of South America, a change he notes from the usual definitions. On January 20 he complains, "Today I was kept in an unusual thing and a mean thing, for they had no business to keep me in."

quite competent imitation of the Spencerian script being taught in these pages, showing herself to be a good student of these lessons. But she also made her own end-paper for her speller, pasting into the cover a piece of black cloth decorated with her whimsical drawings. "Art and Invention," she writes along the edge of the first of these figures, as if to count her doodles among the tropes learned in rhetoric class, and so to insist on her capacity to transform even the dullest of school tasks into a kind of play (fig. 1.8).

The variety of values these children discern in writing and schooling is echoed as well in their records of their reading. Jenny Trumbull keeps track at the end of her journal of all the books she has read. Her list is interesting in itself, ranging from anthologies assembled for children like *The Juvenile Forget Me Not* and Peter Parley books to the novels of Sir Walter Scott, but it also demonstrates the enclosed self-reflexiveness of these literacy practices, how much children too see what they read and the fact that they read as a significant part of who they are. Sam Bigelow boasts of the pace of his reading: "Dexter broart me a piece of a book the name of which was Brislot Bill after I came home I sat down and red it through."[42] I suspect that what Dexter lent him was the *Life and Exploits of the Noted Criminal Bristol Bill,* which would suggest that reading even "bad books" of bank robbery and counterfeiting nevertheless seems to Sam a mark of his goodness—he is, after all, avidly reading.[43] Seven-year-old Grenville Norcross tells how "Florie began the 'Castaways' reading aloud to Willie and myself, Willie and myself taking our turn of reading"—a model of family reading that Lydia Maria Child advocated in *The Mother's Book* as "extremely beneficial," and one that makes Grenville feel proud to take his turn.[44] On another visit from Florie the children "get out the village and played the 'Swiss Family Robinson,'" the pleasure they take in these toy houses structured by their shared reading.[45] The Hale children make a different use of *The Swiss Family Robinson,* basing one of the volumes in their tiny homemade library on these famous adventures;

42. Bigelow, January 27, 1851.

43. The Greenhorn [George Thompson], *Life and Exploits of the Noted Criminal Bristol Bill* (New York: M. J. Ivers, 1851). I have found nothing under "Brislot Bill" in either the collection of the American Antiquarian Society or the Library of Congress, but the date is right and this sort of flipping of letters occurs often in the Bigelow diaries. Like many dime novels, the exploits of Bristol Bill are scattered with moral commentary, in a not very convincing effort to frame this adventure story as a cautionary tale.

44. Child, *Mother's Book,* 88. "Family and Social Reading," *The Mother's Magazine* (March 1848), goes so far as to endorse this practice as an antidote to family dissolution and dissipation: "A book is tenfold a book, when read in the company of beloved friends by the ruddy fire" (98).

45. Norcross, February 9 and March 1, 1861.

Fig. 1.8. Drawings pasted on a bit of black cloth inside the front cover of Lilian Brinstool's copy of Charles W. Sanders, *Sanders's Union Speller* (New York: Ivison, Blakeman, Taylor, and Co., 1871). Author's copy.

indeed, the heroine of "The Desert Island" happened to have a copy with her and consults it as she builds her island home. The Hale family's homemade library is itself a model of communal reading and writing, the children not only enlisting many of their friends to produce stories for the collection, but also selling subscriptions to their little library for a penny. "The readers of the library are often as young as the authors and are not disposed to be critical," Arthur Hale explains in a notice soliciting more writers for the series.[46] Similarly, Mary Allen never mentions a book she has read by herself, it is always "we began to read. . . ."[47] These comments all represent reading and writing as absorbed into family life and children's play, a site of personal pride, relationship, and pleasure. They suggest how much literacy had become a central feature of domesticity, informing both the content and shape of household interactions, homes built out of books. Moreover, these diaries display the role of such literary recreations in forging community between children. Michel de Certeau notes that reading is never a purely passive act of consumption, that however much the reader "is *imprinted* by and like the text," readers nevertheless find in the writings they consume associations of their own, "spaces for games and tricks." By challenging a passive model of consumption, he contends, "we may be able to discover creative activity where it has been denied that any exists, and to relativize the exorbitant claim that *a certain kind* of production . . . can set out to produce history by 'informing' the whole of a country."[48] There are few instances of claims more exorbitant than those of literacy primers, so certain of the receptivity of children and of the capacity of books to mold them aright and through them to reform the nation. Yet these children's accounts of the uses to which they put their reading do indeed relativize such claims. As his friend Dexter passes to Sam the latest installment of *Bristol Bill*, as Florie reads and plays with Grenville and Willie, literacy becomes an important tool in the creation of a culture of childhood enmeshed in but not identical to the culture of the middle-class home.

In Catherine Sedgwick's narrative of domestic advice, *Home*, the ever

46. *The Desert Island* volume of the "Charlieshope Library," the notice is from *The Meteor* 2 (April 29, 1869): 2, a hand-lettered newspaper also produced by the Hale children that often included book reviews for their Charlieshope publications. All in the Hale Family Papers, Sophia Smith Collection, Smith College.

47. Allen, December 3, 1827.

48. Michel de Certeau, "Reading as Poaching," in *The Practices of Everyday Life* (Berkeley: University of California Press, 1984), 167, 174. The tension between the hegemonic impositions of literacy primers and the children's capacity for playful reading is a prime instance of his more general formulation in this text of the differences between "strategies" and "tactics."

sensible Barclays permit in their first modest household but "one luxury, which long habit and well cultivated taste had rendered essential to happiness,—a book-case filled with well selected and well bound volumes."[49] Books, it turns out, are not luxuries at all; they are "essential to happiness," and Sedgwick presents them as the moral and intellectual guarantors of domestic life. William Barclay can afford these full shelves because he furnished his house with a plain five-dollar clock in the kitchen instead of a fancy Geneva timepiece on the mantle, choosing a decorated mind over a decorated parlor. But as he reels off the titles on his shelf, these "well-bound volumes" serve as surely to express the cultural status of their owners as any imported ornaments. Books have not only an affective and moral function in the production of domesticity, but a more material role as well—they are things to buy, own, and display. In a similar manner books are most frequently mentioned in these children's journals simply as possessions, gifts received or pages consumed, with no comment on the content or on how the children felt about reading them. Even if all they give are titles, these children rarely mention reading without naming book or author. At Christmas Grenville reports finding "a list of new and attractive Juvenile Books published by Crosby and Nicols" in his stocking, a gift implying that Santa Claus wished the boy to have some choice over which of these new books he might read. Echoing the language of the advertising flier in his Christmas entry, Grenville's response to this gift registers the commodity status of books. A less circumspect Santa Claus filled Irving and Ames Van Wart's stockings with two books they already owned, "so we are to have them changed," the brothers note. Educators bemoaned the "mental gluttony" of children who rapidly "devoured" books, and Lydia Maria Child had advised that children read fewer books slowly and repeatedly, rather than many books quickly, but it is obvious that neither the publishing industry nor these young readers found this advice appealing.[50] The same Christmas that the Van Wart twins received these redundant books they pooled resources with their classmates to purchase gifts for their Academy teachers; the presents they chose were quite opulent and distinctly literary:

> we gave a handsome book to Mr. Anthon with his name on it which cost $12 &
> a gold pen and pencil to Mr. Miller the assistant teacher (which cost $10) and a

49. Catherine Sedgwick, *Home* (Boston: James Munroe and Company, 1845), 8.
50. "Devouring Books," *The American Annals of Education* 5 (January 1835): 31. Child, *The Mother's Book*, 96.

gold eye glass to Mr. Leaman the French teacher (which cost $6) and when we came away we gave three cheers to each teacher.[51]

There is no way to disentangle these dollars from these cheers. That books function as a commodity, a form of play, a ground of relationships, and a source of status suggests how much those middle-class prerogatives of emotional intimacy and material affluence were tied up in the act of reading, and how literacy training worked to instill these virtues in middle-class children.

Unlike the diaries of adults, which, however hedged round with social expectations, are presumed to be essentially voluntary texts, and usually private, the diaries kept by nineteenth-century children share some of the hierarchies and compulsions of schooling: they are almost always prompted, sometimes required, and often reviewed by adults.[52] Grenville Norcross received his diary as a present from Miss Watte on his seventh birthday along with a number of books from his family and a toy pistol from his friend Willie Tyron. Grenville, in fact, becomes a faithful journal writer, keeping a nearly daily log at least until he is sixteen; he records the source of each year's diary, and it is always given to him by an adult. Louis Gratacap received his diary as a New Year's Day present from his mother and at the end of the first month describes reading from his diary to a neighbor, Mrs. Bards, who rewards him with an apple. Harriet Appleton, age ten, uses a blank book decorated with gold flowers to write stories, poems, and sketches rather than a daily journal, and these pieces are read and evaluated by some adult: "please give me two marks for this one," Harriet writes beneath a poem, "one for the composition and one for good writing." On the first page of her diary Jenny Trumbull records the multiple influences that pushed her toward journal writing: "As the other girls have got journals I thought that I would have one too as mother desired me to write what happens every day."[53] "Mother" and the "other girls"

51. Irving Van Wart, Diary, December 22 and 25, 1854, in the collection of the New York Public Library.

52. Philippe Lejeune finds this also true in nineteenth-century France, where he discovers a complex relation between female education and the rise in diary keeping, noting that while diaries were "often required of girls educated at home" they were frequently prohibited at boarding schools. "The 'Journal de Jeune Fille' in Nineteenth-Century France," trans. Martine Breillac, in Suzanne L. Bunkers and Cynthia A. Huff, *Inscribing the Daily: Critical Essays on Women's Diaries* (Amherst: University of Massachusetts Press, 1996), 114.

53. Norcross, birthday presents reported on entries from February 2 through 6, 1861. At the end of the volume he lists his later journals and their givers through 1870. Gratacap diary for 1863; January 24, 1863. Harriet Appleton, blank book dated 1852; it is possible that this book comprises a collection of school compositions, but I think it unlikely that Harriet would take this kind of tone with a classroom teacher, and she writes in this book that she no longer has a governess "but instead go[es] to Mrs. Dwight's school." Trumbull, November 3, 1829. For

may value diaries for quite different reasons, but in beginning to keep one Jenny accommodates them all.

Jenny Trumbull honors her mother's desire, pledging "I am going to write in this journal every day—Aged 10 years 4 months" as if appending her age would make this promise more binding. Instead she writes fitfully, sometimes filling two or more pages on a single day, at other times leaving the journal untouched for weeks. Once in a large messy hand Jenny writes on the bottom of a page from the month before "March 29 1834 As I am filling up all the places I suppose this must not be left empty" and this proves nearly enough to complete the page.[54] To keep a diary involves an assent to genre, and as a form the diary assumes and asserts the measure of the day.[55] The desire of Jenny's mother that she "write what happens every day" values the daily in two ways: it presumes that the happenings of a day are a worthy subject, that each day matters in some way, and it considers that the development of daily habits, such as daily habits of writing, are good in themselves. For Jenny to leave a blank space in her diary seems almost like a failure to properly fill her days. Yet Jenny's unkept pledges to write every day, and her clumsy efforts to fill each page, suggest as well the artificial nature of these measures and habits. Her life, as she experiences it, does not fit well into such tidy constraints. If one result is irregular entries, another is that when she does choose to write her entries are unusually lively and engaging.

Thomas Augst notes the importance of the practices of mercantile accounting in the ways nineteenth-century clerks used their diaries as a moral ledger of their time.[56] Interestingly, among the diaries I have read, although Jenny may assert the value of daily habits of writing, such concern for reck-

---

what I suspect are similar instances of family tutelage within diaries see the interventions Isabelle Keith makes in the famous diaries of her seven-year-old cousin Marjory Fleming in *The Complete Marjory Fleming: Her Journals, Letters and Verses* (London: Sidgwick and Jackson, 1934), and Alexandra Johnson's excellent discussion of these 1810–11 diaries, "The Drama of Imagination: Marjory Fleming and Her Diaries," in *Infant Tongues: The Voice of the Child in Literature*, ed. Elizabeth Goodenough, Mark Heberle, and Naomi Sokoloff (Detroit, Mich.: Wayne State University Press, 1994), 80–109. See also Louisa May Alcott's childhood diaries, amply commented in by her mother: "I told mother I liked to have her write in my book," Louisa notes in one entry, and she gets maybe more response than she would like. *The Journals of Louisa May Alcott*, ed. Joel Myerson, Daniel Shealy, and Madeline B. Stern (Boston: Little, Brown and Co., 1989), 47.

54. Trumbull, February 13, 1833, and March 29, 1834. It is worth noting that Jenny's mother was also a diarist; her diary is available in the collection of the American Antiquarian Society.

55. See Stuart Sherman, *Telling Time: Clocks, Diaries, and English Diurnal Form, 1660–1875* (Chicago: University of Chicago Press, 1996), on the development of this sense of the daily. By the nineteenth century this conception of life charted by time had become fully naturalized.

56. Augst, *The Clerk's Tale*, especially chapter 1, "Accounting for Character: Diaries and the Moral Practice of Everyday Life."

oning each day does seem to be far more pressing for the boys.[57] Mary Allen and Harriet Appleton do not appear much concerned about the irregularity of their entries, writing more or less when they feel like it, and Harriet's book, not really a diary, is dated only once for the year. Grenville often finds that he has little to tell about his day, but he still feels the need to count them all; his entries for March 27 through 30, 1861, for example, read simply "Nothing important. Nothing Important. Nothing of consequence. Small doings." In September he writes "went to school" on each day for a week, "Nothing worth describing" on Sunday, and then wisely refrains from writing again until the end of the month when he tallies up and writes "went to school steadily ~~of~~ all the month." On May 12, in expectation and explanation of lapses to come, he writes, "Forget to write in Journal til the next day mentioned," as if such warnings would keep his record straight. Out of these charmingly empty entries he is, however, developing habits of order and attention, a sense that time ought to be accounted for and that writing can manage such reckonings. Greely Curtis draws two vertical lines down the pages of his blank book so as to make it into a daily ledger with the date on the left, brief descriptions of his activities in the middle, and any money he spent listed to the right. He heads each page with the name of the month and "Correct Account of Expenses and Occurrences"—a phrase that asserts a kind of symmetry between his financial and narrative accounting. Only when something unusual or exciting happens, like his trip to New York by ship, does Greely cross his ledger lines to write in paragraphs.[58] Sam Bigelow is more meticulous still, writing

57. Two of the boys but none of the girls actually indexed their journals. Grenville reviewed his journals, appending a list of "Principle Events" to each volume, while the Van Wart twins, Irving and Ames, not only listed events at the end of their journal but also used the ruled margin of their leather-bound book to inscribe in fancy print one-sentence summaries of the activities they described at length and in cursive on these large pages. (Van Wart, November 3, 1854–May 11, 1855). The kind of indexing and summarizing skills the boys instance here would be of use to them in school and business, and indeed they may have been taught to do it, though an examination of what they chose to index—the first day Grenville played a certain game with his paper soldiers, for example—suggests that there is pleasure in these activities as well. Grenville in particular, who received "a case for curiosities" as a Christmas present in 1862 and regularly reports in his journal about the number of curiosities in his collection and his manner of organizing them, clearly enjoys these sorts of classifying tasks. On the pedagogical assumptions behind children's cabinets of curiosities see Joyce Henri Robinson, "'And a Little Child Shall Lead Them': American Children's Cabinets of Curiosities," in *Acts of Possession: Collecting in America*, ed. Leah Dilworth (New Brunswick, N.J.: Rutgers University Press, 2003).

58. Curtis, November 24–28, 1846, describing the trip to New York. Augst notes that many clerks treated their diaries as moral and monetary ledgers and that books with such columns were sold for this purpose (28–30 and 49–50). That Greely made his own suggests, as do his "professional" signatures, how he used this diary to impersonate more adult roles. There is real scavenging in this; the paperbound journal Greely uses for his "Correct Accounts" has "The Property of" printed by the stationer on the cover with "H. O. Hooper" written on the line pro-

in his journal every day, a full sheet in the first journal and then half a sheet each day for later volumes. Recording each day is a lesson in orderliness, as significant as anything Sam might learn about writing itself from these efforts, and on some days he will include among his activities "went into the Parlor and wrote yesterday's journal," making sure that there are no gaps. But there are no excesses either. Not once in his thirteen little volumes is Sam so interested in his task or his subject that he permits an entry to overrun its allotted page.[59]

The boys' belief that journals ought to be complete, that they should write every day whether or not they have something to say, and even, as in Sam's case, that every day is deserving of an equal span of lines, all reveal how the literacy skills of the journal work to rationalize time and daily living. For William Potter the whole purpose of his diary becomes keeping track of time:

> As there are 24 hours in a day—I must see how my time is to be apportioned among the 3 principle studies. Algebra—Definition and G. Gramm.—Livy & Latin Gramm.
> —If I sleep 7 hours—there will be 17 left—Vis. 4 to Algebra 2 to Xenophon 2 for Livy—2 for my chores 1 for the Greek and Latin Grammars 1 for writing &c. ¾ hrs for meals and 4 for recitations.[60]

As this adds up to 16 ¾ hours, William has left himself a scant fifteen minutes for anything other than food, sleep, and work. I wished desperately to read "recitations" as "recreations" but his handwriting is, sadly, too clear. Here the value of schooling and the value of time weigh upon each other. If diary keeping offers a means of apportioning time, it also becomes a record of the difficulty of that task: "This is the last month of the year," William writes on December 1, "I must make as much as possible out of it."

The literacy training diaries provide these children is understood by them as a means of ordering their lives, of demonstrating in tidy pages, good grammar, and fully accounted days an accomplishment at once academic and personal. Part of the pleasure, even in William's dreadfully anxious lists, derives from the way in which this writing imitates adult behaviors and forms. Thus by adopting these rules, learning literacy's lessons, these children also form these strictures into a source of power, self-validation, and even play. "It is a

---

vided, and only underneath this mark of prior ownership can Greely write "Now the property of G. S. Curtis."

59. Bigelow, March 23, 1851.
60. Potter, September 30, 1836.

paradox of some interest that nurture always involves compliance," the psy-
choanalyst Adam Phillips remarks, and the proud sense in these pages of education and literacy as nurturing the self clearly rests upon these children's
efforts to conform. Phillips's work gestures toward a vision of education, a
valuation of childhood, that would not require this exchange, yet he is at his
most eloquent and precise in detailing the "complicated clash of internal
ideals" between the child's "wish for competence and the something-to-be-
mourned in its acquisition."[61] These diaries acutely record that act of acquisition, allowing us to trace the process of enrollment in the rules of literacy
and social expectation, to see the wish in these efforts as well as the pressure
and the loss. Their writing displays a capacity to meld conformity and play
that need not only and always view them as opposites.

The moral requirement to "make as much as possible" out of one's days
and one's diary underlies much of these children's writing. Calvinist habits of
spiritual interrogation and Romantic celebrations of the self—opposites in
so many ways, and particularly in their attitudes toward childhood—shared a
commitment to introspection, and the diary's role as an ethical technique derives from its utility in surveying the self.[62] An unidentified student in Massachusetts made himself a book for spiritual self-scrutiny, folding and stitching
two large sheets to form a sixteen-page pamphlet. He begins with a spiritual
autobiography: "My first serious impressions," he writes, "I date from the
time when I was about eight years old"; and he goes on to tell how he was
baptized at fourteen. He evidently started this journal to solemnize his bap-
tism, since the autobiographical narrative is replaced by dated entries at this
point, as he turns to writing to deepen and preserve his religious commitment.
"From coldness in religion I have neglected my journal," he writes after
nearly a year's lapse, voicing this entry as a prayer addressed directly to God:

> I have been so indifferent and hast not been willing to record even thy love! . . .
> Now oh! God will thou help me from henceforth to look into thee and no more
> neglect this important duty.[63]

61. Adam Phillips, *The Beast in the Nursery*, 116, 115.

62. Augst, *Clerk's Tale*, notes the intersection of Christian traditions of self-examination
and concerns of temporal accounting in the way that specific dates—birthdays, New Years—become traditional occasions for such moral evaluations (44). This proves true of the children's
diaries as well, though the calendar markers that most often prompt such self-assessments also
include the beginnings and endings of school terms, another mark of how children experience
ethical assessment and academic assessment as linked.

63. This final entry is dated April 10, 1834, Anonymous Diary for 1833–34 in the collection
of the New York Public Library.

Diary writing stands for this student as a powerful token and responsibility of religious observance. To "look into" God, to examine himself, and to write in his diary are braided strands of his faith. This is the last entry in this anonymous journal, the second signature of folded pages remaining unmarked and uncut, a duty neglected. The anguish of this young man's prayer is undoubtedly greater than any sense of failure found in Grenville's or Greely's lapses in accounting. To read back and forth between these journals is to confront the immense range in the concept of virtue being taught to children during these decades. Much as I found in literacy primers and advice-books, religion and business appear in these pages as simultaneously opposite and identical, both presenting literacy as a means to assess and preserve their so different goods.

Thus even for more secular children, religious rumination is, as Jenny Trumbull put it, the "proper" use of a diary. A blank book invites moral reflection, and Harriet Appleton, who began this passage by describing a sunset, finds herself wandering into theology:

> Whenever I look upon the glorious scene my heart is filled with painful thoughts. That anyone can doubt that there is a God. Who can have made all this? Did it come by chance? But I have wandered from my subject.[64]

Surely even at ten Harriet knows that such thoughts are what one ought to feel in the presence of natural beauty. Far from a digression, her questions are virtually requirements of the form, as is the notion that these thoughts, so unlike the anonymous student's wrenching struggles with his faith, should be considered "painful." In a sense her blank-book provides an opportunity to practice introspection, just as it offers a chance to practice penmanship or composition. Thus it is not surprising that Harriet's musings, like Jenny's hope that she had "not lived in vain," express themselves in conventional, nearly vacuous phrases. Such conventionality should not, however, be understood as a symptom of insincerity. Harriet and Jenny are learning the language of moral life in the forms and phrases that have been taught to them, and they recognize writing as an important part of that learning. Writing, in these terms, allies itself with the true. Even Sam Bigelow, the least introspective of these children, is morally vigilant in his corrections: "I went out and took ~~my~~ George's sled and coasted down the hill," as if the use of the wrong possessive in one's journal were tantamount to stealing—coveting one's brother's sled.[65]

64. Appleton, blank book for 1852, entries are not dated.
65. Bigelow, January 10, 1851.

To recognize diary keeping as an ethical technique, a schooling in moral self-examination, is however to tell only half the story. Just as reading features in these children's journals not only as a mark of virtue and a means of imprinting national ideals, but also as a site of play and cultural making, so too even the most conventionally moral functions of the diary often dissolve into what de Certeau calls "spaces for games and tricks." New Year's Day provides a traditional occasion for rituals of self-assessment. "This morning when I awoke I thought I must write a journal as it is the last day of the year 1851," Sam Bigelow explains, but this sense of special compulsion does not change the content of his entry, which records only the "usual" of going to school, and the "very unusual" of successfully reciting his Latin. Sam's awareness of expectations for New Year's self-examination, and his sense of the appropriateness of journal writing to that task, still does not prompt him to produce the requisite assessments. He ended his previous journal with a poem that even more exuberantly flouts the serious expectations that come with closure:

The end of the book Extending from Sept 14 to ~~Oct~~ Nov 1st

So be it.
    The summer has passed and gone
    And winter has come with its
    snows and storms
    Now for the skating and now
    for the coasting
    Now for the sleigh rides so
    good by nothing

    composed and written by
      [flourish] SAB
      So be it.[66]

The customary obedience to divine will ("so be it"), the literary conventions that mourn the passing of seasons, erupt under Sam's hand into a festival of sledding. So too, though Louis Gratacap begins his journal with the year, his relation to the genre of New Year's resolutions proves as playful as it is earnest:

New Year's Day. I awoke earlier this morning than I generally do; and was on the point of getting up; when I noticed that the light which I took to be day was

66. Bigelow, December 31 and November 1, 1851.

only the light of the Moon; and also that there was a large and fat barrier before me; in the shape of my Brother Tom. and I knew if I attempted to get out while he was there I certainly would get some blowings. accordingly I got into bed . once more, and my thoughts turned to the year that had passed 1862. I thought how I had been saved throughout this dreadful year; and how my Dear Mother and Father and Brother had been also . . . how had I passed the last year. I had passed it disgracefully I had given away to temptations. . . .

I at this moment heard a great noise in the road; and a cry of fire, I jumped up as did also the Barrier; who on looking out found that a pack of loafers had given a false alarm. I got in again ^{and} once ^{more} thought of the past year.[67]

Louis Gratacap's diary is a marvel of disjunctions: the self-assessment and introspection expected of a New Year's entry pivot effortlessly into the pleasures of jokes and narration, the excitement of the cry of fire in the street. Between one sentence and the next the "fat Barrier" can be recast as the "Brother" thankfully "saved throughout this dreadful year" only to become "the Barrier" again a few lines later. The language of morality and theology are not understood or experienced here as at odds with mayhem and play. Instead the tension between the radically different kinds of functions that diary writing might serve becomes, in itself, a kind of game, one of the things Louis plays with as he writes.

The play of children's diaries extends beyond the literary, the pages themselves offering a space for jokes and pranks. Thus this diary not only records the gleeful animosity of the brothers, but becomes another site for their "blowings" as Louis revels in his ability to use his diary to call his brother names. Inside the front cover of Greely Curtis's diary an elaborate warning has been penned:

> Reader, you're a sneaky puppy
> you is
> [flourish]   for looking into
>   other folks business
>   So just stop.[68]

Clearly there is as much pleasure here in the imagined trespass as in the insistence on privacy. Far from serious tools of introspection, these diaries

---

67. Gratacap, January 1, 1863.

68. Curtis. I could not ascertain from the handwriting whether these lines were written by Greely or by the diary's prior owner, H. O. Hooper, who if he did write this warning made no other use of the book. Such warnings are, of course, as conventional as they are fun.

thus also figure as sites and occasions for teasing and disobedience. George Bigelow not only reads but writes in his brother's diary, "How are you bob you little bugger how are you G. B."; and below this infraction, Sam adds a message obviously intended for his brother's eyes: "To the city Marshal Tukey, catch that puppy [that wrote that] if yo can and so good by from S. A. B."[69] The pages of Sam's diary become a game of cops and robbers. So too, while Louis uses his diary as a place to secretly bait his brother, he also records how he stole and read the diary of a neighborhood girl.

> Ros took her Diary out (she carries it in her pocket) and shows it to us Ol and me when we had got it we ran up stairs into his room locked the door and read it all through though after all there was not much in it.[70]

Ros's diary becomes a medium of flirtation and transgression, its content of less interest than its capture. These may be extreme instances of the capacity of diary writing to be an occasion for romps and roughhousing, but even in their most straightforward reporting of each day's occurrences, it is the account of these children's play that almost invariably receives the most detailed and engaged descriptions. Sam will often say little about school, but every day in winter he remarks on whether or not the snow conditions were good enough to allow him to coast there in the morning; in spring his diary reveals a similar obsession with his successes and failures in trapping bobolinks. Grenville devotes pages to accounts of the battles between his toy soldiers, noting by name each of the killed or wounded.[71] In these acts of attention these journals demonstrate and enact a set of values and pleasures that may not always closely mirror adult perspectives and priorities. Adult concerns do remain legible in these diaries, though; Grenville, for example, stages and recounts his battles in the midst of the Civil War, and gives his paper warriors the names of real soldiers—an instance of how play incorporates the real-world concerns that surround it. Rebecca Hogan finds a feminist poetics in the way women's diaries "do not privilege 'amazing' over 'ordinary' events, in terms of scope, space, or selection."[72] Such disregard for conventional standards of importance undoubtedly characterizes the diary genre as a

---

69. Bigelow, the exchange appears below the entry for March 25, 1851.

70. Gratacap, February 1, 1863.

71. See for example Norcross, January 17 and 21, 1862.

72. Rebecca Hogan, "Engendered Autobiographies: The Diary as a Feminine Form," *Prose Studies* 14, no. 2 (September 1991): 103.

whole, but this characteristic gains particular significance and utility for those members of society whose own sense of what matters diverges furthest from the hegemonic line. In their renditions of bobolinks and paper battles, or of Mary Allen's march around the table, these diaries trace the contours of a childhood culture that has its own urgencies and desires. Thus even as the literacy training proffered by diary keeping seeks to inscribe these children in a network of temporal, moral, and literary habits, the children themselves remain capable of using these pages in quite other ways as well.

It is precisely in these departures from adult norms that what Steven Kagle calls the diary's "own distinct identity, its created personality" becomes most evident.[73] I suspect that even in the nineteenth century these diaries were preserved, at least in part, out of appreciation for these childish oddities; it is just when these diaries thwart adult expectations that they most richly fulfill adult desires. The effort to use literacy to discipline and instruct children thus also and simultaneously serves to record childhood's specialness and difference. Carolyn Steedman warns against seeing children's mistakes in spelling or grammar as meaningful parts of these texts: "adult delight in charming childish error is . . . irrelevant to an understanding of children's writing," she contends.[74] Certainly, adult pleasure in such errors—in children's incomplete mastery of literacy's demands—belittles these efforts to write. Yet Grenville's decision to preserve as footnotes the grammatical mistakes he nevertheless corrected in copying over his diary suggests that children themselves might share in this split view of their writing, wishing at once to conform to adult norms and to find pleasure in the ways that they don't fully comply. Mary Allen reveals a similar ambivalence in the many passages in her journal in which she writes about her younger siblings, both celebrating and separating herself from their childish vantage: "Elizabeth was looking out of the window today at the cow, and she said, 'Mama if all the cows were ladies they would come in to dinner.'"[75] In recording her little sister's words, Mary uses her diary to preserve a childhood perspective that already at eight strikes her as funny, charming, naive. Her sister's attempt to understand social conventions highlights Mary's own comparative mastery, but it also invites her to imagine a different world order with cows round the

73. Steven E. Kagle, *Early Nineteenth-Century American Diary Literature* (Boston: Twayne Publishers, 1986). For Kagle such "created personality" is the ideal of the genre, the strongest aesthetic achievement of the diary form.

74. Carolyn Steedman, "The Tidy House," in *The Children's Culture Reader,* ed. Henry Jenkins (New York: New York University Press, 1998), 440.

75. Allen, December 6, 1827.

dinner table. Elizabeth's effort at logic permits Mary a moment of fantasy. Gillian Brown writes movingly and importantly of the vulnerability of children's play—how often it is dismissed and punished by adult imperatives, how imperfect and insecure is the separate world it promises.[76] These children's diaries suggest that children's play is not only vulnerable and permeable to adult interventions, disrupted by them, but that it is in some ways made out of and around these disciplines and conventions. That is, the dualistic construction of child play and adult responsibility misconstrues their relation, missing how children may take for themselves and enjoy the very things adults intended as lessons.

This chapter began with the contradictory way children are used to ward off the novel and yet come to be seen as embodiments of fictional fantasy and play. I find that children's own writing carries similar contradictions, but in a manner that suggests that we may want to look at these tensions differently. Imitation, the trying-on of adult voices and concerns, the virtue of good penmanship and daily habits, conflates conformity and play. Thus in the pages of these diaries, docility to literacy lessons becomes the condition of a certain independence, pleasure, even power. Detailing how children attain their own literary voice through acts of self-making that remain contingent and partial, prompted by adult rules and supervision, these diaries complicate traditional notions of what it means to claim "voice" as a mode of enfranchisement. Thus children's writing unmasks the elements of compliance entailed in all efforts to speak. In particular, I would suggest that these tensions can help us describe the workings of fiction—the interweaving of social compliance and liberation that characterize the new prominence of the novel in the mid-nineteenth-century United States. In the sections that follow I focus on two novelists who, in their very different ways, epitomize this literary evolution, and who do so in a manner that reveals the close links between changing ideologies of childhood and changing attitudes toward fiction.

Childhood and Authority in *Our Nig*

If writing proves for these young diarists a means, however ambivalent, of fitting themselves to the social world, Harriet Wilson's autobiographical novel *Our Nig* inverts these relations, recognizing in childhood a route for gaining access to social place and authorial power. It is a striking irony of literary history that the recovery of *Our Nig* in 1983 and the verification of Harriet Wil-

76. Gillian Brown, "Child's Play," *Differences* 11 (fall 1999): 76–106.

son's racial identity depended upon the death record of her seven-year-old son, George Mason Wilson.[77] In her "Preface," Harriet Wilson claims to have written this book as an "experiment which shall aid me in maintaining myself and child," yet the failure of that experiment, the death of her child a scant five months after this volume was first offered for sale on September 5, 1859, ultimately secured Wilson's position as the first African American woman to publish a novel (3). In her own time, what little we know about the readership of *Our Nig* points to a preponderance of child readers: Miss Mary A. Whitcomb was nine years old when she signed her name in a copy of *Our Nig;* George F. Sawyer was ten when he received his copy in 1860; John H. Colburn was fourteen when he gave a copy to M. Jenne Moar on February 16, 1865, and hence was only eight or nine when the book was published; Flora M. Lovejoy was two then, and surely not yet reading.[78] Much like the children whose diaries I have been discussing, these young readers come from white, middle-class, northeastern homes, and it seems likely that the adults who purchased this book for them saw it as a useful site of moral pedagogy, the purchase itself a lesson in charity and tolerance for a poor black woman in the local community, and the story told a model of Christian fortitude. Surely these purchasers believed this book would be particularly suitable to young readers because for the bulk of its pages the heroine is herself a child. Childhood thus weaves a dense web around the reception of *Our Nig* both in the nineteenth century and in the twentieth. Yet there has been remarkably little attention paid to childhood in the critical studies of Wilson's book.

That Wilson chose both a fictionalized form and a child heroine to structure her "experiment" testifies to the rising cultural power of fiction and its links to childhood. The 1850s saw a significant turn toward fiction as the most promising mode of African American literary expression, a means of navigating what Carla Peterson terms the "essentialized notions of black self-

77. Harriet E. Wilson, *Our Nig; or, Sketches from the Life of a Free Black, in a Two-Story White House, North. Showing that Slavery's Shadows Fall Even There* (New York: Vintage Books, 1983). Henry Louis Gates Jr. recounts the history of the recovery of *Our Nig* and the essential role played by George Mason Wilson's death certificate in his "Introduction" to this volume, xi–xiii. For more information on George Wilson's short life including documents proving his residence at the "Hillsborough County Farm" see Barbara White, *"Our Nig* and the She-Devil: New Information about Harriet Wilson and the 'Bellmont' Family," *American Literature* 65 (March 1993): 21–25.

78. This information is drawn from Eric Gardner's "'This Attempt of Their Sister': Harriet Wilson's *Our Nig* from Printer to Readers," *New England Quarterly* 66 (June 1993), which is still the best account of the reception of *Our Nig.* Gardner surveyed the thirty-four known extant copies of the first edition, only eleven of which bore inscriptions, but more than half of these were the names of children (234–38).

hood" at stake in the slave narrative.[79] The production of these works is itself a strong marker of the growing prestige of the novel, and the increasing recognition that fiction could tell a kind of truth. But Wilson is alone among the African American novelists of this decade in focusing her fiction on the experiences of a child.[80] In her production of young Frado, that "wild frolicky thing" (18), Wilson manifests the complex relations between ideas of child-hood and the possibilities of fiction, finding in child's play the only articulations of freedom in a world of constraints.

Interestingly, groups of schoolchildren appear repeatedly in *Our Nig* as the voice of community, the only real figures of a collective, public weal. They become the indexes of communal value in general, and most strikingly of race:

> As they neared the village, they heard the merry shouts of children gathered round the schoolroom, awaiting the coming of their teacher.
>
> "Halloo!" screamed one. "Black, white and yeller!" "Black, white and yeller," echoed a dozen voices. (20–21)

> As soon as she appeared, with scanty clothing and bare feet, the children assembled, noisily published her approach: "See that nigger," shouted one. "Look! Look!" cried another. "I won't play with her," said one little girl. "Nor I neither," replied another. (31)

These passages are eerily reminiscent of James Baldwin's "Stranger in the Village," where Swiss schoolchildren similarly point and cry "Neger! Neger!" and of Frantz Fanon's lessons in racial objectification: "Look a Negro," "Mama,

---

79. At present count the 1850s produced seven African American novels or significantly fictionalized autobiographies: Frederick Douglass's *The Heroic Slave* (1853),William Wells Brown's *Clotel* (1853), Frank J. Webb's *The Garies and Their Friends* (1857), Harriet Jacobs's *Incidents in the Life of a Slave Girl* (written by 1858, published 1861), Martin R. Delany's *Blake; or, The Huts of America* (1859–1862), Harriet Wilson's *Our Nig* (1859), and Hannah Crafts's *The Bondwoman's Narrative* (written sometime between1855 and 1860). It should be pointed out that this interest on the part of African American writers was not shared by white readers, who continued to prefer factual personal testimony from this source, even as they delighted in slavery novels produced by white authors.

For accounts of this turn toward fiction see William L. Andrews, "The Novelization of Voice in Early African American Narrative," *PMLA* 105 (1990): 23–34; and Carla Peterson, "Capitalism, Black (Under)development, and the Production of the African-American Novel in the 1850s," *American Literary History* 4 (1992): 559–83, quotation from 579.

80. Interestingly, the first African American biography also chose a child–subject; see Susan Paul's *Memoir of James Jackson.* Young James, however, is so honored for his piety and goodness, not for his capacity to play.

see the Negro!"[81] Children stand in all these passages as the enforcers of racial identity, pointing, naming, and othering. To present racial labeling as a task of childhood naturalizes these distinctions, suggesting that they are inherent, unlearned, even though all of these writers present these scenes as a site of learning race. For both Baldwin and Fanon these pointing children mark how they are "sealed into crushing objecthood" "among a people whose culture controls" them, exiled by a history of colonialism and slavery from human agency and identity until "white men have for black men a reality that is far from being reciprocal."[82] At stake for both is the wrestle with what it means to be "black men." This struggle strives to claim a "reality" and autonomy associated not simply with humanity, but quite specifically with adult maleness—a model of identity even harder to imagine for a dark-skinned girl-child. The cries "black, white and yeller" that hail the interracial family of Seth, Mag, and their daughters differ, moreover, in that they recognize a spectrum of racial identity that is pointedly lacking in the binary oppositions of white men and black. Wilson focuses on how these cries are experienced by the white mother, Mag, who "had passed into an insensibility no childish taunt could penetrate" and "did not even turn her head" (21). Far from a triumph over racial categories and prejudice, Mag's "insensibility" to the "childish taunt" coincides with her abandonment of her daughter Frado—her insensibility to parental responsibility and the needs of her child. That Mag does not feel the sting of these words is Wilson's final marker of her fall from social reality.[83]

When eventually Frado returns to the schoolyard without the racial framing of these parents, and with the shabby clothing and bare feet of poverty,

81. James Baldwin, "Stranger in the Village," in *The Price of the Ticket: Collected Non-Fiction, 1948–1985* (New York: St. Martins Press, 1985), 81. Frantz Fanon, "The Fact of Blackness," in *Black Skin, White Masks* (New York: Grove Press, 1967), 77–99.

82. For both Baldwin and Fanon the ways they are seen by whites "poisons"—to use Baldwin's term—self-image. The essays diverge importantly in that from these initial scenes of pointing children Fanon traces a process of individual psychic reclamation, whereas Baldwin is more concerned with the development of a sense of communal history that would replace the ontological invisibility at stake in these children's astonished gaze with a recognition of the reciprocity and mutual entrenchment of black and white pasts. On this last point see Fanon, "the black man has no ontological resistance in the eyes of the white man" (78). Representative quotations from Fanon 77 ("sealed into crushing objecthood"), and Baldwin 82 ("among a people whose culture controls") and 83 ("far from being reciprocal").

83. For a fine reading of this scene as Frado's "entry into the American social symbolic" see Katherine Clay Bassard, "'Beyond Mortal Vision': Harriet E. Wilson's *Our Nig* and the American Racial Dream Text," in *Female Subjects in Black and White: Race, Psychoanalysis, Feminism,* ed. Elizabeth Abel, Barbara Christian, and Helen Moglen (Berkeley: University of California Press, 1997), 192–93.

the children's calls of "yeller" turn to "nigger." As many scholars have noted, Wilson's book not only flaunts that demeaning label as its title, but also employs it to identify the author. "By 'Our Nig,'" reads the title page, transforming a term of denigration into a sign of racial identity and authorial power; "Mrs. Harriet E. Wilson" appears only in the fine print of the copyright.[84] Wilson's use of the word "published" to describe these schoolyard taunts links school and book, and so recognizes enrollment in school and literacy training as a condition of public voice and identity. Wilson's unusual word choice here suggests that this initiation into school, and into the world of reading and writing it permits, not only empowers these children's speech, but also enables Wilson's own act of publication, the production of this book, in which she lays claim to and publishes these schoolyard cries, adopting them for title and pseudonym. In replaying this scene of racial labeling Wilson differs from Baldwin and Fanon. Not only does she adapt the schoolyard taunts for her own use, but in her telling these pointing children are gradually won over by the black girl amongst them: "her speeches often drew merriment from the children; no one could do more to enliven their favorite pastimes than Frado" (32–33), indeed "they enjoyed her antics so fully that any of them would suffer wrongfully to keep open the avenues of mirth" (38). Wilson cannot claim for herself or her heroine the kind of autonomy and historical power that Baldwin and Fanon desire for "black men," or that Sam Bigelow fantasizes when he writes his name "Hon. S. Augustus B." Not only race, but age and gender make this implausible, for the objectification Baldwin and Fanon reject entails a kind of infantilization ("the Negro is a toy in the white man's hands," Fanon complains, 99). Wilson stakes her claims to authorship and authority precisely on this demeaning status of "toy": the enlivening power of Frado's antics.

"Time levied an additional charge," Wilson writes of the births of Frado and her sister, "in the form of two pretty mulattos, whose infantile pranks amply repaid the additional toil" (14). Wilson figures childhood as labor and burden, but insists that these costs are compensated by play and even mischief. What is valued in childhood from this first—still nameless, undifferentiated—mention of Frado are pranks. In this economic equation toil and play achieve a balance not unlike the pull between good handwriting and self-expression in children's diaries. Wilson presents infantile pranks as potent and valuable, a salve to hardship. Here child's play repays a father's toil,

84. For a rich reading of how Wilson inverts the power of this taunt see Claudia Tate, *Domestic Allegories of Political Desire: The Black Heroine's Text at the Turn of the Century* (New York: Oxford University Press, 1992).

but by the very next sentence Frado's father, Jim, has become ill, and "an idler," and finally dead, so that as the book continues the toil turns out to be Frado's own painfully detailed labors, and the compensation play may offer proves less and less ample. Still the logic of this sentence remains, tenaciously, the logic of the book, as Wilson continues to ask her readers to delight like Frado's classmates in her pranks, and clings to them as novelist, offering these brief "frolicky" moments and brave "antics" as her heroine's best claim to autonomy and hence her own best claim to authorship.

Our Nig can be read as an account of the impossibility of agency and voice for a black child, since neither Frado's hard work, quick mind, and playful nature, nor her pious hopes prove capable of alleviating her situation.[85] Certainly, *Our Nig* eschews the usual moral logic of the novel, in which virtues reap rewards. Mrs. Bellmont's brutal punishments frequently include stuffing Frado's mouth with cloth or wood—an "utter repression of the child's voice," as Julia Stern observes.[86] Yet while the plot demonstrates Frado's ultimate powerlessness, Wilson's narrative voice insists on her willfulness and independence, repeatedly claiming for her heroine the kind of control over her life that events relentlessly thwart. Thinking over the plan to leave Frado with the Bellmonts, Mag justifies her decision by noting that her daughter "means to do jest as she's a mind to; she won't go if she don't want to" (18). Indeed, Frado's first words in this book are a screamed "No!" as she knocks Mag's new lover, Seth, to the floor and flees (19). Childhood may be vulnerable, with few options and little effective control, even its cries gagged, but Wilson wields Frado's childhood as a tool of resistance, not docility; it is her own most available "No!" So, for example, Frado's position as child, ignorant of conventions, poised to make her own new sense of all she sees, provides Wilson with a means of articulating the otherwise unacknowledged contradictions of a racist Christianity. When Frado naively asks why God "made [Mrs. Bellmont] white and me black" (51) or whether her dead torturer Mary would find herself blackened in hell—"wouldn't mistress be mad to see her a nigger!" (107)—the pious James and Aunt Abby are stumped by these "knotty questions" (51) but "could not evade them" (107), and neither can Wilson's readers; immune to conventions, the voice of the child becomes a tool of social critique.

85. Ellen Pratofiorito, "'To Demand Your Sympathy and Aid': *Our Nig* and the Problem of No Audience," *Journal of American and Comparative Cultures* 24 (spring-summer 2001): 31–48; on Frado's lack of agency see pages 40–46.

86. Julia Stern, "Excavating Genre in *Our Nig*," *American Literature* 67 (September 1995): 448. See also Gabrielle P. Foreman, "The Spoken and the Silences in *Incidents in the Life of a Slave Girl* and *Our Nig*," *Callaloo* 13 (spring 1990): 313–24.

Despite her detailed telling of all that constrains and punishes Frado, Wilson thus insists on the agency of her child heroine. Endorsing Mag's sense that Frado "won't go if she don't want to," Wilson is careful to present her indenture at the Bellmonts' as a mark of Frado's own reasoned "wanting." Like Mag, Wilson has high stakes in representing her heroine as a free actor, making us deeply aware of the yearning and fragility in these claims. Frado has been abandoned by her mother and commandeered by Mrs. Bellmont, her well-being forfeit to the needs and desires of white adults, but still the narrator frames the choice to stay at the Bellmonts' as Frado's own: "Frado lay, revolving in her little mind whether she would remain or not until her mother's return. She was of wilful, determined nature, a stranger to fear, and would not hesitate to wander away should she decide to" (28). This is the novel's first foray into Frado's "little mind." Earlier the narrator had insisted upon the impossibility of such ingress: "why the impetuous child entered the house, we cannot tell," Wilson writes, juxtaposing the threshold of the Bellmonts' front door and of Frado's mind, the child impetuously crossing where the writer initially cannot (23). Wilson's act of writing thus models itself on the impetuosity of her heroine, locating in childhood a rhetoric of choice and possibility that runs directly counter to the story she has to tell. Given the generic instability of this text, where the novel's third-person narration is ruptured by autobiographical chapter titles (here the painfully ironic "A New Home for Me"), it seems reasonable to presume that the major contours of these events are essentially factual, that a young Harriet stayed to be worked and beaten. Thus what fiction can accomplish for this autobiographical novel pertains less to plot than to characterization and narration. Fiction crosses the threshold into Frado's little mind, and declares her free to "wander away"; autobiography forces her to stay. Such narrative insistence on Frado's autonomy appears poignant in the face of Wilson's inability to use fiction to produce a happy ending. The ambivalent agency of childhood, always hemmed in by necessary dependencies, echoes in the limited possibilities Wilson finds in fiction.

The split genre of Wilson's autobiographical novel thus patterns itself on a split conception of childhood as Wilson's rhetoric of childhood impetuosity, freedom, and power jostles against her recognition of childhood's subjugation and dependency. If Wilson's narration repeatedly insists on Frado's spunky resilience, it is just as clear about all that tests and traps her. Sent to get "some little wood," Frado brings "the smallest she could find," so that when it is deemed too large and she is sent for better kindling,

> the second must be a trifle larger. She well knew it was, as she threw it into a
> box on the hearth. To Mrs. Bellmont it was a greater affront, as well as larger

wood, so she "taught her" with the raw-hide, and sent her the third time for "little wood."

Nig, weeping, knew not what to do. She had carried the smallest; none left would suit her mistress; of course further punishment awaited her. (43)

The incapacity of right, reason, knowledge, even obedience to protect Frado from punishment sharply demonstrates the limits to Wilson's rhetoric of childhood impetuosity. Self-determination simply isn't a possibility for Frado in a world where to be "taught" is to be whipped, and where the tensions over size only emphasize her own hopeless smallness.

The usual compensations of childhood dependency—nurture and care— prove even harder to find than kindling. In her letter of support for Wilson's book, appended to the text, Margaretta Thorn comments:

The writer of this book seems to be a child of misfortune.
  Early in life she was deprived of her parents, and all those endearing asso- ciations to which childhood clings. Indeed she may be said not to have had that happy period; for being taken from home so young, and placed where she had nothing to love or cling to, I often wonder that she had not grown up a monster. (138–39)

Thorn defines childhood as an inherently "happy period"; "childhood clings" to "endearing associations," she explains. Indeed, it seems to be produced by them, for with "nothing to love or cling to" Frado appears to Thorn not to have had a childhood, indeed to risk falling out of the human altogether. Thorn sees the happiness of childhood as inextricably linked to the act of clinging, the result not of resilience, frolic, or willful fortitude but of dependence and care. Wilson clearly holds a wider definition of childhood than the highly depend- ent one Thorn offers. Yet in what Stern calls "a fantasy of maternal concern" Wilson describes how Seth and Mag look for Frado when she runs away, even though they plan to abandon her to the Bellmonts a few days later.[87] In this scene Wilson conjures an image of parental care at the very moment when Mag abdicates her maternal role. Stern fails to recognize, however, that this is also the moment of Frado's most willful act of autonomy, a running away that reveals her competence and independence, an adventure story where

87. See Wilson, 19–20; Stern, 445. One could understand the search for Frado as marking Mag's desire for control as much as it indicates her concern—in hunting for Frado she refuses to let her daughter be the one who chooses their separation.

she "climbed fences and walls, passes through thickets and marshes," and comes to no harm (20). Surely, confronted by Mrs. Bellmont's cruelty, every reader wishes that Frado would run again at least as much as we wish that Mag would return to reclaim her daughter. Thus as Wilson constructs this story she offers fantasies of both dependence and autonomy as the alternative bulwarks of childhood, but the plot itself permits Frado neither one.

The two Bellmont brothers, Jack and James, in their very different ways of valuing Frado embody these alternate notions of what might be desirable in childhood, and yet for all their moments of goodwill, neither proves efficacious at liberating or protecting Frado. Jack takes pleasure in her risky play. Literalizing the economic language of the opening pages, where Frado's pranks were seen as compensation, he throws "Nig" a coin to reward her for a joke played on his mother (72). "Strange, one spark of playfulness could remain amid such constant toil," Wilson acknowledges, as she describes Frado's escapades scrambling up the barn roof or baiting the sheep she was sent to tend, "but her natural temperament was in a high degree mirthful, and the encouragement that she received from Jack and the hired men nurtured the inclination" (53). If their encouragement counts as "nurture" it comes through laughter and cheers that press Frado toward danger, rather than through keeping her safe. Jack's nurture derives from his role as spectator, watching the fun, even paying for it. As such it raises questions about the structures of exploitation at stake in being entertained by the antics of a black child, so that Wilson's critique of Jack reflects back on the audience of her readers, and on whatever pleasure we, like those schoolyard children, take from Frado's play.

James offers readers a different model for watching and appreciating Frado: the sentimental gaze. "A frail child, driven from shelter by the cruelty of his mother was an object of interest to James," Wilson notes (50). This is the mode of interest Margaretta Thorn exemplifies, one that locates the appeal of childhood in its vulnerability and depicts childhood trauma as a failure of maternal nurture. Strikingly, James's interest in Frado arises out of the depiction of Mrs. Bellmont as a cruel "mother" rather than as simply a tyrannical mistress. Thus James roots his fascination with Frado in the ways that her suffering highlights how he too must have lacked a mother to shelter him, a place to cling. James's responses to Frado cast her as a "disconsolate child" (96), and the solace he offers her is the markedly maternal domesticity of a "heavenly home together" with him (95).[88] Yet even for pious James, Frado's personal and spiritual worth remain tied to her sauciness and pranks.

---

88. Foreman discusses how Jim and Mr. John Bellmont are "gendered female" in Wilson's text, and clearly this is true of James as well (see 320).

He felt sure there were elements in her heart which, transformed and purified by gospel, would make her worthy the esteem and friendship of the world. A kind, affectionate heart, native wit, and common sense, and the pertness she sometimes exhibited, he felt if restrained properly, might become useful in originating a self-reliance which would be of service to her in after years. (69)

James's hopes for Frado see her pertness as a basis for self-reliance, asserting the connection between play and autonomy. The restraint James urges here would not come easy; Wilson's first description of Frado notes "an exuberance of spirit almost beyond restraint" (17), and Mag's decision to leave her daughter at the Bellmonts' is confirmed by the thought that "severe restraint would be healthful" for the wild girl (20). The book as a whole can be read as testing the limits of that "almost," gauging the resilience of Frado's exuberance against both the severe restraints of work and punishments and the gentler restraints James refers to here, bonds of spiritual nurture and moral responsibility, strictures associated with growing up.

Our Nig remains clear that dependence and care are not only powerful goods, but basic grounds of community, modeled on maternal nurture. Wilson records her strong sense of the necessity and obligations of care: when Frado falls sick "she felt sure that they owed her a shelter and attention," while Mrs. Bellmont insists that "We shan't pay for doctoring her; you may look to the town for that," selfishly imagining that there could be public responsibilities where private ones fail (120). In her appended letter "Allida" describes Wilson's relation to the white woman who shelters her in terms that conjure childhood, quoting a letter from Wilson in which she exults "O, aunt J____, I have at last found a *home,* — and not only a home, but a *mother*" (133). "Motherhood," Claudia Tate argues, "motivates and justifies Wilson's authorship": Mag's inadequate mothering, Mrs. Bellmont's cruel mothering, the charitable mothering of the woman who harbors Frado, and most of all the adult Frado's own difficult efforts to support and nurture her child, stand as the novel's most secure measures of moral meaning. One role that Allida, Thorn, and perhaps Wilson herself proffer to readers is the task of nurturing this motherless text through the care of our reading. Tate argues that this maternal discourse ultimately enables Wilson's writing "the self-interest of professional literary creation . . . cloaked in the selflessness of mother love."[89] I am suggesting, however, that maternity is not Wilson's only mode for imagining and occupying authorship. Childhood offers another way to write.

Dependency comes to Frado in adulthood. Rather than the *bildungsroman*

---

89. Tate, *Domestic Allegories,* 43, 42.

in which the child grows gradually to independence, or the conventions of the male slave narrative in which the slave claims first psychic and then literal freedom, *Our Nig* recounts the waning of Frado's willful impetuosity.[90] It is as wife, not as child, that Frado is allowed her "first feelings of trust and repose on a human arm"—a feeling that does not last long, as her husband's increasingly frequent absences "compelled" her to "self-dependence" (127). Soon "a still newer companionship would force itself upon her," Wilson writes in her account of Frado's pregnancy, casting the fetus, as she had cast the infantile Frado, as a creature of agency and force in contrast to her own adult passivity—"herself was burden enough" (128). Samuel's failure to provide consistent support and protection to his wife and child demonstrates the precariousness of dependence. The pranks and knotty questions of a willful child may appear remarkably flimsy and insufficient counters of agency, but to be vulnerable, in need of others' care, proves even more dangerous. As the very existence of this book testifies, Wilson's efforts to care for her child, to prove worthy of another's dependency, were heroic and inventive. But her portrayal of this adult self stresses her frailty, and the utter impossibility of "self-dependence" given the "traps slyly laid" (129) by racism and the limitations of Frado's battered and overworked body. In such conditions "repose on a human arm," even her own, offers little security or escape. The book ends with Frado "reposing on God" (130). The appeal to repose, easily understandable in a life so worn by labor, locates solace not in independence or frolic, but in rest. This posture of dependency expresses an ideal of divine and communal responsibility, a culture of care that Wilson reaches for as she appeals to her "colored brethren" to "rally round me a faithful band of supporters and defenders" (Preface). The historical record tells that few if any of these colored brethren bought her book, and that a detached God allowed her son to die. These are only the last in the long line of failed dependencies that haunt *Our Nig.*

    The Frado of the final scenes is a far more pious and conventional figure

---

90. It has become a critical commonplace in accounts of both Harriet Jacobs's *Incidents in the Life of a Slave Girl* and Wilson's *Our Nig* that in these texts gender complicates race, and the strategies of "telling a free story" that had worked for Frederick Douglass or William Wells Brown proved inadequate to the familial enmeshment of the lives of black women. See Frances Foster, *Written by Herself: Literary Production by African American Women, 1746–1892* (Bloomington : Indiana University Press, 1993); Elizabeth Fox Genovese, "'To Weave It into the Literature of the Country': Epic and the Fictions of African American Women," in *Poetics of the Americas: Race, Founding, and Textuality* , ed. Bainard Cowan and Jefferson Humphries (Baton Rouge: Louisiana State University Press, 1997); and Valerie Smith, *Self-Discovery and Authority in Afro-American Narrative* (Cambridge: Harvard University Press, 1987).

than the child of its earlier chapters, this book's movement toward adulthood and dependency coinciding with a movement away from the fictive and novelistic. The two final, "adult" chapters of *Our Nig* (a scant twenty pages, a slim allotment for all that happens after her indenture ends at age eighteen) abandon narrative detail as they take leave of childhood. We are told about the "cricket" six-year-old Frado must stand on "to wash the common dishes . . . a large amount of dish-washing for small hands" (29), but we don't even learn from the text of *Our Nig* that the "valuable recipe" for a "useful article" that supports her in her later years is a method of dying hair (129, and see Allida's letter on 137). The vague swiftness and thinness of these final pages may attest to the increasing desperateness of Wilson's life as she struggles to find a way to support herself and her child, with ever less time and energy to write. But it suggests as well that the act of writing about the present does not empower Wilson in the way that telling her childhood did. Wilson's writing may not be sufficient to succor her son George, but it does give imagined life to the child Frado, just as Frado and childhood itself become for Wilson the grounds and condition of authorship. This leaves us with the questions of what it means for Wilson to figure authorship through childhood, and how this practice might matter, literarily and historically.

Childhood serves in *Our Nig* as a way of coming to terms with disempowerment and making it fruitful. Our ways of figuring authorship and authority are generally triumphant; we see it as a proof of autonomy and control. The interpretation of *Our Nig* as a heroic articulation of motherhood proves so attractive precisely because it confers on Wilson this sort of independent, productive power. As we have noted in the works of child-diarists, early writing is rarely like this; its forms of power and play come entrenched in compliance and suffused with dependence. In identifying her role as novelist less with the pious mother she has become at her story's end than with the exuberant child "almost beyond restraint," Wilson invents a voice and mode of writing that better reflect her historical predicament. As I have argued, one of the important gains from examining childhood derives from how this study illuminates the varieties of imperfect, incomplete autonomy that generally characterize the status of children. Children's partial independence may often prove a more realistic measure of social conditions than can be found in any ideal figure of self-determination—the author included. Harriet Wilson, writing a novel, when she knew of no other African American woman who had done such a thing, when her most basic health and well-being were precarious and unsure, thus finds in childhood a mode not of mastering such insecurities but of playing despite them and with them.

Hawthorne and the Mind of a Child

Of course, what it means for Nathaniel Hawthorne to model his fiction on ideals of childhood is a very different matter. The grown man entering the public sphere hand in hand with a young child, not the abandoned child impetuously stepping into the house of bondage, best figures Hawthorne's authorship:

> If I pride myself on anything, it is because I have a smile that children love; and on the other hand, there are few grown ladies that could entice me from the side of little Annie; for I delight to let my mind go hand in hand with the mind of a sinless child. So, come, Annie; but if I moralize as we go, do not listen to me; only look about you, and be merry![91]

Hawthorne's self-presentation as a writer who wishes to make public on the streets of the town or the pages of a book his connection with childhood provides important insights into his conception of authorship, and more generally into the period's shifting sense of the relation between childhood and fiction. Like Mary laughing over the comments of her little sister, or like Wilson drawing sustenance from Frado's pranks, Hawthorne recognizes the delight to be found in the mind of a child, and he uses this delight as an impetus toward fiction. But unlike Wilson, poised on the threshold of Frado's thoughts, he shows few compunctions about entering in. Hawthorne wrote more pieces directly aimed at a juvenile audience than any other canonical male author of the antebellum period. As many scholars have argued, Hawthorne's preeminence in American literary studies (how he fell into the American canon from the beginning and stayed, until *The Scarlet Letter* became the most ubiquitous of American schoolbooks) derives in large part from the intimate and uncanny power with which his romances express and enforce new national norms.[92]

91. Nathaniel Hawthorne, "Little Annie's Ramble" (1835), in *Twice-Told Tales: The Centenary Edition of the Works of Nathaniel Hawthorne,* ed. William Charvat et al., vol. 9 (Columbus: Ohio University Press, 1974), 122.

92. For accounts of how Hawthorne's fictions work to articulate middle-class domesticity, revealing the complex interdependence of class and gender in family formation, see Michael T. Gilmore, "Hawthorne and the Making of the Middle Class," in *Rethinking Class: Literary Studies and Social Formation,* ed. Wai Chee Dimock and Michael T. Gilmore (New York: Columbia University Press, 1994), 215–38; and T. Walter Herbert, *Dearest Beloved: The Hawthornes and the Making of the Middle-Class Family* (Berkeley: University of California Press, 1993). For an account of how they serve to define the social and intellectual status of authorship, see Richard H. Brodhead, *The School of Hawthorne* (New York: Oxford University Press, 1986). On the way Hawthorne expresses the nature of citizenship, see Sacvan Bercovitch, *The Office of the Scarlet Letter* (Baltimore, Md.: Johns Hopkins University Press, 1991); and Lauren Berlant, *The Anatomy*

One powerful and largely overlooked way Hawthorne's fiction accomplishes this is through the writing of childhood.

Hawthorne's letters reveal his own sense of writing for children as a lucrative and useful means of supporting a literary career. As Elizabeth Freeman and Meredith McGill demonstrate, children often serve in Hawthorne's fiction to figure the avidity of consumer desires—Annie's "pleasure in looking at the shop windows" (9: 123) or the consumptive feats of the little "cannibal" who frequents Hepzibah's shop in *The House of the Seven Gables*—suggesting how closely Hawthorne associates the market with children.[93] In fact this assessment of the literary marketplace proved reasonably true. Hawthorne's combined lifetime earnings from his juvenile fiction, $2,460 plus £50 in British royalties, exceeded the sales of even his most successful adult novel, his lifetime earnings on *The Scarlet Letter* amounting to only $1,500.[94] Hawthorne was often dismissive of these juvenile efforts, noting with humorous sarcasm to his sister Elizabeth that "our pay as Historians of the Universe will be 100 dollars" or explaining to his college classmate Henry Wadsworth Longfellow that he "must scribble for a living, but this troubles me much less than you would suppose. I can turn my pen to all sorts of drudgery, such as children's books etc."[95] There is, moreover, a peculiarly

---

of National Fantasy: Hawthorne, Utopia, and Everyday Life (Chicago: University of Chicago Press, 1991).

93. Elizabeth Freeman, "Honeymoon with a Stranger: Pedophiliac Picaresque from Poe to Nabokov," *American Literature* 70 (December 1998): 863–97; and Meredith L. McGill, *American Literature and the Culture of Reprinting, 1834–1853* (Philadelphia: University of Pennsylvania Press, 2003), 248–52.

94. Laura Laffrado, *Hawthorne's Literature for Children* (Athens: University of Georgia Press, 1992), 135. Hawthorne's initiation into juvenile literature centers on his relation with Samuel Goodrich, the originator of the famous *Peter Parley* series. Many of Hawthorne's early tales were published in Goodrich's literary annual, *The Token*, but Goodrich's publications for the family market also drew upon Hawthorne's talents: Goodrich hired him in 1836 as editor of the short-lived *American Magazine of Useful and Entertaining Knowledge* and as a ghostwriter of one of the Peter Parley books, *Peter Parley's Universal History, on the Basis of Geography, for the Use of Families*. After breaking with Goodrich, Hawthorne tried his own hand at making an institutionally supported income from his writing for children, initially composing his juvenile histories—*Grandfather's Chair, Famous Old People,* and *The Liberty Tree*—in the hope that Horace Mann could be convinced to adopt them as school books for the state of Massachusetts. See *The Letters, 1813–1843, The Centenary Edition of the Works of Nathaniel Hawthorne*, ed. William Charvat et al., vol. 15 (Columbus: Ohio University Press, 1984), 21–26. Showing a similar attitude toward the juvenile market, Ticknor and Fields were quick to capitalize on the critical success of *The Scarlet Letter* not only by reissuing *Twice-Told Tales*, but also by reprinting these failed attempts at school books in a single volume intended for family reading: *True Stories from History and Biography* (1851). Hawthorne's real financial success as a children's author only came, however, in the next few years when Ticknor and Fields urged him to produce and swiftly publish his retelling of Greek myths for children: *The Wonder Book* (1852) and *Tanglewood Tales* (1853).

95. *The Letters, 1813–1843*, 15: 247, 252.

feminine and domestic taint to this literary "drudgery," as Hawthorne shared
with his sister in the production of much of this juvenile work. During his
time as editor of the *American Magazine of Useful and Entertaining Knowledge* the letters Hawthorne sent from Boston to his home in Salem mingle demands that his sisters take care of his laundry and that Elizabeth write for the
magazine: "I have but two clean shirts left. Where is that stock? Ebe should
have sent me some original poetry—and other concoctions." Many of his letters to Salem during these months end not with a signature but with the injunction "concoct—concoct—concoct."[96]

There remains, however, something in this idea of concocting a literature
for children that truly appeals to Hawthorne. He had, after all, published "Little
Annie's Ramble" a year before Samuel Goodrich offered him the editorship of
The American Magazine, and Hawthorne's preface to *Peter Parley's Universal
History* describes the project with remarkable nuance, complexity, and pride:

> To steer clear of bewildering difficulties on the one hand, and repulsive chrono-
> logical brevity on the other—the Scylla and Charybdis which beset the adven-
> turer in this attempt—and at the same time to weave into a few pages a clear,
> vivid and continuous tale of the great human family . . . demands a nicer under-
> standing of the youthful heart and intellect, and more art in the adaptation of
> language to simple minds, than can often be at the command of any man.[97]

Here is not "drudgery" but adventure as fraught with dangers as Greek epics.
Hawthorne's aversion to "repulsive chronologies," his celebration of imagination, sympathy, and understanding intimate the aesthetic project that he
would later call "Romance." Hawthorne clearly wishes in this preface to
mark the difficulty of his task and to celebrate his success in fulfilling it, even
if he equivocates on the gendered terms of that success—unclear whether his
achievement marks him as more or as less than "any man." His description
of the uses he foresees for this history puts further pressure on the concept
of "command":

> I have written for the *Young,* but as I desire that these volumes may not be
> forced upon anybody as a monitor or master, I say in the title page that it is de-
> signed for families. I wish it to be permitted to enter the family circle, and take
> its chance to make its way. If it is placed, not as a task-book, but rather as a

96. *The Letters, 1813–1843,* 15: 239, 230, 240.
97. *Peter Parley's Universal History, on the Basis of Geography, for the Use of Families*
(1837), 2 vols. (New York: S. Coleman, 1839), vii.

storyteller, on the table, perhaps the children may patronize it; perhaps the parents may deign to look into it. (viii)

This new nineteenth-century vision of the family united and disciplined through emotional bonds is the focus of the next section of my study. For the moment it is enough to note how in children's literature, in pedagogy, and in the structure of the family Hawthorne prefers desire to force. The *Universal History* is largely a compendium of facts, each chapter followed by its own quiz, yet despite this traditional didactic form Hawthorne explicitly rejects the anxieties about fiction that suffuse most such texts in the 1830s, and presents the "storyteller" as superior to the "task-book." What becomes clear as we review Hawthorne's early musings on children's literature is how much images of the family structured by love, rather than authority, and epitomized by the ideal "sinless" child become conflated with ideas about pedagogy and the power of storytelling. Hawthorne does indeed see himself, as he put it in a letter to Longfellow, set to "revolutionize the whole system of juvenile literature" (15: 266).

"Little Annie's Ramble" can be read as a meditation on the act of writing for children, and on the conflicting possibilities of monitor and playfellow. The story was first published in the annual *Youth's Keepsake, a Christmas and New Year's Gift for Young People* in 1835, almost a decade before Hawthorne had children of his own, and a few years before his courtship of Sophia Peabody. It is a fantasy of communion with a child that nevertheless remains oddly anti-domestic, telling as it does of Annie's ramble away from home. The *Youth's Keepsake* clearly intended its stories as holiday gifts for children, and the copy at Smith College suggests that the volumes were indeed used in this way: the first page is inscribed "Eliza P. Humphrey, from her father Jan 1st 1835." Hawthorne both addresses and speaks past such young readers; his story is as much for Eliza's father, suggesting the pleasure that grown men should or could take in little girls, as it is for Eliza herself. Ultimately the story would be reprinted in *Twice-Told Tales,* the shift in audience reflecting on the disturbing shifts of tone in the piece itself.

> What would Annie think if, in the book which I mean to send her, on New Year's day, she should find her sweet little self, bound up in silk or morocco with gilt edges, there to remain till she become a woman grown, with children of her own to read about their mother's childhood! That would be very queer. (9: 124)

Such confusions of outside and inside, author and narrator, reader and character, world and book are the principal charm of this story, but also the prin-

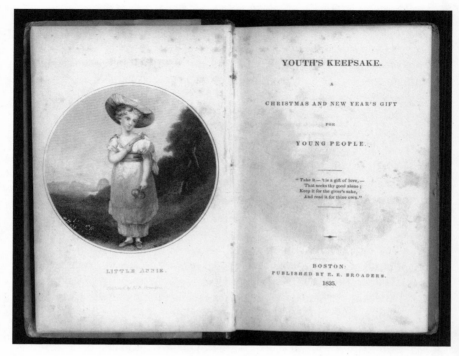

Fig. 1.9. This image of "Little Annie" does not place her on a ramble through town, nor with a stranger, but rather alone in some classical pastoral scene. Courtesy of the Mortimer Rare Book Room, Smith College.

cipal source of threat. The editors of *Youth's Keepsake* were particularly pleased by this conceit and used a picture labeled "Little Annie" as the frontispiece of the entire volume (fig. 1.9). Then, on page 151, immediately below this passage with its playful conflation of child and book, lies a note: "Does not our Frontispiece resemble your 'Little Annie'? EDITOR," calling the author's attention to the Press's fine treatment of his story, calling the readers' attention to the gift-book's expensive plates, but even more offering to make true Hawthorne's whimsical fantasy in the suggestion that Eliza Humphrey and all the daughters of all the fathers that purchased this book could find themselves "bound up" in it. The relation between book, man, and child is, as Hawthorne puts it, "very queer."

In the didactic tradition of early nineteenth-century children's literature the tale of a child who "strayed from her home" (9: 128) is a familiar conceit, one that reveals the dangers of town and affirms that children should be obedient and at home. In such accounts a hearthside pastime like reading would keep a child safe. Hawthorne's story appears to reject such traditional didacticism; the narrator insists that this ramble into the world is a harmless pleasure that leaves Annie "untainted" (9: 129). The story proclaims itself similarly detached from admonitory responsibilities: to "be merry" is better than to "moralize." But the conclusion of the sketch makes clear that the narrator's version of this afternoon ramble is not the only perspective. The bell of the town crier that opened the story, that clang of communal order and public knowledge, ends it as well, this time announcing not circuses but "the loss of a little girl who has not once let go of my hand!" (9: 129).

In the nonchalance with which the narrator discounts the mother's fear of losing Annie, in the worldly cynicism with which he describes all that they see as they roam the streets of the town, and most of all in his obsessive fascination with Annie's "pure, instinctive delicacy of taste" (9: 127), the narrator himself appears as the source of taint. He does not admit that their grasping of hands could be compatible with loss, could indeed be the very sign of loss. "Here we see the very same wolf—do not go near him, Annie!—the self same wolf that devoured little Red Riding Hood and her grandmother" (9: 127), he warns as they tour the caravan, dissolving the bounds between fairytale and real. To the extent that we hear a strain of wolf in the narrator's cajoling tones, the act of storytelling itself appears suspect. In presenting himself as a writer of children's stories, then, Hawthorne suggests the perverse as well as the innocent possibilities of that role. To "go hand in hand with the mind of a sinless child" intrudes hands into minds in a manner that will echo as horror throughout Hawthorne's mature fiction, as "the Unpardonable Sin" of "Ethan Brand," or as the torture Chillingsworth dispenses to Dimmesdale, who "knew that no friendly hand was pulling at his heart-strings."[98]

Presenting itself as an innocent children's story, "Little Annie's Ramble" thus also tells a story of adult lechery and disillusionment: "I have gone too far astray for the town crier to call me back!" the narrator moans (9: 129). Yet even this layered understanding of the story is too simple, for if it distrusts the narrator's self -presentation it still endorses the image of Annie as a "sinless child." One of the most destabilizing things about this story, however, is how Annie is cast as initiating this "strange couple": at least as the narrator sees and describes it, Annie is the one who feels "that impulse to go strolling

---

98. Nathaniel Hawthorne, *The Scarlet Letter,* in *The Centenary Edition of the Works of Nathaniel Hawthorne,* ed.William Charvat et al., vol. 1 (Columbus: Ohio University Press, 1962), 171.

away" and "comes bouncing on tiptoe across the street" to take a stranger's
hand (9: 121), and it is she who "has not once let go" of that hand. One of the
most seductive things about this story, in other words, is how it presents the
little girl as herself the source of seduction.[99] The narrator insists at the story's
end that it is not a story at all, that nothing has happened in it, and that Annie
can return home "with an untainted and unwearied heart, and be a happy
child again" (9: 129). Yet perhaps nothing has happened for the quite different reason that Annie never was such a "happy child" in the first place. The
stroll began, after all, because the narrator could "see that the pretty child is
weary of this wide and pleasant street" (9: 121). The adult life weariness that
he claims at the end can be alleviated by contact with the "still fresh existence" and "sweet magic" of "an hour or two with children" (129) proves part
of childhood itself, since Annie too is weary.

The shifting character of innocence and taint in this story comes to haunt
Hawthorne's experience of parenting. A similar idealization of childhood innocence prompts Nathaniel and Sophia to name their first daughter "Una"—much
against the advice of family and friends—as "the symbol of the one true union
in the world," as Nathaniel put it in a letter to Sophia,[100] and as a harbinger "of
a most delicate spirit, impatient of wrong & ugliness—demanding beauty of all
things & persons—& like the 'heavenly Una' of Spenser," as Sophia noted in the
family journal she and Nathaniel both wrote in sporadically until 1852. She is,
however, careful to counter these beatific predictions for her daughter with the
assurance that "At the same time she will recognize the Real."[101] Sophia began
this notebook on April 3, 1844, exactly a month after Una's birth; Nathaniel
did not write in it until June 20, 1847, when he recorded some of Una's words:

99. See Freeman, "Honeymoon with a Stranger."

100. For Hawthorne's responses to complaints about the name from his sister Louisa and
friend George Hillard see Nathaniel Hawthorne, *Letters 1843–1853, The Centenary Edition of the
Works of Nathaniel Hawthorne,* ed. William Charvat et al., vol. 16 (Columbus: Ohio University
Press, 1985), 20–22, quote 37.

Contemporary critics tend to share these friends' dismay: T. Walter Herbert sees Una's ner-
vous breakdown at the age of fourteen as the psychic costs of the Hawthornes' insistence that
their "home is paradise." See "Nathaniel Hawthorne, Una Hawthorne, and *The Scarlet Letter:*
Interactive Selfhoods and the Cultural Construction of Gender," *PMLA* 103 (May 1988): 285–97;
and "Part Four: Roman Fever," *Dearest Beloved,* 213–56.

101. Patricia Dunlavy Valenti, "Sophia Peabody Hawthorne's American Notebook," in
Studies in the American Renaissance, ed. Joel Myerson (Charlottesville: University Press of Virginia, 1996), 148. The family notebook is a single volume now at the Pierpont Morgan Library,
but the history of publication has split it so that the portions in Sophia's and the children's
hands are printed here, while Nathaniel's portions are reproduced in the *American Notebooks:
The Centenary Edition of the Works of Nathaniel Hawthorne,* ed. William Charvat et al., vol. 8
(Columbus: Ohio University Press, 1972). Subsequent citations of both Sophia's and Nathaniel's
entries refer to these published versions and will be given parenthetically.

"I'm tired of all sings, and want to slip into God. I'm tired of little Una Hawsorne."
"Are you tired of Mama?" "No." "But are you tired of Papa?" "No." "I am tired of
Dora, and tired of little Julian, and tired of little Una Hawsorne." (8: 398)

Tired of nurse and brother and self, here is a world-weariness greater even
than "Little Annie's." Sophia records this scene as well in her different style,
Nathaniel's detached quotation tempered in her version by sympathetic explanation: "Rain & cold. Una had a day of infinite ennui, like a bird with
wings tied to its side. . . . 'I am tired of all ᵗʰ sings'" (151). It is easy to imagine "I am tired of all sings" becoming a kind of family code. What are these
parents doing when they fondly and critically write these remembrances of
Una, the world-weary, self-weary child, moping in the Hawthorne parlor?
The family notebook is full of such observations. There is clearly for both parents a pleasure in recording childish oddities and badness at least as great as
that offered by accounts of the children's goodness. As Sophia puts it, "In
short there never were such divine children, far diviner than if more spotless
of blame—I cannot explain this remark now" (161). What Sophia cannot explain is the way she is charmed by her child, how affection transmutes moral
categories and evades ideology.

Though critics are right to note the idealizing and gendering pressures the
Hawthornes put on their children, and most forcefully on their first child,
Una, the predominant feeling in these notebook entries is one of wonder, of
the uncanny mysteriousness of children.

> But to return to Una, there is something that almost frightens me about the
> child—I know not whether elfin or angelic, but, at all events, supernatural. . . .
> I now and then catch an aspect of her, in which I cannot believe her to be my
> own human child, but a spirit strangely mingled with good and evil, haunting
> the house where I dwell. The little boy is always the same child, and never
> varies in his relation to me. (8: 431)

Hawthorne writes these notes in the days awaiting his mother's death, dis-
comfited in part by Una's fascination with her grandmother's sickroom. Critics often quote this passage because it is so closely echoed in the phrases
Hawthorne will use to describe Pearl in *The Scarlet Letter.* But its portrait of
Una's startling changeability is one that both parents repeat throughout these
pages. Here is Sophia:

> I never knew such a combination of the highest refinement & rudest boorish-
> ness—one lies at the door of the other—When she was a little infant, in one po-

sition as she lay asleep, she reminded ~~me~~ us of Pan—almost Caliban—& in another the most sweet, angelical etherial—spiritual aspect beamed forth. (166)

Sophia's correction from "me" to "us" marks the pressure of family unity—to parent as one—but in so doing it emphasizes the shared sense of this evaluation, how since Una's infancy the couple have been telling stories, assigning symbolic, mythic, literary names to make sense of this life that they have produced but cannot contain or predict. Child-rearing manuals stressed the parental duty to mold the moral being of children. As we have seen in children's diaries, children's own efforts at self-making are deeply marked by their dependency on adult lessons and expectations, but they are not fully controlled by them. Instead they transmute compliance into play. What the Hawthornes record most powerfully in this notebook is the limits to adult command, the autonomy of these beings, the impossibility of control or authorship over what should be "my own human child." That Julian seems less troubling in these terms may be a mark of gender difference (there apparently being less need to explain aggression or wildness in a boy), or even a matter of character. But there is also the difference made by Una's position as first child—how in the parenting of Una the Hawthornes define for themselves what the mysterious relations between parent and child may be. The issues the notebook raises as questions about Una are thus also questions about childhood itself, about how infantile lives come to take a recognizable human form, to be inscribed within moral and social codes, and what role parents might occupy in that process.

Pearl has long fascinated and confused readers of *The Scarlet Letter.* As Barbara Garlitz first noted, the responses of early reviewers described her either as "an embodied angel from the skies" or as "a void little demon," and such polarities have continued to characterize critical response.[102] Garlitz's efforts to make sense of this duality, like those more recently of Franny Nudelman, show how Pearl conforms to nineteenth-century child-rearing doctrine: naturally innocent—"worthy to have been brought forth in Eden" (1: 90)—Pearl had nevertheless imbibed from her mother the passion and sinfulness of the act that conceived her. In *The Mother's Book,* Lydia Maria Child had warned that "it is not possible to indulge anger, or any other wrong feeling, and conceal it entirely. If not expressed in words, a child *feels* the baneful influence. Evil enters into his soul as the imperceptible atmosphere

---

102. Barbara Garlitz, "Pearl: 1850–1955," *PMLA* 72 (September 1957): 698, quoting Henry Giles, *Illustrations of Genius* (Boston: Ticknor and Fields, 1854), 76; and George P. Loring, "Hawthorne's *Scarlet Letter,*" *Massachusetts Quarterly Review* 3 (September 1850): 494.

he breathes enters his lungs" (9). Hawthorne describes Pearl's moral inheritance precisely in terms of such atmospheric transmission.

> The mother's impassioned state had been the medium through which were transmitted to the unborn infant the rays of its moral life; and, however white and clear originally, they had taken the deep stains of crimson and gold, the fiery luster, the black shadow, and the untempered light, of the intervening substance. Above all the warfare of Hester's spirit at that epoch was perpetuated in Pearl. (1: 91)

Drawing on *The Mother's Book* and similar manuals, Nudelman explains that the "intersubjectivity" of mother and child reveals the circular nature of familial authority; in such a system "a mother's efforts to discipline her child cannot be easily distinguished from her efforts to discipline herself."[103] Or as Lydia Maria Child expressed it, "the first rule, and most important of all, in education, is, that a mother govern her own feelings, and keep her heart and conscience pure" (4). Such mutual effects had been apparent to Hawthorne as early as "Little Annie," whose narrator concludes of children that "Their influence on us is at least reciprocal with ours on them" (9: 129). These readings make sense of the doubleness of Pearl, how her spirit, like Una's, is "strangely mingled with good and evil." They suggest as well why it is that Pearl, who "could not be made amenable to rules" (1: 91), nevertheless serves to forestall her parents' flight into lawlessness, why it is she who issues the command "Come thou and take it up!" (1: 210), restoring the scarlet letter and the punitive power of communal judgment to her mother's breast.

In the chapter "The Child at the Brook-Side" Hawthorne stresses the multiple and reflective nature of the child's power. As Pearl reiterates her demand until her mother complies, the narrative voice focuses on the replication of Pearl's gestures and emotions in the reflecting water of the brook.

> At length, assuming a singular air of authority, Pearl stretched out her hand, with the small forefinger extended, and pointing evidently towards her mother's breast. And beneath in the mirror of the brook, there was the flower-girded and sunny image of little Pearl, pointing her small forefinger too. (1: 209)

As many scholars have noted, Pearl's authority here is communal authority, emphasizing the bonds of relationship and responsibility against Hester's an-

---

103. Franny Nudelman, "'Emblem and Product of Sin': The Poisoned Child in *The Scarlet Letter* and Domestic Advice Literature," *Yale Journal of Criticism* 10 (spring 1997): 206.

tinomian vision of personal freedom and escape.[104] Like the schoolyard children of *Our Nig,* Pearl gives voice to social prejudices and norms. The multiplication of Pearls in her reflected image and echoing cries makes her many, "a hidden multitude" (1: 210). But if this doubling serves to conjure communal disapproval, allowing Pearl to express societal claims and enforce Puritan law, it simultaneously manages to mark the mysteriousness of relationship and identity: "This image so nearly identical with the living Pearl, seemed to communicate somewhat of its own shadowy and intangible quality to the child herself. . . . In the brook beneath stood another child,—another and the same" (1: 208). This play of separation and oneness, "another and the same"—how one's own human child can be nevertheless so alien—is mirrored in Hawthorne's writing about his own parenting. Alongside the understanding of the family circle as the source of reciprocal, circular, social discipline runs a sense of the family as "shadowy and intangible," and of childhood as ungraspable as a reflection in a forest pool.

The imagery of "haunting" provides one of Hawthorne's most potent tools for Romance. In the Custom-House introduction to *The Scarlet Letter,* "Moonlight in a familiar room" works this transformation, making "the domestic scenery" of the middle-class parlor into "spiritualized" "things of intellect."

> Nothing is too small or too trifling to undergo this change and acquire dignity thereby. A child's shoe; the doll seated in her little wicker carriage; the hobbyhorse;—whatever, in a word, has been used or played with, during the day, is now invested with a quality of strangeness and remoteness, though still almost as vividly present as by daylight. Thus, therefore, the floor of our familiar room has become a neutral territory, somewhere between the real world and fairyland, where the Actual and the Imaginary may meet and each imbue itself with the nature of the other. Ghosts might enter here without affrighting us. (1: 36)

It seems only fitting that Hawthorne should first work this magic on childhood toys, things which he chooses precisely because they are "trifling" and yet things which were always in their daily usage subject to just the sort of transformation he describes. The normal, expected purpose of doll or hobbyhorse is to become real in a child's imagination, to cry or gallop. The production of this neutral territory, the work of Romance, not only transforms the domestic scene, but is modeled on it and particularly on the play of chil-

---

104. See Bercovitch, *Office of the Scarlet Letter,* 9–10; Richard H. Millington, *Practicing Romance: Narrative Form and Cultural Engagement in Hawthorne's Fiction* (Princeton, N.J.: Princeton University Press, 1992), 90–93; and Nudelman, "'Emblem and Product of Sin,'" 208.

dren. Thus Hawthorne's sense of the relation between literary romance and children's play gestures toward the sort of middle space Winnicott theorizes. Hawthorne may be disquieted by his daughter's way of "haunting the house where I dwell," but it is a discomfort tinged with wonder and desire, and it is, moreover, a practice that he seeks to emulate in his writing of Romance.

The Wonder Book, the most successful of Hawthorne's children's books, largely imagines the idealization of childhood and the expectations of society as seamlessly united. Written in Lenox during the summer of 1851, in the light of the critical success of *The Scarlet Letter* and *The House of the Seven Gables,* it marks Hawthorne's most sanguine literary period, a moment when he feels most confident that his creative vision might indeed coincide with the public taste.[105] Here the innocence of children, the felicity of literary production, and the clarity of authorial control all appear certain. In this book the college student Eustace Bright tells six stories based on Greek mythology to a group of loosely related children with such simultaneously prosaic and blossomy names as "Milkweed," "Squash-Blossom," and "Dandelion." The frame narrative of Eustace and the flower-children is lively and detailed, presenting a year's worth of storytelling on hillside walks and by a winter fire and providing one of Hawthorne's fullest literary portraits of affluent and pleasurable domesticity. It is a domesticity clearly propped up by this storytelling, suggesting how much literary enjoyment and the kind of shared cultural norms carried by Greek mythology inform the ideal middle-class household. Just as Grenville used his toy houses to play the Swiss Family Robinson, Sophia writes in the notebook about acting out these myths with the children, Una cast as Pandora and Julian in "a jaunty cap" as Mercury (158). Eustace Bright titles his narration of the myth of Pandora "A Paradise of Children":

> ". . . when the world was as new as Sweet Fern's bran-new humming-top. There was then but one season of the year, and that was the delightful summer; and but one age for mortals, and that was childhood."
>
> "I never heard of that before," said Primrose.
>
> "Of course, you never did," answered Eustace. "It shall be a story of what nobody but myself ever dreamed of,—a Paradise of children,—and how by the naughtiness of just such a little imp as Primrose here, it all came to nothing."[106]

---

105. Nina Baym, "Hawthorne's Myths for Children: The Author Versus His Audience," *Studies in Short Fiction* 10 (1973): 35–46; and Laffrado, *Hawthorne's Literature for Children,* 66–99.

106. Nathaniel Hawthorne, *A Wonder Book and Tanglewood Tales, The Centenary Edition of the Works of Nathaniel Hawthorne,* ed.William Charvat et al., vol. 7 (Columbus: Ohio University Press, 1972), 63.

It tells of how "troubles" come into the world together with aging, so that childhood appears to predate pain. Still, of course, Pandora's "vexation" at the mystery of the box, her "naughtiness," precedes and prompts the act of opening it. It arises, moreover, from domestic unhappiness, from Pandora's inability to play happily with little Epimetheus and the other children. The Paradise of childhood thus rests upon obedience and domestic accord. It is worth noting that Primrose is chastised—the "little imp"—for questioning the authority of the storyteller. At the end of the volume Hawthorne himself figures as a character, "That silent man, who lives in the old red house near Tanglewood avenue, and whom we sometimes meet, with two children at his side"; and Eustace makes clear that his authority is not to be doubted:

> If our babble were to reach his ears and happen not to please him, he has but to fling a quire or two of paper into the stove and you, Primrose, and I, and Periwinkle, Sweet Fern, Squash-Blossom, Blue Eye, Huckleberry, Clover . . . would all turn to smoke, and go whisking up the funnel! Our neighbor in the red house is a harmless sort of person enough, for aught I know, as concerns the rest of the world; but something whispers to me that he has a terrible power over ourselves, extending to nothing short of annihilation. (7: 169–70)

In a sense *A Wonder Book,* though perhaps the most "sunny and happy" of Hawthorne's books,[107] is also the most deluded, since it wins that sunniness through a dual simplification that imagines both parenting and writing as acts of simple fiat. Here childhood appears truly as a parental paradise, Locke's *tabula rasa* offered literally as a blank page on which the father-author can write.

Hawthorne mailed the manuscript for *A Wonder Book* to his publisher, Ticknor and Fields, on July 15, 1851, and on July 28 Hawthorne records in the notebook "at seven o'clock, A.M. Wife, E. P. P. [Sophia's sister Elizabeth Palmer Peabody], Una, and Rosebud, took their departure, leaving Julian and me in possession of the Red Shanty" (8: 436). The notebook account "Twenty Days with Julian & Little Bunny, By Papa" is full of the glee of domestic inversions—Julian shrieking because he can with "baby gone" (8: 436), or Nathaniel smoking and taking "the little man" on a picnic with Melville and the Duycknicks where Julian eats only gingerbread (8: 464).[108] There are

---

107. Praise from a review in *Graham's Monthly Magazine,* quoted in *A Wonder Book,* 6: 306.

108. These journal entries have just been published as a separate little volume, for a popular audience—a testament, as Paul Auster puts it in his fine introduction, to Hawthorne's skill as a "private" writer. Nathaniel Hawthorne, *Twenty Days with Julian & Little Bunny by Papa* (New York: New York Review of Books, 2003), ix.

some domestic trials as well: "The little man woke me with his exclamation between two and three o'clock; and I found him, wonderful to say, in a perfectly soppy state. There had been a deluge in his bed and nowhere else" (8: 452). But there is no sense of authorial omnipotence, rather if anyone is the wielder of words it is Julian,

> Either I have less patience to-day than ordinary, or the little man makes larger demands upon it; but it really does seem as if he had bated me with more questions, references, and observations, than mortal father ought to be expected to endure. He does put me almost beside my propriety; never quitting me, and continually thrusting in his word between the clauses of every sentence of all my reading, and smashing every attempt at reflection into a thousand fragments. (8: 454)

The Hawthorne children do scribble in the pages of this notebook, their own words, drawings and wildly wielded pens erupting around their parents' words, insisting on being part of this writing thing that their parents do. Clearly they know that one way they matter for their father is as a subject of writing.

> Enter Una—"Where is little Julian?" "He has gone out to walk." "No; but I mean where is the place of little Julian that you've been writing about him." So I point to the page, at which she looks with all possible satisfaction; and stands watching the pen as it hurries forward. "I'll put the ink nearer to you," says she. "Father are you going to write all this?" . . . I tell her that I am now writing about herself—"that's nice writing," says she. (8: 403)

Una, with narcissistic satisfaction, finds the writing that is about her "nice writing" indeed. Pearl seems herself "the scarlet letter in another form; the scarlet letter endowed with life!" (1: 102). In this mirror bond between child and writing, Hawthorne stakes the nature and meaning of authorship, both for the family and for fiction.

Jacqueline Rose argues that children's fiction continues to be based on a "philosophy which sets up the child as a pure point of origin in relation to language, sexuality, and the state."[109] I suggest in this chapter that childhood underlies mid-nineteenth-century attitudes toward writing more generally; concepts of fiction and of authorship entwine with the figure of the child in multiple and surprising ways. The chapters that follow will put similar pres-

109. Jacqueline Rose, "Introduction," in *The Case of Peter Pan* (London: Macmillan, 1984), 9.

sure on the workings of the family and of the state. Hawthorne's sense of mystery about the dynamics of parenting, of what it means to claim another as "one's own human child," hints at the complexity of relations within the mid-nineteenth-century household, and how, in families structured by affection, dependency can be a kind of power. The patterns of compliance and autonomy we have found in children's writing, and in the claiming of literary voice, presage the part children play in individual households, in social institutions, and in national formation as a whole.

PART TWO

The Child and the Making of Home:
Questions of Love, Power, and the Market

CHAPTER TWO

Temperance in the Bed of a Child

And now she saw that Joe had crept into the bed behind the
sick child, and that her arm was drawn tightly around his
neck.

"You won't let them hurt me, will you, dear?" said the
poor frightened victim of a terrible mania.

"Nothing will hurt you, father," answered Mary, in a voice
that showed her mind to be clear, and fully conscious of her
parent's true condition.

She had seen him thus before. Ah! What an experience for
a child! . . .

"I knew I would be safe where you were," he whispered
back—"I knew it, and so I came. Kiss me, love."

How pure and fervent was the kiss laid instantly upon his
lips! . . . Now the sphere of his loving, innocent child seemed
to have overcome, at least for the time, the evil influences that
were getting possession even of his external senses.[1]

Over and over again, nineteenth-century temperance fiction
tells this story of a drunken father creeping into bed with his

An earlier version of chapter 2 appeared as "Temperance in the Bed of
a Child: Incest and Social Order in Nineteenth-Century America," *American
Quarterly* 47 (March 19995): 1–33. Reprinted with the permission of the
Johns Hopkins University Press.

1. Timothy Shay Arthur, *Ten Nights in a Bar-Room, and What I Saw
There* (1854; facsimile reprint, Cambridge: Belknap Press, 1964), 78–79.

young child.[2] This is not, of course, the only plot available to temperance fiction. Indeed, from my readings, the single most dominant temperance plot was one of degeneration from first misguided sip to destitution and death. Still, this scene of conversion wrought by the embraces of a young child appears at least as a vignette in fully one-quarter of the more than three hundred tales I have read; it is a favorite device in a literature generally characterized by formulaic writing.

Narrative formulas index cultural obsessions, and this scene repeats throughout temperance fiction as obsessively and fervently as the caresses with which—in another story—little Debby Colt greets her father, "eager lips . . . kissing him over and over again."[3] Just returned from the foundling hospital, Debby is newly healed of the broken bones caused by her father's frequent beatings; Mary may promise her father that nothing will hurt him while he lies in her arms, but her sickness was caused by being hit on the head by a beer tumbler an angry tavern-keeper had thrown at Joe. There is every reason to suspect that in nineteenth-century America, as now, the drunken father's demand for such caresses was—along with beatings and flying beer mugs—simply another, more secret form of abuse. With those suspicions so amply corroborated by twentieth-century analysis of childhood sexual abuse, it is hard not to read the insistence that Joe is only "safe" in Mary's bed, that "nothing will hurt" him there, as an inverted trace of how these embraces must have hurt her, how they strip her of all safety. "Ah! What an experience for a child!" the narrator exclaims. And yet what I find most startling about these scenes is the vehemence with which they define this hardly veiled erotic contact not as abuse but as the surest and best antidote to abuse. With their kisses, Debby and Mary ultimately convert their drunken fathers into good, temperate men. In their rhetorical insistence on

2. On August 4, 1836, at the annual convention of the American Temperance Union held in Saratoga, New York, the members voted to endorse the use of fiction and "the products of fancy" in their campaign against intemperance; by the 1850s fiction had clearly become the favored form for temperance propaganda. See Herbert Ross Brown, *The Sentimental Novel in America, 1789–1860* (Durham, N.C.: Duke University Press, 1940), 201–3. In her Ph.D. dissertation, Joan Silverman reports that the National Temperance Society's Publication House, founded in 1865, alone produced "over two billion pages of temperance literature." "'I'll Never Touch Another Drop': Images of Alcoholism and Temperance in American Popular Culture, 1874–1918" (Ph.D. dissertation, New York University, 1979), 1. My own coverage of this voluminous material has relied simply on those temperance tales that have found their way into the collections of the American Antiquarian Society and the Amherst College, Mount Holyoke College and Forbes Libraries—312 in all.

3. "Debby Colt: What She Did, and How She Did It," in *The Old Brown Pitcher and Other Tales,* ed. Elizabeth Prentiss (New York: National Temperance Union and Publication House, 1863), 169.

the potency of a child's caress, these stories epitomize the culture's most cherished fantasy about childhood—that dependency and vulnerability could be a form of power.

These conversion stories are structured by their own logic of conversion; they make drunks temperate by transforming scenes suffused with the lurking dangers of pederasty and incest into loving mechanisms of redemption. In noting the double valence of these plots—at once culturally subversive and culturally conservative—my work runs counter to what meager literary analysis such texts have already received. Temperance fiction has been damned and (occasionally) praised, along with other forms of nineteenth-century reform literature, for its adherence to sentimental conventions, like that of the lovingly redemptive child, or for its grotesque fascination with such alcoholic effects as delirium tremens and spontaneous combustion.[4] My concern is not to choose between these reform rhetorics but to recognize the violence and sensuality embedded within even the most angelic and sentimental generic conceit, and so to explore the cultural and ideological implications of this strange redemption plot—and the particular conception of childhood at its core.

In this chapter, I ask why temperance fiction locates its scenes of salvation in the bed of a child. My answers will suggest the erotic potential of the new stress on disciplining through love as the nineteenth century's chosen model of child-rearing and how this emphasis on love rather than punishment works to ally domesticity both with self-control *and* with the fulfillment of desire. The easy conjunction of restraint and indulgence characteristic of this redemption plot will, moreover, prove integral to the structures of bourgeois capitalism. Thus this section on the making of the family inevitably points outside the middle-class household toward the political and economic requirements of the nation. The forms of authority assumed by these fictional children replicate patterns already familiar from the tactics Frado or child diarists employ in their efforts to wring agency out of dependency and compliance. The children in these stories, however, unlike Jenny Trumbull or Louis Gratacap or even the semi-autobiographical Frado, are purely the product of

---

4. David S. Reynolds, *Beneath the American Renaissance: The Subversive Imagination on the Age of Emerson and Melville* (New York: Alfred Knopf, 1988), chapter 2, still contains the most comprehensive discussion of nineteenth-century temperance fiction to date. Reynolds would decidedly exclude the stories I discuss here from the category of the subversive, to castigate them as does Brown and others as simplistically and conservatively maudlin. The essays collected in *The Serpent in the Cup: Temperance in American Literature,* ed. David S. Reynolds and Debra J. Rosenthal (Amherst: University of Massachusetts Press, 1997), begin to suggest the influence of temperance writing on a wide range of American issues and genres, especially anti-slavery writing.

adult invention. They are fantasy children; the alchemy that transforms their vulnerability into power carries no grain of self-making. Instead, the redemptive power of these fictional children proves a rhetorical ploy, a pawn in somebody else's game. Children's own efforts at self-expression are largely obscured, lost beneath a general cultural idealization of childhood as expressive. In turning to these fantasies of childhood power, I am interested precisely in the gap between American cultural figurations of childhood and the experiences of any individual child, a chasm all the more harrowing when the issues in question are alcoholism, domestic violence, and sexual abuse. Thus, although this fiction depicts children successfully disciplining their fathers, the child's ability to domesticate and even feminize male desires does not fundamentally alter the structures of power. As the loving domestic scene is proffered as a replacement for the dissipation and excesses of drunkenness, the child's love works to enforce a bourgeois patriarchal order that leaves the child as vulnerable as ever.

Love and the Law

We tend to forget that "temperance was the most popular, influential and long-lived social reform movement of the late nineteenth and early twentieth centuries."[5] I will not detail this history here, but stretching between the 1810s and the passing of the Eighteenth Amendment in 1919, the evolving methods and goals of temperance reform indicate changing attitudes toward the social power of domesticity. In particular, the shifting strategies of the temperance movement reveal a fundamental tension between a belief in "moral suasion" (that the reform of individual sinners would precede and produce the purification of society as a whole) and a reliance on prohibition (that only through state action—such as the "Maine Law" of 1851 which forbid the manufacture or sale of intoxicating liquor—could the problems of drunkenness be alleviated for individual or state). This debate on tactics has an obvious gender bias, as arguments over the efficacy of moral suasion implicitly assess the social efficacy of the American family in the face of a problem that—as temperance workers were quick to remind the public—rendered women and children particularly vulnerable.

Moral suasion is woman's work both because it depends upon women's presumed skill at nurturing the good and because it conforms to women's limited access to public power. "What then is the aid that woman can most fitly

5. Jed Dannenbaum, "The Social History of Alcohol," *Drinking and Drug Practices Surveyor* 19 (1984): 11.

lend to the noble science of being 'temperate in all things'?" Lydia Sigourney asks in the introduction to her collection of temperance verse. "Not the assumption of masculine energies, not the applause of popular assemblies; but the still small voice singing at the cradle-side."[6] Describing the Washingtonians' goal of redeeming the drunkard through example and moral suasion, John Hawkins relies upon maternal metaphors: "we don't slight the drunkard; we love him, we nurse him, as a mother does her infant learning to walk."[7] Hawkins's manner of reclaiming individual drunkards presumes that maternal love wields social power; but though they claimed to work "as a mother" Washingtonian meetings, with their public and histrionic confessions, clearly breached domestic norms of privacy and decorum. All too aware of the limits of such maternal politics, the women's suffrage movement gained most of its early adherents among women who wished to vote for prohibition.[8]

This national ambivalence over the efficacy of moral suasion as a means of public reform coincides with its rising preeminence as a mechanism of internal domestic discipline.[9] Prohibition might deem the law, not familial love,

6. Lydia Sigourney, *Water Drops* (New York: R Carter, 1850), v.

7. Quoted in Jed Dannenbaum, *Drink and Disorder: Temperance Reform in Cincinnati from the Washingtonian Revival to the WCTU* (Urbana: University of Illinois Press, 1984), 38. Hawkins, a former hat-maker and reformed drunkard, was one of the national leaders of the Washingtonians. Founded in 1841, the Washingtonians relied heavily on the example of their already reformed members; their open meetings consisted of "reformed drunkards" telling the highly dramatic stories of their past dissipation and the happiness and prosperity that total abstinence had brought to their lives. Although public events, Washingtonian meetings bear a striking resemblance to the "twelve-step" program of today's Alcoholics Anonymous. In terms of the relation between temperance and pederasty, it is worth noting that contemporary groups working with either the victims or perpetrators of childhood sexual abuse frequently employ similar therapeutic procedures.

8. For a historical account of the temperance movement's gradual abandonment of moral suasion sensitive to these gender issues, see Lori D. Ginzberg's chapter "Moral Suasion Is Moral Balderdash," in her *Women and the Work of Benevolence: Morality, Politics and Class in the Nineteenth-Century United States* (New Haven, Conn.: Yale University Press, 1990). Ruth Bordin, in *Woman and Temperance: The Quest for Power and Liberty, 1873–1900* (Philadelphia: Temple University Press, 1981), describes the complex of goals, activities, and political philosophies developed by the Woman's Christian Temperance Union (WCTU) in the later part of the century: "women used the WCTU as a base for their participation in reformist causes, as a sophisticated avenue for political action, as a support for demanding the ballot, and as a vehicle for supporting a wide range of charitable activities" (xvi). This range of activities continues to work both for legislative prohibitions and for individual reform.

9. The passing of the Maine Law in 1851 marks the initial upsurge of support for prohibition. It is harder to provide a precise date for the adoption of disciplinary intimacy as the favored mode of child-rearing; still, as I suggest in the preface, domestic manuals of the 1830s through the 1850s become increasingly consistent and assured in their preference for affectionate persuasion over punitive coercion. Moreover, during this period, mothers, not fathers, were increasingly represented as the parent primarily responsible for child-rearing and child discipline. For discussion of this transition in American culture see Bernard Wishy, *The Child and*

to be the best way to rule the nation's drunkenness, but love was clearly the best way to rule the home. What Richard Brodhead insightfully labels "disciplinary intimacy" reorganized the order-inducing structures of the American home on the basis of affection rather than authority—with the result of an increasingly internalized and perfect domestic discipline: "love's beauty as a disciplinary force, is that it creates a more thorough order of subjugation."[10] Love's thoroughness, as we have already seen in the example of the Hawthornes, stems in part from its implicit reciprocity: love's new familial order figures children not only as objects of discipline but also, and more interestingly, as its agents. This chapter focuses on the disciplinary possibilities of the child and demonstrates how the figure of the child functions in the making of homes, effectively imposing domestic order. Thus, although disciplinary intimacy provides a domestic configuration of the reform methods of moral suasion, it overlays the gender bias of moral suasion with issues of age and innocence. The salvific effects of children's love are a sentimental norm, but one that complicates normative adult models of social control. In this way children's love proves much like children's writing: the process of socializing and controlling children easily inverts, affording childhood a peculiar kind of cultural power. I want to stress, however, the distinctions between the kind of agency child writers cull from their acts of studious compliance and the celebration of vulnerability-as-power that characterizes these texts. The romanticization of childhood vulnerability at the heart of these stories may well serve, after all, as a highly effective means of keeping children dependent. When, in one temperance story, "Phoebe's love had saved" her father, who pledging abstinence "kissed her passionately and burst into tears," the narrator concludes that "what reason, persuasion, conscience, suffering, shame, could not do, the love of a little child had wrought. Oh! love is very

---

the Republic: The Dawn of American Child Nurture (Philadelphia: University of Pennsylvania Press, 1968); Mary Ryan, Cradle of the Middle Class: The Family in Oneida County, New York, 1790–1865 (New York: Cambridge University Press, 1981) and The Empire of the Mother: American Writing about Domesticity, 1830–1860 (New York: The Institute for Research in History, 1982); Steven Mintz, A Prison of Expectations: The Family in Victorian Culture (New York: New York University Press, 1983); and Richard Brodhead, "Sparing the Rod: Discipline and Fiction in Antebellum America," Representations 21 (winter 1988): 67–96. The writings of John Locke and Jean-Jacques Rousseau provide the Enlightenment foundations for this shift, so that Philippe Ariès can argue in Centuries of Childhood that the West's reorganization of the family around love rather than authority began as early as 1700.

   10. Brodhead, "Sparing the Rod," 87. Though my work is largely inspired by Brodhead's essay, I want to mark how our understandings of "disciplinary intimacy" diverge. Taking the "intimacy" of Brodhead's term literally, I am interested in the erotic dimensions of thus producing domestic order. I therefore construe the disciplinary forces evoked by love as more complexly multi-directional than those he describes.

strong."[11] These conclusions celebrate the power of a child's love; they distinguish it not only from the public and masculine purview of reason but also from such feminine tools of moral suasion as persuasion, conscience, suffering, and shame. As Phoebe's strong love suggests, differentiating the power of vulnerable women from the power of even more vulnerable children reimagines moral suasion in a newly transcendent guise. Temperance authors know that the weaker the agent of reform, the more spectacular is love's success. Of course, in lauding children's strong love such stories affirm and reinforce the dependencies of childhood.

Speaking about the family and about the state, temperance fiction assumes a mixed allegiance to the discourses of law and love and to masculine, feminine, and childlike strategies of reform. The demands of genre require that temperance fiction align itself with moral suasion—after all, it is the aim of these sentimental tales to touch their readers' hearts—and so insist that social change rests upon the loving regeneration of individual drunkards or readers. There is no narrative motive in prohibition; the law is its own last word. Thus, although many tales do endorse the closing of taverns, the rhetoric of temperance fiction runs counter to the increasing political preference for legislative solutions.[12] Temperance fiction includes stories that call for social and legislative—not individual—reform: in *The Sedley Family; or, The Effect of the Maine Liquor Law,* pledges and family love prove insufficient to redeem Mr. Sedley from intemperance, so the family moves to Maine where, Mrs. Sedley hopes, "the law might save her husband."[13] Yet though the reforming tactics advocated in such stories may have changed to reflect national interest in prohibition, the rhetoric remains grounded in emotional persuasion—and particularly in the strong love of a child. In the story of "The Red Frock," for example, father, repentant after having thrown little Molly's new red dress into the fire in a fit of drunken temper, takes the pledge. But "the pledge alone wouldn't save him" and his bouts of drunkenness only end

11. T. S. Arthur, "Phoebe Grey," in *The Pitcher of Cool Water and Other Stories* (New York: National Temperance Society and Publication House, 1873), 131–32.

12. Reading this fiction I was struck by the persistence of scenes of redemptive child-love from the height of moral suasion in the 1830s through the prohibitionary successes of the 1850s and into the founding of the WCTU in the 1870s. Both in style and in professed political goals, temperance fiction changed a great deal during this half-century, yet this formulaic plot device remained present and powerful throughout. My discussion of this fiction ranges widely through these decades in an effort to demonstrate this continuity, both as an instance of the recalcitrance of narrative convention and as an index of the persistence of the familial structures that link love and abuse—regardless of shifts in political methodology.

13. *The Sedley Family; or, The Effect of the Maine Liquor Law* (Boston: T. O. Walker, 1853); note that the publication date is only two years after the passing of the Maine Liquor Law. Quoted in Ginzberg, *Women and the Work of Benevolence,* who discusses this novel on 117–18.

once "he had got us a new home in a place where no liquor was sold." "You will bless God, with me" father writes, "that there are places to be found where no license can be had to send men to perdition." This prohibitionary tale ends, however, by celebrating not only the efficacious law but also the initiatory and invisible blessing of a drunkard's redeeming love for the little girl whose red dress—need I insist upon its erotic symbolism?—he burned. Leaving off its praise of prohibition, the narrative's last sentence recalls Molly, now grown and a schoolteacher, but still innocent in her ignorance, "who does not know the story of the little red frock—the turning point of her life."[14]

Even when little girls explicitly choose public and political temperance strategies, these stories invariably locate their power in contradistinction to prohibitionary laws. In the story "What Two Little Girls Did," Katy and Ellen bewail their powerlessness to combat intemperance:

> "O my! If we were men!" exclaimed Katy, her face flushed with excitement.
> "But we are only little girls," answered Ellen mournfully.
> "Maybe little girls could do something, if they tried," suggested Katy.

What they did was write a letter to the newspaper explaining that they are "puzzled" by "something very bad"—the willingness of the town's leaders to sanction the selling of alcohol. Their letter does "rouse up a whole town," prompting action among the men Katy wished they were, and, within two weeks, every drinking-saloon has been closed. Yet even here, the letter succeeds because it is, as the newspaper's editor observes, "the artless, earnest appeal and protest of two children."[15] In short, it produces prohibition not with votes and laws, as men would, but with the sentimental appeal of moral suasion. Yet, no longer devoted to reforming individual drunkards, these tactics of sentimental persuasion work instead to prompt legislation. Though the story insists that these little girls derive their efficacy from the political innocence of their domestically circumscribed position, it nevertheless takes the logic of disciplinary intimacy full circle by presenting moral suasion not as merely enforcing, but as actually revising the law of the father.

Relying on sentimental appeals, the genre of temperance fiction presumes the power of a domestically based campaign of moral suasion to transform the public soul. Temperance fiction's depiction of family discipline, however, destabilizes the family's alliance with the tactics of moral suasion. Instead,

14. Kruna, "The Red Frock," in *The Drinking Fountain Stories* (New York: National Temperance Society and Publication House, 1873), 177, 178.

15. T. S. Arthur, "What Two Little Girls Did," in *The Pitcher of Cool Water*, 77, 82, 79, and 88.

this fiction reveals the social inversions inherent in relying on domesticity to correct a failure internal to the domestic scene—a failure of patriarchy. Dedicated to maintaining conventional familial order, temperance fiction is conservative; nevertheless, in these tales family love cannot simply uphold patriarchal rule, since it is the wife, and even more the children, who must bring the erring man under discipline. Granting moral authority to childhood inevitably compromises paternal authority.

The campaign for "Home Protection" vividly portrays drink as perverting family order so that affection is replaced by violence. Working for the New York Temperance Society, Samuel Chipman attempted to document such claims by visiting jails, asylums, and poorhouses throughout the state in order to ascertain the correlation between domestic violence and inebriation. The society published the results in 1834:

ALBANY COUNTY: Of the intemperate, at least twenty have been committed for abuse to their families.

BROOME COUNTY: One of the intemperate was committed for whipping his wife; and two on charges of rape.

NIAGARA COUNTY: Of the intemperate a considerable number have been committed repeatedly; one man has lain in jail for two-thirds of the time for three years past, for abuse of his family when intoxicated; when sober, is a kind husband and father.[16]

By 1850, Elizabeth Cady Stanton argued that alcoholism ought to be valid grounds for divorce. As she saw it, the dissolution of the conventional family would be far preferable than to "come into daily contact, with a coarse, beastly, disgusting drunkard, and consent to be the partner of his misery and rage through a long weary life."[17] Or, as she put it to the New York State Legislature in February 1854 in an argument about custody laws, "Instead of your present laws, which make the mother and her children the victims of

16. Samuel Chipman, *The Temperance Lecturer* (Albany, N.Y.: n.p., 1834). In *The Politics of Domesticity: Women, Evangelism and Temperance in Nineteenth Century America* (Middletown, Conn.: Wesleyan University Press, 1981), Barbara Leslie Epstein quotes this material but cautions that "Chipman's reports do not, of course, tell us how many sober men were incarcerated for beating their wives or children, nor do they give us any hint of how many men beat their wives or children without being incarcerated" (109–10).

17. Published in *The Lily* 2 (April 1850): 31. The piece is signed simply "S. F." for "Sunflower," one of Stanton's frequent pseudonyms during this period.

vice and license, you might rather pass laws prohibiting all drunkards, libertines and fools the rights of husbands and fathers."[18] Urging divorce, she warned the drunkard's wife, "be not misled by any pledges, resolves, promises, prayers or tears. You cannot rely on the word of a man who is, or has been the victim of such an overpowering appetite."[19] Temperance fiction was never so radical. After all, its moral goals rested upon the presumed efficacy of promises, prayers, tears, and—most of all—the appeal of the loving family. But while this sentimental aesthetic was fundamentally committed to maintaining traditional domestic and patriarchal structures, its depiction of the drunkard's devastated home largely echoes Stanton's critique of patriarchy itself.

Like temperance fiction's relation to patriarchy, the incest discernible in the plots of these stories proves ambiguous; it serves both as the most extreme mark of familial disintegration and as the mechanism best able to produce family order and happiness. This redemption plot thus seems to be a cultural and narrative reaction-formation, as it reconfigures trauma into the possibility of moral triumph. There is ample historical evidence that in the last decades of the nineteenth century incest was a relatively frequent occurrence and that its dominant form—at least as reported to child-protection agencies—was coercive relations between fathers and their pre-adolescent daughters. Evidence from earlier periods, where we do not have the benefit of agency records, is more scanty. The case records of child-protection agencies, and the painful testimony of diaries, provide a real but inadequate measure of incest's trauma.[20] That this history remains fragmented and partial, that there is much that has been silenced and much that we do not and cannot know, is in itself part of that trauma. It is clear, however, that child advocates and

18. Stanton's speech was reprinted in *The Una* 2 (May 1854): 260.

19. Quoted in Elizabeth Pleck, *Domestic Tyranny: The Making of Social Policy against Family Violence from Colonial Times to the Present* (New York: Oxford University Press, 1987), 57.

20. Linda Gordon's *Heroes of Their Own Lives* rests on research into the records of three Boston child-protection agencies that confirms the prevalence of coercive incest within nineteenth-century families and the predominance of sibling and father/daughter relations. Although child-protection agencies were first organized in the 1870s, Gordon's discussion suggests that these patterns of family violence have a far longer history. See also Linda Gordon and Paul O'Keefe, "Incest as a Form of Family Violence: Evidence from Historical Case Records," *Journal of Marriage and the Family* 46 (February 1984): 27–34. The earliest autobiographical account of incest I am aware of is *Religion and Domestic Violence in Early New England:The Memoirs of Abigail Abbot Bailey*, ed. Ann Taves (Bloomington: Indiana University Press, 1989); first published in 1815, this text alludes to Major Bailey's sexual abuse of their daughter. For a record of family violence in the 1860s, including sexual relations between the diarist's husband and a series of young nieces, see *A Private War: Letters and Diaries of Madge Preston, 1862–1867*, ed. Virginia Walcott Beauchamp (New Brunswick, N.J.: Rutgers University Press, 1987).

temperance reformers believed that such abuse was linked to, if not completely caused by, alcoholic excess, and thus, that they recognized scenes of a drunken father in bed with his child as all too real.[21] For us, in the absence of more historical data, the incestuous patterns suggested and disguised by these stories can provide at most only elusive access to actual behaviors.

In reimagining scenes of drunken sexual abuse as sites of moral redemption, temperance writers were engaged in an act that disavows actual behaviors and individual abuses. Yet this very denial works to reveal some of the contradictions that infuse familial order and affection. Incest is central to the confrontation between the disciplinary forces of law and love I am describing precisely because of its double role as both what the family must prohibit and what constitutes and maintains the family. Foucault asserts "that sexuality has its privileged point of development in the family; that for this reason sexuality is 'incestuous' from the start," and hence that, for the family, incest is both "a dreadful secret and an indispensable pivot."[22] Recent work on incest and pedophilia in Victorian culture, both American and British, provides these generalizing structures with literary and historical particulars and suggests that a "monstrous" sexual attraction to children, however strenuously denied and demonized, nevertheless informs nineteenth-century conceptions of desire, domesticity, and even innocence itself.[23] The new regime of disciplinary intimacy illustrates these arguments by demonstrating how incestuous bonds actively function to hold the family together and to endow the home with affective meaning.

Foucault's focus on how incest functions in the maintenance of social order fails to acknowledge the pain of individual abuses. Conversely, therapeutic discussions only depict incest as the infliction of individual pain and as a mark of familial dysfunction—as if admitting the socializing effects of the circulation of incestuous desires would endanger the creation of the "safe

21. In terms of the relation between incest and alcoholism, Linda Gordon convincingly observes that "familial sexual abuse was rarely a crime of uncontrolled, momentary passion to which the lowering of inhibitions by alcohol might contribute; but a longer-term, calculated relationship perpetuated during sober as well as drunken moments." Nevertheless, her correlation of stress factors for family violence reveals alcoholism to be by far the most significant stress factor for incest. In all events, it is clear from her readings of case reports that late nineteenth-century child-protection agents considered drunkenness to be a prime cause of child sexual abuse, and there is every reason to believe that temperance writers shared this view. *Heroes of Their Own Lives,* 218 and table 6, 174.

22. Michel Foucault, *The History of Sexuality, Volume I: An Introduction* (New York: Vintage Books, 1978), 108–9.

23. See James Kincaid, *Child-Loving: The Erotic Child and Victorian Culture* (New York: Routledge, 1992); and G. M. Goshgarian, *To Kiss the Chastening Rod: Domestic Fiction and Sexual Ideology in the American Renaissance* (Ithaca, N.Y.: Cornell University Press, 1992).

families" so integral to the recovery process.[24] The difference stems from a division between the symbolic and the enacted: the incest that structures the family is an incest more felt and disciplined than acted upon; the incest that destroys the family is one that has been acted out. The shock of these temperance plots lies in their conflation of such categories so that recognizably incestuous acts—however innocently portrayed—yield social order. In my readings of these stories, I intentionally imitate temperance fiction's own practice of fusing the real and the symbolic in order to uphold incest's individual and cultural meanings: to acknowledge the child's vulnerability and incest's trauma while still recognizing the eroticized child as an effective disciplinary agent. By insisting on the individual and cultural significance of temperance's incestuous redemption plots, I find individual abuse to be not merely an evil ignored by patriarchy but one assimilated into—indeed, necessary to—the construction and maintenance of patriarchal power.

If father/daughter incest has been found to be most prevalent in practice, erotic relations between mothers and sons has long dominated the symbolic discourse of incest. Myth, anthropology, and psychoanalysis may have labeled such relations as taboo—the prohibition that constitutes culture—but it is equally clear that this incest orders and "instructs" culture, and so permeates the rhetoric of the ideal nineteenth-century American family.

> *Every son, "Behold thy mother!"* Make love to her, and her your first sweetheart. Be courteous, gallant, and her knight-errant, and your nearest friend and bosom confident. Nestle yourself right into her heart, and her into yours. Seek her "company" and advice, and imbibe her purifying influences. Learn how to court by courting her. No other society will equally sanctify and instruct.[25]

---

24. In *Trauma and Recovery* (New York: Basic Books, 1992), Judith Lewis Herman argues that the willingness of societies to acknowledge trauma, including childhood abuse and incest, is contingent on political conditions: "To hold traumatic reality in consciousness requires a social context that affirms and protects the victim and that joins victim and witness in a common alliance. . . . For the larger society, the social context is created by political movements that give voice to the disempowered" (9). But while her discussion of the ability to acknowledge trauma is thus highly conscious of the import of social context, her discussion of trauma itself and the process of recovery effaces this context. Consequently, though she describes how discourse about sexual trauma can have a social function, she does not admit that incestuous desires are in any way integral to family order. See, for example, her description of how a therapeutic group ritually "welcomed [an incest survivor] into a 'new family' of survivors" (228–29). In pointing out this gap, I do not mean to criticize Herman's powerful book; rather, my intention is to demonstrate how, even in what I consider to be the most socially engaged discussion of incest's trauma, such silences hold.

25. O. S. Fowler, *Perfect Men, Women, and Children, in Happy Families* (Boston: n.p., 1878), 170, one of many paeans to mothers by the famed phrenologist and temperance advocate. This passage is quoted in Bryan Strong, "Toward a History of the Experiential Family: Sex and Incest in the Nineteenth-Century Family," *Journal of Marriage and the Family* 35 (August 1973): 462.

The gendered division of incest into violent, family-disabling relations between fathers and daughters and loving, family-propping relations between sons and mothers suggests that incest serves patriarchy both as a sign of male coercive power and as a promise of sexually satisfying domestic love. In their stories of redemption through the love of a child, temperance writers have actually crossed these two cultural versions of incest, and reimagined male violence as domestic love.

Readers and Drinkers

We are left, however, with the question of who is served by such a reimagining of familial abuse as familial redemption. This question has far-reaching social implications, but before it is possible to even begin postulating responses, we need to know who in nineteenth-century America actually read these stories, for surely this plot would carry different meanings for audiences of different class, age, gender, and domestic status, and for sober or drinking readers. Ascertaining readership remains a largely speculative business, and what we do know suggests that reading patterns were far more eclectic and the structuring of knowledge far more chaotic than has been commonly assumed; men often prove, for example, to be nearly as avid readers of sentimental fiction as women.[26] What clues I have found for the readership of temperance tales does, however, imply a division between authorial hopes that these stories would convert drunkards and the realization that their primary readership lay in the already temperate home. Moreover, recognition that temperate men, women, and especially children constituted the major audience for these stories links the ability of temperance fiction to reform drunkards with the ability of domestic love to pass on this saving lesson. Thus, assertions of the genre's efficacy oddly echo the plot of individual temperance tales: both genre and plot imagine the good child-reader as the means of redeeming the drunken man.

The National Temperance Society founded a publication house in 1865 to publish and distribute temperance fiction, and at that year's National Temperance Convention James Black voiced the society's expectations for this proposed venture:

Although I find Strong's conclusions about the sexual anxieties of nineteenth-century men reductive and unconvincing, I do concur with him in discerning a sexual "undercurrent flowing beneath the sentimental cult of motherhood."

26. Ronald Zboray supports these findings through an analysis of the charge records of the New York Society Library; see "Gender and Boundlessness in Reading Patterns," in *A Fictive People: Antebellum Economic Development and the Reading Public* (New York: Oxford University Press, 1993).

> We must have publications spread broadcast over the land, or many more
> thousands of drunkards' graves will be filled, many more families broken up,
> many more hearts, hopes, and joys crushed, many more children made or-
> phans, to grow up a curse to themselves, a disgrace to friends, and a burden
> to society. . . .

As his talk progressed to goals for distribution, this "broadcast" proved more
and more narrow in its reach: from the public "booksellers," the imagined
site of distribution contracts first to "house-hold and Sabbath-School libraries" and then to the "sales of publications made at the close of an interesting [temperance] lecture" that, Black argues, would not only spread the
word but also raise money to support the lecturers' travel.[27] Society advertisements selling collections of temperance books at a discount ("48 volumes
specially adapted to Sunday-School Libraries, written by some of the best authors in the world"); the practice of selling pamphlets in batches of one thousand; and the financial reports of the Publication House all suggest that in
practice distribution occurred mainly through Sunday schools and local temperance organizations.[28] Nevertheless, the discussions of the Publication
House that appear in the proceedings of all subsequent conventions continue
to assert evangelical success; they boast the number of pages published and
celebrate an immense and essential demand: "the demand of the present
is *books,* BOOKS, **BOOKS!** Men *must* have books, women *will* have books,
and children *should* have books."[29] The gradient of auxiliary verbs hints,
however, at the gender imbalance of their actual audience, for while "will"
confidently assumes a female readership and "should" implies the ease with
which such moral lessons can be imposed on children, the fundamentally internal obligations of "must" are both most strongly desired and most difficult
to impose. Indeed, by 1873, the Society itself had begun to acknowledge
openly that temperance literature rarely reached drunkards:

> Our mission is not merely nor mainly to rescue the drunkard, but to save every
> boy and girl from the drunkard's sin and shame. . . . Our literature is not to be

---

27. "National Temperance and Tract Publication House," paper presented by James Black, in
*Proceedings of the Fifth National Temperance Convention, Saratoga Springs, New York, August 1,
2 and 3, 1865* (New York: National Temperance Society and Publication House, 1865), 51, 52.

28. All of these materials can be found in the National Temperance Society and Publication
House files of the American Antiquarian Society.

29. J. R. Syper, "Temperance Literature," in *Proceedings of the Sixth National Temperance
Convention, Cleveland, Ohio, July 29, 1868* (New York: National Temperance Society and Publication House, 1868), 113.

the life-buoy flung out to the man already sinking in the death tide, but the baby-tender, if you will, to train and strengthen the least of the little ones.[30]

Temperance was in fact a familiar nineteenth-century "baby-tender," even outside adamantly "cold water" circles. In the general moral pedagogy of *The Good Boy's and Girl's Alphabet,* for example, it is no surprise that "D was a Drunkard" or that "V was a Vintner, who drank all himself," or that these—along with a host of other sinful letters—should stand as warnings to Y, "a Youngster that loved not his school."[31] Temperance writers continued to claim, moreover, that thus producing pro-temperance children could itself save drunkards. If temperance stories could not reach the fathers directly, who was to say that they could not rescue them through their sons and daughters?

The juvenile temperance tale "The Snow Storm; or, What Jennie Scott Did" is subtitled "a true story," but what it offers is a wishful emblem of how such juvenile fiction might work to reduce adult alcoholism. Given a copy of *The Youth's Temperance Banner* on a train, Jennie Scott reads about a middle-class family who aids the destitute children of a drunkard. In the *Banner* story,

> the tears began to flow from all the children's eyes, and from those of their dear Mama too. . . . Jennie also cried when she read this story, then she asked her father [who likes a glass of wine after dinner] to read it. . . . By and by putting her arms around her father's neck, and pulling his head down, so that she could whisper in his ear, she said in a most loving tone,—
>
> "O my dear papa, will you let anybody say [like the child of the story] that 'MY father drinks?'"
>
> . . . For a moment he made no reply, but little Jennie saw the tear-drops glistening in his eyes, and took courage. In another moment he brushed away the tears, and pressing his arm tighter around his child's waist, he said,—
>
> "No, Jennie, no!"[32]

30. A. G. Lawson, "Temperance Literature," in *Proceedings of the Seventh National Temperance Convention, Saratoga Springs, New York, August 26 and 27, 1873* (New York: National Temperance Society and Publication House, 1873), 140.

31. *The Good Boy's and Girl's Alphabet* (Philadelphia: B. Bramell, 1841). This "A was an Archer" rhyme was one of the most popular and often reprinted of alphabets. Not all of its versions were so moralistically aimed at "good" children, and even this one, as Patricia Crain points out, spans "the extreme poles of discipline and festivity," ending as it does with a playful and disruptive "Z was a Zany." Crain, *The Story of A: The Alphabetization of America from* The New England Primer *to* The Scarlet Letter (Palo Alto, Calif.: Stanford University Press, 2000), 114–15.

32. Peter Carter, "The Snow Storm; or, What Jennie Scott Did," in *The Old Brown Pitcher,* 178, 180, 181.

As the tears spread from the *Banner* story, to Jennie, to her father, and presumably to her young reader and then (why not?) to her reader's father, this sentimental deluge—waters *mise en abîme*—promises to sweep all wine and liquor away. Jennie need not even write like Katy and Ellen; all she need do to end intemperance is read and cry.

This faith that temperance tales could reach drunkards through their children is not an isolated fantasy;[33] it may indeed be the inaugural fiction of the genre. Lucius Manlius Sargent wrote a series of "Temperance Tales" beginning in 1833 that, if not the earliest such stories, were certainly among the genre's first successes. In the preface to his first tale, Sargent urges his reader,

> When you have read it, if, among all your connections and friends, you can think of none whom its perusal may possibly benefit—and it will be strange if you cannot—do me the favor to present it to the first little boy that you meet. He will no doubt take it home to his mother or father. If you will not do this, throw it in the street, as near to some dram-seller's door as you ever venture to go.[34]

Sargent himself gave a two-volume, elegantly bound copy of the *Temperance Tales* as a gift, inscribed to "David Eckley, Esq. from his old friend L. M. Sargent." David Eckley, however, left no mark in the books; it is "May Belle Eckley" (sister? wife? daughter?) who writes her name inside the covers of both volumes. Passing from parent to child and not—as Sargent wished—the other way around, another set of the tales is inscribed to "Freddie—from his mother E. C. Brown."[35] The tales' own images of transmission—through little boy or side-

---

33. For a novella-length version of this fantasy see Jenny Marsh Parker, *The Story of a Story-Book* (New York: General Protestant Episcopal Sunday School Union, and Church Book Society, 1858), which traces the moral influence of a book from a Sunday school library as it is read by a series of sinners young and old.

34. Lucius Manlius Sargent, *My Mother's Gold Ring; Founded on Fact* (Boston: Ford and Damrell, 1833), iii–iv.

35. The Eckley copy is in the collection of the American Antiquarian Society. The Brown copy is in the collection of the University of Virginia. For an illuminating discussion of what we can learn about past readers from the signatures and marginalia they leave behind, see Davidson, *Revolution and the Word: The Rise of the Novel in America* (New York: Oxford University Press, 1986), chaps. 1–4.

The temperance movement's own claims for Sargent's tales presume a very different readership. Charles Jewett asserts, for example, that "thousands of men before the year 1840 had been converted to the doctrine and practice of abstinence by their perusal—many of them by the perusal of a single number of the series." Jewett, *Forty Years Fight with the Drink Demon; or a History of the Temperance Reform as I Have Seen It and of My Labor in Connection Therewith* (New York: National Temperance Society and Publishing House, 1872), 217. Whether or not thousands were converted, there is no question that these tales were extremely popular in temperance circles. The first tale had sold 114,000 copies by 1843, and there are multiple editions both of in-

walk—feel less convincing than even such anecdotal marks of readerly propri-
etorship. Indeed, the preface already figures the tale's dismal incapacity to reach
an alcoholic readership, for if no little boy will carry it, Sargent's suggestion
for how to circulate his pamphlets would leave them trampled in the gutter.

No doubt inadequate to their temperance goals, these fantasies of effective literary dissemination are striking for how closely they mirror the plot of
redemption-through-a-child's-love these stories so repeatedly tell. It seems to
make remarkably little difference whether the child rescues a drunken father
through the sharing of caresses or the sharing of temperance tales. Indeed,
as is the case with Jennie Scott, caresses and stories are easily and frequently
combined. In their insistence that children—and therefore fiction read by
children—can save despite family violence and the threat of the gutter, these
redemption-love stories serve to buttress the genre's own claim to efficacy.[36]

---

dividual tales and of collected volumes. Yet, in a "Prefatory Sketch of Their Origin and History"
he wrote for a complete edition of his twenty-one tales, *Temperance Tales* (Boston: American
Tract Society, 1863), Sargent draws all his evidence for their emotional power, and every testimony to their efficacy, from responses garnered within temperance circles, which suggests once
again, the limits of distribution, even for such popular tales. One quoted testimony begins:

> I write you from the office of the New York State Temperance Society. Mr. Delavan informs
> me that you have recently prepared a tract, entitled the "Gold Ring," which he thinks bet-
> ter calculated to promote the cause than anything he has yet seen. Several of his friends, as
> well as himself, had read it, with the deepest emotion; but, afraid of trusting entirely their
> own judgements on a subject where their feelings had been so deeply enlisted, they re-
> solved to have it read in a very crowded temperance convention. The effect produced upon
> the audience he described as overwhelming. They were not simply in tears, they were con-
> vulsed with emotion. (4–5)

36. Interestingly, a frequent contemporary criticism of temperance fiction—a heightened
version, as we have seen, of the dangers associated with all fiction—was that it might corrupt
innocent young readers rather than permit them to purify the world.

> [many temperance novelists] of refined sentiments and delicate nerves are employing their
> talents in describing minutely the scenes of drunkenness which are said to occur at public
> hotels, and in bringing to light the secret sins of individuals, which, for all the good that
> can be anticipated from their exposure, might well be left in the darkness and privacy in
> which they were committed. The object which these good and gifted ladies have in view,
> as understood, is to teach morality. But would it be safe, think you, for a prudent mother,
> in order to impress upon the still pure heart of her daughter a warmer regard for the beauty
> and dignity of virtue to introduce her to the companionship of the vulgar, the obscene and
> the vicious, even admitting that she kept her guarded by the presentation of the most vivid
> contrasts? Would not the experiment be dangerous, we ask, the end and good effect doubt-
> ful to say the least?

Quoted from a review in *Godey's Lady's Book* (September 1854) in Nina Baym, *Novels, Readers
and Reviewers: Responses to Fiction in Antebellum America* (Ithaca, N.Y.: Cornell University
Press, 1984), 180. For a discussion of this immoral or "subversive" potential in reform fiction
more generally see Reynolds, *Beneath the American Renaissance,* especially chapter 2, "The Reform Impulse and the Paradox of Immoral Didacticism"; and R. Laurence Moore, "Religion, Secularization, and the Shaping of the Culture Industry in Antebellum America," *American Quarterly* 41 (June 1989): 216–42.

Thus, to return to the question with which this section began, the links temperance fiction draws between familial abuse and familial satisfaction serve to mask the inherent powerlessness of child and story to end social abuse—discursively endowing both abused child and temperance tale with a power they too often and too painfully lacked. But if these images of sentimental power rarely converted drunkards, it need not follow that the good child reading in a Sunday school library or an already temperate home did not find such fictions compelling. Indeed, as a closer examination of these redemption scenes will show, much of the cultural importance of this fiction lies in the tightly enmeshed doubleness with which it figures the child as simultaneously victim of abuse and agent of discipline.

Restraint and Indulgence

Juvenile temperance fiction regularly asserts that its purpose is to teach children the ethos of self-denial, which will protect them from alcoholism and other sins. This ethos, associated with the wise parent, finds expression in a notion painfully familiar from our reading of *Our Nig:* the repetitive, unrestrained touting of "restraint."

> My darling child, be thankful every day you live that you have parents wise
> enough to restrain you in your childhood . . . the time will come when you will
> be grateful that you learned self-denial when you were young.
>   . . . For instance, when you awake on a cold morning, don't lie still in bed,
> thinking how warm and pleasant it is there, until you fall asleep, but jump up at
> once; don't indulge yourself. All these little victories will help you in fighting
> with greater temptations as you grow older.[37]

Yet the stories in this collection—the National Temperance Society's 1868 "special effort for the children"[38]—rarely tell of childhood self-restraint. Rather, they tell of children's efforts to regenerate drunken men, their successes often linked not with self-discipline but with the indulgences of a warm and pleasant bed. In these stories the love of a child undeniably functions to enforce self-restraint and social order, but it does so through the promise not of delimiting, but rather of fulfilling desires.

Suggestively, *The History of a Threepenny Bit* ends with the reformed tavern-keeper setting up a new establishment "in the windows of which might

37. "The Sleigh Ride," in *The Old Brown Pitcher,* 75, 77.
38. Introductory "Note," *The Old Brown Pitcher.*

be seen marbles, lollypops, toys, picturebooks, and other articles likely to tempt the youth of a country village."[39] The transformations wrought by little Peggy's love have altered the content of temptation, but they have not rejected its pleasures or its profits. Far from denouncing temptation, this fiction depends upon it, since the love of a child becomes itself the most potent object of desire. More than toys or candy these stories offer the child's love as the one temptation stronger than the love of drink. When, at closing time, the tavern-keeper finds Peggy sleeping in front of his fire—where she hid cold, heartbroken, and exhausted after her father had taken her last "threepenny bit" to spend on drink—he experiences her purely as temptation, as something he tries but cannot resist.

> "I'm not going to be made a fool of like this. Don't I know them? . . . It's no use," he went on, shaking his fist at the unconscious Peggy; "you'll be as cruel and as bad as the rest some day, for all yer soft little voice, and yer, 'Daddy, daddy!' You don't come over me like this,—d'ye hear?"
>
> And he waited again for his answer. . . . She moaned in her sleep and repeated:—
>
> "Daddy, please don't."
>
> The little voice was so hopeless and appealing, that it reached again the hidden chord in the publican's heart, and he knelt down and whispered soothingly:—
>
> "No—no—no, dearie, I won't."
>
> The little sleeper was calmed for the moment; but directly he moved, she burst out again:—
>
> "Daddy, please don't."
>
> "Don't what?" whispered the publican bending over her.
>
> "Don't spend it." said Peggy, with a sobbing sigh.
>
> Closer and closer he bent, till his lips almost touched her cheek; and gently he repeated:—
>
> "No—no—no, dearie, I won't."
>
> Whether the answer penetrated through the mists and shadows of sleep, I know not; but the child stirred no more. But long after she was wrapped in her peaceful slumber did the old man remain with his cheek against hers, dreamily repeating:—
>
> "No—no—no, dearie, I won't." (85–87)

39. *The History of a Threepenny Bit* (New York: n.p., 1873), 211. In this story too, the tavern-keeper's reform and a host of other reconciliations are all brought about by the love of little Peggy. She is not, however, completely omnipotent—her father dies of delirium tremens.

The pleasure the publican cannot resist, the pleasure that will ultimately compel him to shut down his tavern, is the pleasure of whispering "no" into the cheek of a sleeping child. In Peggy's hopeless and appealing "No, Daddy don't" the spending of a daughter's pennies echoes against all the other things a father ought not to do to his little girl. Thus the refusal of profligacy has its own satisfactions; there is an erotic charge to abstention, to saying "no."

My reading of this passage may seem to eroticize a familiar sentimental scene, but it is my contention that an insistence on the sexual innocence of children and of the disciplinary intimacy they are enlisted to enforce is precisely what enables these erotics to function; the suppression gives these scenes their sexual charge. It is the refusal to acknowledge childhood sexuality—either as subject or as object of desire—that makes a Mary, Debby, Phoebe, or Peggy so irresistible, so sexually vulnerable, and, at the same time, so strategically capable (at least within the logic of juvenile fiction) of disciplining the father. I am suggesting not merely that the practice of disciplining through love has erotic content, but indeed that this eroticism is essential to its functioning. This observation has far wider ramifications for our understanding of the social power of American domesticity; here, it is sufficient to note how a domestically confined juvenile sexuality displaces an anti-domestic, dissipating alcoholism.

The alliance of domestic discipline with the fulfillment of desire would seem to function as a means of luring wayward men home—a promise that their own hearth could be as intensely pleasurable as any barroom. Yet, as we have seen, there is little reason to believe that such undomesticated men read these tales; this testimony to the seductions of home is finally better understood as a story domesticity tells about itself to itself. The already domestic family avidly imagines the well-regulated home as an erotically saturated space. But if viewing home—and particularly the good child—as a temptation that can save proves a self-referential domestic fantasy, it does not serve merely domestic ends. In particular, the promise that the fulfillment of desires will yield not chaos but good order suggests provocative connections to the social and economic agenda of an industrializing nation. After all, the belief that there need be no tension between social discipline and consumerist indulgence underlies claims for the social and moral efficacy of consumer-capitalism. Desire, both home and market agree, need not result in dissipation; it might instead produce a domestic, economic, and even national good. Thus, temperance fiction's assertion of the compatibility of restraint and indulgence is not an isolated freak of reformist discourse; rather, it is constitutive of the newly dominant American middle class.

Temperance fiction's obsession with the sexual dynamics of the family is matched only by its obsession with money. On this point all temperance writing agrees: drink results in destitution. In this fiction, men are forever spending their last pennies on rum instead of on much-needed bread; there is no more evil spot than that commercial establishment, the dram-shop. This might suggest that the public sphere of economic exchange should be understood as a threat to domestic happiness, and, like all sentimental fiction, these stories voice anxiety about the moral taint of the marketplace.[40] Yet, as with the tavern-keeper's new shop of tempting toys, the drunkard's salvation invariably appears fully ensconced in capitalist structures of industry and exchange. Just as surely as a drunkard's sad end lies in poverty, the clearest mark of redemption is signaled in these tales by the attainment of an adequately prosperous home.

The centrality of money for temperance fiction is literalized in *The History of a Threepenny Bit* through a narrative trope (quite conventional in nineteenth-century juvenile fiction, however bizarre it may seem to twenty-first-century readers), for this story is actually told by Peggy's cherished coin.[41] This narrative strategy requires that, throughout the novel's 216 pages, the coin circulate primarily among the small group of socially quite diverse characters with whom the story is concerned. The social mobility of a threepenny bit, capable of passing from a wealthy lady to a beggar girl, does not, however, work to suggest the dangerous promiscuity and volatility of market economies. Instead, this sequence of financial transactions connects characters who, it not surprisingly turns out, already bear more intimate, if unrecognized, domestic relations: Peggy's invalid mother once worked as the wealthy Mrs. Ogilvie's maid, and this lady's present maid proves to be the tavern-keeper Timothy Craig's long-alienated daughter. The ties that link shopkeepers, servants, and mistress, moreover, are consistently figured as loving and familial rather than economic. Thus the very structure of this novel—both in narrative technique and in plot—depends upon refusing to uphold distinctions between the economic and the domestic: virtually all the relations in the novel involve both the exchange of coin and the exchange of affection. At the novel's end, Peggy's happy cottage home, a short walk from Craig's new store

40. See Gillian Brown, *Domestic Individualism: Imagining Self in Nineteenth-Century America* (Berkeley: University of California Press, 1990), for the seminal explanation of how, despite the pervasive rhetoric of separate spheres, American domesticity actively organizes the possessive individualism of American capitalism.

41. For another example of a narrating thing see *The Biography of a Bottle, By a Friend of Temperance* (Boston: Perkins, Marvin and Co., 1835).

and on Mrs. Ogilvie's land, is in a very real sense made out of the circulation of a threepenny bit. Indeed, the coin is not a detached, economic narrator of these emotional scenes but is itself an object of affection; Peggy awakens in the tavern to find that Craig had "slipped me [our narrator-coin] into one of her little hands. . . . [Peggy] pressed the little coin to her lips, and hugged it close up to her, exclaiming, as she did so, 'It's come back—it's come back to me! Peggy's own—Peggy's very, very own!' "[42]

The confusion between the erotic and the economic that leads Peggy to kiss her coin appears completely benign, for both Peggy's ability to love and her money secure the domestic bliss of the novel's end. This can only happen because the novel has so fully succeeded in domesticating the economic realm; it is, after all, on the barroom floor that Peggy and Timothy Craig make their cozy and redemptive bed. Shorn of such domestic security, the links among barroom, sex, and money may be far less tidy or comfortable. In *Ten Nights in a Bar-room*, Mary tells her groaning father a dream that nearly bursts with the effort to encompass this complex mesh of connections:

> I thought it was night, and that I was still sick. You promised not to go out until I was well. But you did go out; and I thought you went over to Mr. Slade's tavern. When I knew this, I felt as strong as when I was well, and I got up and dressed myself and started out after you. But I hadn't gone far before I met Mr. Slade's great bull-dog Nero, and he growled at me so dreadfully that I was frightened and ran back home. Then I started again and went away round by Mr. Mason's. But there was Nero in the road, and this time he caught my dress in his mouth and tore a great piece out of the skirt. . . . But I . . . kept right on until I came to the tavern and there you stood in the door. And you were dressed so nice. You had on a new hat and a new coat; and your boots were new and polished just like Judge Hammond's. I said—"O father! is this you?" And then you took me up in your arms and kissed me, and said "Yes, Mary, I am your real father. Not old Joe Morgan—but Mr. Morgan now." It seemed all so strange, that I looked into the bar-room to see who was there. But it wasn't a bar-room any longer; but a store full of goods.[43]

Mary's dream has soaked the tavern with images of sexual threat, sexual attraction, and the pleasures of bourgeois status and procurement. This passage is dense with meanings, convincingly like those of real dreams in that

---

42. *History of a Threepenny Bit*, 87, 94–95.
43. Arthur, *Ten Nights in a Bar-room*, 92–93.

they are at once so overdetermined and so contradictory. Rather than attempt to create a coherent interpretive order out of this tangle of dog-torn skirts and shiny new boots, I want to focus on the tangle itself, on the ways in which the sexual and the financial, the frightening dog "Nero" and the desirable "real" father, the evil barroom and the "store full of goods," all seem surprisingly and yet inextricably bound up with one another. If this passage makes clear that what Mary wants most is the embrace of a father who is "dressed so nice" and the riches of the storeroom, it seems just as evident that these domestic rewards of affluence remain contingent upon the violent sexual initiation of barroom barter and ripped skirts. Not only are sex and money impossibly entangled in one another, but the moral valence of both also appears drastically unstable.

Social historians have convincingly argued that the temperance movement was an important agent in nineteenth-century articulations of class conflict: that the middle class attempted to use temperance rhetoric and laws as a means of disciplining the working class and particularly the leisure activities of Irish and German immigrants.[44] In noting the congruence between temperance fiction's depictions of family sexual and economic dynamics, I expand upon this sense of how temperance serves middle-class interests. The prevalent image of the temperate home as the place capable of reconciling restraint and indulgence installs and affirms as dominant the elasticity of the middle-class position (stretched to encompass both producers and consumers) within capitalism's new, swiftly industrializing national order. Thus these images of the temperate home domesticate, and so naturalize, the strains that result from capitalism's double call to work and play, to save and spend, to be temperate and profligate. Childhood is itself an expression of this elasticity, since it is precisely during these decades that children's role in the household economy shifts, as the value of children comes to be located less in their labor than in their capacity for affection and play.

---

44. Paul E. Johnson discusses the authority Rochester's leading families evoked to repress workplace drinking, and the fervor evangelical revivals wielded against alcohol—a fervor Johnson describes as "very much like class violence." Johnson, *A Shopkeeper's Millennium: Society and Revivals in Rochester, New York, 1815–1837* (New York: Hill and Wang, 1978), 79–83 and 113–15. Roy Rosenzweig's ethnically differentiated account of the politics of leisure in nineteenth-century Worcester explores these issues in terms of working-class resistance. Rosenzweig, *Eight Hours for What We Will: Workers and Leisure in an Industrial City, 1870–1920* (New York: Cambridge University Press, 1983), chapter 2. For antebellum accounts of similar dynamics in Philadelphia and Boston see Bruce Laurie, *Working People of Philadelphia, 1800–1850* (Philadelphia: Temple University Press, 1980); and Jill Seigel Dodd, "The Working Classes and the Temperance Movement in Ante-Bellum Boston," *Labor History* 19 (fall 1978): 510–31.

Submissive Daughters, Absent Women, and Effeminate Men

That the middle-class, temperate home bolsters factory and marketplace should not surprise, despite the nineteenth century's insistent rhetoric of separate spheres—exclusively male or female, public or private, economic or sexual, disciplined by law or by love. But if, as the stories of Peggy and Mary suggest, such rhetorics of separation obscure the dynamics of identity and power in the American middle class, it nevertheless remains clear that the deconstruction of this divide remains fraught with anxiety—predominantly gender anxiety. For while the collusion of home and market are essential to the very existence of consumer capitalism in America, patriarchy has rested on the presumption of separate spheres.

The temperance stories of redemption through the love of a child are heavily gendered: Mary, Debby, Phoebe, Molly, Katy, Ellen, Jennie, and Peggy are all little girls. In a fundamental way, these stories of disciplinary intimacy offer the profoundly patriarchal promise that feminine sexual docility—the loving compliance with caresses, however drunken or aggressive—will be rewarded. The celebration of submissiveness at stake in this plot is, oddly enough, most transparent in a version of this familiar storyline that occurs not in the guise of sentimental fiction but in that of biography. In writing *Hannah Hawkins: The Reformed Drunkard's Daughter,* Rev. John Marsh quotes from newspaper reports and John Hawkins's famous Washingtonian lectures in an effort to relate factually how this temperance hero attained "his rescue, from the fangs of the rumseller, through his own child." This is how John Hawkins describes Hannah's ministrations:

> I would come home, late at night, open the door, and fall prostrate on the floor, utterly unable to move. My daughter Hannah, sitting up for me . . . would come down with a pillow and a blanket, and there, as she could not raise me and get me upstairs, she would put the pillow under my head and cover me with the blanket, and then lie down beside me like a faithful dog.

What Marsh finds so admirable and efficacious about this scene is Hannah's dog-like docility. Her loving submissiveness, he repeatedly explains, enables her to reform her father; if she acted differently—defiantly—John Hawkins

> would never have suffered her to say, "Father, don't send me for whisky to-day." She would have received a blow which would have felled her to the floor, and her father himself would have drank the more fiercely for it. But when his little Hannah, who had sat up late for him at night, and who had covered him with a

blanket, put a pillow under his head and laid down by him, as he expressed it, like "a faithful dog," said, in tones of daughter-tenderness, "Father, don't send me for any whisky to-day" it was more than he could bear.[45]

The redemptive power of "daughter-tenderness" serves as a mark of the daughter's obedience. Her submissiveness protects the father from the "fierce" need to combat the threat of being disciplined by his child. Her submissiveness enables him to submit.

In his preface Marsh compares the "fancied" scenes of redemption in "My Mother's Gold Ring" with the actual salvation story he intends to share. The comparison is interesting because Sargent's tale enacts the blow Marsh hypothesized for a less perfectly docile child. I wonder, however, whether here the familiar redemptive scene of drunken paternal caresses can appear as a more probable moment of battering, precisely because the child—judgmental instead of submissively loving—is a boy. The mother narrates this scene, her voice domestically located at the kitchen sink:

> . . . while I was washing up the breakfast things, I heard our little Robert, who was only five years old, crying bitterly; and going to learn the cause, I met him running towards me with his face covered with blood. He said his father had taken him on his knee, and was playing with him, but had given him a blow in the face, only because he had said, when he kissed him, "Dear papa, you smell like old Isaac, the drunken fiddler."[46]

This story appears more concerned with little Robert's capacity for telling the truth than with the father's swift salvation. The juxtaposition of these two scenes postulates that feminine submissiveness, not masculine honesty, can most effectively discipline the father.

In *A Million Too Much* (1871) an alcoholic young man defends his drinking with the assertion "I don't intend to reform. . . . I am not domestic."[47] But such a reform into domesticity is precisely what this fiction intends. The discipline produced by sexually submissive little girls has the effect of creating

45. Rev. John Marsh, *Hannah Hawkins: The Reformed Drunkard's Daughter* (New York: American Temperance Union, 1848), vi, 21, 45.

46. Sargent, "My Mother's Gold Ring," 6–7.

47. Julia McNair Wright, *A Million Too Much, A Temperance Tale* (Philadelphia: Porter and Coates, 1871), 257. Indeed, this novel blames the youth's alcoholism, dissipation, and eventual death on his lack of a properly domestic upbringing: not only is he orphaned at birth, but from infancy his nurse pours gin in his milk. Such stories suggest some of the ways in which the temperance plots of youthful temptation and those of paternal redemption may intersect.

submissive, domestic, and indeed feminized men; men who won't drink and won't hit. It was the same John Hawkins, we should recall, who would later describe his own efforts to save drunkards as the nurture "a mother [gives] her infant learning to walk." These maternal men are, of course, a fundamentally feminine fantasy. One of the few little boys to voice the wish that his drunken father "would let me lay my cheek to his, once more, as he used to do, when I was a babe" can expect no male readers, since he speaks from the pages of Lydia Sigourney's *Book for Girls*.[48] In the midst of this project of domesticating men, traces of anxiety about emasculation can, of course, be found. The temperance ballad "Learn to Say No," for example, strives, like the similarly named twentieth-century anti-drug campaign, to represent domesticity and abstinence as macho. The ballad concludes the story of John Brown's poverty-producing and home-destroying drunkenness with this hopeful verse:

> John Brown took the pledge, and asked help from above
> That he still might provide for those he should love;
> He went back to work, determined to show
> That John Brown was a man when he learned to say NO.[49]

Yet, even here, *The Temperance Speaker*'s advertisement that the poems, dialogues, and addresses there collected were intended "for the use of temperance organizations, schools, bands of hope, etc . . ." and its publication in 1873 at the advent of the "woman's campaign" (WCTU) suggests that John Brown's assertion of his maleness was often declaimed in the higher voices of women or children—feminized once more.

Although temperance reform may emulate maternal nurture, it is rarely mothers who do this feminine, redemptive work; this disciplinary task falls instead to little girls. In a literature espousing "Home Protection," wives are frequently absent or ineffective. Peggy's mother is ill, Debby's mother is dead, Phoebe's mother can do nothing to match her daughter's "strong love." For sentimental fiction, the appeal of these structurally motherless homes stems both from the consequent increase in the vulnerability of the child and from the therefore more pressing need to make the abusive father into a good,

---

48. Lydia H. Sigourney, "Wife of the Intemperate," in *A Book for Girls in Prose and Poetry* (New York: n.p., 1843), 131.

49. "Learn to Say No," in *The Temperance Speaker: A Collection of Original and Selected Dialogues, Addresses and Recitations, for the Use of Temperance Organizations, Schools, Bands of Hope, Anniversaries Etc.*, ed. J. N. Stearns (New York: National Temperance Society and Publication House, 1873), 67.

loving, and effectively maternal parent. Indeed these two advantages prop one another up, since in the absence of a mother, and countered only by a vulnerable and submissive child, it becomes easier to imagine a genuinely domesticated father as compatible with patriarchal power.

One problem with figuring adult women as disciplinary agents is that their power within the domestic sphere, however circumscribed, remains relatively real. Children, by comparison, can claim no actual arena of control—they wield only the power of fantasy, play, and affection. For temperance fiction, it is this very powerlessness that makes children, not wives, the ideal agents of home protection. A suggestive counterexample, Sargent's tale of "Kitty Grafton," tells the story of a wife who actively opposes her husband's cider-drinking and child-battering ways. As Kitty's responses to her husband's behavior grow more aggressive—sharp words are gradually replaced by such violent acts as hitting him over the head with a poker or pushing him down the basement stairs, until the house becomes "a battleground"—Sargent's sympathy with his heroine wanes. By the tale's end Kitty's unwomanly violence, not her husband's drunkenness, stands as the most damning sign of domestic dysfunction. Better no woman at all, temperance fiction seems to propose, than one as threatening to patriarchal control as Kitty Grafton.

Another advantage children bring to these tales of disciplining the father is their supposed sexual innocence. The stories discussed in this essay may represent incest, but they do not acknowledge it. The historical record suggests that absent or ineffective mothers were characteristic of incest situations. One form of child sexual abuse especially prevalent in the nineteenth century is what Linda Gordon calls "domestic incest," in which "girls became virtual housewives, taking over not only wifely sexual obligations but also housework, child care, and general family maintenance."[50] Within temperance fiction, where the incest plot remains masked by avowals of children's sexual innocence, domestic incest's penchant for replacing wives with daughters has the ostensible result of desexualizing disciplinary intimacy. The innocence of children—their supposed exclusion from the erotic—permits the child to domesticate adult sexuality, and so to feminize the father.

In "The Baby in the Brown Cottage," after their mother's death two little girls take on responsibility for their home, including the redemption of their alcoholic father. But in their housekeeping role even these little girls, with their pledge to do "everything to make it comfortable for him," are too much

---

50. Gordon, *Heroes of Their Own Lives*, 212, 225. Gordon describes domestic incest as being far more common before 1930 and the changes in the norms of childhood household labor that followed from mandatory secondary education.

like adult women to serve as a sufficiently strong—sufficiently vulnerable, sufficiently innocent—alternative to the allure of the barroom. Instead they proffer their baby brother as a more potent lure for paternal rectitude. As little Hetty explains:

> "Father loves baby, and . . . we'll always keep baby looking so sweet and clean that he'll love to come home just to see him, instead of going to the tavern when he shuts down the mill. If Mrs. Florence would give baby a nice white frock, and one with a pink or blue spot in it, and a pair of new shoes, I could keep him looking, oh! so lovely. Father couldn't help coming right home from the mill to see him; and who knows, Mrs. Wilder," Hetty continued, growing warm and hopeful, "but father might stop drinking altogether."[51]

To further ensure that Father will indeed "love baby," his attractions must be propped by decidedly fine clothing—unaffordable for a drunkard's child.[52] With his new pink or blue spotted frock the gender of this baby boy appears as yet unmarked. I would submit that it is precisely because the indecipherable gender of baby garments and babyhood would seem to bespeak the complete absence of sexuality that loving baby provides the perfect antidote to father's intemperate desires.[53]

Regardless of dress, the story remains quite clear that baby is indeed a boy, so that the father's love for him feminizes not only because it removes the erring father from the tavern and the purportedly more sexual embraces of adulthood to relocate him in that most feminine of spots, the cradle-side, but also because it evokes that other threat to patriarchy: homosexuality. That, in this instance, the baby is a boy reminds us of how the merest suggestion of homoerotic desire underscores the feminization at stake in all these tales of salvific pederasty. I want to insist that, for this fiction, going to bed with

51. T. S. Arthur, "The Baby in the Brown Cottage," in *The Pitcher of Cool Water and Other Stories,* 60–61.

52. Boston child-saving agencies understood the effect of putting fine middle-class garb on their "waifs." Before-and-after-photographs were a standard feature of their fund-raising brochures; these displayed the children dressed first as they had been found and then in elegant, lace-trimmed clothes. Gordon, *Heroes of Their Own Lives,* 36. A sample photograph is opposite page 51.

53. In nineteenth- and early twentieth-century America, red and pink were considered stronger, more masculine colors, while blue was thought to be feminine; but even this color-coding, the inverse of our present practices, was not thought to hold for young children. Clothing for children under the age of five was entirely genderless, an absence of sex-markers that implied the child's sexual innocence. See Jo B. Paoletti and Carol L. Kregloh, "The Children's Department," in *Men and Women: Dressing the Part,* ed. Claudia Brush Kidwell and Valerie Steel (Washington, D.C.: Smithsonian Institution Press, 1989), 22–41.

little boys is not essentially more feminizing than going to bed with little girls; just as baby's genderless frock does not distinguish his sex, both scenes place the father in the same maternal, feminine role of loving a small child. For the purposes of these temperance tales, then, homosexuality functions predominantly as an index of feminization, not as a sign of distinct sexual desires. Nevertheless, such production of homosexual meanings does mark the possibility that the feminization of the father this fiction seeks may prove irreconcilable with the privileged heterosexual mythos of the domestic scene. In this fiction's essentially conservative model of domesticity, the desire to bring the man home conflicts with normative definitions both of the home as woman's sphere and of the man as, well, manly. The difficulty these stories have in representing such a feminized father as a positive figure—their reluctance to keep a wife alive and present and so to consummate a fully domestic marriage (for what is heterosexual about the union of two such feminine figures?)—provide fictional markers of cultural contradictions. What these temperance writers want, and cannot imagine without ambivalence, is a universalizing of domestic virtues—virtues the culture has coded as feminine—that would not alter traditional gender roles or hierarchies. Temperance fiction's efforts to create a patriarchal home actively occupied by the father thus falter in the uncertainty of what it would mean to be a fully domesticated man. Might this domesticated man not be a man at all?

In his temperance story "The Child's Champion," Walt Whitman obviously cares about the homoerotic possibilities of staging the standard redemptive love scene between a man and a boy. Viewed in the context of temperance fiction's pedophilic conventions, the homoerotic energies of this story provide an insightful vantage on the genre's widespread concern with the creation of effeminate men. Especially in the earliest version of this story, Whitman is abundantly clear about the sexual urgency of the love the young man feels for little Charles.

> Why was it that from the first moment of seeing him, the young man's heart had moved with a strange feeling of kindness toward the boy? He felt anxious to know more of him—he felt that he should love him. O, it is passing wondrous how in the hurried walks of life and business, we meet with young beings, strangers, who seem to touch the fountains of our love, and draw forth their swelling waters.

The fountains and swelling waters of love have a rhapsodic quality familiar from the later poems. What is more surprising, especially for those who have not read much of Whitman's early prose, is this story's commitment to the structures of disciplinary intimacy I have been describing—the ways in which this sexual, and specifically homosexual, intensity is enlisted in the decidedly conservative and bourgeois project of reforming the profligate young man to a productive and apparently heterosexual domestic life—"head of a family of his own":

> It was now past midnight. The young man told Charles that on the morrow he would take steps to have him liberated from his servitude; for the present night, he said, it would be best for the boy to stay and share his bed at the inn; and little persuading did the child need to do so. As they retired to sleep, very pleasant thoughts filled the mind of the young man; thoughts of worthy action performed; of unsullied affection; thoughts too—newly awakened ones—of walking in a steadier and wiser path than formerly. All his imaginings seemed to be interwoven with the youth who lay by his side; he folded his arms around him, and, while he slept, the boy's cheek rested on his bosom.[54]

Whitman found these passages too open an expression of male-male desire and censored them from later versions of the story, although the basic erotic structure of the plot remains in place even as man and boy are safely tucked into separate but neighboring beds. Whitman's self-censoring here serves to acknowledge the sexuality of a scene temperance fiction as a whole avows as powerfully but not erotically sentimental.[55] As Whitman makes clear, however, the aim of these bedroom conversions is to domesticate men not simply by removing them from the bar to the bed, but by actually transforming their desires and replacing the dissipations of drink with the pleasurable containment of enfolding a child in one's arms. Such pleasures are at once sexual and feminizing. The young man's imaginings of a "steadier and wiser" life are "interwoven" with, indeed indistinguishable from, the pressure of the boy's cheek on—not his chest—but his "bosom."

The clear current of homosexual desire in Whitman's story lays bare both

---

54. "The Child's Champion," in *Walt Whitman: The Early Poems and Fiction*, ed. Thomas L. Brasher (New York: New York University Press, 1963) 74 n., 79, 76 n. Whitman published a total of four versions of this story. While the suggestion of a heterosexual happy ending appears in all versions, the two longer passages appear only in the original *New World* (1841) version.

55. In *Disseminating Whitman: Revision and Corporeality in* Leaves of Grass (Cambridge: Harvard University Press, 1991), 26–36, Michael Moon treats the self-censorship evident in Whitman's revisions of "The Child's Champion" as a model for the strategies that, both here and in the later *Leaves of Grass*, would permit Whitman to voice culturally proscribed sexual and power relations. While Moon's discussion of this story richly explores its coding of homosexual desire, he does not situate this plot in relation to the pedophilic conventions of the temperance genre.

Figs. 2.1 and 2.2. "Home of the Intemperate" and "Home of the Temperate." Paired frontispieces to Jane E. Stebbins, *Fifty Years History of the Temperance Cause* (Hartford, Conn.: L. Stebbins, 1876). Copyright © American Antiquarian Society.

the sexual intensity of this conventional conversion scene and its feminizing potential. Thus, despite all its submissive daughters, temperance fiction's plot of redemption in a child's bed evokes a double threat to patriarchal norms: these are at once stories of male violence that would disable family structures and stories of an equally destabilizing homoerotic emasculation. Juxtaposing a world in which everyone has been feminized with one in which male power victimizes women and children, this fiction strives to imagine male consent to a domestication women have always and already undergone. However, while such imaginings may reorganize and generalize patriarchal control, they do not dispense with it. That an explicitly feminine and feminizing love serves to cover fundamentally patriarchal practices of sexual abuse makes clear the relation between love and power. In these stories children may prove effective disciplinary agents, but in reforming their fathers they do not empower themselves.

I end with a pair of images that stunningly codify temperance fiction's reorganization of patriarchal norms—how the child remains as vulnerable as ever, even as he or she figuratively takes on the work of enforcing a new bourgeois order. The "Home of the Intemperate" (fig. 2.1) and the "Home of the Temperate" (fig. 2.2) appeared as paired frontispieces to Jane Stebbins's *Fifty Years History of the Temperance Cause*.[56] In the home of the intemperate, father is there breaking tables, knocking out daughters, and threatening the wife and son who would confine him. In the home of the temperate, there is no father at all, though the luxury of the room implies that he is out producing wealth, not out consuming gin. Still, the fully domesticated male proves unrepresented and unrepresentable. In his place, his children embody the mechanisms of middle-class domestic order. While the daughter, a benign and enabling presence, stands behind the chair, one son reads (intellect), one pulls a wagon (industry), and baby holds the whip.

56. Frontispiece to Jane E. Stebbins, *Fifty Years History of the Temperance Cause*, published in the same volume with T.A.H. Brown, *A Full Description of the Origin and Progress of the New Plan of Labor by the Women Up to the Present Time* (Hartford, Conn.: L. Stebbins, 1876).

CHAPTER THREE

The Death of a Child and the Replication of an Image

Dying is what children do most and do best in the literary and cultural imagination of nineteenth-century America. These ubiquitous deaths epitomize the disconnection between childhood's fictional power and the vulnerability of children. That the figure of the dead or dying child proves so common, such a narrative cliché, stands in marked opposition to the acute pain, the unassimilable wrench of an individual child's death. The sort of narrative cover-up I have traced in temperance fiction, where sexual abuse may be reimagined as a source of efficacious reform, appears even more starkly here. The death of a child stands as the quintessential example of how the helplessness of any actual individual child can be converted into cultural influence. The power that adheres in the figure of the dying child may be used to enforce a wide array of social issues, and any reader of nineteenth-century fiction can easily produce a list of the lessons—temperance, abolition, charity, chastity, and most of all piety—underscored by the death of a child. The loss of a child must be one of the most intimate of griefs, a fundamentally familial loss that makes little apparent rent in the social fabric. And yet

An earlier version of chapter 3 appeared as "Then When We Clutch Hardest: On the Death of a Child and the Replication of an Image," in Mary Chapman and Glenn Hendler, *Sentimental Men: Masculinity and the Politics of Affect in American Culture.* Copyright © 1999 The Regents of the University of California. Reprinted with the permission of the University of California Press.

the constant reiteration of this figure, from Mary Morgan, Eva St. Clare, and Beth March to the myriad of child elegies that—at least in terms of numbers—dominate the poetic production of nineteenth-century America, suggests that the death of a child serves a public function as well, enacting a loss the culture needs to evoke and repeat. The repetitive portrayals of a dead or dying child work to articulate anxieties about growth and loss for a young nation characterized by abundance, geographic expansion, and industrialization but also threatened by economic instability and sectional divisions. In this chapter I pay particular attention to how the deaths of children serve to express cultural bereavement over the commodification of affect and social relations in an ever more urbanized, industrialized, and impersonal America.

The deaths of children are not only or centrally allegorical in this way; they are also and most immediately sites of personal trauma, grief, and mourning. My aim in this chapter is to explore the connections between what Esther Schor calls "the exquisite pain of bereavement" and "the calm commerce of condolence."[1] In the nineteenth century's proliferation of mourning paraphernalia (clothes, jewelry, tombstones, portraits, and verse), condolence is quite literally commercial. I want to suggest that this replication of the figure of the dead child, its mass production as it were, may point to new ways of thinking about the relation between personal emotion and the commerce of the public sphere. Thus the sorts of questions I raise in part one about how ideas of childhood influence nineteenth-century attitudes toward fiction, manifest here in terms of both how childhood shapes the culture of emotion and how this emotionally laden figure personalizes the market economy. Making an individual child into a replicable and saleable memento literalizes the tensions between personal and iconic childhoods at stake in my study. What happens to each of these dead children happens to childhood as a whole.

The untouched drawer, the empty cradle, the vacant chair—these standard nineteenth-century figurations of loss all represent the death of a child as a gap in the domestic scene. And yet the more I have examined the nineteenth century's reiteration of this trope, the less convincing this common-sense interpretation seems.

> Ah! there is an empty crib in the nursery; there is an untenanted chair at the
> table; there are little frocks hanging up in the wardrobe, there are half-worn

---

1. Esther Schor, *Bearing the Dead: The British Culture of Mourning from the Enlightenment to Victoria* (Princeton, N.J.: Princeton University Press, 1994), 3. Schor's interest is in how a psychological focus on mourning has obscured its social and cultural form, and her work strives to invert that process of elision and to look at the social structures of mourning rather than the individual grief. My intention is to describe the links between the social and the personal.

shoes about; there is a little useless straw hat in the entry, there are toys that have borne its wearer happy company; there are little sisters left,—and they are loved. But, O, not like the dead![2]

In this passage, Fanny Fern shows how the presence of things asserts what is absent, and fills this emptiness with the words, images, and emotions of mourning until love for the child who has died ultimately proves more perfect and intense than any love that can be offered a living child. In this way the loss of a child tends rather to confirm the family, and the multiple representations of a child's death serve to secure and extend domestic affect, filling the house with feeling, so that even chairs and shoes become haloed with emotion. The first section of this chapter explores how the death of a child is seen to constitute the family as the locus of affect.

Such an argument recognizes the role of grief in producing and valuing the private: both the home and the feeling individual cherished there. Contending, however, that the figure of the dead child is not only deeply privatized but also endlessly circulated and reproduced, I focus my discussion on such media of circulation: mortuary photographs of dead children and the sentimental and highly formulaic writing that memorializes the death of a child across a wide range of genres, from consolation books to sentimental fiction to elegiac verse. The new technologies of photography, with their increasing capacity to replicate objects and turn them into images, help to make evident characteristics of figural replication also at play in the many pieces Americans wrote about child death. The final section of this chapter asks what happens to grief in the whir of mass production and commercial circulation. One answer lies in aesthetics, and I suggest that we may best understand sentimentality as the expression of the family multiplied and commodified.

I have placed a discussion of Emerson's essay "Experience" at the middle of this chapter, a fitful bridge between my exploration of how the death of a child gives form to the private intimacy of family emotion and my discussion of how the sentimental figuration of this loss sends domestic affect into commercial circulation. In its opening pages Emerson's essay touches on his son's death in ways that would seem to refute both of these formulations: the essay famously fails to find in grief any capacity to confirm the reality of the feeling self ("the only thing grief has taught me, is to know how shallow it is") and describes a subsistence economy for the self that would inhibit commerce ("we have enough to live and bring the year about, but not an ounce to im-

2. Fanny Fern [Sara Parton], "Incident at Mount Auburn," in *Fern Leaves from Fanny's Port-folio* (Buffalo, N.Y.: Miller, Orton, and Mulligan, 1854), 260.

part or invest").[3] If sentimentality is an aesthetics of affect and excess, then Emerson's essay would appear as a rejection of the sentimental. And yet I find Emerson's "Experience" useful precisely because in this apparent rejection it articulates an economy of grief, and so asks, as I would here: how does personal sorrow enter into a system of production, possession, and exchange?

Keeping Loss in Drawers Full of Graves

In a *carte de visite* photograph made by the Squyer Studio in Auburn, New York, in 1864 (fig. 3.1), a boy and his smaller sister lie cuddled together, his arm around her shoulder, her whole small body in a fancy checkered dress resting against him; their eyes are closed. It is a picture of tender love between brother and sister, and it is a picture of tragic loss, for both are dead. The Squyer Studio—most likely at the family's request—mounted this image in an oval frame, as if the children were held in cupped hands, treasured in an egg, or reflected, as indeed they are, in the oval of the viewer's eye. We know that brother and sister were placed in this loving posture, that the tenderness with which they hold one another registers the care of other hands that dressed them, brushed their hair, and laid one small corpse in the arms of the other. In depicting the love between these children, the photograph thus alludes to the love of the family that had this picture taken. This tableau has been arranged, staged. The articles on making postmortem portraits that daguerreotypists and later photographers wrote for the trade press reveal that in practice arranging the bodies of the dead is a necessary but quite "unpleasant duty."[4] The aim of these manipulations is to produce out of these dead bodies a meaning that exceeds the fact of death. This tableau performs

---

3. Ralph Waldo Emerson, "Experience," in *Essays and Lectures* (New York: The Library of America, 1983), 472 and 471. All further citations will be given parenthetically in the text.

4. Charles E. Orr, for example, wrote an article for the *Philadelphia Photographer* in 1877 to give "assistance to some photographers of less experience, to whom it might befall the unpleasant duty to take the picture of a corpse." He explains that photographers should "secure sufficient help to do the lifting and handling, for it is no easy matter to bend a corpse," and advises that mourners should be "politely request[ed] . . . to leave the room to you and your aides, that you may not feel the embarrassment incumbent should they witness some little mishap liable to befall the occasion." Quoted in Jay Ruby, *Secure the Shadow: Death and Photography in America* (Cambridge, Mass.: MIT Press, 1995), 58. In "An Address to the National Photographic Association," published in the *Philadelphia Photographer* (June 1872), Albert S. Southworth recalled his first postmortem daguerreotypes, reporting how by repeated bending the joints can be made pliable so that "you may do just as you please so far as handling and bending the corpses is concerned," and going on to detail his procedures for removing fluid from the mouth of the corpse so that none will be "ejected" during the sitting. Collected in Merry A. Foresta and John Wood, *Secrets of the Dark Chamber: The Art of the American Daguerreotype* (Washington, D.C.: Smithsonian Institution Press, 1995), 308.

Fig. 3.1. *Carte de visite*, Squyer Studio, Auburn, New York, 1864. Courtesy of the Fogg Art Museum, Harvard University Art Museums, on deposit from the Carpenter Center for the Visual Arts. Photo by Allan Macintyre, © 2004 President and Fellows of Harvard College.

a valuation of the family, whose love and intimacy is here poignantly confirmed, even in a sense produced, in the image of the children it has lost.

This sense of the dead child as the most powerful sign of right sentiment—
for the family and for the individual—is itself one of the founding tropes of
sentimentalism. Karen Halttunen argues that "death had come to preoccupy
sentimentalists, who cherished it as the occasion for two of the deepest 'right
feelings' in human experience: bereavement, or direct mourning for the dead,
and sympathy, or mournful condolence for the bereaved."[5] Harriet Beecher
Stowe, for example, would offer the experience of bereavement as the deepest truth of her individual heart and as the means of forging a sympathetic
connection with both the lives of slaves and the lives of her readers. *Uncle
Tom's Cabin*, she averred, began in the death from cholera of her eighteen-
month-old son Charley:

> It was at *his* dying bed, and at *his* grave that I learnt what a poor slave mother
> may feel when her child is torn away from her. . . . I felt that I could never be
> consoled for it, unless this crushing of my own heart might enable me to work
> out some great good to others . . . much that is in that book ("Uncle Tom") had
> its root in the awful scenes and bitter sorrows of that summer.[6]

In the novel, this "root" becomes the central mechanism and emblem for
Stowe's abolitionist project, and so grounds public political change on personal
domestic feeling. It is important to note, however, that before Stowe can proffer the family as a model for national life she must affirm its good heart, and
she does this most often and most forcefully by detailing its capacity to mourn.[7]

In a scene that explicitly enacts Stowe's own novelistic procedures, the

5. Karen Halttunen, "Mourning the Dead: A Study in Sentimental Ritual," in *Confidence
Men and Painted Women: A Study of Middle-Class Culture in America, 1830–1870* (New Haven,
Conn.: Yale University Press, 1982), 124. Halttunen's argument focuses on the ironies of seeking to perform sincerity in both of these right feelings, and how such performances become a
means of claiming genteel status. My concern with the relation between commercialism and
mourning would see nineteenth-century expressions of grief less as a tool of status than as in-
terdependently bound to it.

6. Harriet Beecher Stowe, Letter to Eliza Lee Cabot Follen, December 16, 1852, in Charles
Edward Stowe, *The Life of Harriet Beecher Stowe Compiled from Her Letters and Journals* (Boston:
Houghton and Mifflin, 1889), 198–99.

7. I quite agree with Gillian Brown that the family, in its present form, is not offered by
Stowe as itself an adequate model for national life, and that Stowe's project of reforming the
polity in *Uncle Tom's Cabin* is dependent upon the concomitant reforming of the family. I con-
tend, however, that the familial ideal toward which such reforms are tending is epitomized not
only by the abundance of Rachel Halloway's kitchen but also by the mourning of children who
have died. See Gillian Brown, *Domestic Individualism: Imagining Self in Nineteenth-Century
America* (Berkeley: University of California Press, 1990), 13–38.

escaping slave-woman Eliza Harris elicits sympathy and succor by respond-
ing to Senator and Mrs. Bird's questions as to why she ran away with a question of her own: "Have you ever lost a child?" Mrs. Bird feels the question as
"unexpected . . . and thrust on a new wound." But Stowe is clear that Eliza's
question is also calculated, for Eliza had "looked up at Mrs. Bird, with a keen,
scrutinizing glance, and it did not escape her that she was dressed in deep
mourning."[8] Like Eliza, scrutinizing Mrs. Bird's black dress, Stowe's knowledge of her readers is cultural knowledge; she knows (as we historicist readers
of nineteenth-century sentimental fiction are always reminding ourselves) that
one out of six children in the 1850s died before reaching the age of five. Her
task is to make those broad cultural statistics novelistically and politically efficacious, to replace the undifferentiated mass of death with the more precise
connections of condolence—to make of the corpse a love-affirming tableau.

In making such a connection Senator Bird, too, thinks about clothes:

> "Mary, I don't know how you'd feel about it, but there's that drawer full of
> things—of—of—poor little Henry's." So saying, he turned quickly on his heel,
> and shut the door after him.
>
> His wife opened the little bed-room door adjoining her room and, taking the
> candle, set it down on the top of a bureau there; then from a small recess she
> took a key, and put it thoughtfully in the lock of a drawer, and made a sudden
> pause, while two boys, who, boy like, had followed close on her heels, stood
> looking, with silent, significant glances, at their mother. And oh! mother that
> reads this, has there never been in your house a drawer, or a closet, the opening
> of which has been to you like the opening again of a little grave? Ah! happy
> mother that you are, if it has not been so. (153–54)

Stowe's image of a bureau drawer, "the opening of which has been to you like
the opening again of a little grave," imagines that all homes are built, like
Stowe's novel, around a child's grave. This image does not denote a rupture
in the domestic, or imply that the abysses of loss accessed through bureau
drawers are antithetical to the protective goals of home, but rather that this
capacity of drawers to become like graves, of homes and hearts to harbor
loss, is precisely what constitutes the ideal sentimental reader and the ideal
nineteenth-century American family. Indeed, only when Mrs. Bird approaches
her grave-drawer and puts the key in the lock are her living sons suddenly con-
jured into the text. The grave locked within the home serves to produce and

8. Harriet Beecher Stowe, *Uncle Tom's Cabin; or, Life among the Lowly* (New York: Penguin, 1981), 149. Subsequent citations will be given parenthetically in the text.

focus the family tableau. Stowe ends by imagining some other home, a home without graves. But when she offers as an alternative to her searing question the exclamation "Ah! happy mother that you are, if it has not been so," this affirmation feels full of doubt and threat. Can such happy ignorance ever last? Indeed, can this "happy mother" truly be a mother if she has known no loss?

Explicitly adding the readers' presumed losses to the novel's chain of mourning, Stowe casts the reader as a participant both in Eliza's pain and in Mary Bird's capacity for sympathetic action.[9] That Eliza's and Mary's two little boys have the same name and can fill the same clothes would erase the racial divide, and insists on the overdetermined, almost tautological nature of these links; all children mean the same once they are gone. What they mean is, ego-centrically perhaps, your own child, your own loss, your own pain. David Marshall defines sentimentality as "not just the capacity for feeling, but more specifically the capacity to feel the sentiments of someone else," and goes on to conclude—following Adam Smith—that this poses "an epistemological and aesthetic problem: since we cannot know the experience or sentiments of another person."[10] The figure of Mrs. Bird standing before the bureau drawer is an instance of just such a projection of the self. In a letter to Sarah Allen, who had also lost a child, Stowe described her own scene of mourning—"I cannot open his little drawer of clothes now without feeling it through my very heart"—and then asked: "How is it with you in your heart of hearts when you think of the past—I often wonder how your feelings correspond with mine."[11] Like Marshall, Stowe realizes that she cannot know another's heart of hearts, that one person's grief may not correspond to another's, and yet in assigning the scene that cuts through her very heart to the character of Mrs. Bird, in asking her readers the same wounding question that Eliza asks Mrs. Bird, indeed in imagining that the "crushing of [her] own heart" at Charley's death "may" feel like the separations of slavery and "might enable

9. As Elizabeth Barnes notes, such chains of identification end up "equating democracy with similarity"; Stowe's narrative strategies create a "democratic readership" through "the subordination of physical difference to psychological and emotional sameness." See Barnes, *States of Sympathy: Seduction and Democracy in the American Novel* (New York: Columbia University Press, 1997), 92.

10. David Marshall, *The Surprising Effects of Sympathy: Marivaux, Diderot, Rousseau, and Mary Shelley* (Chicago: University of Chicago Press, 1988), 3 and 5.

11. Letter to Sarah Allen, December 2, 1850. The Allens had been the Stowes' next-door neighbors in Cincinnati, and Diarca Howe Allen taught with Calvin Stowe at the Lane Seminary. In 1844 Sarah and Harriet worked together as midwives delivering the baby of one of the Stowes' boarders. See Joan D. Hedrick, *Harriet Beecher Stowe: A Life* (New York: Oxford University Press, 1994), 158–62, 199.

[her] to work out some great good to others," Stowe risks offering her readers just such a mesh of correspondence. At once calculated and unexpected, the "new wounds" of grave and drawer suggest that the site of mourning is not only secret and deep (unknowable), but also and importantly open.

Marianne Noble astutely links Stowe's treatment of sentimental identification as a "wound" with Roland Barthes's assertion that he was "interested in Photography only for 'sentimental' reasons; I wanted to explore it not as a question (a theme) but as a wound."[12] The open wound provides a site where internal pain remains internal and yet becomes externally visible. What I find most lacerating about the Squyer photograph is the tension between what is held close and what is laid open: the two children appear so protectively enclosed in this image (curled around each other, encircled by the frame, wrapped by death), and yet the oval aperture permits us to see into this intimate space. Such photographs are memorial treasures, carried in purse or pocket, kept secret in a bureau drawer; what they keep is not only the particular lost loved one, but more the loss itself. They work to keep the wound open, as it were. Stowe had a daguerreotype of her son Charley taken after his death (fig. 3.2). Her letters tell how tormenting the cholera was: "I have just seen him in his death agony, looked on his imploring face when I could not help nor soothe nor do one thing, not one, to mitigate his cruel suffering, do nothing but pray in my anguish that he might die soon."[13] The daguerreotype confirms her anguished hope that death might be, for Charley, an end to pain; it represents him lying peacefully on a bed or sofa, his head resting, smooth-browed, on a soft white pillow, a small bouquet clasped in his hands. In the daguerreotype image there is no agony, no imploring face, no cruel suffering. Death and the daguerreotypist have made him instead into a memorial object, a small material thing with which to keep and cherish loss.

In the anonymous magazine verse "The Baby's Drawer," the image of the dead child's full but unused drawer claims the act of cherishing and preserving, of keeping the wound open, as the quintessential maternal task.[14]

---

12. Roland Barthes, *Camera Lucida: Reflections on Photography,* trans. Richard Howard (New York: Hill and Wang, 1981), 21. See also Barthes's sense of the "punctum" or pricking detail of a photograph producing a physical response, "tiny jubilations as if they referred to a stilled center, an erotic or lacerating value buried in myself" (16). For Marianne Noble, this connection between Stowe and Barthes points to the psychological and erotic content of wounding as central to the pleasures of sentimentality. See Noble, *The Masochistic Pleasures of Sentimental Literature* (Princeton, N.J.: Princeton University Press, 2000), 77.

13. Letter to her husband, Calvin Stowe, July 26, 1849. Stowe, *The Life,* 124.

14. "The Baby's Drawer," in Mrs. L. B. Hancock, *A Mother's Scrap-book Only* (Cincinnati, Ohio: Hitchcock and Walden, 1878), 95–96.

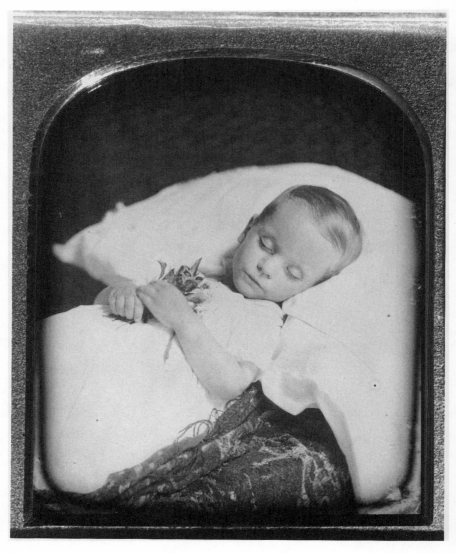

Fig. 3.2. Daguerreotype of Samuel Charles Stowe, 1849. Courtesy of The Schlesinger Library, Radcliffe Institute, Harvard University.

There's a little drawer in my chamber
    Guarded with tenderest care,
Where the dainty clothes are lying,
    That my darling shall never wear.
And there, while the hours are waning
    Till the house is all at rest,
I sit and fancy a baby
    Close to my aching breast.

My darling's pretty white garments!
    I wrought them sitting apart,
While his mystic life was throbbing
    Under my throbbing heart.
And often my happy dreaming
    Breaks in a little song,
Like the murmur of birds at brooding,
    When the days are warm and long.

I finished the dainty wardrobe,
    And the drawer was almost full
With robes of finest muslin,
    And robes of whitest wool.
I folded them all together,
    With a rose for every pair,
Smiling and saying, "Gem fragrant,
    Fit for my prince to wear."

Ah the radiant Summer morning,
    So full of a mother's joy!
"Thank God, he is fair and perfect,
    My beautiful newborn boy."
Let him wear the pretty white garments
    I wrought while sitting apart;
Lay him so sweet and helpless,
    Here, close to my throbbing heart.

Many and many an evening
    I sit, since my baby came,
Saying, "What do the angels call him?"
    For he died without a name;

> Sit while the hours are waning
>> And the house is all at rest,
> And fancy a baby nestling
>> Close to my aching breast.

No drawer that held the clothes of a living baby could ever preserve its contents so perfectly dainty and white. Like the drawer itself, where fullness and disuse both contradict and support each other, this mother's value as a mother is confirmed not by the one verse that describes her holding her "sweet and helpless" living son, so much as by the four surrounding it that depict her anticipating the birth and mourning the death of her child. In this poem motherhood is enacted most purely and perfectly in dreams, and if there is real pathos in the woman who fancies her dead baby nestling at her breast, there is also real power in that act of imagination. "Often my happy dreaming / Breaks in a little song," the woman says of her pregnant self in a passage otherwise cast completely and appropriately in the past tense; this "break" into the present, even as an unintended grammatical error, absorbs the dreams of pregnancy into the fancy of mourning. To mother the not-yet-born and the already-lost amount to the same thing, and although clearly the author intends a contrast between the "throbbing heart" of the happily expectant mother and the "aching breast" of the bereaved one, throbbing cannot be sufficiently differentiated from aching. The bureau drawer and its dainty contents connect her hope and her mourning much as it serves to link Stowe, her readers, Mrs. Bird and Eliza. The poem recognizes how grief can inhabit material things, and asserts that these "pretty white garments" are not, finally, unused objects; rather, they are used—as Senator Bird suggests using the contents of their household's similar drawer—to produce sympathetic connection and sentiment. If the baby had lived the mother would, no doubt, have enacted the loving labors of mothering; the drawer and its dainty clothes would have been worn rather than "guarded with tenderest care." Yet by dying the baby does not rupture these familial ideals, or leave these clothes without use, but rather enshrines them in the imagination, the bureau drawer, and this poem.

Roland Barthes writes of "that rather terrible thing which is there in every photograph: the return of the dead." What Barthes recognizes here is the uncanny nature of photography, an uncanniness to which we may have grown so accustomed that it has come to feel almost familiar, but which was felt with gothic intensity in the years of photography's invention. "What the Photograph reproduces to infinity has occurred only once: the Photograph mechanically repeats what could never be repeated existentially."[15] (The daguerreotype, of course, reproduces a moment only once, upon a single unique plate; but when Daguerre unveiled his and Niecep's invention in 1839, that single act of replication astounded its viewers far more intensely than the infinite repetitions of the postmodern simulacrum are felt by us now.) Even two decades later, when daguerreotypes had been displaced by the infinitely replicable process of negative-positive photography, Oliver Wendell Holmes described for his *Atlantic* readers the process of making a photographic portrait in the occult imagery of "the ghost we hold imprisoned in the shield we have just brought from the camera."[16] As Barthes's notion of the returning dead suggests, there may indeed be no more accurate name for a photograph than "ghost."

In a story on the "Lights and Shadows of Daguerrean Life" he wrote for *The Photographic Art-Journal,* the daguerreotypist Gabriel Harrison literalizes the connection between photography and a child's death. He tells of being called to the basement home of a poor woman in order to photograph her dead daughter. When he arrives he finds the mother "giving way to low heart-rendering choking sobs" and is himself overwhelmed by her "thousand, thousand thanks." The conditions of poverty are not the best conditions for photography. As the daguerreotypist sets up his equipment, the technical concerns (how to get enough light into the basement) and the stillness of photography seem the antithesis to this swirling grief.

> The mother held up a white cloth to give me reflected light to subdue the shadows. All was still, I took the cap from the camera. About two minutes had elapsed, when a bright sunray broke through the clouds, dashed its bright beams upon the reflector, and shedding, as it were, a supernatural light. I was startled—the mother riveted with frightful gaze, for at the same moment we beheld the muscles around the mouth of the child move, and her eyes partially open—a smile played upon her lips, a long gentle sigh heaved her bosom, and as I replaced the cap, her head fell over to one side. The mother screamed.
>
> "She lives! She lives!" and fell upon her knees by the side of the couch.
>
> "No," was my reply; "she is dead now, the web of life is broken."
>
> The camera was doing its work as the cord of life that bound the gentle be-

15. Barthes, *Camera Lucida,* 9 and 4. See also Susan Sontag's contentions on the graveyard quality of a photographed world, in Sontag, *On Photography* (New York: Penguin, 1978).

16. Oliver Wendell Holmes, "Doings of the Sunbeam," *The Atlantic Monthly* 12 (12 July 1863), collected in Beaumont Newhall, ed., *Photography: Essays and Images, Illustrated Readings in the History of Photography* (New York: Museum of Modern Art, 1980), 66.

ing to earth snapped and loosened the spirit for another and better world. If the earth lost a flower, Heaven gained an angel.[17]

Here the moment of photography actually is the moment of death, as if the camera that would memorialize the child must require her to die. The daguerreotypist's response to the sudden burst of sun is to clap the cover on his camera so as not to overexpose his plate. He views this light technically as the medium of his work, not as the celestial promise and sanctification that sunbeams conventionally proffer for the sentimental deathbed scene. In the opposition between the photographer's technical concerns and the mother's emotional intensity, photography might appear antithetical to mourning. But I am suggesting instead that, occupying as it does in this story the precise point where the lower-class child becomes an "angel," photography offers to replace a chaotic "shocking," "choking" grief with a more genteel mourning object, a picture that in promising to hold and focus loss ensures that the death of the child will not destroy the family but rather secure it with a material memory.

As this story demonstrates, the relation between death and photography appears particularly poignant and pressing when it comes to the problems of photographing children. In a poem that Anna L. Snelling, wife of the editor of *The Photographic Art-Journal,* published in her husband's magazine, the "laughing, bouncing" living child is presented as inimical to photography:

> What! put *her* in daguerreotype,
>   And victimize the pet!
> Those ruby lips so cherry-ripe,
>   On lifeless silver set!
>
> The frisking, laughing, bouncing thing,
>   So full of life and glee—
> A restless bird upon the wing—
>   A sunbeam on the sea! . . .
>
> Now she is still—fly to the stand;
>   The smiling features trace!
> In vain—up goes a tiny hand,
>   And covers half a face.

17. Gabriel Harrison, "Lights and Shadows of Daguerrean Life," in *The Photographic Art-Journal* 1 (March 1851): 179–81. My thanks to Laura Wexler for telling me of this story.

Give up the task—let childhood be
    Nature's own blooming rose!
You cannot catch the spirit free,
    Which only childhood knows.

Earth's shadow o'er that brow will pass
    Then paint her at your will;
When time shall make her wish, alas!
    She was a baby still.[18]

The sense of the preciousness of childhood, and hence the desire to preserve it, conflicts in this poem with the acknowledgment that the preservation photography offers is precisely the "lifeless" silver-plate stillness of death. The last verse recognizes that childhood is always about loss—all children are precarious and fleeting, whether they die or simply grow up.[19] Here—evoking the techniques and idiom of "sun-painting"—it is only once the "sunbeam" child has been touched by "shadow" that it becomes possible to photograph her. For portrait photographers, whose work was precisely the task of preserving an ephemeral face, it is quite clear that at least through the early 1850s the dead child is a far better photographic subject than a live one, and estimates suggest that certainly for infants, and perhaps even for young children, the mere number of mortuary images exceeds that of photographs taken of living children during this period. The first daguerreotypes required a fifteen-minute exposure; this was quickly reduced to thirty seconds, and by the mid-1850s the switch to a collodion or wet-plate process had reduced exposure times to as little as half a second. Yet even this is a long time to expect stillness from a living child.[20] If they lack other definite markers or inscriptions, contemporary historians of photography routinely conclude that a sharply focused early daguerreotype of a baby is likely to be postmortem.[21]

As the bouncing, face-covering antics of the girl in Snelling's poem indi-

18. Mrs. Anna L. Snelling, *The Photographic Art-Journal* 1 (February 1851): 126.

19. Generalizing the "bloom" of pedophilic desire and the way the vanishing of childhood prompts a particularly intense desire to look at children, James Kincaid notes how "Photographing children before they slip away, before that 'bloom' can no longer be caught, is a need felt by Lewis Carroll, by J. M. Barrie, and, judging by the television and magazine advertisements of film companies like Kodak and Polaroid, by nearly everyone today." James R. Kincaid, *Child-Loving: The Erotic Child and Victorian Culture* (New York: Routledge, 1992), 227–28.

20. For a table of exposure times from the 1840s see Beaumont Newhall, *The Daguerreotype in America* (New York: Duell, Sloan and Pearce, 1961), 124.

21. Bill Jay, "Infantry Tactics," in Sue Packer, *The Babies* (Manchester, Mich.: Cornerhouse, 1989).

cate, photography not only imitates death, but requires a deathlike stillness to make that replication possible. Nineteenth-century photography journals frequently published articles sharing tactics for photographing restless infants ("arrangements for the babies should be made so as not to interfere with their daily sleep, as they look and feel so much better and sweeter after a nap"), while advertisements claimed skill in photographing children ("We are always glad to take a reasonable amount of pains with children. They are subjects that make lovely pictures, but they are often difficult to secure. We can always get *something* of them"), and many child photographs reveal restraining sashes or even hands.[22] The uncomfortable iron stands used to hold the heads of adults still—often blamed for the stoic expressions characteristic of daguerreotype portraits—were found to produce only pictures of wailing youngsters. Explaining what he considers a more successful procedure "if a very young child is to be taken," Edward Tompkins Whitney describes an elaborate apparatus for tying a child into a special cushioned chair so that the strings are "hugging it close to the cushioned back rail . . . held as in its mother's arms."[23] Indeed, such devices proved more trustworthy than mothers, since even seated on her mother's lap a squirming child could seemingly dematerialize into a blur (fig. 3.3). As late as 1874 George Rockwood printed a humorous booklet to entertain sitters waiting their turn in his New York studio, including a series of cartoons on the frustrations of photographing babies (fig. 3.4).[24] That such complaints extend well beyond the long-exposure days of the 1840s or 1850s only emphasizes how in more than a straightforward, technical way the dead baby proved a far more satisfactory photographic subject, even when the goal of such mortuary photography was to produce a lifelike image.

In his 1855 article "Taking Portraits after Death," N. G. Burgess acknowledges that "all likenesses taken after death will of course only resemble the inanimate body, nor will there appear in the portrait anything like life itself, except indeed the sleeping infant, on whose face the playful smile of innocence sometimes steals even after death. This maybe and is oft-times transferred to the silver plate."[25] The lovely Southworth and Hawes photograph of a dead child, nestled on a soft pillow with seemingly relaxed, gently crossed

22. Edward L. Wilson, "To My Patrons" (Philadelphia, 1871). Collected in Newhall, *Photography: Essays and Images,* 130 and 133.

23. Edward Tompkins Whitney, "On Taking Daguerreotypes of Children," *The Photographic and Fine Art Journal* (March 1855): 76.

24. George G. Rockwood, *Rockwood's Photographic Art-illery Manual and Infantry Tactics* (New York: n.p., 1874).

25. Ruby, *Secure the Shadow,* 69 and 44, emphasis added in the Burgess quotation.

Fig. 3.3. "Frances Helen M. Stevens and daughter Mary," 1852. Courtesy of the Minnesota Historical Society, St. Paul, Minnesota.

limbs and a peaceful, innocently "sleeping" face, testifies to the truth of these claims (fig. 3.5). Especially for children, mortuary photography promises to preserve the ideal of childhood, to present a child more pliant and open to adoration than any live subject could be. The coercion that is death preempts the need for the photographic coercions of sash, drug, hand, or rod. That Burgess knows that such an appearance of life rarely characterizes post-mortem photographs of adults suggests in part that the desired image of adulthood—certainly for adult men, but even for adult women—is never so

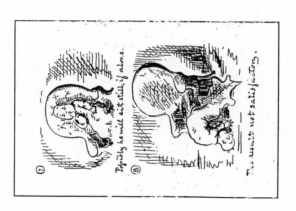

Fig. 3.4. Illustrations from George G. Rockwood, *Rockwood's Photographic Art-illery Manual and Infantry Tactics* (New York, 1874).

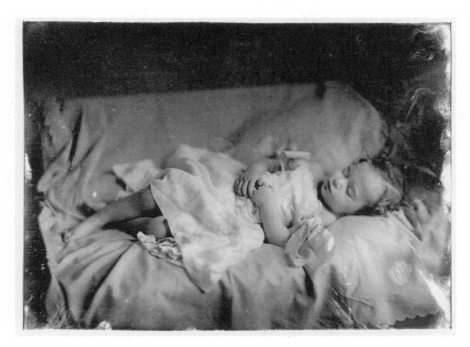

Fig. 3.5. Daguerreotype, Southworth and Hawes, Boston, ca. 1850. Courtesy George Eastman House.

passive. If the dead child serves better than the live one, it may well be because of the very ways a child is imagined like a drawer, an empty receptacle waiting to be filled with familial values.

From the first the miracle of photography has been understood as a miracle of memorialization, the capacity to preserve a bit of the present, to let us see again, as it were, a moment that is in all other ways irretrievably past. For a parent to commission a photograph like the Southworth and Hawes image must involve contradictory emotions: the image invites its viewers at once to deny death—to retain the living child at least as an image—and to record the fact of death, to acknowledge that the child has died. The girl in the Southworth and Hawes print clasps the ribbon of a small crucifix, half-obscured by the folds of her white dress, ensuring that however skillfully the photographers have arranged her corpse to imitate sleep, no viewer could long mistake the image for that of a living child. A family might well take a postmortem portrait of their child, even when they already had a picture of the living child. In one image—a *mise-en-abîme* of childhood made still—a dead boy is actually posed holding a daguerreotype of himself when alive. Simi-

Fig. 3.6. Daguerreotype, father and mother holding dead infant. 1850s–1860s. Courtesy of the Strong Museum, Rochester, NY (2004).

larly, there are family portraits that include a child corpse. Some explicitly constitute the family around the fact of the child's death, while others pose as for any family portrait, looking not at the child but at the camera, recording the family as a whole that simply, poignantly, includes this small corpse (fig. 3.6). Each of these pictures may display the child's death somewhat differently—some foregrounding it, some masking it—but in every case the image emphatically functions to include the dead child as a central and essential member of the family. The death of the child is, after all, the occasion of each picture.

Emerson's Vain Clutching

In a journal entry of October 24, 1841, Ralph Waldo Emerson writes of having his own daguerreotype portrait made:

> Were you ever daguerreotyped, O immortal man? And did you look with all
> vigor at the lens of the camera, or rather, by direction of the operator, at the

brass peg a little below it, to give the picture the full benefit of your expanded and flashing eye? and in your zeal not to blur the image, did you keep every finger in its place with such energy that your hands became clenched as for fight or despair, and in your resolution to keep your face still, did you feel every muscle becoming every moment more rigid; the brows contracted into a Tartarean frown, and the eyes fixed as they are fixed in a fit, in madness, or in death? And when at last you are relieved of your dismal duties, did you find the curtain drawn perfectly, and the hands true, clenched for combat, and the shape of the face or head?—but, unhappily, the total expression escaped from the face and the portrait of a mask instead of a man? Could you not by grasping it very tight hold the stream of a river, or of a small brook, and prevent it from flowing?[26]

Here, all the daguerreotype can image is death. Expression, the immortal soul of "O immortal man," proves to be precisely what this technology seems unable to grasp. Photography can thwart death only by imitating its stillness. The ironic barb of Emerson's questions points, of course, to how little faith men have in their immortality, and hence at the desire to be daguerreotyped, to preserve at least a death-mask face against an uncertain future. Emerson may ridicule this desire for photographic immortality, but he also shares it; he too has gone before the operator. Most significantly, his final image for the futility of photography—the absurd goal of stopping the flow of a river with one's grasping hands—returned to haunt him just three months later when, on January 27, 1842, his only son and beloved first child, Waldo, died of scarlet fever.

Emerson speaks explicitly of Waldo's death in only one paragraph of his essay "Experience," yet, as Sharon Cameron and others after her have argued, Waldo's death is not simply "set forth and set aside, in fact the essay is a testament to the pervasiveness of a loss so inclusive that it is suddenly inseparable from experience itself."[27] Emerson follows his specific words on his son's death with this same, no longer foolish, image of hands vainly clutching at an ungraspable flow: "I take this evanescence and lubricity of all objects, which lets them slip through our fingers then when we clutch hardest, to be the most unhandsome part of our condition" (473). What is "unhandsome" is indeed our "hands": both that they would clutch at life—where clutching

26. Ralph Waldo Emerson, *The Journals and Miscellaneous Notebooks of Ralph Waldo Emerson,* ed. William H. Gilman and J. E. Parsons (Cambridge: Harvard University Press, 1970), entry of 24 October 1841.

27. Sharon Cameron, "Representing Grief: Emerson's 'Experience'," in *The New American Studies: Essays from Representations,* ed. Philip Fisher (Berkeley: University of California Press, 1991), 202.

is useless—and that for all their clutching they will never grasp.[28] The daguerreotyped hands clenched in combat or despair gain a new poignancy. The fight to possess and the despair of possessing, how hands are unhanded, characterizes our condition by locating it in the body, and more specifically locating it in that portion of the body that differentiates the human capacity to manufacture the objects of our world. All our making cannot grant possession. The death-mask daguerreotype of immortal man is one instance of such vain clutchings, an instance clearly grounded in a market economy where daguerreotype portraiture sells. The impossibility of preventing Waldo's death, or more, of keeping him truly present once he has died, is another. The unhandsomeness of our hands characterizes both the consumerist quest for ever more having and the grief of bereavement.

The pain of no longer being able to have his son is the theme of many of Emerson's letters and journal entries in the days after Waldo's death:

> For this boy in whose remembrance I have both slept and waked so oft decorated for me the morning star, & the evening cloud, how much more all the particulars of daily economy; for he had touched with his lively curiosity every trivial fact & circumstance in the household, the hard coal and soft coal which I put in my stove; the wood of which he brought his little quota for grandmother's fire, the hammer, the pincers, & file, he was so eager to use, the microscope, the magnet, the little globe, & every trinket & instrument in the study; the loads of gravel of the meadow, the nests in the henhouse and many & many a little visit to the doghouse and to the barn—For everything he had his own name & way of thinking, his own pronunciation & manner. And every word came mended from that tongue.[29]

These pages are imbued with a sense of how Waldo's presence permeated his father's life. The belief that Waldo's touch endowed the world with value characterized his role in the family all along; it was not simply a response to his death. So, for example, in a journal entry written when Waldo was not yet two, Emerson quoted his wife Lidian's maternal prizings of two apples the boy had carried home "one in each hand. . . . 'See where the dear little Angel has

---

28. Stanley Cavell calls attention to the connection between "the hand in unhandsome and the impotently clutching fingers" of this passage, although he sees the unhandsome only in the desire "to deny the standoffishness of objects by clutching at them," a desire he associates with language and one I wish to associate with the urge to possess that characterizes consumerism. Cavell, *This New Yet Unapproachable America: Lectures after Emerson and Wittgenstein* (Albuquerque, N.M.: Living Batch Press, 1989), 86–88.

29. Emerson, *Journals,* entry of January 30, 1842.

gnawed them. They are worth a barrel of apples that he has not touched.'"[30] But if Waldo had "touched" and "mended" all this—both with his hands and tongue, and with the "lively curiosity" of his mind—he himself is no longer lively and can no longer be touched, so that the question of what it would mean to mend such a loss straddles the gap between all the specific, graspable things Emerson can list and the ungraspable thing he has lost.

A few days after Waldo's death, Emerson would write to Caroline Sturgis:

> I chiefly grieve that I cannot grieve; that this fact takes no more deep hold than other facts, is as dreamlike as they; a lambent flame that will not burn playing on the surface of my river. Must every experience—those that promised to be dearest & most penetrative—only kiss my cheek like the wind & pass away?[31]

Following Cameron, it is important to see this grief over the loss of affect as a displacement of grief over the death of the son that incorporates and reiterates that loss: it is not only an abstract "experience" that has "passed away," but also the boy who used to kiss his father's cheek. Still, this pattern of displacement as reiteration differs from the idea of mourning that characterizes the sentimental ideology detailed in the first section of this chapter: mourning as a keeping of loss, a clutching at loss. Not only does Emerson fail, in this account, to grasp evanescent experience, but neither can the "fact" of his son's death "hold" him. The vainness of clutching and the impossibility of being held prove one and the same. In "Experience" Emerson elaborates it this way:

> So it is with this calamity: it does not touch me: some thing which I fancied was part of me, which could not be torn away without tearing me, or enlarged without enriching me, falls off from me, and leaves no scar. It was caducous. I grieve that grief can teach me nothing, nor carry me one step into real nature. The Indian who was laid under a curse that the wind should not blow on him, nor water flow to him, nor fire burn him, is a type of us all. The dearest events are summer-rain and we the Para coats that shed every drop. (473)

This image of a ripping of flesh that "leaves no scar" is the perfect antithesis of the sentimental cultivation of the new and open wound. Mrs. Bird has no

---

30. Emerson, *Journals,* entry of July 16, 1838. See also Lidian's adoration of a tower Waldo has built, entry of April 29, 1838, 4. In both of these cases the "fit of affection" is depicted as Lidian's—a maternal valuation—but the father writing presents his words as an endorsement of her effusions.

31. Ralph Waldo Emerson, letter to Caroline Sturgis, February 4, 1842, in *The Letters of Ralph Waldo Emerson,* ed. Ralph Rusk, vol. 3 (New York: Columbia University Press, 1939), 9.

scar not because her loss has seamlessly healed, but rather because the wound will not close. Stowe offers Mrs. Bird (in a scene that recapitulates her own personal experiences of loss) as "a type of us all," assured that readers reading this passage will claim and feel Mrs. Bird's wound as their own. In claiming no scar, Emerson asserts his loss as an utter loss. "It was caducous," like (as my dictionary says, offering notably sentimental examples) the sepals of a flower or a baby's milk teeth, a palpable part of the self that is early shed and leaves no mark of the initial connection. Similarly, the connection to his readers that Emerson proffers, what he finds "of us all," is not shared feeling but rather the shared curse of an inability to feel.

In passages like these Emerson clearly and strongly rejects the sentimental conception that the cherishing of the dead can in any way relieve loss or produce emotional ties. "Intellect always puts an interval between the subject & the object," he would muse in his journal some months later. "Affection would blend the two. For weal or for woe I clear myself from the thing I contemplate: I grieve, but I am not a grief: I love but I am not a love."[32] Death and grief, especially for what is loved, are simply loss: they do not remake the self in their own image, they build no connections, they teach nothing. Yet as Emerson's imagery reveals, this very claim of impermeability and disconnection—"the Para coats that shed every drop"—simultaneously expresses how grief and loss permeate the world; the mourner may believe that loss will not bring him "one step into real nature," nor forge the precise connections of sentiment, but the skies themselves cry in summer-rain the father's tears.[33] This double sense of loss as both caducous and diffusely all-permeating clearly differs from the sentimental conception of loss as grounding both individual affective identity and precise emotional bonds to others. It is, however, this Emersonian conception of loss—ungraspable and all-permeating—that best reveals the way grief, even in the sentimental guise of "Affection" that Emerson disavows, bears on issues of production, commerce, and possession.

From his earliest writings, Emerson had aligned himself, and his call for a national rebirth, with childhood and in opposition to mourning. Mourning entails homage to the dead: "Our age is retrospective. It builds the sepulchers of the fathers," he asserts in the first lines of *Nature,* and famously goes on to ask "Why should not we also enjoy an original relation to the universe?"

32. Emerson, *Journals,* undated entry of September 1842.

33. See Cameron, "Representing Grief," 210 and 215–16 for more extended readings of these passages that have deeply influenced my work, including the recognition that the kiss of the wind and the tears of summer rain evoke Waldo and the act of grieving him in passages that might seem to mourn the loss of affect and not the loss of a son.

(7). Emerson's scorn for retrospect, sepulchers, and fathers sees in mourn-ing's attachment to the past, in its effort to keep the dead present in the feel-ings and thoughts of the living, a profound threat to the original relation he imagines. He wants not a remembrance but a making new, even if it must be, as his "also" admits, always only the repetition of making new again. But what happens when the sepulcher proves not for the fathers but for the son, when what is mourned is not the past, but the future? "It is true that the Boy is gone," Emerson writes to Lidian when he is away lecturing in Providence a scant two weeks after Waldo's death, "the far shining stone that made home glitter to me when I was farthest absent—for you & I are passing, and he was to remain."[34] The lost boy is figured as "far shining" future, but he is also the source, the buried past, and no doubt the "little man" of the poem which be-gins "Experience," to whom nature whispers "The founder thou! these are thy race!"(469).

Part of what Waldo has founded for his father is precisely this refusal to hold on to grief. "We are finding again our hands & feet after our dull & dread-ful dream which does *not* leave us where it found us," Emerson wrote to Mar-garet Fuller in the week after Waldo's death. He goes on to admonish himself for being thus altered by bereavement, so that what follows this passage al-ready points to the claim in "Experience" that even the most grievous loss "would leave me as it found me" (473).

> Lidian, Elizabeth, & I recite chronicles words & tones of our fair boy & magnify our lost treasure to extort if we can the secretest wormwood of grief, & see how bad is the worst. Meantime the sun rises & the winds blow Nature seems to have forgotten that she has crushed her sweetest creation and perhaps would admon-ish us that as this Child's attention could never be fastened on any death, but proceeded still to enliven the new toy, so we children must have no retrospect, but illuminate the new hour if possible with an undiminished stream of rays.[35]

It is the child, particularly the child who has died, who together with nature teaches the parent not to fasten onto death. And so the mourning parents— to whom what is lost is a treasure—become instead "we children," relin-quishing retrospect by returning to youthful origins, and claiming each "new hour" as a "new toy" so as to find not loss but abundance in the passage of time that makes us mortal. Thus one way that Emerson fastens onto his son, even as he "if possible" (this lesson is in no way easy) resists fastening onto

---

34. Emerson, letter to Lidian Emerson, February 15, 1842, in *Letters,* 3:12.
35. Emerson, letter to Margaret Fuller, February 2, 1842, in *Letters,* 3:9.

death, is by recording this capacity to let go as one of the things his child
taught him.

There is much that is disturbing about Emerson's notion of "Compensation," as he titled his essay on loss as a source of abundance. The confidence
in redress Emerson offers here can feel like a callous discounting of loss.
"Compensation" was published in *Essays: First Series,* and so was written
long before Waldo's death, but in the wake of the deaths of Emerson's first
wife, Ellen, and his brother Charles.[36] Comparing the soul to a shellfish that
must periodically quit its "beautiful stony case, because it no longer admits
of its growth and slowly forms a new house" (301), Emerson writes:

> A fever, a mutilation, a cruel disappointment, a loss of wealth, a loss of friends,
> seems at the moment unpaid loss and unpayable. But the sure years reveal the
> deep remedial force that underlies all facts. The death of a dear friend, wife,
> brother, lover, which seems nothing but privation, somewhat later assumes the
> aspect of a guide or genius; for it commonly operates revolutions in our way of
> life, terminates an epoch of infancy or of youth which was waiting to be closed,
> breaks up a wonted occupation, or a household, or style of living and allows
> new ones more friendly to the growth of character. (302)

Emerson undoubtedly found this deep remedial force harder to believe in by
the time he wrote "Experience," but this is at most a shift of emphasis.[37] The
recompense claimed here is, after all, nothing more sanguine than the recognition that our lives are not fractured by deprivations but made whole
through them, because ultimately everything is subject to loss, all ways of life
are "waiting to be closed." The sense that even the gravest calamities can be
assigned meaning and thus transmuted into value, that loss may prove the
source of abundance, remains Emerson's most insistent response to death.

36. See James Cox, "Ralph Waldo Emerson: The Circle of the Eye," in *Emerson: Prophecy,
Metamorphosis and Influence,* ed. David Levin (New York: Columbia University Press, 1975),
on how the deaths of Ellen and Charles inspired and empowered Emerson's writing.

37. Stephen Whicher's seminal study of Emerson, *Freedom and Fate: An Inner Life of Ralph
Waldo Emerson* (Philadelphia: University of Pennsylvania Press, 1971), posits Waldo's death as
the pivot that turns Emerson from optimism to skepticism. This basic structure still organizes
most critical work on Emerson, although increasingly critics—including myself—have focused
on the continuity of Emerson's thought and the way fate haunts even such early work as "Nature" and "Self-Reliance." See Cavell, *This New Yet Unapproachable America,* and Richard
Poirier, *The Renewal of Literature: Emersonian Reflections* (New York: Random House, 1987) on
the pervasiveness of Emerson's skepticism. Christopher Newfield's *The Emerson Effect: Individualism and Submission in America* (Chicago: University of Chicago Press, 1996) takes such a
revision farther than I find convincing in depicting Emerson's fatalism as his most significant
(and damning) contribution to the nature of American liberalism.

There is a chilling solipsism here—the mirror image of the sentimental ego-ism that would absorb all losses in one's own bereavement. In both these cases loss and grief become sources of value, more "payable" than one had ever imagined. Letting go of the dead, the very opposite of the sentimental preservation enacted by photographs and bureau drawers, ultimately shares with sentimentalism the recognition that loss confers worth, that it enriches and empowers the self because it prompts new beginnings and the work of self-making.[38] Emerson finds in the "epoch of infancy or of youth" a clear model for the fabrication of identity because they prove so fleeting. The changeability of childhood that sentimentalism mourns becomes for Emer-son its chief attraction.

Critics have found the way Emerson writes of Waldo's death in "Experi-ence" as scandalous as they find sentimental responses trite, because Emer-son insists on the insufficiency of grief and, worse yet, depicts the loss of a child with peculiarly economic analogies:[39]

> In the death of my son, now more than two years ago, I seem to have lost a beautiful estate,—no more. I cannot get it nearer to me. If tomorrow I should be informed of the bankruptcy of my principal debtors, the loss of my property would be a great inconvenience to me, perhaps for many years; but it would leave me as it found me,—neither better nor worse. So it is with this calamity: it does not touch me. (473)

I realize that I may risk sounding like Emerson's original audience: young men of the new commercial classes who, Mary Kupiec Cayton argues, misconstrued Emerson's message and applauded his examples ("Steam was as abundant 100 years ago as now but it was not put to so good a use as now. [Applause]") while remaining oblivious to the "higher theory" Emerson intended such ex-amples to illustrate.[40] Still, it seems to me that Emerson's comparison of the

---

38. Michael Lopez, *Emerson and Power: Creative Antagonism in the Nineteenth Century* (DeKalb: Northern Illinois University Press, 1996), in chapters on "The Doctrine of Use" and "The Uses of Failure," richly explores Emerson's conviction that loss should be apprehended as a source of power.

39. Mark Edmundson gets well beyond the "shock" in noting how these economic figura-tions of loss "anticipate Freud's own economic tropes for the psyche." See "Emerson and the Work of Melancholia," *Raritan* 6 (spring 1987): 128, and specific economic comparisons with "Mourning and Melancholia" on 131.

40. Mary Kupiec Cayton, "The Making of an American Prophet: Emerson, His Audiences, and the Rise of the Culture Industry in Nineteenth-Century America," *The American Historical Review* 92 (June 1987): 612–13. The quote is from a report on Emerson's lecture "Wealth" by the *Daily Cincinnati Gazette*, 13 December 1852.

death of his son to the loss of an estate and the bankruptcy of debtors is significant, not only because it jars sentimental expectations, but more because
it insists upon a relation between grief and economic possession. What the
boom-and-bust cycles of the 1830s amply illustrate is the insecurity of possession: how easily beautiful estates may be lost; how—in the figure of the
debtor whose bankruptcy incurs losses for others—possession is not singu-
lar but rather forges flexible and multiple links. This is not, of course, the vision of commercial progress that mechanics, clerks, and aspiring merchants
would want to applaud, but it is an understanding of the economic world that
stresses the exchange and fluidity of America's new commercial structures
and suggests that these could be reimagined as a source of renewal.[41]

The impossibility of securing possession is not only a general economic
fact, but one Emerson recognized as specifically relevant to his own work as
a lecturer and writer. As he wrote in "Experience":

> So many things are unsettled which it is of the first importance to settle,—and,
> pending their settlement, we will do as we do. . . . Law of copyright and interna-
> tional copyright is to be discussed, and, in the interim, we will sell our books for
> the most we can. Expediency of literature, reason of literature, lawfulness of
> writing down a thought is questioned; much is to say on both sides, and while
> the fight waxes hot, thou, dearest scholar, stick to thy foolish task, add a line
> every hour, and between whiles add a line. Right to hold land, right of property,
> is disputed, and the conventions convene, and before the vote is taken, dig away
> at your garden, and spend your earnings as a waife or godsend to all serene and
> beautiful purposes. (481)

Here the joy of what "we do" is identified not with possession but with
expenditure. Emerson's own early collections of essays—tellingly titled
"series"—circulated far more widely and successfully through pirated British
editions and the often inaccurate and certainly fragmenting reprint mechanisms of periodical notices and reviews than in authorized editions.[42] If

41. I share Richard F. Teichgraeber's sense that in his use of economic imagery Emerson is
not merely illustrating philosophical and ethical issues outside the market economy, but also offering ways of reimagining that economy. Teichgraeber, *Sublime Thoughts / Penny Wisdom: Situating Emerson and Thoreau in the American Market* (Baltimore, Md.: Johns Hopkins University Press, 1995).

42. See Teichgraeber, *Sublime Thoughts / Penny Wisdom*, esp. 173–99. Lawrence Buell's
account of antebellum balancing acts between the increasing commercialization of authorship
and "the persistence of the ideal of art as a form of cultural service" finds in Emerson a perfect
instance of the capacity to have it both ways, as he simultaneously "resisted depicting art as a
commodity" and yet made Transcendentalism into "an eminently marketable commodity that

Emerson takes pleasure in how "things are unsettled" and how the "right of property" is unrealizable, it is clear that this pleasure derives from how the inability to grasp leaves unhindered the ability to sell and write and spend. Susan Stewart has argued that the memento or souvenir—of which the post-mortem photograph is a particularly affect-laden example—is like a book in "the way in which an exterior of little material value envelopes a great 'interior significance.'" "Yet at the same time," she adds, "these souvenirs absolutely deny the book's mode of mechanical reproduction. . . . Because of its connection to biography and its place in constituting the notion of the individual life, the memento becomes emblematic of the worth of that life and of the self's capacity to generate worthiness."[43] In contrast, I argue that most souvenirs, including mementos of the dead, are in fact collaborations between the modes of commercial and mechanical production and the emotions and desires of an individual life.[44] Books and mementos are both instances of how thought and memory may be endowed with a commodifiable form. What Emerson concludes of his books—that commercialization and replication are valuable not as a means of (re)possession but as ways to facilitate both circulation and production ("and between whiles add a line")—proves equally true of his grief.

I am finally suggesting reading "Experience," and its sense of bereavement's failure to confirm the reality of the feeling self, as a critique of the notions of memorialization and preservation characteristic of nineteenth-century sentimental mourning practices, including mortuary photography. But I am also suggesting that Emerson's critique is strongly marked by the wish that sentimental claims might be true, and hence that one could, as photography advertisements urged, "secure the shadow ere the substance fades," and find in replication and commodification a form of keeping.

> This morning I had the remains of my mother & my son Waldo removed from the tomb of Mrs. Ripley to my lot in "Sleepy Hollow." The sun shone brightly on the coffins, of which Waldo's was well preserved—now fifteen years. I ventured to

(as legions of late-century imitators found) lent itself to mass production." Buell, *New England Literary Culture: From Revolution through Renaissance* (New York: Cambridge University Press, 1986), 62–65.

43. Susan Stewart, *On Longing: Narratives of the Miniature, the Gigantic, the Souvenir, the Collection* (Durham, N.C.: Duke University Press, 1993), 139.

44. Helen Sheumaker's study of hair fancy work provides a particularly rich example of how even so personal and "authentic" a memento as a lock of hair could be made into a sentimental consumer object. A prime use of hair wreaths, of course, was to frame memorial photographs of the dead. See Sheumaker, *"A Token that Love Entwines": Nineteenth-Century Human Hair Work and the American White Middle Class* (Ph.D. dissertation, University of Kansas, 1999).

look into the coffin. I gave a few white oak leaves to each coffin, after they were put in the new vault, & the vault was then covered with two slabs of granite.[45]

Enacting his own most shocking comparison, Emerson would make the reinterred body of his child a physical part of the "beautiful estate" of Concord's Sleepy Hollow Cemetery. But if this effort at preservation seems more absolute than any keepsake memento—insisting as it does on the actual body rather than accepting the mediations offered by reproduction—it is also and necessarily undermined by this very materiality. Emerson does not say what he finds in that coffin, but surely it is not preservation. Peering into the grave Emerson embodies sentimental efforts to keep the dead present and so proves the disintegration of the dead, ungraspable but also therefore uncontainable even by slabs of granite.

There is nothing to possess but dust. Yet if having must always be an occasion for loss, it is equally true for Emerson that loss will always be an opportunity for production and renewal. What Emerson accomplishes is a reimagining of possession as a limitless circulation, a quest for the new that he associates with childhood. Emerson explains in "Experience" that "when I receive a new gift I do not macerate my body to make the account square, for, if I should die, I could not make the account square. The benefit overran the merit the first day, and has overran the merit ever since" (491).[46] The image of his son as something "I fancied was part of me, which could not be torn away without tearing me," haunts this passage, for the father had wished in those lines for a body that could be macerated, for experience that could be clutched and in the touching produce wounds. The inability to square the account suggests not debt or loss but rather excess, a world overrun with "new gifts." Years later Emerson would write about gifts in his journal, offering as one "capital example" a birdhouse that has housed bluebirds each of the years since its giving. He then "thinks of another" example,

> quite inestimable. John Thoreau, Junior, knew how much I should value a head of little Waldo, then five years old. He came to me, & offered to carry him to a daguerreotypist who was then in town, & he, Thoreau, would see it well done. He did it, & brought me the daguerre which I thankfully paid for. In a few

45. Emerson, *Journals,* entry of July 8, 1857.

46. Wai-chee Dimock uses nineteenth-century economic debates to elaborate on how the self's felt lack, what she calls its "constitutional scarcity," distinguishes it from the abundant world and permits it to receive endlessly. Her essay makes a strong case for the centrality of economic concerns to "Experience," to which my notion of an economy of grief is largely indebted. See Dimock, "Scarcity, Subjectivity and Emerson," *Boundary* 2, no. 17 (spring 1990): 83–99.

months after, my boy died, and I have ever since had deeply to thank John Thoreau for that wise & gentle piece of friendship.[47]

In Emerson's economy, what is valued in the daguerreotype of the now dead child is the capacity to overrun, to renew and multiply like the generations of bluebirds. What is valued is the excess that replication permits and loss initiates. Thus, even as we may read "Experience" as a critique of sentimental-ism and its vain clutching at what is gone, Emerson's theory of bereavement expresses more explicitly than sentimentalism itself how the structures of ex-cess, replication, and circulation that characterize sentimentality reflect not only the repetitive characteristics of mourning, but also the commercial and replicating mechanisms that place those feelings in circulation. Photography and bureau drawers can never really preserve the dead, but they can make of loss a "new toy."

The Sentimental Surplus of Smitten Households

Memorialization and mourning may be accomplished not simply in the heart, but also through the commercial mechanisms of the market. Daguerreotypes offer a perfect instance of how desire and the market create each other. In 1838 there was no such thing as a daguerreotype, and though itinerant artists could produce fairly inexpensive portraits, such portraits were still far too costly to let most Americans afford a likeness of themselves or of those they loved. A decade later "there were already 2000 daguerreotypists in the country . . . by 1853, three million daguerreotypes were being made annually and there were eighty-six portrait galleries in New York City alone," and nearly everyone could afford to have their portrait made. This tremendous popularization and growth made it clear that to have one's portrait taken was both to participate in the creation of a new market and to act on a new desire (one rarely prac-ticable before this new technology).[48] John Berger remarks on the wide range of uses photographers found for this new technology—from family albums to police records, from travel postcards to military reconnaissance—and con-cludes that "the speed with which the possible uses of photography were

47. Emerson, *Journals,* entry of January 17, 1862.
48. John Tagg, "A Democracy of the Image: Photographic Portraiture and Commodity Pro-duction," in *The Burden of Representation: Essays on Photographies and Histories* (Minneapolis: University of Minnesota Press, 1899), 43. Richard Rudisill calculates that more than 95 percent of the daguerreotypes made in the United States were commercially produced portraits of indi-viduals or groups. Rudisill, *Mirror Image: The Influence of the Daguerreotype on American Soci-ety* (Albuquerque, N.M.: University of New Mexico Press, 1971), 198.

seized upon is surely an indication of photography's profound, central applicability to industrial capitalism."[49] In his 1862 *Atlantic* article Oliver Wendell Holmes pushes photography's applicability to capitalism one step further, claiming that "card portraits, as everybody knows, have become the social currency, the 'greenbacks of civilization.'"[50] As a new commodity form—if not as currency itself—photography made the relation between consumerist desire and the market more obvious because of this newness, and more glaring because the thing to be purchased was the replication of a beloved face. Perhaps more perfectly than any other object offered for sale, daguerreotype portraits meld commercial replication and unique, emotional individuality—for what is replicated and commodified by these portraits is not the unique plate or the individual's image so much as a form, the standard poses, accoutrements, and presentation of the daguerreotype portrait. The daguerreotype of the mother holding both her dead child and an elaborate hat displays the ambivalence at stake in making a visit to a portrait studio into a ritual of bereavement (fig. 3.7). This is not a funereal hat; indeed, the family paid extra to have its ribbon hand-colored a festive blue. Thus as the mother literally balances on her lap the dual rites of grieving for her child and dressing for the photographer, she epitomizes the relation between memorialization and this new commodity—the daguerreotype portrait. After all it is the hat, that incongruous effort to assert status and make a good picture, that most distinguishes and individualizes this image, letting us glimpse something of what it meant for this woman to use photography as a means of posing and preserving her grief.

The image of young Max Anderson lying in his perambulator provides a similar instance (fig. 3.8). It reminds us, moreover, that the same argument holds for the way the manufacture of goods specifically for children—also a new mid-nineteenth-century development—allies the creation of marketable desires with familial affection and status.[51] Cribs, high-chairs, child-chairs, baby-swings, perambulators, and the myriad commercially manufactured playthings required for safe and happy middle-class childhoods were, begin-

49. John Berger, "The Uses of Photography," in *About Looking* (New York: Pantheon Books, 1980), 48.

50. See Alan Trachtenberg, *Reading American Photographs: Images as History, Matthew Brady to Walker Evans* (New York: Hill and Wang, 1989), 18–19.

51. Carol Mavor notes that "the child and the photograph were commodified, fetishized, developed alongside each other: they were laminated and framed as one." Mavor, *Pleasures Taken: Performances of Sexuality and Loss in Victorian Photographs* (Durham, N.C.: Duke University Press, 1995), 3.

Fig. 3.7. Postmortem daguerreotype, ca. 1850. Courtesy of Stanley B. Burns, M.D., and the Burns Archive.

ning in the 1830s, all either entirely new or radically reconceived forms.[52] In 1868 when this card was made, this fine carriage would have been almost as recognizably new a commodity in Xenia, Ohio, where the photograph was taken, as was the *carte de visite* itself.

   The commodification of childhood and photography reveal how deeply the processes of commercialization depend upon emotions traditionally

52. See Karin Calvert, "Cradle to Crib: The Revolution in Nineteenth-Century Children's Furniture," in *A Century of Childhood: 1820–1920* (Rochester, N.Y.: The Margaret Woodbury Strong Museum, 1984), 33–64.

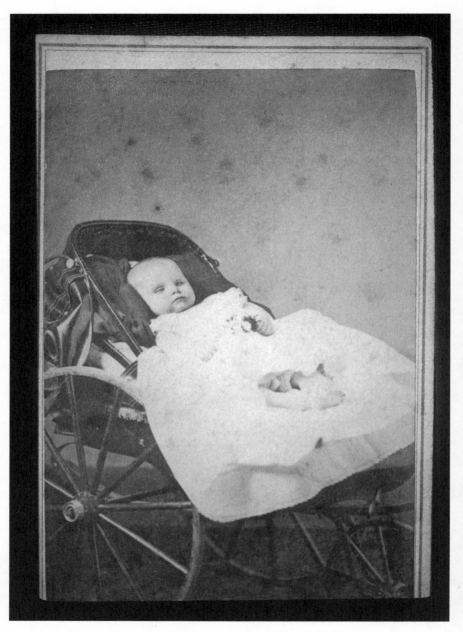

Fig. 3.8. Postmortem *carte de visite* of Max Anderson, ca. 1868. D. D. Randolph, Xenia, Ohio. Courtesy of Stanley B. Burns, M.D., and the Burns Archive.

understood as inherently individual, intimate, and therefore noncommodifiable. Of course, this understanding of mourning is itself a new product of that era, the legacy of nineteenth-century discourses of sentiment and domesticity that would claim in heart and hearth a lone haven from commercial taint. The scorn with which most scholarship has viewed the nineteenth-century commercialization of death and mourning rests on the assumption that mortality and grief are incompatible with commerce, and therefore that the creation of these new commodities and their professionals (funeral directors, embalmers, and cemetery designers, as well as daguerreotypists) ultimately functions to strip bereavement of its emotional authenticity.[53] Anne Douglas, for example, interprets the cult of death and its sentimental commodifications as a symptom of the feminization of American culture: "the dying infant was made supremely to flatter [women and clergymen] . . . he shared their weakness while he dignified and extended their authority."[54] This argument sees in the dead child a self-indulgent fixation on and inappropriate projection of private emotions that simultaneously robbed grief of sincerity and contaminated the public realm. There is much that I find convincing and important about this argument, but also much that I believe it misses, both about the experience of grief and about the implications of putting that grief in circulation. As the examples of photography and childhood make clear, however, the commercial, the public, and the emotional need not be viewed solely in oppositional terms. If commodification exploits feelings to yield profit, it is equally possible for emotions to use the commercial as a means of expression and a form of circulation.

The marketing of photography was from the very beginning quite conscious of these tensions. Marcus Aurelius Root paradoxically proposed in his

53. Both *Passing: The Vision of Death in America,* ed. Charles O. Jackson (Westport, Conn.: Greenwood Press, 1977) and *Death in America,* ed. David E. Stannard (Philadelphia: University of Pennsylvania Press, 1975) organize their essays so as to tell an overarching story about the fall from the colonial period's authentic and communal (if rather grim) relation to mortality, through the nineteenth century's sentimental and lamentable commercialization and beautification of death, to the twentieth century's attempt to deny death or at least make it invisible. This is, of course, an American elaboration of the trajectory traced by Philippe Ariès's *Western Attitudes toward Death: From the Middle Ages to the Present,* trans. Helen Weaver (New York: Alfred A. Knopf, 1981).

54. Anne Douglas, "The Domestication of Death," in *The Feminization of American Culture* (New York: Avon, 1977), 246. For accounts of how the nineteenth-century "cult of death" uses bereavement—both the proofs of emotional depth and sincerity it produces, and the purchase and consumption of mourning accessories it prescribes—as means of claiming gentility and class status, see also Halttunen, "Mourning the Dead," and Elizabeth A. Petrino, "Feet so Precious Charged: Dickinson, Sigourney and the Child Elegy," *Tulsa Studies in Women's Literature* 13 (fall 1994): 317–38.

influential defense of the art that daguerreotypes should be seen as a commercial antidote to commerce:

> In a world where incessant competition and struggle tend to produce a selfish egotism, whatever serves to vivify and strengthen the social sentiments should be hailed as a blessing to our race. Daguerreotype works indirectly, but not the less powerfully, to this important result. The moderate price of sun-linings, as compared with that of all previous portraiture, has induced multitudes of all classes and degrees of culture to procure portraits of relatives and friends.[55]

The claim that the purchase of a commodity is desirable for noncommercial reasons is, of course, one of advertising's most persistent ploys. The market succeeds in large part through such acts of disavowal. Yet I cannot help wondering in what ways these marketing claims might be true—that though surely it is possible to "keep the memory of loved ones" without any such material aids, yet it is also evident that the existence of such aids changes how we remember. Photography makes memory material and external.[56] Walter Benjamin suggests that portrait photography is one of the last sites in which the "aura" of uniqueness and "cult value" that are for him defining attributes of the original "work of art" persist into "the age of mechanical reproduction." "The cult of remembrance of loved ones, absent or dead, offers a last refuge for the cult value of the picture. For the last time the aura emanates from the early photographs in the fleeting expression of a human face."[57] But for this very reason such mechanically produced portraits also become a first site for the entry of what have previously been understood as unique sentiments into the multiplying mesh of replication and commodification.

The commodification of remembrance that photography permits, and particularly the marketing of these products as prods for fidelity, love, and grief, as aids in the perpetuation of right sentiment and a warm heart, worked, as Root implies, to associate these feelings with the attainment of class status. The performance of mourning, Karen Halttunen demonstrates, served "to establish the mourner's claim to his or her due status as one of the sentimental

---

55. Marcus Aurelius Root, "The Various Uses of the Daguerrean Art," in Foresta and Wood, *Secrets of the Dark Chamber,* 262.

56. Berger remarks that the most revealing answer as to "what served in the place of photography; before the camera's invention" is not manual forms of rendering but memory. "What photographs do out there in space was previously done within reflection." Berger, "Uses of Photography," 50.

57. Walter Benjamin, "The Work of Art in the Age of Mechanical Reproduction," in *Illuminations,* ed. Hannah Arendt, trans. Harry Zohn (New York: Schocken Books, 1969), 226.

genteel."[58] Similarly, even as daguerreotypes swiftly became cheap enough
to attract "multitudes of all classes and degrees of culture," daguerreotype
"parlors" and "palaces" became opulent enough to make most portraits taken
against their rich curtains or in their carved chairs appear elegantly bourgeois.[59] To note that photographs and mourning practices can function as
means of claiming class status suggests one way in which affect can be of use
to the market, but the acceptance of these arguments in no way invalidates
the alternative possibility that the market may be of use for the bereaved. Indeed, what I find most fascinating and revealing about such affect-laden commodities as these photographs of dead children is precisely this doubleness,
how they bind grief to the market and the market to grief.

The new technology of photography exaggerates the externalization and
materialization of memory, but memory has always housed itself in things.
The differences are significant: the utility of the photograph is explicitly this
act of preservation, while baby's shoes were purchased for walking and rattle
for shaking even if—once these uses are no longer possible—these objects
may become cherished containers for the memory of those acts. Like "Baby's
Drawer," child elegies are filled with—generally commercially procured—
objects that prompt mourning. If for Emerson grief itself could become a
"new toy," in these poems toys become material vehicles of grief. Here mass-
produced objects are recognized as carrying the unique personal meanings
that come from individual usage, and unique anecdotal significance. Once
taken home, the mass-produced thing may be produced again, as it were, as
a uniquely personal possession. An anonymous poem titled "Broken Playthings" is largely a catalog of such objects: "dolls with their robes all tar-
nished," "rattles all taken to pieces, / To see what occasioned the sound," and

> Rubber rings, where memory lingers
>   On four little teeth of pearl,
>   That sometimes shut on our fingers,—
>   The weenie, mischievous girl![60]

Where memory lingers is not exactly in the rubber rings, although the rings
may well bear small dents made by those little teeth, nor even in the teeth

58. See Halttunen, "Mourning the Dead," 136.

59. This opulence is a decidedly American feature of photography; daguerreotype studios
in London and Paris were generally far simpler, just as European daguerreotype cases were
mostly plain card as opposed to the quite elaborate range of American cases. See Rudisill, *Mirror Image*, 200–203.

60. "Broken Playthings," in *A Mother's Scrap-Book Only*, 82–84.

themselves, but in the whole "weenie, mischievous girl." The difficulty of
these transformations, the piecemeal nature of the process whereby first metonymy and then synecdoche—the toy, the teeth—sequentially produce the
memory of the child, suggests how desperately memory needs such props.
That the poem contains four eight-line stanzas concerned only with the cat-
aloging of such anamnestic objects reveals not only the excess and ease of
memory—how the now dead child permeates the household, memorialized
by any and all things—but also how painfully inadequate even this glut of
objects is to the task of preservation.

In "Mourning and Melancholia," Sigmund Freud's account of "normal
mourning" suggests a conversely piecemeal process, where what is mourned
can only be relinquished in a partial and repetitive manner. He suggests that
because there is so much "understandable opposition" to acknowledging
"that the loved object no longer exists," reality's orders to withdraw all such
attachment "cannot be obeyed at once. They are carried out bit by bit, at great
expense of time and cathectic energy."[61] Thus Freud describes the work of
mourning as accomplished through repetition, in a manner that bears significantly on nineteenth-century America's success in harnessing the replicating capacities of industrialization and commercialization to the expression of
grief. If the deaths of children became sites of mass production—the source
of seemingly endlessly reiterative images and artifacts—this may be in part
because mourning expends itself in just such repetitions. The notion of expenditure is Freud's as well, and the resonances I am suggesting here between his psychological theories and American commercial practices are further supported by his own persistent recourse to economic metaphors and
the explanatory power of what he calls "general economic experience."[62] The
metaphor of a psychic economy does not, however, fully account for how grief
functions in the marketplace, since a psychic economy describes a closed system, and precisely what is gained in the commodification of mourning is the
capacity to link one's grief to a system of circulation that extends well beyond
the individual psyche or the particular family circle.

---

61. Sigmund Freud, "Mourning and Melancholia," in *The Standard Edition of the Complete
Psychological Works of Sigmund Freud*, trans. and ed. James Stratchey, vol. 14 (1914–1916)
(London: Hogarth Press, 1957), 244–45.

62. Freud, "Mourning and Melancholia," 254. Thus, for example, Freud explains the relation between melancholic and manic states through an economic example ("when, for instance,
some poor wretch, by winning a large sum of money, is suddenly relieved from chronic worry
about his daily bread . . ."—254), speaks of "economies of pain" (244), and speculates on "the
economic means by which mourning carries out its task" (255), et cetera. Moreover, the very
notion of mourning as "work" (*Trauerarbeit*)—a mode of production that should elicit compensation—is itself an economic metaphor.

The economics of replication as a mode of mourning capable of carrying personal grief into the public domain organizes Mrs. L. B. Hancock's work of collecting poems about the deaths of children (including "The Baby's Drawer" and "Broken Playthings") into *A Mother's Scrap-Book Only.* Addressed "to the Bereaved Mothers in the Great Household of the Sorrowing and in Memory of the Angel-child who passed to his heavenly home Dec. 7, 1874," her double dedication suggests the dual commercial and cathartic functions of this volume, its goals of both attaining an emotionally identified market (a niche) and expressing her own individual loss in the death of her son, Freddie Hancock. In her preface to the anthology Mrs. Hancock explains her reasons for assembling the volume:

> It has been said, and I believe truthfully, that he who speaks or writes of the death of little children will never lack for auditors or hearers; but never did I fully realize this, or the darkness of the shadow cast by one little grave, till death entered my own home-circle—invaded my own fireside—and robbed me of my own precious boy.
>
> The following selections consist of some original thoughts and some tender loving contributions from dear friends; but mainly they are "waifs," gathered from newspapers, magazines, or our standard authors, selected and prized in the freshness of *my own grief,* and designed then as a "Scrap Book," in which a weeping mother found vent for her own sad emotions; but at the solicitation of friends I have concluded to send them out on a mission of sympathy to other smitten households. (5–6)

This description of the genesis of *A Mother's Scrap-Book Only* is paradigmatic of the complex interrelations between private mourning and public audience, between the unique claims of personal grief and the ubiquitous and swift circulation of generic comforting words. The title, with its odd disclaimer "only," emphasizes how this volume no longer is, if it ever truly was, "only a mother's scrap-book."[63] The glut of mourning poetry waiting to be culled from news-

---

63. Indeed, twenty years later Hancock published a second, similar collection, *Heart's-ease: A Mother's Offering* (Cincinnati, Ohio: Curtis and Jennings, 1899). Both anthologies collect poems written significantly earlier, *A Mother's Scrap-Book,* for example, containing pieces Lydia Sigourney wrote in the 1820s.

Such anthologies remain popular. Wendy Simonds and Barbara Katz Rothman's book *Centuries of Solace: Expressions of Maternal Grief in Popular Literature* (Philadelphia: Temple University Press, 1992) augments a scholarly essay comparing maternal consolation literature of the nineteenth and twentieth centuries with an anthology of pieces of both periods intended for a more general readership. *Out of Season: An Anthology of Work by and about Young People who Died,* ed. Paula Trachtman (Amagansett, N.Y.: Amagansett Press, 1993), is another contemporary example.

papers, magazines, and such nineteenth-century favorites as Sigourney, Longfellow, Piatt, Whittier, Lowell, and Mrs. Browning, as well as from local pens
(the author of two poems about "Freddie Hancock" is identified simply as
MAMA), suggests this genre is itself a site of surplus production. Calling the
verses she has collected "waifs" casts the assembling of the "Scrap-Book" as
an act of domestic philanthropy that would rescue children. In adopting these
wandering expressions of grief and giving them a home and the solicitude of
her own maternal tears, Mrs. Hancock can be seen as re-privatizing mourning. But then what of her decision to publish this collection—even if now
nicely housed in gilt-edged pages—and so to launch these sentiments once
more into the public domain?

The poems Mrs. Hancock collected in her "Scrap-Book" replicate each
other, starting with their titles: three "Empty Cradles," four slight variants on
"A Little Grave," another four "On a Curl of Child's Hair," and an equal number of "Angels," et cetera. These have proved a culturally durable imagery for
child death, and recent anthropological work suggests that even in a high-
tech world of sonograms, parents grieving miscarriages can still find the imagery of angel-babies relevant and comforting.[64] Of course the predictability
of such imagery is much of what can make these poems, as poetry, so dreadfully trite. Even the publisher of *The Smitten Household; or, Thoughts for the
Afflicted,* a collection of essays offering "sweet consolation" from five cler-
gyman, feels the need to explain that "the authors who have written these essays are not to be held responsible for the sentiment or taste of the poetical
selections with which the book is interspersed."[65] Yet interspersed they are,
as it proves somehow impossible to publish a book about mourning without
such poetry, just as Mrs. Hancock and the clergymen all seem bound to address "smitten households." Such compulsions reflect the force of genre as a
mold for production. Excess and repetition prove characteristic of much of

64. Linda Layne notes the use of angel imagery among parents who talk of their stillborn
babies, and examines how this language intertwines with the scientific language of sonograms
and fetuses. "Though angels would normally be considered symbolic, the image of one's own
baby as an angel is more concrete and personal . . . it is precisely this pivotal nature of iconic
images . . . highly personal but embedded in and informed by more abstract systems of meaning—which makes them so effective in linking together the disparate discursive domain of tech-
noscience, the everyday, and religion." Layne, "Of Fetuses and Angels: Fragmentation and Integration in Narratives of Pregnancy Loss," *Knowledge and Society: The Anthropology of Science
and Technology* 9 (1992): 50.

65. S. Irenaeus Prine, D.D., W. B. Sprague, D.D., J. B. Waterbury, D.D., and C. M. Butler,
D.D., *The Smitten Household; or, Thoughts for the Afflicted* (New York: Anson D. F. Randolph,
1860), publisher's note.

this verse, but they are also characteristic of mourning itself. As Jerome Neu observes, "emotions are not natural kinds. They have conventional boundaries," so that the transformation of a unique grief into a formulaic and infinitely replicable mourning artifact should be understood, at least in part, as an expression of what was always already conventional and repetitious about the trauma of bereavement.[66]

The lines fourteen-year-old Delia Perry wrote "On Visiting the Grave of a School-Mate" are remarkable for their absolute conventionality. A good student, Delia has said what she was supposed to say about death, and every phrase reads like a dutiful quotation (fig. 3.9). This exercise was published as a broadside to memorialize not the unnamed "school-mate" but Delia Perry herself; her words on her friend's death, so blandly general that they could apply to any schoolgirl, easily become her own elegy. Here death clearly has an authorizing power: Delia's words are valuable and publishable because they were written "just before her death" and are thus sanctified by her dying. The repetition that is death is expressed in the repetitions of convention and publication.

The diary Louisa Jane Trumbull started when she was seven is, as we have seen, a far more idiosyncratic and personal document. Like Delia, Jenny Trumbull recognized death as an appropriate subject for her compositions, and from its earliest pages her diary reveals an informative, matter-of-fact interest in death. Jenny regularly reports who died in the town and of what, mentioning for example after her grandmother's death that "they had cut off all her hair as almost everyone would wish for a lock." There is nothing morbid about Jenny's accounts; death is simply one of the more important things that happens in her town, and she mentions it much as she reports how many chickens hatched or what kind of fabric her mother is using for her new dress. The death of her brother Johnny means something different, however, and she fills pages with stories about him that range from the funny to the holy.

He was, as she writes with the precision that measures fragility and loss, "four years, six months and three days old when he died." She was nine.

---

66. Jerome Neu, "A Tear Is an Intellectual Thing," *Representations* 19 (summer 1987): 40. Neu's discussion of the clinical notion of "display rules"—what is socially acceptable as a way of displaying emotion rather than any natural notion of emotion itself—further suggests how the expression of grief is always in a sense fabricated, tears proving nearly as much a cultural product as black bands or mortuary photography (cf. 42). For accounts of the particular political and cultural work that tears do in the early nineteenth century, see Julia A. Stern, *The Plight of Feeling: Sympathy and Dissent in the Early American Novel* (Chicago: University of Chicago Press, 1997); and Julie Ellison, *Cato's Tears and the Making of Anglo-American Emotion* (Chicago: University of Chicago Press, 1999).

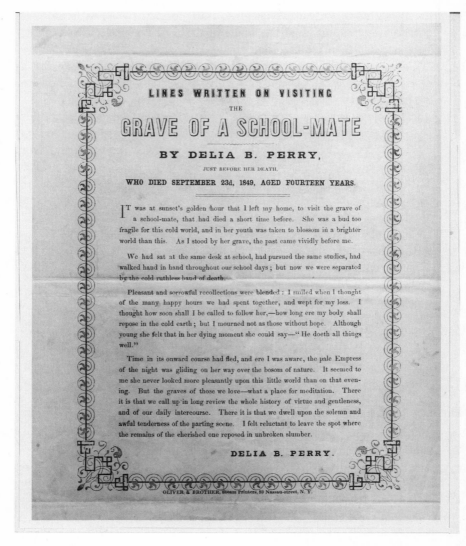

Fig. 3.9. Delia Perry, "Lines Written on Visiting the Grave of a School-Mate," 1849. Copyright © American Antiquarian Society.

February 9th, 1833

Wednesday it was very unpleasant; it snowed all day until Johnny's coffin, was let down into the ground, when the sun broke through the clouds, and everything looked beautifully. Perhaps it was Johnny's happy spirit so bright. The last time he ever was at Aunt Bradsh's was, when he went in to tell her that "we had

got a new pair of yellow bellows and that she must come in and see them soon."
That was the last time that she ever saw him.

What this diary reveals with humorous and wrenching clarity is how the literary conventions of the dying child serve to organize Jenny's experience of
her brother's death, and that they are not her only way of speaking about or
understanding this loss. The passage I quoted above epitomizes this tension,
as Jenny revises her prose, first with a conventional piety, writing of "Johnny's
happy spirit so bright," and then rejecting this somehow to her not convincing explanation for the appearance of the sun at the lowering of her brother's
coffin. My point is not that there is one authentic voice of mourning (the one
that remembers Johnny's excitement over the yellow bellows) and one pious
and artificial voice of mourning (the one that takes recourse to spirits bright).
Jenny, with her care to speak only of what is "probable," clearly means it when
she writes a few pages earlier that "it is probable that he is now a little angel
singing the praises of his almighty God and Father." Both registers of bereavement are available to Jenny, and in her commingling of these ways of speaking her brother's death she reveals how this death is both uniquely, specifically individual and still circulating within a general culture of mourning.[67]

Photography again provides a useful analogue to these tensions between
individual loss and the mechanisms and conventions of replication. The memorial card for Maria Jane Hurd (fig. 3.10) shows a picture of her face above
a list of New Year's resolutions "found in her little portfolio after her death,"
as is explained in a footnote across the bottom of the card. Just as the card
authenticates the list by noting its origins in Maria's portfolio, it identifies the
picture as a "copy of Daguerreotype taken at six years of age." Daguerreotypes produce unique images: the plate in the camera, once exposed and then
fixed, is the plate protected and framed in the daguerreotype case. Daguerreotypes can be copied, but each plate is a unique object. Maria Hurd died at age
twelve in 1849. Two years later Frederick Scott Archer would invent the wet
collodion process that produced negatives from which multiple positive paper prints could be made. Thus for this card two unique private objects, the
daguerreotype portrait and the handwritten portfolio, are lithographed to

67. Louisa Jane Trumbull's diary is in four volumes, running from 1829 to 1837. Her comments on Johnny's death cited here all come from February 1833, though she continues to mention his death throughout the rest of the journals. One particularly poignant moment written a
few weeks after his death occurs during an account of her own discomfort because of the cayenne
and rum rub her mother had given her for croup: "it felt as hot as could be and smarted dreadfully. Poor little Johnny had a great blister on his poor little breast and it was as raw as could
be" (February 20, 1833).

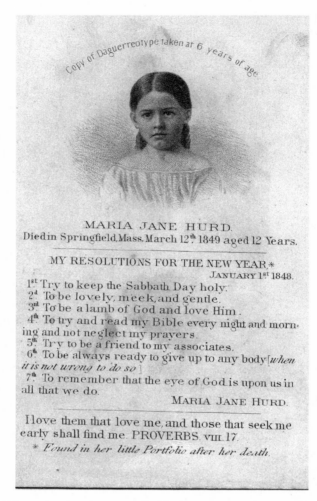

Fig. 3.10. Lithograph, 1849, "Memorial Card for Maria Jane Hurd," Jay Ruby Photograph Collection. Reproduced with the permission of the Historical Collections and Labor Archives, Special Collections Library, The Pennsylvania State University Libraries, University Park, PA.

produce multiple copies that could be given or sent to family and friends, extending and demarcating relations in mourning and memorialization well beyond the immediate circle of the bereaved. That this manually produced lithograph should be explicitly identified as a copy of a daguerreotype suggests the desire to extend to this drawing the facticity, the capacity for exact replication, associated with photography. So too, while Maria's parents felt the need to correct her sixth resolution, appending "[*when it is not wrong to do so*]" after her promise "to be always ready to give up to any body," they employed italics and brackets to make the fact of alteration legible. Memorialization inevitably alters the thing it seeks to repeat, yet what I find so moving about this card is the way in which the desire to replicate the face and words of their dead daughter and the recognition of her irreplaceable uniqueness collide in the manufacture of this memorial object. Maurice Blanchot says of the particularity of death that it is unshareable even as it is also what every individual has in common with all others.[68] Walter Benjamin writes that "death digs most deeply the jagged line of demarcation between physical nature and significance."[69] This sense that death's power derives from its ultimate uniqueness, and that it is therefore in a fundamental way resistant to representation, may be true of death, but it is the function of mourning—and of sentimental conventions in particular—to acknowledge publicly what cannot be shared, to trace again and again that jagged line.

Even before the draftings that substituted a lithograph for a daguerreotype, the wide-eyed face of Maria Jane Hurd at age six undoubtedly looked quite different from that of the nearly adolescent girl who died. Growing up is not only achievement, it is also loss, childhood (like death) eliciting, "bit by bit," continuous acts of separation. Loss and bereavement are inherent to a process of growing up that is also a growing away.[70] This is perhaps especially true in an America that privileges independence as the mark of national identity, and even more so at a time when rapid urbanization and westward expansion meant that adulthood brought geographical separations far more frequently than it had in earlier periods. Indeed, as Caroline Leslie wrote in another poem collected in Hancock's *Scrap-Book,* the child who dies is more stable, and hence more easily preserved, than the child who lives and leaves, claimed not by Heaven but by the world:

68. Maurice Blanchot, *The Writing of the Disaster,* trans. Ann Smock (Lincoln: University of Nebraska Press, 1986).

69. Walter Benjamin, *The Origins of German Tragic Drama,* trans. John Osborne (London: Verso, 1977), 166.

70. Simonds and Rothman suggest that for this reason maternal consolation literature proves resonant for all mothers: "There is a sense in which all motherhood is loss, an ongoing continual separation, an unending grieving . . . it is this universal experience of loss, as much as the universal fear of child death, that explains the appeal of this consolation literature well beyond the narrow audience of grieving parents." Simonds and Rothman, *Centuries of Solace,* 9, 13.

Historicizing this "universal experience of loss," Carolyn Steedman writes with precision and subtlety about the ways in which nineteenth-century studies of physiological science came to link growth with death, and childhood with both. See Steedman, *Strange Dislocations: Childhood and the Idea of Human Interiority, 1780–1930* (Cambridge: Harvard University Press, 1995), esp. chaps. 3–4.

Yet, when the world our own would claim,
    It doth not greatly grieve us;
We calmly see as days go by,
    Our little children leave us,
And, smiling, heed not how the swift
    Soft-footed years bereave us.

Oh mother hearts! I count you rich
    beyond mere earth possessing,
Whose little babies never grow
    Away from your caressing;
Safe-folded in His tender arms
    Who gives again with blessing.[71]

Or, as the concluding lines of another poem put it, "*Oft* children *living* are children *lost;* / But our children *dead,*—ah, we keep them *all!*"[72] A vision of the world as a dangerous place informs these assertions that death is a safer, surer form of keeping than that offered by even the best mothers' caressings. Living children may be lost in these accounts because what the world has to offer—temptations of excess, anonymity, and greed, allures habitually associated with urbanization and commercialization—are perceived as simultaneously separating the child from both parental and divine precepts. Here what is "safe" is what is "folded," like the spotless clothes in "Baby's Drawer," closed in ways that inhibit both the reception of experience and the unfolding and expansion of growth. The stasis of the dead, safely folded child thus stands in opposition to the multiplying growth of an expanding nation. Ironically, in what I presume is a typographical error, Mrs. Hancock gives the title of Leslie's poem as "Self-Folded," as if this relinquishing of growth were the child's choice, or characteristic of childhood itself.

Sentimentality is, among other things, the genre that accompanied American expansion and industrialization. The literary preference for producing tears, for voicing what we often describe as "excessive," repetitive emotion coincided with the advent of mass production and its way of making surplus. Connections between sentimentality, mass production, and commercialism have often proved grounds for aesthetic critique, and those literary critics who have wished to revalue the sentimental have often done so by insisting

71. Caroline Leslie, "Self-Folded" [*sic?*], in *A Mother's Scrap-Book Only,* 116–17.
72. "A Little Dead Prince," by "the Author of John Halifax, Gentleman," in *A Mother's Scrap-Book Only,* 113–16.

on its separation from the marketplace—its capacity to locate in the grieving maternal heart an alternative sphere of "sentimental power."[73] My aim in this chapter has been to set aside questions of aesthetic value and to ask instead about the social utility of repetition, to think about what mass production and wide circulation accomplish as a response to death. As a technological capacity, as a goad to commerce, and as an aesthetic practice, replication acknowledges the repetitive characteristics of grief while providing a structure for circulating emotion that expands the lineage of feeling. Thus I understand sentimental conventions as an aesthetic grounded simultaneously in the emotional and the commercial.[74] Sentimentality is the expression of the family commodified, and that act of commodification makes pain more public and more shareable.[75] Of course, the market is also a site of alienation and inauthenticity. It may well be that in turning to the commercial sphere to express personal loss, nineteenth-century Americans reveal their cultural bereavement—the gradual loss of more personal and communal forms of connection. But while the market may be a weak substitute for such nostalgically idealized links, it does substitute.

The child who dies, the child who does not grow into the world, figures a resistance to the national enterprises of commerce and expansion, hallowing the emotional intensity of heart and home. Yet as the figure of the dead child becomes itself a commodity of sorts, and as the market tools of replication and circulation are harnessed to the act of mourning—that is, as a figure innocent, intimate, static, and unique becomes an object of mass production—the dead child carries intimacy and affect into the commercial, industrial world where such feelings appear most threatened. Appealing to a mass audience, often characterized by conventional, repetitive forms, sentimentality nevertheless

73. See Jane Tompkins, "Sentimental Power: *Uncle Tom's Cabin* and the Politics of Literary History," in her *Sensational Designs: The Cultural Work of American Fiction, 1790–1860* (New York: Oxford University Press, 1985).

74. Fredric Jameson asserts that the goal of Modernism is "*not* to be a commodity, to devise an aesthetic language incapable of offering commodity satisfaction, and resistant to instrumentalization"; in this way he depicts "modernism as reactive, that is, as a symptom and result of cultural crises, rather than a new 'solution' in its own right." Jameson's attempt to articulate the symptomatic relation between a certain set of commercial and aesthetic practices has been an important impetus for my efforts in this chapter. Jameson, "Reification and Utopia in Mass Culture," in *Signatures of the Visible* (New York: Routledge, 1990), 16.

75. For a moving discussion of how pain requires acknowledgment, and therefore establishes the importance of public mourning rituals, see Veena Das, "Language and Body: Transactions in the Construction of Pain," *Daedalus* 125 (winter 1996): 67–98. The recent anthology *Loss*, ed. David L. Eng and David Kazanjian (Berkeley: University of California Press, 2003), centers on mourning as a public and political act, asking what it would mean to "address loss not as an individual but as a collective process" (ix).

preserves intimacy by celebrating the private and feeling subject. For this reason I see the sentimental, and in particular its ways of wielding the trauma
of children's deaths, as a means of mediating between the private mourner
and a commercial world that proves not without feeling, but actually capable
of circulating emotion. Telling again and again the deaths of children thus
serves at once to affirm the family as a unique locus of affection and to ally
both the family and its emotional value with America's newly commercial
sense of public culture. To say this is not to abstract and disavow the pain of
a child's death; the intensely and almost exclusively emotional loss that is the
death of a child and the more diffuse and public trauma of national and commercial progress can elaborate each other because in nineteenth-century
America both are real and urgent sites of bereavement.

PART THREE

Rearing a Nation: Childhood and the
Construction of Social Identity

Playing at Class

Class and childhood are highly visible yet often under-
theorized features of nineteenth-century American identity,
perhaps for the same reason: national ideologies of class promise that in the United States poverty, like childhood, is merely
a stage to be outgrown. In this chapter I consider class conversely as an identity to be grown into, and childhood as a
powerful site for such growth. In the previous section I explored how the figure of the child orders and haloes the middle-
class family, childhood's effect extending outward to imbue
both social reform and commercial exchange with feeling.
These arguments are haunted by the abuse and death of individual children, but they focus on discourses of childhood that
cover and compensate for these specific pains. I am concerned,
that is, with how the psychological manifests in the social. This
final section turns explicitly to the construction of the social—
to questions of class, race, religion, and nation. That childhood is individually our most important period of identity formation has been a stable presumption of psychological theory.
In this chapter I argue that how childhood is imagined and inhabited similarly provides one of the most potent mechanisms
of class formation, and one comparatively little explored.[1]

An earlier version of chapter 4 appeared in *ELH* 67 (2000): 819–842.
Reprinted with the permission of the Johns Hopkins University Press.
    1. Considering the vast array of studies that have explored childhood
as a site for the construction of gender or racial identity, it is striking how

Not only is class identity constructed in childhood, but in nineteenth-century America childhood itself is increasingly recognized as a sign of class status. The invention of childhood entailed the creation of a protracted period in which the child would ideally be protected from the difficulties and responsibilities of daily life—ultimately including the need to work. "For the history of children," Priscilla Clement explains, "the legacy of industrialization was the hardening of class lines," with middle-class families' exemption of their children from labor as one of the strongest markers of their difference from the lower classes.[2] Thus to the extent that childhood means leisure, having a childhood is in itself one of the most decisive features of class formation. Yet since the "work" from which children were exempted never fully includes household labor, these general shifts in the definition of childhood function quite differently for girls than for boys.

Historians of leisure have charted the rising valuation of play throughout the nineteenth century while, as we have seen, historians of the family have described the period's idealization of childhood.[3] My concern here is with the links between these trends, as the same patterns of urbanization and industrialization that separate workplace from home, and labor from leisure, simultaneously function to commodify leisure time and to idealize middle-class domesticity, especially that of childhood. "Play," explained Bronson Alcott in justification of his pedagogical proposals, "is the appointed dispensation of childhood." This wonderfully unplayful phrasing presents child's play as part of the created order of things. "Appointed dispensation" emphasizes in its very redundancy the guiding wisdom—divine and/or social—that regu-

---

very little work has approached class identity in this way, especially since the recognition that class is a social construction rather than a natural state is far more widespread. Mary Ryan's historical analysis of the production of middle-class identities in the home in *Cradle of the Middle Class: The Family in Oneida County, New York, 1790–1865* (New York: Cambridge University Press, 1981) is a significant exception here, acknowledging as it does the important role changes in child-rearing practices played in the consolidation of middle-class values. Also see Carolyn Steedman, *Landscape for a Good Woman: A Story of Two Lives* (New Brunswick, N.J.: Rutgers University Press, 1987), for an account of how paying attention to class alters the psychoanalytic norms of ego formation in children.

2. Priscilla Ferguson Clement, *Growing Pains: Children in the Industrial Age, 1850–1890* (New York: Twayne Publishers, 1997), 7.

3. On shifting valuations of play see Foster Rhea Dulles, *America Learns to Play: A History of Popular Recreation 1607–1940* (New York: Peter Smith, 1952); David Nasaw, *Going Out: The Rise and Fall of Public Amusements* (New York: Basic Books, 1993); and Kathryn Grover, *Hard at Play: Leisure in America 1840–1940* (Amherst: University of Massachusetts Press, 1992). Bill Brown, *The Material Unconscious: American Amusement, Stephen Crane, and the Economics of Play* (Cambridge: Harvard University Press, 1996), and William A. Gleason, *The Leisure Ethic: Work and Play in American Literature 1840–1940* (Stanford, Calif.: Stanford University Press, 1999), assess the manifestation of these changes on literary production.

lates human affairs, and Alcott's discussion of children's play focuses on how teachers should use play to ready children for the "loftier claims" of "instruction" and "advancement."[4] Not only do these changes in social organization produce new conceptions of childhood and of play, but, as we have seen in the relation between childhood and fiction, these new conceptions prove mutually reinforcing (if play is valuable, then children must be valuable; if children are valued then play must be too), and both formulations work to idealize and naturalize class consciousness and to affirm the desirability of middle-class practices.

Alcott, writing in 1830, was among the nation's earliest champions of children's play, and his defense of its "designed purpose" shows the marks of the culture's general view of leisure as a largely suspect activity and childhood as besmirched by infant depravity and original sin.[5] By the time Macy's opened the nation's first toy department in 1875, the merchandising of children's toys epitomized how leisure, not work, would drive the consumption patterns of mature industrial capitalism. The 1870 census would be the first to track children's employment, and it would also be in the 1870s that states would begin passing laws regulating child labor.[6] These are enormous and extremely swift shifts in the cultural understanding of childhood, work, and play. I focus my exploration on the decades of the 1850s through the 1870s— the verge of transition—and on the figure of the working child, whose need to labor stands in potent opposition to the burgeoning idealization of childhood as a life-stage appointed for play.[7]

4. Amos Bronson Alcott, "Observations on the Principles and Methods of Infant Instruction" (1830), in his *Essays on Education, 1830–1862* (Gainesville, Fla.: Scholars Facsimiles and Reprints, 1960), 5.

5. Alcott, "Observations," 5.

6. See Clement, *Growing Pains,* chapter 5; on the census see 133. For a provocative account of how "the expulsion of children from the 'cash nexus' at the turn of the past century . . . was part of a cultural process of 'sacralization' of children's lives" in which emotional value comes to preclude economic utility, see Viviana A. Zelizer, *Pricing the Priceless Child: The Changing Social Value of Children* (New York: Basic Books, 1985), 11.

7. Daniel T. Roberts concludes his historical survey of nineteenth-century trends in middle-class child-rearing with the observation that "what seems clearest about formal child shaping is the fact of repeated change." See Roberts, "Socializing Middle-Class Children: Institutions, Fables, and Work Values in Nineteenth-Century America," *Journal of Social History* 13 (spring 1980): 364. Roberts divides the century roughly in thirds, with the first thirty years stressing obedience to authority, the middle decades devoted to developing self-control, and the final decades of the century valuing imagination over systematization. What I find most valuable in his schema is his nuanced sense of the unevenness of transitions between these models so that in the disparate settings of home, storybook, and school widely differing ideals and expectations could be set upon the same child. In picking these decades I am focusing on the transition from self-control to imagination.

This is not a simple story of playtime's haves and have-nots, for with re-markable consistency it is the working child who is seen to embody play, and who hence teaches the middle class about fun. By the end of the century, play, and the worlds of the imagination, would become cultural markers for what was marvelous about childhood, and this culturally valuable play would be recognized as an attribute of middle-class affluence and leisure. Yet (and this is the crux of my argument) it is through depictions of working-class chil-dren that these middle-class ideals are first and most forcefully articulated.[8] In particular I focus on the paradigmatic example of the street child, and most especially the newsboy. With paper sales one of the largest and most visible forms of child employment in American cities, the newsboy figured largely in literary and reform discourses as the representative child laborer, and one no-torious for mischievous play, while among the new toys manufactured for the entertainment of middle-class children were novelty presses, enabling well-to-do youth to play press laborers themselves.

Newsboy Narratives

The newsboy is America's paradigmatic child laborer. The "shrewdest and sharpest" of street children,[9] the newsboy figures a wide array of cultural anx-ieties about childhood, cities, print culture, the communal life of the nation, economic possibility, and even the relations between leisure and labor. In

8. Melvin L. Kohn's influential mid-twentieth-century study of what values parents strive to inculcate in their children finds a significant divergence between working- and middle-class families: working-class parents emphasize "*behavioral conformity*" (obedience, cleanliness, and good behavior), while middle-class parents stress "internal process" (curiosity, happiness, and empathy). See *Class and Conformity: A Study in Values, with a Reassessment, 1977* (Chicago: Uni-versity of Chicago Press, 1977), 21. Clearly in the nineteenth century all classes would put more stress on conformity to authority than now; still it seems plausible that the tendencies Kohn de-scribes may well reflect on the class-differentiated attitudes held within actual nineteenth-century families, even as literary representations would apportion obedience and curiosity quite differ-ently, producing well-behaved middle-class children and playful working-class children.

9. *First Annual Report of the Children's Aid Society* (New York, 1854), 6. In 1854 the New York Children's Aid Society was founded in the charitable hope of mitigating the social and in-dividual dangers of child poverty and homelessness. It initiated a flurry of experimental pro-grams: industrial workshops, Sunday "meetings," schools, clothing distribution, and most fa-mously a placing-out system that sent urban children to work in rural households and a series of Newsboys' Lodging Houses that provided cheap but clean room and board for children work-ing on the streets of the city. The annual reports of the Society are one of my most important sources; subsequent citations will be parenthetical and will give the year of the report and page number. I have worked from the complete run of these reports available at the New York Histor-ical Society, but the first ten reports are more readily available in a facsimile reprint, *Annual Reports of the Children's Aid Society: Nos. 1–10, Feb. 1854–1863* (New York: Arno Press, 1971).

one sense, the newsboy is a generic figure: "the term 'Newsboy' . . . properly embraces all those of either sex, in our great cities, who at a tender age
are compelled to rely upon their own wits and exertions for support." When
John Morrow writes his life story at sixteen, after years of selling matches and
stationery—but never newspapers—on the streets of New York, he titles his
book *A Voice from the Newsboys.*[10] When the New York Children's Aid Society founded their first shelter for homeless children, they called it "The Newsboys' Lodging-House," even though, as Charles Loring Brace explains, "it is
not restricted to lodging newsboys," and their data suggest that only about a
quarter of the children staying in the house actually sold papers (1858: 24).
Moreover, many children who hawked the news alternated that work with
other street trades. Thus, much of my material ranges rather broadly among
street children regardless of specific occupation. But in other ways the newsboy is a highly specific figure, whose job quite literally places the child as the
disseminator of all that is most important for the nation, or as one nineteenth-
century observer grandiloquently put it, "those awful personages whose
movements move the hearts of millions and whose voices agitate communities by the slightest syllables. . . . The most important and active agent in
supplying the world with intelligence—the Newsboy."[11]

The newsboy is such an important and active figure in the mid-nineteenth-
century imagination because he embodies the urbanization of American life.
The employment of newsboys began in 1833 with the production of the first
"penny papers," dailies whose low price made distribution through traditional
adult salesmen no longer profitable.[12] Thus, like the papers they hawked,
newsboys were one of the first products and "agents" of an urban-based national culture. Their voices did indeed agitate communities: their cries of the
"Extras" were a sound of the city that insisted on the significance of events,
making profit and community out of scandal and disaster. Unlike the middle-

10. John Morrow, *A Voice from the Newsboys* (New York?: Published for the author, 1860),
1, from the introduction by "W.B.D. Englewood NJ."

11. George G. Foster, *New York by Gas-Light and Other Urban Sketches* (Berkeley: University of California Press, 1990), 112.

12. For accounts of the rise of the daily paper that debate its formative role in the reshap-
ing of urban culture and democratic politics, see Alexander Saxton, *The Rise and Fall of the
White Republic: Class, Politics and Mass Culture in Nineteenth-Century America* (New York:
Verso, 1990), chapter 4; Michael Schudson, *Discovering the News: A Social History of American
Newspapers* (New York: Basic Books, 1978), chapter 1; and David M. Henkin, *City Reading:
Written Words and Public Spaces in Antebellum New York* (New York: Columbia University
Press), chapter 5. In these accounts the shift to newsboys as distributors appears as a minor
note in larger discussions centered on technology, literacy, and politics.

class child ideally protected from the happenings of a dangerous world, the newsboy literally lived off such dire events. "'How's business now?'" Frederick Ratchford Starr, one of the directors of the Philadelphia Newsboys' Lodging House, "inquired of one of the lads. 'Very dull sir; so few accidents.'"[13]

In an economic pattern that maximized the press's profits, newsboys bought papers at a small discount in the morning with no possibility of returning unsold copies. Thus they only made money once their sales exceeded their initial investment. Such a system required shrewd decisions by the newsboys, gauging weather and the appeal of the day's events so as to have enough papers to satisfy regular customers and none left over at day's end. "A lad of mere ordinary capacity," Starr concludes after detailing the economic strictures on the newsboy, "would starve at the business."[14] Under these conditions, newsboys were not simply passive disseminators of information; they were knowledgeably involved in evaluating the news and giving it voice. Considering these economic motivations, it is not surprising that observers frequently complained that newsboys were too noisy and too willing to lie, fabricating disasters when actual headlines produced inadequate sales.[15] I want to stress the extremely exploitative nature of this economic system; still, in terms of my concern with figurations of work and play it is striking how much the strategies of economic survival newsboys developed under this system depended upon making noise and making up news, the raucousness and imagination that we associate with play.

If, as Benedict Anderson claims, newspapers bind disparate events and accounts into a shared ritual of daily reading, enabling the imagination of a national community, the newsboy interposes a child between the projections

13. [F. Ratchford Starr], *John Ellard: The Newsboy* (Philadelphia: William S. and Alfred Martien, 1860), 7.

14. Starr, *John Ellard: The Newsboy*, 6. David Nasaw describes the same economic pressures for newsboys of the early twentieth century in *Children of the City at Work and Play* (New York: Oxford University Press, 1985), 75–76. Joseph Holt Ingraham goes into great detail in describing the economics of newspaper sales in the late 1830s. In Ingraham's novel, a newsboy can buy six papers for four cents, thus making a two-cent profit when he sells them. Ingraham, *Jemmy Daily: or, the Little News Vendor a Tale of Youthful Struggles* (New York: Sun Office, 1843), 27. Johnny Morrow's memoirs reflect the tighter economics and larger volume of the job twenty years or so later: "I had fifty-six papers for my morning's stock, for which I paid eighty-four cents. For the sale of these I have received one dollar and twelve cents, leaving me a profit of twenty-eight cents; nine of these I am going to spend for my breakfast, and I shall then have nineteen to spare." Morrow, *A Voice From the Newsboys*, 129.

15. Nasaw cites a *New York Times* article of 1917 headed "Police Move to Stop Noise of Newsboys: Public Annoyed by Shouting of War Calamities for which There Is No Basis," in *Children of the City*, 78. But as Georgeanna Muirson Woolsey's letters suggest, "real living and lying 'Extra' boy[s]" were just as much relied upon during the Civil War. Quoted in Henkin, *City Reading*, 112. Accounts of fabricating news and learning to shout are staples of newsboy fiction.

of print culture and its community of readers.[16] Urbanization, industrialization, and immigration all functioned, of course, to erode older, more interactive notions of what "community" might mean. The public spaces of American cities created new situations of anonymous proximity where class difference was more visible and yet also more chaotic and insecure.[17] Newspapers, whose columns similarly juxtaposed remarkably diverse material, provided one means of mediating and comprehending such social heterogeneity, while the newsboy—with his "territory" preferably staked out in affluent business streets, and his regular customers of various political allegiances and social status—created and maintained patterns of cross-class circulation.[18] As children, newsboys both embodied the chasm of class (since middle-class children would not occupy the streets in this unsupervised way) and made that divide appear less frightening. For whatever New York's chief of police, George Mastell, might say about the "idle and vicious children of both sexes, who infest our public thoroughfares," whatever Charles Loring Brace might warn about the ways children "grown up ignorant of moral principle . . . will poison society" (1854: 12), infestation and poison pose largely future threats, while the adult poor appear far more immediately dangerous.[19] To street-children, as children, accrued much of the charm the middle class associated with childhood, along with the pathos of lacking most of the material conditions that made such charming childhoods possible. For these reasons images of newsboys proved a popular means of representing and humanizing all that was troubling but attractive about urban spaces. Consistently drawn against a backdrop of posted bills, in these paintings the boy and the papers he would

16. Benedict Anderson, *Imagined Communities: Reflections on the Origins and Spread of Nationalism* (New York: Verso, 1991), 32–36.

17. See Christine Stansell, *City of Women: Sex and Class in New York, 1789–1860* (New York: Alfred A. Knopf, 1986); and Eric Homberger, *Scenes from the Life of a City: Corruption and Conscience in Old New York* (New Haven, Conn.: Yale University Press, 1994) for detailed discussions of the class contestations over public space in nineteenth-century New York. Karen Halttunen, *Confidence Men and Painted Women: A Study of Middle-Class Culture in America 1830–1870* (New Haven, Conn.: Yale University Press, 1982), explores some of the social meanings of living in such heterogenous and anonymous cities through an account of the strategies adopted for demonstrating social status in a world of strangers where class had to be constantly reenacted because it could no longer be intimately assumed.

18. See Henkin, *City Reading* for a wonderful account of New York as a printed, legible space. In his rendition the orality (and flesh) of the newsboy is largely treated as an anachronism, the newsboy's power resting in the written authority of the papers he sells (112).

19. Mastell is quoted in Stansell, *City of Women*, 194. Brace's annual reports for the Society and his book-length summary of the Society's efforts, *The Dangerous Classes of New York, and Twenty Years' Work among Them* (New York: Wynkoop and Hallenbeck, 1872), are filled with attempts to convince the wealthy that homeless children are indeed dangerous and that they are worthy of charity—an ambivalence I explore in this chapter.

sell seem to arise out of and give focus to a more chaotic city of print.[20] (See figs. 4.1, 4.2, 4.3.)

Of the examples shown in figures 4.1–4.3, only James Henry Cafferty's newsboy is actually working at selling papers; he is also the youngest and most vulnerable-looking of the three. The viewer looks down at him and he looks back with large, immigrant eyes. Among the bills pasted behind him is one for a lost dog, and for all his earnest efforts to make his sale the boy appears lost too. But even he stands beside a table of apples—a "treat" of urban life,[21] and a nod toward that most housebound of genres, still-life painting, that would dominate Cafferty's artistic output. Thomas LeClear's *Buffalo Newsboy* is actually eating his apple, and F. R. Spencer's *Newsboy* has a dog of his own. These two boys are lounging rather than working; they appear handsome and intelligent, emitting a sense of street-life as a free, generally pleasurable adventure. Leisure, in these pictures, becomes visible largely as the absence of work. "By Railroad" but "O.K." reads the crate on which the Buffalo newsboy sits, and the clearest banner above Spencer's boy proclaims "Something Coming"—"a reference," Joan Murray suggests, "to the boy's future success" (27). These benign images of street life are not, however, unambiguous. There are other bold words on the wall in Spencer's painting as well, words Murray does not note, including RIOT. My point is that these images all associate newsboys with play as well as labor, although the emphasis may vary from one artist to the next and although the social consequences of such play—pleasure or riot—remain undecided. These ambiguities express the instability, the cultural uncertainties, of the assignation of class identity to street children. Distributors rather than producers, they pose as independent agents (however exploited); their labor evades the routinization of factory, office, or domestic work. Thus, despite their extreme poverty and the harshness of their work conditions, street children are frequently evoked to represent a

20. Other notable paintings in this genre, all with a background of posted bills, include William Page, *The Young Merchants* (c. 1834), Academy of Fine Arts, Philadelphia; Henry Inman, *The Newsboy* (1841), Addison Gallery of American Art, Andover, Mass.; James Henry Cafferty, *Weary Newsboy* (1861), present location unknown; and in an interestingly classicized version, Martin Johnson Heade, *Roman Newsboys* (1848–49), Toledo Museum of Art (the wall in Rome is mostly covered with graffiti, but it does include two small advertising bills). Joan Murray, in "Rags to Riches: The Newsboy in Nineteenth-Century American Art," *Canadian Collector: A Journal of Antiques and Fine Arts* 17 (September/October 1982): 26–31, reproduces some of these works. See also David Stuart Hull, *James Henry Cafferty, N. A. (1819–1869)* (New York: New York Historical Society, 1986), 17–18. Sean Shesgreen recounts the British tradition of street hawker or "Crier" iconography in his *Images of the Outcast: The Urban Poor in the Cries of London* (New Brunswick, N.J.: Rutgers University Press, 2002).

21. At the Children's Aid Society giving out apples is treated as an entertainment—not part of a regular meal. See Brace, *Dangerous Classes*, 111.

Fig. 4.1. James Henry Cafferty, *Newsboy Selling New York Herald Tribune,* 1857. Oil on canvas. Courtesy of the Collection of Walter and Lucille Rubin.

Fig. 4.2. Thomas LeClear, *Buffalo Newsboy,* 1853, 24 x 20, oil on canvas. Courtesy of the Albright-Knox Art Gallery, Buffalo, New York, Charlotte A. Watson Fund, 1942.

kind of liberty from the constraints and abjection of labor. Marx would count "orphans and pauper children" among the "surplus-population," that "industrial reserve army" required for the "free play" of capital.[22] His analysis

22. Karl Marx, *Capital: A Critique of Political Economy* (1867; New York: Modern Library, 1936), 697 ("orphans and pauper children"), 707 ("surplus population" and "industrial reserve-army"), and 696 ("free play").

THE NEWSBOY, 1849

Fig. 4.3. Frederick R. Spencer, *The Newsboy,* 1849. Oil on wood. Courtesy of the Collection of Peter B. Rathbone.

suggests how these figurations of street trading as a form of play present a romance of the market, one that emphasizes the swirl of circulation and disre-
gards the wasting of "surplus" lives. In a more conservative version of social
critique, reformers like Charles Loring Brace see in these children the clearest
mark of social disintegration. Wai Chee Dimock's observation that "leisure is
class-inflected" not because "it is tied to one particular class" but because it
is "variously nuanced and accented, when it is invoked as the salient characteristic for different groups" can thus be pressed one step further, under the
recognition that street children are seen to occupy simultaneously a number
of quite "different groups" with quite differently "accented" conceptions of
leisure: they are workers, children, unproductive scamps, and entrepreneurs
(or, as they were often called by apologists for the press, "little merchants").[23]

In a similar way, the association of these children with the streets, the
ease with which their portraits serve as potent figurations of urban life,
stands in conflict with the traditionally domestic accents of childhood. Imag-
inatively unsettling though they may be, such portraits appear demographi-
cally accurate. The majority of city-dwelling adults during this period had
grown up in rural areas, so that in a very real way the children who lived and
worked on the streets understood urban life and urban spaces far better than
did adults.[24] One of the stock scenes in literature about newsboys is that of
the lost adult—often newly arrived from the country—who must rely on the
newsboy for directions and information.

> "Can you tell me, my lad, the way to Broadway?"
>
> "Another insult by gorry," thought Bob, and quick as thought he touched his
> thumb to the tip of his nose, and wheeling his fingers in the air answered, "no
> you don't, you don't come it over this child"; and he looked back and relieved
> himself of a great laugh, while the questioner remained standing and looking af-
> ter him in utter amazement. "Just as if he didn't know he was in Broadway,"
> thought Bob, and he gave an extra key to the compass of his voice to show his
> contempt for all fooling.[25]

23. Wai Chee Dimock, "Class, Gender and a History of Metonymy," in *Rethinking Class:
Literary Studies and Social Formations*, ed. Wai Chee Dimock and Michael T. Gilmore (New
York: Columbia University Press, 1994), 84.

24. Chapter 5 of David Nasaw's *Children of the City at Work and Play* gives a fine sense of
"newsies'" comfort and competence in the city, although his work is devoted to the early twentieth century, not the mid-nineteenth.

25. Elizabeth Oakes Smith, *The Newsboy* (New York: J. C. Derby, 1854), 36. Such stories of
lost adults are standard features of Horatio Alger's street-boy series. See for example the opening scene of *The Young Outlaw* where Sam Barker asks ten cents for directing to Canal Street a
country deacon already standing on it (Boston: Loring, 1875), 9–12.

A world where adults must ask the aid of children is a topsy-turvy place, one in which traditional models of deference, due to age or class, no longer hold. In a clash of cultures, Bob is as unwilling to recognize the depths of this gentleman's ignorance of the city as the gentleman is incapable of recognizing Broadway or comprehending Bob's response to his question. Bob's insistence that "you don't come it over this child" rejects all middle-class notions of what a child should be—innocent, ignorant, docile—and instead represents the child as the master of urban spaces; thumbing his nose at the very notion of deference, he is himself the champion of "fooling."

As even this one scene from Elizabeth Oakes Smith's 1854 novel *The Newsboy* amply illustrates, the fictional newsboy is a deeply ambivalent literary figure; such cultural ambivalence bespeaks the strains of fitting these working children to middle-class definitions of childhood. In this scene the joke is on the gentleman who doesn't even know where he is, and Bob's own fooling is recorded with fond pleasure. Still Smith and her readers know something that Bob does not—that in thumbing his nose at this request for help Bob is also rejecting any possibility of seeing the city as a community of trust and mutual aid, or at least as a place where such bonds could cross class lines. Bob's rejection of trust, indeed his complete unwillingness to even acknowledge such a possibility in the exchange, simultaneously ridicules the naiveté of a middle-class perspective that can imagine the city in such terms and bemoans the realism of a working-class perspective that cannot.

Smith's ambivalence is characteristic of the genre.[26] Literary representations of newsboys ricochet between seeing these street children as vulnerable and exploited (childhood innocence abused by economic and urban circumstances) and seeing them as spunky and resourceful (childhood insouciance simply taking the city and the labor it requires as conditions for a new kind of play). The alternative to Bob's jeering autonomy is sympa-

---

26. Smith's very modes of literary production are suggestive. Her plot in this 300-page novel works relentlessly to attach Bob to middle-class values and opportunities, and her narrative voice obviously positions her as a middle-class author writing to middle-class readers: "I with my conventional life, and years of training, and ancestors of forecast—how could I comprehend a being who had stood up naked from the hands of nature?" (9). Yet Smith also wrote "Dime Novels" for Beadle and Adams—series read mostly by working-class boys—and there is something surprisingly convincing in her detailed account of and high regard for newsboys' literary tastes: "I would rather stand the ordeal of the Newsboys, were I to write a play," Smith concludes, "than any other audience in the world" (27).

For an account of the working-class readership of Dime Novels see Michael Denning, *Mechanic Accents: Dime Novels and Working Class Culture in America* (London: Verso, 1987), chapter 3. Albert Johannsen discusses Elizabeth Oakes Smith and her participation in the genre in *The House of Beadle and Adams and Its Dime and Nickel Novels: A Study of Vanished Literature*, vol. 2 (Norman: University of Oklahoma Press, 1950), 259.

thetic pain. "I had not gone far," writes Lydia Maria Child in one of her *Letters from New York,*

> when I met a little ragged urchin, about four years old, with a heap of newspapers, "more big as he could carry," under his little arm, and another clenched in his small red fist. The sweet voice of childhood was prematurely cracked into shrillness, by screaming street cries at the top of his lungs; and he looked blue, cold, and disconsolate. . . . I stood looking after him as he went shivering along. Imagination followed him to the miserable cellar where he probably slept on dirty straw. . . .[27]

Child's *Letters* blend social criticism with rich accounts of the development of a moral and aesthetic imagination. They are thus engaged simultaneously in creating and elevating bourgeois subjectivity and in critiquing the social inequities that have historically made that subjectivity possible. Thus this letter, in which Child invites her readers to follow her imagination as it fabricates a future of abuse and ultimate criminality for the newsboy, presses on to ask: "When, oh when, will men learn that society makes and cherishes the very crimes it so fiercely punishes and *in* punishing reproduces?" (84). The surprising word here is "cherishes," a word that seems deeply descriptive of Child's own imaginative procedures, and unsettlingly perceptive of the ways society may foster crime. To be cherished is just what the nineteenth-century middle class had understood as the child's ideal but necessary role. The lisping child voice, with its awkward grammar that proclaims the pile of newspapers "more big as he could carry," is not, of course, the newsboy's. It speaks in the third person; and besides, among the first things that Child notices about this newsboy is that he lacks "the sweet voice of childhood." By interpolating such a "sweet voice" into her letter, by the evident fondness with which she produces its little errors, Child demonstrates how a cherished childhood should sound.

One literary use of the newsboy is thus to define and value middle-class childhoods through the depiction of their antithesis. In Louisa May Alcott's "Our Little Newsboy," the possessive and the diminutive function to claim the newsboy for the middle-class home, and indeed the scene of the story is not Jo's encounter with the newsboy, but her retrospective telling of that meeting as a bedtime story.

> "If I saw that poor little boy, Aunt Jo, I'd love him lots!" said Freddy, with a world of pity in his beautiful child's eyes.

27. Lydia Maria Child, *Letters from New York* (New York: Charles S. Francis and Co., 1843), 83, "Letter XIV" dated February 17, 1842.

And believing that others would be kind to little Jack and such as he I tell
the story.

When busy fathers hurry home at night I hope they'll buy their papers of
the small boys. . . . For love of the little sons and daughters safe at home, say a
kind word, buy a paper, even if you don't want it; and never pass by, leaving
them to sleep forgotten in the streets at midnight, with no pillow but a stone.[28]

Here the middle-class child's response to the story of a homeless newsboy is itself definitive of a childlike vision—Freddy has "beautiful child's eyes"—and
this vision urges charity upon busy middle-class men. In this realm of middle-
class benevolence, commercial interactions come to seem like moral attributes,
and to buy "even if you don't want it" becomes a mark of virtue. It is after all
just as preposterous an imposition of possession for fathers to speak of "their
papers" as it is for Aunt Jo to claim "our little newsboy," but middle-class identity is being constituted in scenes like these so as to make the emotional traits
of interest and concern indistinguishable from the economic processes of purchase and ownership. Read sentimentally, it is the middle-class child's com-
passion that marks him as a good child. It is the middle-class father's love of
this child that affirms the father's class position and inaugurates the charitable social responsibilities of that position. Read commercially, middle-class
affluence buys both comfort (material distance from need) and conscience
(empathic proximity to need). Aunt Jo's bedtime terms—from Freddy's nursery to the newsboy's stone—resonate with the end of Child's letter, which finds
her unable to sleep. The voices of street hawkers outside her window "proved
too much for my overloaded sympathies. I hid my face in the pillow and wept;
for 'my heart was almost breaking with the misery of my kind'" (Child, 86).

Class identity, it seems, is largely a question of pillows. Soft beds support
sentimental suffering; they create a safe space for imaginative identification
and so teach the comfortable virtues of feeling for someone else the very pain
that this class position, this soft pillow, protects one from feeling in one's own
person. As Child represents herself weeping into her pillow, the "confusing
elision between sentimentality and domesticity" that June Howard incisively
charges us to interrogate appears remarkably palpable, suggesting how very
much the material conditions of middle-class households provide the contours
and possibilities of sentimentality's imaginative form.[29] It is these comfortable and private spaces that enable reader and writer to luxuriate in feeling.

28. Louisa May Alcott, "Our Little Newsboy," in *Aunt Jo's Scrap Bag* (Boston: Robert
Brothers, 1872), 191–92.

29. June Howard, "What is Sentimentality?" *American Literary History* 11 (spring 1999): 73.

The hard beds of street children are perceived as teaching other lessons, but they are just as certainly the source of class identities to be learned. "I know an old wagon, up an alley, where I can sleep like a top," Horatio Alger's bootblack Tim explains to Sam Barker, a greenhorn newly escaped to city life from the abundance and hard work of a New England farm. At day's end the boys climb into the wagon together: "There is everything in getting used to things, and that is where Tim had the advantage. He did not mind the hardness of his couch, while Sam, who had always been accustomed to a regular bed, did."[30] This lesson of hard beds produces a certain hardiness and resilience that Alger marks as an "advantage." Clearly the recognition that "there is everything in getting used to things" proves a comfortable antidote to the tears brought on by "overloaded sympathies." But it is also true that such hardiness is one of the strongest attractions of Alger's fiction. Sam's sly resilience does after all keep him and the novel's plot "adrift in the streets"; his scams carry him and his readers humorously from one scrape to the next while Alger's anxious narrator "warn[s] my boy readers that I by no means recommend them to pattern after him" (84). Thus, as with Bob thumbing his nose, such stories of badly-behaved boys celebrate the play of street life even as they press their young heroes toward softer beds and office jobs.

Novelistic images of the "child wage earner as an urban folk hero" and "seedling entrepreneur" run, of course, counter to the historical record: very few if any children actually prospered through street trading.[31] But to note the falsity of such images, or on the other hand to question the presumptions that underlie Lydia Maria Child's imaginings of the newsboys' dismal prospects, should initiate, not foreclose, explorations of the representational work done by street children. The simultaneous popularity of these two opposing images, in their very opposition, produces a middle space of exploitation and survival that may more accurately represent the discontinuous manner in

---

30. Alger, *The Young Outlaw*, 158 ("I know an old wagon") and 164 ("There is everything in getting used to things"). The two-volume life of Sam Barker told in *The Young Outlaw* and *Sam's Chance and How He Improved It* deviate somewhat from Horatio Alger's usual formula of the worthy street boy raised by "luck and pluck" to the lower rungs of respectability, in that Sam begins where Alger and the Children's Aid Society would have such boys end, as an adopted rural laborer in a pious home. Thus the pair of volumes must narrate Sam's descent to the allures and vices of street life as well as his gradual reformation from them.

31. Adrienne Siegel, *The Image of the American City in Popular Literature, 1820–1870* (Port Washington, N.Y.: Kinnikat Press, 1981), 82, from which these phrases come, provides a useful survey of street child stereotypes and decries their inaccuracy. David E. Whisnant, in "Selling the Gospel News, or: The Strange Career of Jimmy Brown the Newsboy," *Journal of Social History* 5 (spring 1972): 269–309, goes further, arguing that this benign mythology of newsboy life actually functioned to exempt newsboys from child-labor protections well into the twentieth century.

which class identity is lived. Thus while these stock figures tell us a great deal about middle-class constructions of class identity, they do not end there, for as I will show, street children themselves learned how to move within and manipulate these stereotypes.[32] The annual reports of the Children's Aid Society were bolstered with appendices of miscellaneous documents, examples of newspaper coverage of the Society's work, reports and diary excerpts by visitors and Society staff detailing specific daily events, and most remarkable of all, large collections of letters written by children who had been helped by the Society and by the families that took in such children. These are obviously biased and mediated sources, but for all their limitations they provide a rich cache of documentation about the attitudes and experiences of particular, individual, nineteenth-century street children. The understandings of childhood work and play voiced by these children overlap with and diverge from the representations offered by philanthropists and novelists. Thus the standard stories of street-child pathos or hardiness do not simply prove false, but rather provide a projected context that actual street children strove to use as best they could.

Critics of Alger's tales have pointed out not only the gap between his novels and the real conditions of street children in New York, but also, more surprisingly and interestingly, the divergence between his novels and the "rags to riches" mythos that has grown out of them. Not only do Alger's heroes rarely achieve riches, settling rather more often for the humble rewards of office jobs, but even this small success is never dependent upon the skill and industry with which they work their street jobs. Rather, Alger's heroes get their "chance" at respectability through extra-professional services rendered to the wealthy: it is the finding and rescuing of wallets and children that most often wins Alger's street boys their patrons. This is not to say that work is irrelevant; the newsboy Rufus, for example, is called "Rough and Ready" because of his readiness in hawking papers, while Ragged Dick easily supports himself as a bootblack because he is "energetic and on the alert for business."[33] But Alger is not, in fact, so naive as to represent a change in work habits as able to do more than increase a boy's income within his street trade and indicate his capacity for success in other, more respectable jobs once

32. My argument here parallels Vincent DiGirolamo's wonderful analysis of newsboy funerals, in which middle-class mourning practices are adapted to produce working-class solidarity. "Newsboy Funerals: Tales of Sorrow and Solidarity in Urban America," *Journal of Social History* 36 (fall 2002): 5–30.

33. Alger, *Rough and Ready* (1896; reprint, Philadelphia: Porter and Coates, n.d.). *Ragged Dick* (1867; reprint, New York: Collier Books, 1962), 46.

luck has intervened to move him there. Moreover, the new positions as clerks and office boys to which Alger's heroes rise are not represented as more richly remunerative than their street work. When Rufus quits selling newspapers to work for Mr. Turner, the businessman offers to pay his new clerk "the same you have been earning by selling papers,—that is eight dollars a week. It is nearly double what I have been accustomed to pay" (297). As Alger explains, the difference between clerk and street boy derives not from the difference in their earnings but from their different habits of expenditure. In the case of Ragged Dick,

> There were not a few young clerks who employed Dick from time to time in his professional capacity, who scarcely earned as much as he, greatly as their style and dress exceeded his. Dick was careless of his earnings. Where they went he could hardly have told himself. However much he managed to earn during the day, all was generally spent before morning. He was fond of going to the Old Bowery Theater, and to Tony Pastor's, and if he had any money left afterwards, he would invite some of his friends in somewhere to have an oyster stew; so it seldom happened that he commenced the day with a penny. (43)

This is to say that Alger's project—the narrative of fitting street boys for the middle class—proves to be all about redirecting play rather than teaching work. In the process of these novels Alger's boys learn to save in newly opened bank accounts, and to spend the cash they accrue not on swiftly consumed pleasures, but on more lasting markers of status and domesticity: suits of clothes and regular beds.[34] Alger's heroes thus shed not only their "rags" but also their "riches," if by riches we mean the luxuries of consumption, leisure, and play. If the audience for these books was primarily middle-class boys, might not such readers remember them as rags to riches stories precisely because in their renditions of street-boy excesses and pranks they offer such riches—teaching middle-class children to play and spend?[35] Mr.

34. The Newsboys' Lodging Houses shared this ethos, often providing the boys with better clothes, and by their second year of operation they opened a makeshift savings bank, "a table in which each boy should have his own money-box numbered, where his earnings could be deposited. . . . This has given the first taste of the pleasure of saving" (1855: 14).

35. See Michael Moon, "'The Gentle Boy from the Dangerous Classes': Pederasty, Domesticity and Capitalism in Horatio Alger," *Representations* 19 (summer 1987): 87–110. Moon writes about the ways Alger's narrative structures articulate the modest rewards and homoerotic bonds that impel corporate/capitalist culture. In this account the "rags to riches" formula speaks a truth about capitalism that is, I think, deeply consonant with the constructions of childhood and class identity at stake in my analysis here. In both cases the misreading of Alger's stories correctly asserts the sources of pleasure and attraction within them.

Turner's son, Walter, envies Rufus his income from selling papers; "I only get fifty cents a week for spending money," he whines (262).

In 1867 Benjamin Woods invented a treadle printing press that was small enough to fit on a parlor table and inexpensive enough to be marketed as a toy. Woods advertised his "Novelty Press" in the most popular juvenile periodicals, and soon hosts of wealthy boys like Walter were busy selling papers of their own.[36] In terms of the discourses of class and leisure that concern us here, these juvenile papers are fascinating for how adamantly they figure their efforts at parlor newspaper production as labor. These costly toys epitomize a middle-class notion of play that would be productive rather than frivolous. The editors of these amateur papers are constantly explaining and complaining about how hard they work: "it is well enough to spend one or two nights in the week making up a monthly paper, but it requires constant and unrequited labor to issue a weekly regularly and punctually," the editor of *The Boys' Own Weekly* boasts in this paper's fourth number. By the seventh he has decided to turn it into a monthly after all; "we are not millionares, nor have we the time to continue as we have commenced, nor *would we* even had we the time, continue to work as we have worked."[37] The Van Wart twins report that they "bought a little printing press for $2 ¼ and we printed til bedtime"; the next morning they note in their diary, "we printed til breakfast," but after that they seem to lose interest in the press, or at least don't mention it again in their fairly extensive list of recreational practices.[38] Far less dilettante, *The Juvenile Key* takes for its masthead "a man's arm with the hand

36. Dennis R. Laurie, "Amateur Journalism," *Collectible Newspapers: Official Journal of the NCSA* 6 (April 1989): 6. Laurie notes that prior to Wood's "Novelty Press" there were some juvenile newspapers produced by hand, or by homemade presses, but that in the decade after this invention the numbers rose to over a thousand such papers, many short-lived. The American Antiquarian Society has an extensive collection of these papers: more than 50,000 issues of 5,500 different papers, almost all produced by juvenile pressmen. These papers sold for a few pennies and some had more than a hundred subscribers. They were often exchanged, and much space is spent on reviews of other juvenile newspapers; see for example the New York paper *The Boys of Gotham* 1 (March 1876), which gives three of its nine columns to intra-paper references. Nathaniel Hawthorne, by the way, was one of the many middle-class boys to make his own paper; "The Spectator" (1820) was carefully hand-lettered to imitate print. The original is in the collection of the Peabody Essex Museum, Salem, Mass.

37. The New York paper *The Boys' Own Weekly* 1 (June 11 and July 2, 1877). Similarly *Ours,* which in fact ran for over two years, a very long time for a juvenile paper, contrasts the paper's beginning "in the soft unclouded skies of a vacation" with the decision to stop publication "overwhelmed in the stormy deep of an arduous school-life!"—the work of the paper requiring leisure. *Ours* 5 (March 1873). The paper was begun in November 1870, also in New York City.

38. Irving Van Wart, Diary, in the collection of the New York Public Library, diary entries for December 14 and 15, 1854.

grasping a mallet or hammer, raised as in the act of labor. It is called the *working man's sign*," and it is chosen by the young editors, "one but seven, the other nine years of age," to celebrate "the importance of early habits of industry" instanced by their own press labor. Though a few numbers later they print the working man's sign upside down:

> Perhaps the reader will think the hammer has been *up* long enough. I think so too, and have therefore brought it down this week where we will let it rest for a little while, because the editor has nothing to say particularly at this time on the subject of industry. He remembers the old adage. "All work and no play makes Jack a dull boy."[39]

But evidently all play and no work seems equally dull.

Charles Wiggin kept a diary during the year that he was producing *The Carrier Pigeon,* in his "office" in one of the family's parlors. The diary documents his constant anxiety about getting each paper finished in time, yet running ahead of schedule makes Charles anxious too:

> Saturday 17, March
> . . . just think, I'm *two weeks* ahead this month—besides having part of the May number set up.

> Monday 19, March
> Worked in office as much as I dared to, but the fact is, I am afraid I shall get entirely out of work if I keep on—that would be a *dreadful* state of affairs. . . .

> Tuesday 20, March
> Rainy—Worked in office a little—I'm wrong. I *did* work a considerable—that's all I did through the day

Alger's lessons of discipline and industry were clearly familiar to his middle-class readers. Charles spends his Christmas money not on oyster dinners but on additional typeface. If there are middle-class stakes in imagining the work of street children as a kind of play, they are tightly paired with a desire to recast middle-class play as a kind of work. Well aware of these ironies, Charles

---

39. *Juvenile Key or Child's Newspaper,* Brunswick, Maine, 1 (September 18 and October 9, 1850). This paper was produced by the sister-and-brother team of Z. J. and G. W. Griffin. They claim to have done most of the typesetting themselves using the press in the printing office of their father, J. Griffin.

admits his enjoyment in watching the real hammers of the working men renovating the house next door: "not feeling particularly like working, I was in the next house seeing others work."[40]

"We Must Have a Little Fun"

There is some evidence that street children, at least those who relied upon Newsboys' Lodging Houses, read Alger's novels as well. In 1870 a New York Children's Aid Society table of statistics on the children who had stayed in the Lodging Houses in the previous year found only 10 percent to be illiterate.[41] Alger advertises in his preface to *Fame and Fortune* that his publisher, A. K. Loring, would "send a gratuitous copy of the two volumes of the *Ragged Dick Series* already issued to any regularly organized Newsboy's Lodge within the United States," and some Lodging Houses appear to have taken him up on this offer:

> The manager of the Newsboy's Home in St. Louis writes, "when on East last year, I got a copy of *Ragged Dick*, and the boys have enjoyed it so much, that it will not last much longer, and are continually asking for the second volume. You will oblige us very much by sending us a copy of both *Ragged Dick* and *Fame and Fortune*."[42]

I have no more detailed account of what it was about these books that the boys in St. Louis so enjoyed, but their consumption of Alger's stories attests to the ways that their self-making was in conscious dialogue with fictional images of street boys. Clearly, in the terms offered by the Lodging Houses

40. The diary of Charles H. Wiggin runs from June 1859 to December 1860, in the collection of the American Antiquarian Society. Charles describes his Christmas expenditures on January 1, 1860. His remarks about seeing others work are from an entry made April 4, 1860. For examples of Charles's worries about his press work see the entries of July 22–26, 1859. The American Antiquarian Society also has a few copies of *The Carrier Pigeon*. I should note that Charles is an invalid; he will in fact die in 1861, and there is a clear sense in the diary that he and his family feel this precariousness, viewing the miniature press purchased a decade before such things are mass produced as a substitute for the adult career he may never live to have.

41. "Number able to read and write 4,423; read only 2,371; unable to read and write 1,861; total 8,655 or 10% illiterate" (1870: 18). It is not clear whether it is Brace's math or his data that is off, but even a 20 percent illiteracy rate is not only impressive, but also convincing once one considers what a crucial survival skill literacy must have been for street traders, and especially for newsboys.

42. Alger, "Preface," in *Fame and Fortune* (Boston: A. K. Loring, 1868), viii; and "At Our Desk," *Student and Schoolmate* 24 (November 1869): 530. Both passages are quoted from Carol Nackenoff, *The Fictional Republic: Horatio Alger and American Political Discourse* (New York: Oxford University Press, 1994), 195.

(which quickly came to contain small libraries) and by Alger's fiction (where the decision to spend an evening reading, rather than squandering earnings on oysters and vaudeville, is one of the strong markers of a boy's rise), such enjoyment is itself a sign of reformation. But given the instability of riches and play in these books it is hard to be sure which pleasure is which.

When in the *Second Annual Report of the Children's Aid Society* Charles Loring Brace describes the sort of boys he hoped to reach through the founding of Newsboys' Lodging Houses, he emphasizes the non-domestic nature of their lives, and is evidently more troubled by their choices in play than by their exploitation in work.

> The class of newsboys were then apparently the most wild and vicious set of lads in the city. Many of them had no home, and slept under steps, in boxes, or in corners of the printing-house stairways. . . . Their money, which was easily earned, was more quickly spent in gambling, theaters and low pleasures, for which, though children, they had a man's aptitude. (1855: 13)

Writing this account in the Society's *Second Annual Report*, Brace's use of the past tense suggests the possibility of reform. Indeed, Brace happily reports that since the founding of the Lodging Houses this "man's aptitude" for forms of play which strike him as inappropriate to childhood has been largely redirected; for example, "the game of chequers" was introduced into the Lodging House "as a check to gambling . . . serving to exercise harmlessly that incessant mental activity and love of venture peculiar to the class" (1855: 14). Of course, the Lodging House also provided regular beds and baths.[43] Yet despite such efforts to reshape the newsboys' leisure, and the sharp charge of viciousness, it remains clear that it is precisely the newsboys' peculiar love of venture that made this "class" such a potent embodiment of the play of entrepreneurial speculation, and similarly that made these street children so attractive to reformers.

Frederick Starr explains that at the Philadelphia Newsboys' Lodging House "pains is taken gradually to refine their tastes by entertaining lectures, readings, dramatic or otherwise, and innocent games."[44] Yet the Lodging House game he describes with greatest detail does not appear very likely to refine its players:

---

43. "At the first opening of the Lodging House, it was made the condition of lodging that every boy should take a bath. To this there was great reluctance. Now it is prized as a privilege" (1854: 14).

44. Starr, *John Ellard*, 39.

A certain game, admitting of no euphemism in its suggestive title has possession of the floor. This is no other than "The Pile of Maggots," and its nature is that of a vortex, drawing in all appreciative spirits with an irresistible offer of fun. The rule is for all to "pile in," the best fellow keeping on top without injuring his competitors. Of course the party who supposes himself uppermost has but brief time for exaltation, soon finding himself at the bottom of the heap, and made thoroughly to *feel* his position. The struggle is generally of short duration, for as the fun grows fast and furious, the smaller boys shouting "Ouch! Get off uv me, you fellers," the superintendent taps a bell, and all is quiescent instanter.[45]

"The Pile of Maggots" does not appear in William Newell's *Games and Songs of American Children* (1883); Newell, after all, holds that children's games almost "invariably came from above, from the intelligent class," and that while many games and songs "still common in our cities, judging from their incoherence and rudeness, might be inventions of 'Arabs of the streets;' these invariably prove to be mere corruptions of songs long familiar on American soil," not immigrant made.[46] In Starr's telling, the game has the feel of a parable, but one in which Alger's stories of *"struggling upwards"* are shown to require that others tumble downward.[47] Thus "The Pile of Maggots" plays at the inversion of the social order, and locates pleasure as much in the squirming and toppling as in any capacity to secure the "top." I find the language of Starr's account rather like the game itself in that his absurdly elevated phrasing vies for supremacy with the words he quotes from the boys, so that this description is itself a shifting pile of values and vocabularies. Starr's obvious falsifications in claiming that such a game could be played "without injuring" the boys below and that one tap of a bell could reduce a heap of boys to "quiesence instanter" ultimately function to acknowledge the limits of staff control. If "The Pile of Maggots" indicates the boys' capacity to make squalor into play, and so imposes a kind of imaginative control over the hardships of street life, Starr's narration of this game reveals a similar tendency among the philanthropists: a capacity to find "fun" and pleasure in those boys' activities they cannot manage to refine or reform.[48] The vision of the street boy

45. Ibid., 42.

46. William Wells Newell, *Games and Songs of American Children* (1883; reprint, New York: Harper and Brothers, 1903), 7, 2. Newell does devote one chapter to "playing at work," but the games and dances he cites all imitate agricultural and artisan labor.

47. Alger, *Struggling Upwards* (1890; reprint, New York: Hurst, n.d.).

48. Vermin are a staple feature of Brace's *Annual Reports*. Long passages are devoted to detailing the process, for example, of removing lice from the head of a boy: "a sight sufficient to make the strongest nerves quiver. Every hair on his head was alive with vermin." But Mr. Macy,

playing offers a salve to middle-class consciences and a fantasy of the vicissitudes of the market as a game, even as images of the street boy's vulnerability helped form those consciences. After all, few in the middle class could say of themselves, as Alger can of Sam, that without debts or assets they are "just even with the world" (251–52).

Mr. Tracy, superintendent of a Newsboys' Lodging House in New York, while claiming that the House is "working harmoniously . . . and its arrangements are popular with the boys," nevertheless recognizes the limitations of its appeal. "The temptations of a street life to such boys, and its excitements are so strong, that it is exceedingly difficult to get them in here, and induce them to stay," he reports (1857: 17). His accounts of the Lodging House are full of examples of such difficulties in reforming the street boys' models of pleasure and consumption.

> These boys always live well when they have the money. This evening, while a number of them were telling each other what they had for supper, I undertook to reason with them about their diet,—that they should avoid some of the nice things which they had mentioned, and live more upon plainer food, as that was healthier and cheaper. That they should allow their reason instead of their appetite to control them in the selection of their food, "Ah sir," said one boy, "when a feller is hungry and has a good diner smokin' before him, its no time to **reason**; and I have made up my mind that them ruffled shirt 'quills' (clerks) shant eat up all the good things, no how!" I concluded to let the matter drop for the present, and took another subject. (1855: 25, from a section titled "Extracts from Mr. Tracy's Diary")

This street boy understands himself to be engaged in a contest of status and pleasure with the city's other horde of working youth—"them ruffled shirt 'quills.'" Thus the boy is clear that Tracy's terms of reason vs. appetite, and the system of moral values they imply, are an ethical gloss on what is in fact a class conflict. The boy knows that the issue is not learning to "control" desires, but who gets to have their desires fulfilled. Starr makes a joke of the Philadelphia newsboys who upon learning that a Lodging House was to be opened in that city "made tours of the west end of the city, and brought back fantastic reports of several of the costly mansions there, which exactly met

---

though "nearly sickened at his task . . . persevered for about three hours with shears and comb, and soap and water" (1858: 54). Such passages record the quivering nerves of a middle-class sensibility, so as to mark the heroism of the Lodging House staff who must overcome such disgust in order to tend to these boys. In this context what are we to make of Lodging House games that blatantly play upon the aspects of street life that sicken the House staff?

their lofty ideas." What they got instead were "plain, yet comfortable, lodging rooms in Pearl Street."[49] I suspect that in suggesting more illustrious addresses these boys were jesting themselves—pointing out the gap between the wealth of their benefactors (whose addresses appear in the subscription lists) and the modest nature of their grandly offered largess. Why is it that what is appropriate for one appears absurdly "lofty" for another? In these pranks the boys talk back to middle-class philanthropic presumptions. Such responses suggest that the acceptance of these dinners and these beds does not necessarily mean concurrence in the process of reforming appetites nor gratitude for the beds and meals bestowed.

The boys are highly aware of the ways in which their lives and desires do and do not conform to the philanthropist's understandings. When, for example, Johnny Morrow first came to the Lodging House he falsely claimed to be an orphan, since he had heard of the house as "the place for boys to sleep who haven't got any father or mother." Not wanting to stay with his drunken father and stepmother, he and his brothers put on the identity they thought the institution required.[50] In other instances, the boys appear delighted to demonstrate their benefactors' misunderstandings about the conditions of street life. Visitors to the Philadelphia Lodging House posed a math problem to the boys: "'If I purchase 20 papers at 3¢ each, and sell 12 at 5¢ each, do I make or lose by the transaction?' Several voices at once exclaimed 'Why you make!'" Such tests are, of course, all about power—the school drill, like the analysis of language or dress, gives a measure of the boys' neediness. But in this case multiplication facts prove an insufficient grounds for answering such queries: "These gentlemen knew but little of the profession, and required to be informed that the remaining eight copies 'could be sold for old paper!'" Here Starr reveals his own precarious balance of allegiance between the boys he helps and the gentlemen whose money makes such help possible, his narration of this scene showing him to be as gleeful over the visitors' discomfiture as were any of the boys there.[51]

In another encounter with philanthropic visitors, this time to a News-

---

49. Starr, *John Ellard*, 18. The New York Children's Aid Society *Annual Reports* contain lists of benefactors and their gifts, making it clear that the Society drew many donations of clothing and gifts of $1 or less (the list of donations to the Newsboys' Lodging House in 1855 includes one dollar from "Lod the Newsboy"; in 1857 "Tillie and Winnie" gave fifty-six cents, and at separate times that year five cents and one penny were "found in box" and duly counted toward the year's total), as well as gifts like Mrs. J. J. Astor's annual $100–$150 for Sunday dinners or the nearly $4,000 that was left to the Society by Mr. J. B. Barnard's estate.

50. Johnny Morrow, *A Voice from the Newsboys*, 62.

51. Starr, *John Ellard*, 122–23.

boys' Lodging House in New York, the newsboys' skill in balancing docility
with provocation is even more apparent. After hearing their visitor speak, the
newsboys were asked to treat him with a speech in return. Brace published
an account of "Paddy's" speech in his *Annual Report* for 1861, noting that he
had taken it "from the *Daily Times.*" Brace printed it again in *The Dangerous
Classes of New York,* there identifying it as taken "from the journal of a visitor from the country." Presuming that both sources are true—that a visitor's
journal entry was published in the *Daily Times*—the disparity in attribution
points to Brace's shifting sense of which kind of source gives more authority
to his account: the prestige of newspaper coverage or the immediacy and authenticity of a diary. In all events, these multiple publications make it evident
that Brace recognizes this scene as peculiarly useful advertising for the Lodging House. So it is remarkable how much of the newsboy's ironic relations to
the charity offered by Brace and the Children's Aid Society remains legible
through all of these beneficent publications:

> "Bummers," said he, "snoozers, and citizens, I've come down here among ye to
> talk to yer a little! Me and my friend Brace have come to see how ye'r gittin'
> along, and to advise yer. You fellers what stand at the shops with yer noses over
> the railin' smellin' ov the roast beef and hash—you fellers who's got no home—
> think of it how we are to encourage ye. [Derisive laughter, "Ha-ha's," and vari-
> ous ironical kinds of applause.] I say, bummers—for you're *all* bummers [in a
> tone of kind patronage]—*I was a bummer once* [great laughter]—I hate to see
> you spendin' your money on penny ice-creams and bad cigars. Why don't you
> save your money? You feller without no boots, how would you like a new pair,
> eh? [Laughter from all the boys but the one addressed.] Well, I hope you may
> get 'em, but I rayther think you won't. I have hopes for you all. I want you to
> grow up to be rich men—citizens, Government men, lawyers, generals, and in-
> fluence men."[52]

Paddy's speech cavorts in "the area between mimicry and mockery," as Homi
Bhabha calls it;[53] his performance for a philanthropic visitor permits him
to imitate just such visitors, to play one of those "rich men" who can claim
Brace as "my friend" and dole out advice and encouragement to hapless
newsboys. For what is so very funny about Paddy's identificatory claim that
"*I was a bummer once*" is the group's knowledge that the speaker had been

---

52. "A Visit to the Newsboys" (1861: 74–75), excerpted in Brace, *Dangerous Classes,* 110–11.
53. Homi K. Bhabha, "Of Mimicry and Man: The Ambivalence of Colonial Discourse," in
The Location of Culture (New York: Routledge, 1994), 86.

a bummer—"roving about the streets of night without sleep"—in the recent past, and no doubt could soon be one again.[54] Thus it is in the gap between the actual present tense and this fictive past tense of progress and reform that Paddy's play doubles into critique. Paddy pleases both his audiences. The newsboys delight in this parody of their benefactors; with their "derisive laughter" and "ironical kinds of applause" they join in the game of mimicry, playing at being a good audience, and thus record the pleasures of ridiculing this oh-so-familiar good advice. But the visitor and Brace clearly appreciate the performance as well, hearing not mockery but intimacy in this capacity teasingly to reproduce their moral lessons. In a way that Bhabha's account does not quite recognize, it is clear that this mimicry is itself a mark of both inclusion and its limits: it is only in being part of this institution that Paddy can so knowingly mock it, and it is only to the extent that he remains outside its redemptive program that his words are funny. The appeal of Paddy's speech lies in the multiplicity of its targets, joking at the expense of the boy with no boots and the well-heeled philanthropist. The newsboys' famed capacity for play affectionately crosses class bounds, yet it is not without its barbs for both parties. As Paddy goes on to tell his life story of escapes from drunken and abusive parents, his audience grows ever more raucous.

> "Well, boys, I wint on till I kim to the 'Home' [great laughter among the boys], and they took me in [renewed laughter], and did for me, without a cap to me head or shoes to me feet, and thin I ran away, and here I am. Now boys [with mock solemnity], be good, mind yer manners, copy me, and see what you'll become."
>
> At this point the boys raised such a storm of hifalutin applause, and indulged in such characterizations of delight, that it was deemed best to stop the youthful Demosthenese, who jumped from his stool with a bound that would have done credit to a monkey. (1861: 75)

The visitor will write down his memories of this speech and Brace will have them thrice published, yet (hiding the philanthropists' power within the passive voice) "it was deemed best to stop" the performance as the game of imitation becomes contagious and the newsboys' play at being a "hifalutin" audience threatens to turn into a "storm." If play makes the newsboy attractive to middle-class benefactors, it nevertheless remains precisely the characteristic that such philanthropies seek to contain. It may be the visitor's own penchant for irony that leads him to call Paddy "a youthful Demosthenese," but

54. This definition of "bumming" comes from "Newsboys' Dictionary or Glossary" (1855: 26).

it is his anxiety about the uncivility of such play that leads him to turn the classical orator into a monkey.

The stories Brace tells of street girls are quite different, and it is a difference of which he is himself acutely aware.

> A girl street rover is to my mind the most painful figure in all the unfortunate crowd of a big city. With a boy "Arab of the streets," one always has the consolation that, despite his ragged clothes and bed in a box or hay barge, he often has a rather good time of it, and enjoys many of the delicious pleasures of a child's roving life, and that a fortunate turn of events may at anytime make an honest, industrious, fellow of him. . . . With a girl vagrant it is different. She feels homelessness and friendlessness more; she has more of the feminine dependence on affection; the street-trades too are harder for her, and the return at night to some lonely cellar or tenement room, crowded with dirty people of all ages and sexes, is more dreary. . . . Then the strange and mysterious subject of sexual vice comes in.[55]

Even here, Brace cannot quite let himself imagine a street girl sleeping in a box. Homelessness, crowds, and dirt may offer boys delicious pleasures, but they never offer such to girls. Femininity, in Brace's often repeated intensifier, requires "more." That is, for a street girl, Brace sees the loss of the accoutrements of domesticity without ambivalence, simply and purely as loss—pathos without play. Yet while the domesticity offered by Newsboys' Lodging Houses was imagined as refuge, that same domesticity clearly figures in the Lodging House for Homeless Girls as the product of their feminine labors. The matron complains of the girls' "foolish pride or prejudice against housework," but boasts that under her administration "All were taught that this Lodging House was merely a stepping-stone to getting on in the world [no long-term stays], and that nothing was so honorable as industrious *house-work*" (1863: 12–13). The sort of resistance boys show through play and consumption appears among these girls as a more radical antipathy to domestic norms.

> A young girl in our Lodging House was relating to us recently how she had been attracted to another young girl there by hearing her answer our Matron "No, Ma'am! I don't know where my parents are. I don't care—*I hate them!*" This was at once a common bond of sympathy between the poor creatures! (1858: 4)

That the "bonds of sympathy"—the emotional trait that underlies philanthropic labors like those of the Children's Aid Society—could be forged out

---

55. Brace, *Dangerous Classes*, 114–15.

of the hatred of parents threatens to explode the domestic ideals of these charitable Homes. Brace's exclamation of pity ("poor creatures") insists on casting that bonding hatred as a mark of vulnerability and need, in a sentimental attempt to contain the reality that the family might be a site of animosity, not succor. After all, the entire structure of this charitable enterprise depends upon the presumption that domesticating these children will suture the social wounds of class.

Indeed, the Society's favorite project was not these temporary lodging houses but rather its placing-out system, which largely relied on its city charities to identify street children who could be relocated to work in rural families.[56] A highly innovative (and intrusive) program, the placing-out system was a self-conscious effort to invert the historical shifts in the practices and definitions of childhood. By transporting children who epitomized the new urban-based cultural patterns in order to provide agricultural labor in rural communities, it recapitulated the time when children's work formed a normal and regular part of the middle-class household economy. Significantly, in many cases the labor of the transported children served to decrease the amount of work expected of other children in the family, and thus helped produce the ideal of middle-class childhood leisure even within these rural settings.[57] In a letter written by a child placed out with a family in Indiana descriptions of the hired child's labor alternate with accounts of how the children of the family play: "I can saw and split wood for the fire. The little boy's father has given him a cannon." There is no rancor in this letter; the child writing it is quite matter-of-fact about which children in the household have the leisure and material support for play. The writer is clear too about the ambivalent nature of his inclusion in this household—sometimes speaking of a familial "we" and yet referring to the members of the family with oddly distant nouns: "the lady," "the man," "the little baby" (1863: 62). In this way letters written to the Children's Aid Society by children who had been placed out powerfully document the children's own acute sense of class identities and differences and the ways they manifest themselves in daily patterns of intimacy, work, and play. These letters regularly detail the children's farm and school work, sometimes in pride ("I am busy now grafting our roots. Perhaps you would like to know something about gardening. I will tell you some

56. For fine historical accounts of this placing-out system see Marilyn Irvin Holt, *The Orphan Trains: Placing Out in America* (Lincoln: University of Nebraska Press, 1992), and Miriam Z. Langsam, *Children West: A History of the Placing-Out System of the New York Children's Aid Society, 1853–1890* (Madison: State Historical Society of Wisconsin, 1964).

57. See Clement, *Growing Pains*, 149, on how children in prosperous farm families benefited from the work of hired boys and girls.

kind of apples we have grafted" [1859: 49]) and sometimes in complaint ("Had to be up early to chop wood, fetch water and feed the pigs, and water the horse. . . . Hadn't I a time of it with that there horse—he used to kick up his heels so. I stayed one week there—couldn't stand the work" [1858: 53]).

Though deeply aware of how much their own days are structured by labor, the children who wrote these letters are remarkably consistent in the adamance with which they assert their need to play. Much like some children's unwillingness to "stand the work," constraints on play prove a significant rational for leaving placements: "I have left Mr. S__. Mrs. S__ has been troubled with her head for about forty years, and she would not stand any noise, and I was very fond of singing, and sometimes I would sing, and not think anything about it, and she would scold me, and that was more than I could bear" (1863: 66). "Fun" figures in these letters as a defensible right in a way that seems to me quite unlike the attitudes toward play expressed in even the period's most permissive and celebratory texts of middle-class childhood. "They say I am a good girl, but too wild and daring, and will get me neck broke if I do not stop; but I must have some fun" (1863: 75), one girl writes. "You know we can't be silent all the time, you know, so we must have a little fun once in a while" (1861: 59), another child comments. In such letters the need to play figures as a powerful site of identity; the demand for at least a little fun is ardently claimed as a characteristic of self that survives these children's quite drastic geographic and class relocations. These children share with the classic play theorists a sense of play as the best measure of identity, since it presents the self at its least constrained, for as Johan Huizinga famously defined it, "the first main characteristic of play" is "that it is free, is in fact freedom." Play functions at such moments as mark of identity and site of resistance. And yet their letters demonstrate, as cultural critics were quick to do with the ideal assertions of *Homo Ludens,* that this self-articulated play is never fully a "stepping out of 'real' life," but rather that the nature and possibilities of play are always socially constructed and constrained, bounded by the changed social conditions of these children's lives.[58] These children understand play as a basic need for the maintenance of self, but their letters are equally clear about how the difficulties of meeting that need—the real limitations on their mode and time for play—alter with their new environment.

Just as these letters defend the children's right to fun—to wildness, daring, and noise—against the expectations of the middle-class homes in which

58. Johan Huizinga, *Homo Ludens: A Study of the Play Element in Culture* (Boston: Beacon Press, 1950), 8.

they now dwell, the remarks directed to the street children still living in Society Lodging Houses counter work-centered preconceptions of farm life and
insist that fun is possible outside of New York: "I think there is as much fun
as in New York for nuts and apples are free," one boy writes, though the letter goes on to suggest that less edible aspects of the New York entertainment
may be harder to find in Indiana: he asks whether "FATTY" could send him
"pictorials to read, especially *The Newsboys Pictorial.* . . . I want something
to read" (1860: 84–85). Another boy, while asking of news from the Lodging
House, vividly advertises the fun of horses and hunting:

> Please let me know how the boys in the Eleventh Ward Lodging House are get-
> ting along. Tell them we are happy, and we hope they are also; if not, let them
> come out to see us, and we will make them happy. We will let them ride on our
> mustangs, or hunt with our double-barreled shot-guns, and we will go along
> with them and show them where there is lots of game, and then they will be
> happy. I bet. (1872: 58)

Clearly, one purpose of these correspondences was to help the Lodging
Houses "secure," as the 1854 *Annual Report* put it, other children for the
placing-out program (24). Children's letters speak often of the rewards of
placing out that are consonant with the arguments mounted by the Society itself—testifying to their "good homes" (1861: 66), access to schooling, moral
reform, and monetary success. But it is clear from letters like this one that the
children also have an agenda of their own, and one as committed to preserving identity as it is to acculturation. In this boy's fantasy of leading a battalion of street children on a hunt the one-upmanship of competition with
city pleasures is speckled with nostalgia for the Lodging House community
of boys: this boy locates his happiness in the imagined possibility of mingling
in play the parts of his life that have been severed by his move west.

Because their labor in these new families is largely domestic in nature, the
assertion of this need to play appears more disruptive and troubling in girls.
In a long letter a man in Peoria lays out the *"pro* and *con"* of keeping a girl
named Elizabeth (1857: 51). The pros include her intelligence, "musical genius," physical weakness, and moral need (1857: 52). Of the cons he writes:

> She is a very bad girl. I cannot say that she is *immoral.* I have had fears and sus-
> picions, but she assures me that she is not guilty of indecency in speech or con-
> duct. She is bad in the sense of impudent, stubborn, disobedient, hot tempered,
> and ungrateful. . . .
> And now, dear sir, when I tell you that I have young children, of whom it is

necessary that Elizabeth should take charge, and that I am burdened with anxiety with regard to the influence such a girl must exert on them, you will understand why I am not desirous to keep her. I say nothing of the peace of my family
or the trouble the girl causes me; but the question is—*Is it my duty to risk the
ruin of my children?* . . .

   With regard to her position in my family, I have not adopted her as my
child, but we wish to make her, and have her consider herself, as one of the
family; not as a servant. And just in this particular, we have great difficulty with
her; she persists in the closest intimacy with our kitchen servant, which for her
own sake and for the sake of order in our household, we cannot allow.

   With regard to my treatment of her . . . I have on two occasions, inflicted a
slight punishment. . . . I would not treat a *servant* so; but my children often
need and receive chastisement. (1857: 51–52)

Charged with care of the children but not a servant, one of the family but not
adopted—this letter is riven by the contradictory nature of Elizabeth's place
in the household. How much simpler and freer to be a servant—permitted
the intimacies of kitchen friendships and safe from the rod. As this letter
makes abundantly clear, there are no imaginative structures that can accom-
modate the wild play of the street into the proper domestic work of girls.
Girls' impudence cannot be recuperated for a capitalist enterprise, but rather
threatens to disrupt the order of the household and ruin the children.
   An unusually indulgent western family, with no children of their own,
writes to the Children's Aid Society that the boy they have taken in "is full of
fun and play; and seems to be as happy as the happiest." This letter recognizes and approves the child's sense of play and presents those traits in easy
balance with the industry and piety that the family also prizes. The letter goes
on to describe the boy's work habits, schooling, and church attendance, and
concludes with the observation that "we feel that it is a great responsibility
to train a child for the active duties of this life, but much more responsible for
the never-ending ages of eternity" (1860: 75). The boy writes too, and his letter similarly juxtaposes work and play, his responsibilities for the cows, his
successes at school, and his boast-worthy collection of toys.

   My large top will spin four minutes; I have got an India-rubber ball, and a boat
   that I made myself with a man on it, such as I used to see in New York. I have
   got a kite and a windmill, besides a good many other playthings. . . . I have got
   a large, nice sled—it is the nicest sled but H___'s; you can't think what good
   times we had sliding down hill last winter on the snow. (1860: 76)

His toys are an interesting mix of the made and the bought, the rustic and the commercial. His attitudes toward play appear similarly double, as clearly for this boy the "good times" of sledding cannot be fully disentangled from the consciousness of having one of the nicest sleds. If the play on city streets appears largely to be about expenditure—of energy and resources—this middle-class play appears to be more about possession.

A family who has taken in "a daughter of a drunken mother," as Brace puts it in his header to this letter, appears similarly doting:

> Being a cabinet-maker myself, I have furnished her with a small bureau, bedstead, &c., and she has learned to take care of her own and her doll's clothes, and seems to take pride in keeping her things nice. We call her S__ A__, and consider her our own. (1862: 48–49)

Yet this letter need not balance work and play, since for this girl play is itself a kind of domestic apprenticeship, where the girl learns the household skills her "drunken" mother could not teach her. If the cabinet-maker and his wife have made of her a doll of their own, even to the extent of changing her name, this is only possible because the non-domestic family from which she comes can be so easily and thoroughly discounted.

Letters like these elaborate the ways in which play—which marked street identities—can also express incorporation into rural and middle-class values, and hence how conceptions of play themselves change with shifting class position. The letters these children send back to their Lodging Houses thus participate to a surprising degree in the chiasmic imaginings of class and play that characterize middle-class discourses on childhood. The children recognize how their new lives within middle-class households gain them far greater access to material conditions that facilitate play (toys, horses, and the security of meals and homes) and yet find in these comfortable settings a far more anxious conception of what it means to play.

Through the philanthropic publication of their life-stories and letters the children furnished a kind of real-life sentimental narration: allowing middle-class readers to imagine and sympathize with the horrors of the street, and to feel beneficent satisfaction over accounts of rescue and reform made possible by their contributions. The 1857 *Annual Report* included, for example, a detailed vignette describing a twelve-year-old orphan's efforts to support herself "by selling wax-matches" and recounting her gratitude at being relocated by the Society to "a fine home" in Pennsylvania (1857: 42). The report ends with a touching letter from the girl that affirms the Society's reformist agenda: "I have got acquainted with good girls who do not say bad words. . . . I hope I will never see the bad girls of New York again," she writes (1857: 42–43). Yet in the *Report* for 1858 there is another letter "from the little match girl" which, although it certainly attests to her pleasures in her new life, nevertheless suggests this sentimental tale of reform might be read slightly differently by the children themselves: "[Mr. Jessup] gave me one of your reports. I could not help laughing when I saw my letter there. . . . I should be glad to have you send me some of your Reports, they are so interesting to me" (1858: 64). What accounts for her laughter? Is it amusement at her own younger self, delight in seeing her words in print, or a recognition—not unlike the laughter of the newsboys listening to Paddy's speech—of the ways in which her letters play along with the Society's program, knowingly producing the patterns of gratitude and reform that the situation requires? Even as her first letter affirms her separation from the "bad girls of New York," her interest in the *Reports* indicates how these publications often functioned for the children as a kind of community newspaper, a means of preserving past relations and identities, a way to keep track, as one letter put it, of "how they are all in the City, and how times are there" (1859: 45). One boy, who clearly views the *Reports* in these terms, voiced his dissatisfaction with the Society's protective practice of publishing children's letters anonymously. His letter appears under the all-caps heading "LETTER FROM L. D. SMITH, ELLSWORTH O":

> But I want to tell you something, that is, when a boy writes a letter to you, do you put it in the book that has the letters from the boys printed, the Annual Report, because my people out here would like to see my name in it, and I want you to send me a record, when they are out, for 1861, and try to have my name in it; well I guess I have said all about that I do know now, and I must bid you good-by for a while. (1861: 57)

In thus cooperating with young Smith's aspirations the Society figures itself as an indulgent parent, and the *Annual Reports,* for all their altruistic and business concerns, function as a kind of toy, the street children's version of the juvenile newspapers that were circulated and exchanged among young "pressmen."

    "The Pile of Maggots," the oyster dinner, the child who "must have some fun," the children the Lodging Houses repeatedly fail to "secure," all testify to the inability of reformist discourse to fully contain these unruly subjects. Just so the girl's laugh intimates that the publication of these letters serves for her a different function than the reformist and sentimental harvest of donations and tears. Given the conditions of cultural production and preservation, it is hardly surprising that I have evidence for a far more detailed account of how the play of street children shapes middle-class identity than I do for how it matters to the children themselves. Images of the street child at play teach the middle class about the pleasures of circulation and expenditure and justify the "free play" of capital. Stories of street children's vulnerability and pathos elicit the generous sympathy of middle-class readers—distinguishing each caring individual from the exploitive system that produces such suffering. Which is to say that these apparently opposing images functionally support each other in exonerating the middle class's increasing self-identification with childhood leisure. For street children, however, play serves not as a measure of leisure but as a mechanism of resistance, a means of claiming autonomy and pleasure on their own, nonproductive terms—of thumbing their noses at the middle-class values that this same play nevertheless helps to install. And yet in recognizing this resistance we see as well the difference that is gender: how for girls—who have no imaginable place in the play of the market, except in the terms of sexual vice at which Brace shudders—there is no way to figure work as a game.

Raising Empires Like Children

Domestic Empires: Questioning the Boundaries of the Home

In the rearing of each and every child the processes of social formation are reproduced in miniature. Earlier chapters detail what this entailed in the construction of class identity, household economies, and familial feeling, as well as in the validation of literary culture. Here I focus on the forging of national identity, under the combined pressures of geography, religion, and race. The analogy between nation and nursery, which in the nineteenth century motivated the production of a veritable sea of cheap moral tracts for children, also informs my critique of these writings. As the title of this chapter suggests, I am interested in these tracts because in the didactic baldness of their rhetoric they explicitly articulate the felt similitudes between the national projects of raising good, white, middle-class, Christian, American children and raising an economic and cultural American empire. In particular, Sunday school stories about mission work—with their emphasis on national, religious, and racial difference—provide an acutely legible account of anxieties over national identity and of the hope that the properly reared child might

An earlier version of chapter 5 appeared as "Raising Empires Like Children: Race, Nation, and Religious Education," *American Literary History* (November 1996): 399–425. Reprinted by permission of Oxford University Press.

resolve all such troubles. Thus in these stories, concerns about foreign heathens and America's global role reflect upon a whole host of internal worries
over how to incorporate the nation's own racial and religious others. African
Americans in slavery and then emancipation, Native Americans and the policies of Indian removal, non-Protestant immigrants arriving in unprecedented
numbers—all of these populations put intense pressure on the nation's future, and hence on its vision of childhood. The image of American imperialism I find in these stories is in many ways quite familiar, but in other ways it
offers significant challenges to our usual assumptions about the relations between world, nation, and household and locates the threats posed by otherness not so much outside as within.

By the 1880s the United States was the world's largest source of Protestant
missionaries to the "heathen." Increasingly, these missionaries were women,
missionary wives and unmarried female missionaries together accounting
for 60 percent of the American mission force by 1890. This feminization of
the foreign mission movement coincided both with the rapid growth in American missions abroad and with the United States' increasing interest in international expansion. Transporting their Victorian bric-a-brac and their domestic behaviors and ideals to Asia and Africa as well as to the un-Christian tribes
and slums within United States territory, these women are clear embodiments of a domestic empire.[1] Their evangelical expansionism suggests the
inadequacy of those discussions of American imperialism that would cast the
adventures of empire-building as a reaction against, and a manly alternative
to, the bourgeois, feminine home culture of sentimentality and domesticity.[2]
It also reveals the limits of most accounts of the nineteenth-century domestic ideal. Although critical analysis of the culture of domesticity has proven

---

1. Jane Hunter, *The Gospel of Gentility: American Women Missionaries in Turn-of-the-
Century China* (New Haven, Conn.: Yale University Press, 1984), xiii. Hunter's book provides
the richest account of the meanings of foreign mission work for evangelical American women,
including the concept of "domestic empire" (chapter 5). Peggy Pascoe, in *Relations of Rescue:
The Search for Female Moral Authority in the American West, 1874–1939* (New York: Oxford
University Press, 1990), reveals similar patterns of self-empowerment and self-sacrifice, cultural
empathy, and cultural chauvinism in the work of female missionaries during this same period
in the western United States.

2. The literature of American imperialism repeatedly enacts a rejection of domesticity, but
the best recent discussions of this literature reveal that such reactions are linked and are cultur-
ally dependent upon each other. See Lora Romero, "Vanishing Americans: Gender, Empire, and
New Historicism," in *The Culture of Sentiment: Race, Gender, and Sentimentality in Nineteenth-
Century America,* ed. Shirley Samuels (New York: Oxford University Press, 1992), 115–27; Amy
Kaplan, *The Anarchy of Empire in the Making of U.S. Culture* (Cambridge: Harvard University
Press, 2002), especially chapter 1; and Laura Wexler, *Tender Violence: Domestic Visions in an
Age of U.S. Imperialism* (Chapel Hill: University of North Carolina Press, 2000).

increasingly concerned with the permeability of the period's putatively separate—male or female, public or private—spheres, for the most part the
nineteenth-century "Empire of the Mother" remains conceptually unencum-
bered by the continental and global projects of building an American Empire.[3] In studying the stories about missionary work published at mid-century,
I demonstrate that these manifestations of imperial domesticity were already
anticipated in the relations Sunday school stories construct between the
American child, home, nation, and the world beyond.[4] Such narratives precede and produce the complexly gendered contours of American international imperialism and coincide with America's continental expansion. The
childhood reading of two generations of empire-builders, male and female,
these stories inform both the rhetoric of extreme gender division and the
reality of intertwined institutions that would characterize America's global
posture by the end of the century.

On the copyright page of his 1849 collection *Tales for Little Readers, about
the Heathen,* Dr. John Scudder advertises his ambitious goals for this volume:

> Should the eye of any Christian father or mother rest upon [this book] I would
> ask them if they have not a son or daughter to dedicate to the *missionary* work.
> The duty of devoting themselves to this work of Christ, or at least, of consecrat-
> ing to it their money, their efforts, and their prayers, is the great duty to be per-
> severingly and prayerfully impressed on the minds of our children. A generation
> thus trained would, with aid from on high, soon effect the moral revolution of
> the world.[5]

The belief that individual and domestic piety can change the world underlies
all sentimental writing; it is, for example, what Catharine Beecher and Harriet Beecher Stowe claim for "Christian families" as they "go forth to shine
'as lights of the world' in all the now darkened nations." There is hardly any
need to stress the imperialistic correlative in the grandeur of such visions. Cit-

3. Mary Ryan's *The Empire of the Mother: American Writing about Domesticity, 1830–1860*
(New York: Harrington Park Press, 1985), for example, never discusses "empire" in its geopolitical sense.

4. Laura Wexler argues for the importance of extending our analysis of sentimental and
domestic fiction beyond the 1870s—when literary production declines—into the period of "its
concrete social institutionalization in schools, hospitals, prisons, and so on, whose building,
staffing and operation quite naturally had to lag behind the literary imagination." My practice
here inverts this project, looking back in time from the burgeoning of missionary activity to its
literary sources in didactic juvenile fiction. Wexler, *Tender Violence,* 102–3.

5. [John Scudder], *Dr. Scudder's Tales for Little Readers, about the Heathen* (New York:
American Tract Society, 1849), 4.

ing this passage, Jane Tompkins speaks in celebratory tones of *The American Woman's Home* as "a blueprint for colonizing the world in the name of the 'family state.'" She can applaud domestic expansion without irony, because she is convinced that the Beecher sisters' domestic colonization offers an "alternative" to the nationalist and capitalist varieties of imperialism.[6] Scudder's tales from specific "darkened nations" inhabited by dark-skinned people substantiate the racial content of Beecher's and Stowe's domestic vision and suggest that, far from alternatives, the moral revolution of the world in the image of American, Christian domesticity and the more traditionally recognized economic and political forms of American imperialism are reciprocally interdependent. Depicting the child as a world evangelizer, Sunday school writing on mission work makes explicit the connections between domestic order and international order. My readings of these texts, unlike Tompkins's approach to sentimental fiction, are essentially ironic. The irony stems from the recognition that connections between domesticity and world mission, home and nation, faith and race that Sunday school stories find unproblematic nevertheless work to prop repressive imperialist policies and practices. Indeed, their very stance of innocence and the children who embody it are what make Sunday school stories such useful tools of empire.[7]

In a characteristic instance of such masking, while Sunday school stories of mission work may stress devotion, the primary activity asked of missionary children is collecting money. Religious educators believed that the exoticism of missionary tales would attract child readers unmoved by the more standard—and generically local—Sunday school lessons. Among "objects which appeal with special interest to the young," a writer observed in the *Sunday School Times,* "we may name two which always interest them,—missions to the heathen, and missions which have for their object the establishing of Sunday Schools in neglected neighborhoods."[8] Such interest was often pecuniary as well as literary, and by mid-century collections for both varieties

6. Jane Tompkins, *Sensational Designs: The Cultural Work of American Fiction, 1790–1860* (New York: Oxford University Press, 1985), 144. Tompkins quotes from Catharine E. Beecher and Harriet Beecher Stowe, *The American Woman's Home: or, Principles of Domestic Science; Being a Guide to the Formation and Maintenance of Economical, Healthful, Beautiful, and Christian Homes* (New York: J. B. Ford and Co., 1869), 458–59. It is worth noting that Hunter's study of missionary women at the turn of the century begins with a similar quotation from Catharine Beecher's 1842 *Treatise on Domestic Economy* (xiii).

7. In this way the child readers and characters of Sunday school fiction provide for missionary work the kind of "innocent eye" that Laura Wexler locates in the similarly domestic and imperial project of female photographers. See *Tender Violence*, 6–7.

8. "Missionary Collections in the Sunday Schools," *Sunday School Times* 12 (October 8, 1870): 648.

of mission work were a regular part of most Sunday school curricula, justified by the hope that the habit of donating pennies would teach self-denial.[9]
The double claims of economics and devotion are emblematized in the praises
one story bestows on a little girl whose three-cent pieces, kept in a red leather
purse "with a gold lettered motto on it to—'be economical' . . . have been
rubbed up with chalk Saturday afternoon, on purpose to have them bright to
put in the missionary box."[10] If the rather luxurious leather and gilt purse
with its economical motto embodies the contradictions of the bourgeoisie,
the carefully shined pennies that fill it demonstrate the success of the missionary endeavor in sanctifying and separating itself from the commercial
realm. These coins brightened by a child's hand are no longer mere imple-
ments of exchange; they have become tokens of faith. Like Peggy's "Threepenny Bit" or the "money" Scudder puts first—before efforts or prayers—in
his list of what children should consecrate to mission work, these pennies suggest how, through the evocation of a child, economic concerns can be transformed into domestic piety.

In *Self-Denial; or Alice Wood and Her Missionary Society,* donating money
constitutes the story's entire plot.[11] Alice Wood founds a sewing society, pro-
posing that "while we sew . . . one reads aloud from some interesting book
or paper about missions and benevolent societies, and thus we shall all become interested in the intelligence, and be more willing to work and save to
help the needy" (8). What they sew would raise money for missionary work.
But more money derives from acts of self-denial—the group's decision to
forgo the candy shop, or individual pledges like that of Clara Hall:

> her father had promised her a quarter of a dollar if she would have an ugly
> double tooth drawn that had ached for some time. . . . "But," said she, "Alice

9. Anne M. Boylan, *Sunday School: The Formation of an American Institution, 1790–1880*
(New Haven, Conn.: Yale University Press, 1988), 46–48. On page 47 Boylan reprints an elegant
1869 certificate of "Life Membership" in a Sabbath School Missionary Society acknowledging
one girl's donations to missionary work. Such documents suggest that mission charity could
have its own social rewards.

10. Aunt Fanny [Frances Elizabeth Mease Barrow], *All Sorts of Pop-guns* (New York: Sheldon and Co., 1864), 77. These shiny pennies are donated at a Presbyterian "Anniversary Missionary Meeting" where it is reported that over the year the children had raised $910 to support
mission work, supplying not only tracts and Bibles but also the salary of "Rev. Mr. Lewis, the
good Western missionary. Only think how grand! A real minister supported in his noble work
by the children themselves! I can tell you what, when they think of *their own missionary* they
feel just as happy and proud as can be" (81).

11. *Self-Denial; or Alice Wood and Her Missionary Society.* This tiny anonymous volume,
barely three inches high, lists no place or date of publication, but the American Antiquarian Society postulates that it was printed by the American Sunday School Union in Philadelphia, in 1846.

the very next time it aches as hard in the day as it does sometimes in the night, I
shall come with the tooth in one hand, and the quarter of a dollar in the other,
for the society." (15–16)

An offering in each hand, Clara gives both a bit of her body and the money
it yields "for the society." Like Christ, she would trade her own pain for the
spiritual salvation of others, though in the ugliness of the tooth, and in
Clara's strategies of deferral, her gift retains decidedly mundane limits. The
concluding pages of this little book affirm, however, that the good thus ac-
cumulated in intelligence and quarters will ultimately prove limitless.

> we shall never know, till the secrets of the last great day are disclosed, how
> much good such an association may have accomplished; how many souls the
> Bibles thus sent forth may have converted; and then, too, how much good these
> converts may have done in teaching the way of life to others, and these again to
> hundreds and thousands more. (26–27)

This faith in expansion, secret but unerring, characterizes both evangelical
Christianity and the hopes for a more global market that flourished in a
swiftly commercializing America. The role of missionaries in tapping raw
materials and producing new markets has long been a historical commonplace. What interests me is how the figure of the child comes to occupy, and
so domesticate, this rhetoric of evangelical and economic expansion.

For child missionaries like Clara and Alice, heathen children—those un-
numbered recipients of their domestic largess—prove desirable commodities. Lydia Sigourney suggests that supporting the mission education of a
heathen child "is a delightful charity for the children of a Christian land. If a
number of them join and pay the annual expense, they may be permitted to
give a name to the child, and have the pleasure of feeling that they are its
benefactors."[12] Society members may be asked to walk past the penny-store
or to have their teeth pulled; but such acts of self-denial yield compensatory
pleasures, enabling them to redeem—that is, to buy—a heathen child.

The stories these tracts tell merge the sentimental, feminine, religious basis of domesticity with the aggressive, masculine, economic, and military
project of imperialism in both ideological and rhetorical terms. As a genre
they blur traditional gender boundaries, commingling accounts of violence
and danger with the conventionally domestic rhetoric of sentiment and piety.

---

12. [Lydia Sigourney], *How to be Happy. Written for the Children of Some Dear Friends. By
a Lady* (Hartford, Conn., 1833), 60.

Captain Frederick Marryat produced two juvenile retellings of the *Swiss Family Robinson,* that most famous instance of the construction of a home as an adventure. He prefaced *The Mission: or Scenes in Africa Written for Young People* with a celebration of this very combination as the source of his scenes' "most salutary tendency; for while they inculcate many profound principles of revealed truth, adapted especially to juvenile and domestic readers, they also encourage the noblest spirit and exertions of active philanthropy."[13] In such remarks the active and the domestic may seem in opposition, as they often do in Marryat's descriptions of warriors turned Christian where the many pages precisely and gleefully depicting "a Mantee fighting wildly against numbers with ten or twelve arrows and spears pierced in his body" (2: 38) contrast with the bland lack of detail in the single paragraph that portrays a warrior chief once "he became a peacemaker and a Christian . . . his whole life was devoted to acts of kindness and charity—to instructing and exhorting" (2: 58). But though the warrior may be felt to produce more readerly and writerly pleasure than the peacemaker, such pleasure is itself understood as the lure that would induce children to learn the lessons of Christianity by suffusing the Sunday school regime of instructing and exhorting and the domestic virtues of kindness and charity with the exotic exhilaration of African warfare. Sunday school stories work to forge rhetorical links between what remain distinctly separate cultural arenas. The resulting imagery can, however, prove quite disquieting, as when in Aunt Fanny's *Pop-gun* anthologies each piece is introduced by the image of a woman with raised rifle, whose gun—"Make Ready, Present, Fire"—shoots off a fitting moral for the narrative that follows (fig. 5.1). The woman's "BANG" purports to rid the household of evil, and so to protect the children clinging to her skirts. Yet this image of a fully martial domesticity must have been far from comforting for its child readers, since her targets are also children, arrayed like caught criminals with their hands raised. They were perhaps intended to represent childish vices, but there are no clear symbolic markings that would let us read one as vanity and another as greed, and so dismiss as allegory the little corpse shot down by this didactic gun.

The difficulty in interpreting Aunt Fanny's pop-guns as either a defense or an explosion of the domestic suggests the remarkably complex—even contradictory—flexibility of the relation between the domestic and the adventurous that structures these missionary tales. If in Marryat's scenes adventures serve to attract readers to quite unadventurous virtues, in Mrs. Lovechild's

13. Captain Frederick Marryat, *The Mission: or Scenes in Africa Written for Young People,* 2 vols. (New York: Geo. S. Appleton, 1845), 1: prefatory note.

The illustration contains the following text: LITTLE BEN. / "BE GRATEFUL FOR HAPPY HOMES." / BANG! / FIRE! / MAKE READY / PRESENT! / ABOUT a year ago, a little old gentleman was walking in Fifth Avenue, in the city of New York. He had a hooked nose, with a pair of gold spectacles sitting on the top of it, and

Fig. 5.1. Shooting out the moral "be grateful for happy homes," this illustration introduces the story of "Little Ben," which describes urban mission work in the notorious Five Points area of New York City, where "happy homes" are deemed impossible. Aunt Fanny [Frances Elizabeth Mease Barrow], *All Sorts of Pop-guns* (New York: Sheldon and Co., 1864), 121. Copyright © American Antiquarian Society.

"The Missionary" a domestic sensibility leads to African exploits.[14] The tale
begins by describing a young boy who "thought more and more on the miserable ones who had no Bible. He bought all the books which told of their
condition, and often his mother found him in his room weeping" (85). This
proclivity to tears, this sentimental capacity to be affected by the representation of another's suffering, has a distinctly domestic locus: the boy's sentimental response is concealed within his room and discovered by his mother.
But this is not ultimately a story of interiority where the tears of identification count as action; instead the boy becomes a missionary and the story becomes an account of adventures.

> Often he had to swim rivers and walk over burning deserts in order to reach vil-
> lages in which he hoped to do some good. Once he was bitten by a serpent and
> nearly lost his life, at another time he lost his way in a jungle, or thicket of
> brakes, and was saved from a tiger only by creeping under the matted roots, and
> concealing himself until the animal had passed by. (87–88)

The desert, the jungle are no place for tears; one who cries concealed among
matted roots risks not a mother's but a tiger's detection. This apparent replacement of sentiment with action does not, however, conform to the anti-
domestic imperialist model in which manly adventures are understood as a
rejection or fleeing from the too sentimental and feminine home. After all,
the "good" for which the missionary swims rivers and crosses deserts is the
good exemplified by the American Christian home. Indeed, the good the
missionary brings may prove to be the very ability to cry. In *Scenes in the
Wilderness,* the account of Zeisberger's mission to "a tribe of Indians living
on the banks of the Susquehanna" is full of "toil and danger" compensated
finally by the Indians' conversion to a Christianity most clearly marked by
softhearted tears:

> "Whenever," said one of the converts, "I saw a man shed tears, I used to look
> upon him with contempt. I would not have wept though my enemies had cut
> my flesh from my bones. It is of God that I now weep, who has made my hard
> heart soft."[15]

14. Mrs. Lovechild, "The Missionary," in *The Christmas Tree and Other Stories for the
Young* (Boston: William H. Hill Jr., 1863).
15. *Scenes in the Wilderness* (Philadelphia: American Sunday School Union, 1846), 7, 9,
and 14.

Thus in these stories weeping can not only prompt adventure, but serve as its telos. Sentimental tears are themselves what missionary action brings to the wilderness.

Domestic Empires: Questioning the Boundaries of the Nation

The notion of a domestic empire seems oxymoronic not only because it would conflate—as these stories do—home and world, faith and pennies, inward sentiment and expansionist adventure, but also because in geopolitical terms it would erase the distinction between the national and the international. Empires occur, the modern European model has taught us, when a nation's reign extends beyond national boundaries—that is, when its hegemony exceeds the domestic. For a nation constructed through the displacement of native peoples and the accretion of a diverse immigrant population—both voluntary and involuntary—the otherness that classic colonialism would continue to regard as foreign remains still other and yet somehow inside the national home. Marryat and Mrs. Lovechild describe missions to Africa, Aunt Fanny's story of "Little Ben" tells of an urban mission in New York, and Zeisberger's missionary work lies along the Susquehanna. The fluidity of American identity and borders, which allows these stories to locate the otherness in need of civilizing both within and without, differentiates American imperialism from most European models and exempts the United States from most theoretical accounts. The acquisition and permanent control of colonies was only an explicit aim of United States policy between 1898 and 1912, yet America's mid-nineteenth-century rhetoric of national identity and expansion reveals, as Amy Kaplan succinctly puts it, "United States nation-building and empire-building as historically coterminous and mutually defining."[16] Indeed, the very contested (domestic) nature of American imperialism makes it an important site for historical and theoretical analysis: in a fundamental way the case of the United States of America embodies

16. Amy Kaplan, "'Left Alone with America': The Absence of Empire in the Study of American Culture," introduction to *The Cultures of United States Imperialism,* ed. Amy Kaplan and Donald Pease (Durham, N.C.: Duke University Press, 1993), 17. Kaplan argues that there have been "three salient absences that continue to structure the way we think about the cultures of U.S. imperialism . . . the absence of culture from the history of U.S. imperialism; the absence of empire from the study of American culture; and the absence of the United States from the postcolonial study of imperialism" (11). In this chapter I seek to participate in the project of redressing these absences. To note these exclusions in U.S. historiography may say much about the myths of exceptionalism America tells about itself, but it does not imply that the United States' national/imperial formation is necessarily exceptional.

what Benedict Anderson describes as "the inner incompatibility of empire and nation."[17]

Although these Sunday school texts clearly depend on European and especially British precedents—many tracts published in America simply reprint European material, and the most famous British missionaries (David Livingston, Robert Moffat, etc.) are familiar presences even in tracts written in the United States—the internal, domestic contours of American imperialism make even an identical tract mean differently once it has crossed the Atlantic. For example, *Ten Books Beautifully Illustrated for Children*, printed and distributed by the Protestant Episcopal Society for the Promotion of Evangelical Knowledge in New York, speaks of "our little English children" in a manner which indicates the collection's origin in the Anglican church; yet surely the meaning of tales titled "The Wild Karen Boy," "The Little Hindoo," or the "Little Bushman" is different for an American reader. It differs not only because the American child's relation to these "little heathens" is less straightforwardly colonial than that of the English child, but also because the collection contains the story of "A Missionary in North America" and his praise for a "little Indian [who] thought nothing of going back 100 miles over a stormy lake, in his little canoe, where he was tossing about for nine days, *alone* to recover his Bible." It differs, that is, because although there are no representations of heathen children in England, the place of the American child is produced as a site of missionary action, a place where children must still be civilized into a bravely devout Christianity.[18]

Even within tracts written in America, a description of New York City can sound virtually indistinguishable from one of Calcutta:

17. See Benedict Anderson, *Imagined Communities: Reflections on the Origins and Spread of Nationalism* (New York: Verso, 1991), 88–89.

18. *Ten Books Beautifully Illustrated for Children* (New York: Protestant Episcopal Society for the Promotion of Evangelical Knowledge, 1861). Each "book" has its own pagination, and the phrase "our little English children" appears frequently—see especially "The Little Hindoo," 8 ("How many of our little English children have not the dread of sin, nor yet the love of God, which was shown by this little Hindoo?"). The story of the American Indian boy is titled "Love for the Bible"; quotations are from pages 2 and 6.

Other English collections do describe urban mission work and even juxtapose it with tales from missions abroad, but in these cases though there may be a strong sense of class difference, the "Ragged Scholars" of London are in no way represented as un-English. See the American republication of three British tracts: *The Ragged Scholars, Perils in the Desert,* and *The Avenger Stayed* (Philadelphia: Presbyterian Board of Publications, n.d. [1850–57?]). Stories of urban missions to cities in the contiguous subject nations of Ireland, Scotland, and Wales occupy an ambiguous middle position—not so other as India, but just as surely not English. See, for example, Robert Boyd, *Wee Willie; or Truth Sought and Found* (Chicago: Henry A. Sumner, 1870), for the American reprinting of a tale about mission work in Edinburgh.

This mission-school was opened in one of the many dreary moral wastes in the city of New York where there is no Sabbath, no church, and no Sunday-school; where scarcely a Bible can be found in any habitation; where the houses are crowded with emigrants; where the streets swarm with miserable, ragged, half-civilized children; and where the haunts of sin and shame are seen on every side.[19]

Indeed, many suggested that such a "half-civilized" child was "worse off than the heathen, for he lived in a Christian land, and yet had no one to tell him of Jesus."[20] Where in the midst of this "swarm" can national identity be located? What makes this a "Christian land"?[21] The notion of a "half-civilized" child thus marks a fault-line in America, suggesting the partial nature of national identity in a nation built by expansion and immigration. Moreover, the situation of this "half-civilized" child evokes connections between the two meanings of "domestic" at play in my readings. For, as Charles Loring Brace similarly asserted when founding his Newsboy Lodging Houses, part of what makes New York seem so foreign and these children only partially or ambivalently American is the absence of homes. The narrator speaks of "habitations," of "houses . . . crowded with emigrants," of "streets" and "haunts," all explicit signs for the lack of that tranquil and loving familial enclosure the Beecher sisters celebrated as the American Home.

The succor the mission school promises to bring to a half-civilized, homeless, and decidedly alien New York is not one that fully extinguishes other-

19. *Maria Cheeseman or the Candy Girl* (Philadelphia: American Sunday School Union, 1855), 15–16. Writing of New York, Christine Stansell remarks that "By the 1830s, the enclosures of laboring people were coming to constitute separate territories, so extensive and distinct that they seemed to genteel observers something like a foreign domain." This sense of foreignness only increased as the century progressed. Stansell, *City of Women: Sex and Class in New York, 1789–1860* (New York: Alfred A. Knopf, 1986), 41–42.

20. Barrow, "Little Ben," in *All Sorts of Pop-guns*, 139.

21. The problem was intensified, moreover, by the narrowness with which these Protestant missionaries defined Christianity quite explicitly to exclude the Catholics who were migrating to America in ever-increasing numbers. [Helen Cross Knight], *The Missionary Cabinet* (Boston: Massachusetts Sabbath School Repository, 1847), for example, offers a case-by-case description of "idols" now housed above the Boston Mission Society offices and collected by missionaries from converts who have learned "to pray to Jesus" instead of worshiping these "bits of wood, clay or stone"; the collection includes not only relics and figures of saints but even images of the crucifixion:

Old coats and old bones cannot save your souls, can they, my dear children? No, nothing but what Jesus has done for you can do that. You must pity the Catholics very much. . . . Here is a stone with Jesus on the cross carved on it used by Catholics. . . . They really worship *that image,* and say their prayers to it, without much thought of the Jesus who is in heaven. (38–39)

ness. A few pages later the same narrator who saw "haunts of sin and shame" offers to replace that "dreary moral waste" with this visionary idyll:

> Let the eye wander over the area from river to river, on any Sunday looking in upon a band of German children here, reading the Bible in the language of their fatherland; and there upon a school of Jewish children, reading the New Testament. Farther on is a collection of ragged news boys and in another place a class of Chinese. . . . In the instruction of these schools some of the best energy, talent, and piety of the church is acting upon the worst and most degraded elements of society. It is like the sunlight breaking in upon the clouds and chaos of an unfinished creation.[22]

Differences of language, original religion, class, and race all seem reconcilable before the Christianizing and Americanizing force of these mission schools. A finished creation, a perfected nation, would not contain such "chaos." Yet ranged in their separate classes, this vision offers not a New York rid of its heterogeneity, nor a city that thrives upon difference, but rather a diverse population put in good (Christian) order. Anxiety over how to achieve such order—how to create and preserve a national identity capable of containing (in both senses of the word) swarms of internal aliens—informs these Sunday school stories about mission work. The solution imagined here seems to lie in refraining from fully absorbing this otherness—in continuing to identify the alien as alien. The very fact of a mission school oddly serves to un-Americanize its students by marking them as others in need of conversion. Thus the paradoxical task of consolidating a domestic empire accounts for one of the most striking features of these Sunday school stories: how little it seems to matter whether the missionary subject is located inside or outside United States borders. Or better yet, I should say that it is precisely because the contested nature of American borders and American identity matters so much that these stories refuse to distinguish between internal and external "heathens."

Coloring American Faith

The project of consolidating a national or racial American identity I have traced within these stories may seem at odds with their explicit evangelism. After all, the goal of a world mission evokes a global Christianity that would seem to dissolve rather than confirm national divisions. Similarly, the pro-

22. *Maria Cheeseman,* 26–27.

cess of conversion affirms the spiritual value of national and racial others, insisting on the significance of "not race, but grace" for mission work. Indeed, historians of nineteenth-century American missionaries have noted that in their discourse—if not always in their practice—mission workers generally rejected the biological determinism that characterized scientific racialism during the second half of the nineteenth century. In opposition to the scientific and increasingly popular contention that, as George W. Stocking summarized it, "race and culture were linked in a single evolutionary hierarchy extending from the dark-skinned savage to the civilized white man," mission workers distinguished between race and culture, affirming that dark-skinned people were capable of embracing Christian beliefs, values, and even behaviors.[23] What Christianity entailed for American missionaries, however, remains not only spiritual but also cultural: their strategy of conversion appears antithetical to racial determinism but it fully supports an ethnocentric cultural imperialism.[24] These poles merely delimit the spectrum of missionary practice, enabling, for example, Alexander Crummell and other black American missionaries to link the celebration of a pan-Africanist culture with the "evangelization and enlightenment of heathen Africa."[25] The categories for

23. George W. Stocking Jr., *Race, Culture and Evolution: Essays in the History of Anthropology* (New York: Free Press, 1968), vii. For other important studies of scientific racialism see William Stanton, *The Leopard's Spots: Scientific Attitudes toward Race in America, 1815–1859* (Chicago: University of Chicago Press, 1960); John S. Haller Jr., *Outcasts from Evolution: Scientific Attitudes of Racial Inferiority, 1859–1900* (Urbana: University of Illinois Press, 1971); and Thomas Gossett, *Race: The History of an Idea in America* (Dallas, Tex.: Southern Methodist University Press, 1963).

Michael C. Coleman, "Not Race, but Grace: Presbyterian Missionaries and American Indians, 1837–1893," *Journal of American History* 67 (June 1980): 41–60, and Peggy Pascoe, "Home Mission Women, Race, and Culture: The Case of Native Helpers," in her *Relations of Rescue,* 112–46, both argue that mission work entailed rejecting or simply ignoring the tenets of scientific racialism. Pascoe's argument is both more complex and more convincing in that she details how—despite explicit theoretical and practical rejections of racialism—hierarchical linkings of race and culture could in practice continue to limit racial equality within the mission homes. On such debates over the import of "race" vs. "civilization" Etienne Balibar writes, "I fail to see any difference [between racism and ethnocentrism], once it is a matter of the absolute, innate, 'natural' superiority of the white race, Western values, and so on." See "Paradoxes of Universality," trans. Michael Edwards, in *Nation and Narration,* ed. Homi K. Bhabha (New York: Routledge, 1990), 287.

24. American missionaries imbued this equation of Christian beliefs with nationalism, chauvinistically imagining the United States as the culmination of Christian civilization—the ideal Christian nation. See Robert Handy, *A Christian America: Protestant Hopes and Historical Realities* (New York: Oxford University Press, 1984), and James H. Moorhead, *American Apocalypse: Yankee Protestants and the Civil War, 1860–1869* (New Haven, Conn.: Yale University Press, 1978), for detailed accounts of nineteenth-century evangelical Protestants' millennial vision of creating a fully Christian America.

25. Alexander Crummell, *The Future of Africa: Being Addresses, Sermons, etc., etc., Delivered in the Republic of Liberia* (New York: Scribner's, 1862), 148.

identity provided by race, nation, and religion jostle each other, refusing to combine in any simple or predictable way. The United States' political traditions of resistance to the institutionalization of a state religion do not resolve such conflicts, but rather position everyone as a potential convert—structurally inviting internal evangelisms even as they protect religious minorities. Thus the very gap between church and state may have made the missionaries' depiction of America as the quintessential Christian nation not only more amorphous and precarious, but also more anxiously fervent.

The Red Brothers emphatically asserts the irrelevance to mission work of racial and geographic divisions:

> The European with his white skin, the olive-colored Chinaman, the tawny Hindoo, the brown Malay, the black Negro, and the red Indian of America are all alike the children of Adam. . . . If, then, we are all brothers and sisters, surely we ought to love the whole human family, and help them if we are able, though our skins may differ in color, and wide seas may divide us from one another. And in what better way can we help those we love, than by sending them the gospel of our Lord Jesus Christ?[26]

Published by the American Sunday School Union, this text does not list the white-skinned American citizen who constitutes its audience. However, the meaning of the word "we" seems to shift in this passage from the all-inclusive "whole human family" to those unlisted white Christian Americans who already possess the gospel, who read the publications of the American Sunday School Union, and who should therefore "help those we love." The odd instability of this "we" suggests the tension between a truly global Christian identity and a more localized personification of Christian virtue. Etienne Balibar, theorizing on the relation between racism and nationalism, observes that "the racial-cultural identity of the 'true-nationals' remains invisible, but it is inferred from [and assured by] its opposite, the alleged, the quasi hallucinatory visibility of the 'false nationals': 'Jews,' 'wops,' immigrants, *indios*, *natives*, blacks."[27] Thus *The Red Brothers'* apparently inclusive list of the

---

26. *The Red Brothers* (Philadelphia: American Sunday School Union, 1846), 5–6.

27. Balibar, 285. See also his "Racism as Universalism," in *New Political Science* 16 (fall/ winter 1989): 9–22, especially his discussion of how racism functions in the "process of building a community . . . creating lived ties and affects and common evidences among people in a society where, for example, kinship has ceased to be a central social structure" (18). I find Balibar the most compelling theorist of the role racism plays in the construction of nationalism. For other historical accounts of this relation that parallel and inform my work here, see: on South Africa, Kate Manzo, *Racial Nationalism and the Politics of Exclusion* (Boulder, Colo.: Lynne Rienner, 1994); on England, Paul Gilroy, *There Ain't No Black in the Union Jack* (London: Hutchinson, 1987).

"Sons of Adam" can be seen as working to infer and assure the importance of the unlisted, invisible, white, Protestant American.

The Red Brothers is just as concerned about distinguishing this American from the "European with his white skin" as from the "red Indian of America." Thus the book explains that "those who first visited [our red brethren] did not act as missionaries do now: they did not seek to do good to their souls, but to possess the country" (6). While this tract is rare in its explicit condemnation of imperialism, this very anomaly serves to emphasize how even those texts most committed to a global spiritual "family," and most critical of the strategies of conquest, remain engaged in the project of delimiting a national identity. The Europeans "who acted so unjustly and cruelly were from Christian lands" (11), and the central task of this tract is to compare their false claims to Christian practice with the true Christianity ("like their blessed Lord") of American missionaries: "instead of selling to them guns with which to shoot one another; and rum to make them drunkards, they give them the Bible, and tracts, from which they learn to be sober, and to dwell together in love" (18–19). Significantly, this tract never mentions Jacksonian policies of Indian removal—neither the "Indian Removal Bill" (1830), nor the suffering of the "Trail of Tears" (1838), nor the paternalism with which Jackson justified these forced migrations can be acknowledged in this effort to affirm America's position as the true Christian nation where the various children of Adam might dwell together in love.[28]

28. See Ronald T. Takaki, "Jackson: Metaphysician of Indian-Hating," in *Iron Cages: Race and Culture in Nineteenth-Century America* (Seattle: University of Washington Press, 1979), 92–107; and Michael Paul Rogin, *Fathers and Children: Andrew Jackson and the Subjugation of the American Indian* (New York: Knopf, 1975), for seminal discussions of how Jackson's paternalism toward his "red children"—his desire "to protect them from the mercenary influence of white men" (Takaki, "Jackson," 101) by moving them west of the Mississippi—served to disguise and justify his brutality in taking possession of Indian lands. Missionaries frequently functioned as quasi-governmental agents in the implementation of U.S. policies of acculturation and removal. Yet white missionaries had also actively participated in tribal resistance to these policies. Most famously, in 1830 eleven white clergymen working with the Cherokee were imprisoned for refusing to comply with the expulsion decree; the resulting Supreme Court ruling in *Worcester vs. Georgia* held that state law did not apply within Indian territories, and proved unenforceable under the Jackson administration. See Henry Warner Beecher, *American Indians and Christian Missions: Studies in Cultural Conflict* (Chicago: University of Chicago Press, 1981), 173–78; and William G. McLoughlin, *Cherokees and Missionaries, 1789–1839* (New Haven, Conn.: Yale University Press, 1984) on the Cherokee tactic of resistance through acculturation, including reliance on missionaries. Priscilla Wald, "Terms of Assimilation: Legislating Subjectivity in the Emerging Nation," *Boundary 2* 19 (fall 1992): 77–104 provides a chilling account of how *Worcester vs. Georgia* constructs the rights and subjectivity of American citizenship by eliding the racial and national others within United States territory.

Sunday school texts remain blithely silent on these conflicts in the missionary's role. For example, *The Choctaw Girl* (Philadelphia: American Sunday School Union, 1835) begins by ex-

"Denial," Homi K. Bhabha writes of the contradictions of postcolonial identity formation, "is always a retroactive process; a half acknowledgement that otherness has left its traumatic mark." The trauma for national identity that the *Red Brothers'* silence would deny is simultaneously racial and religious, for if Christian civilization gives content to American identity, racial distinctions provide the borders of that identity. Thus these Sunday school stories depict American mission work as simultaneously converting and reaffirming racial difference. Bhabha describes the colonialists' paranoid ambivalence— "alternating between fantasies of megalomania and persecution"—in the demand "turn white or disappear."[29] Yet in the face of its internal racial others, white, Protestant America seems less ambivalently, more gratuitously to insist that these others both "turn white *and* disappear": for what else is asked by, say, the policy of simultaneously civilizing and exterminating the Cherokee, or by the American Colonization Society's double goal in shipping ex-slaves to Liberia of both Christianizing Africa and ridding America of free blacks. The problem for national identity, the anxiety that underlies so many of these tracts, is that the otherness within America will not disappear; instead these years are marked by its ever increasing and increasingly multiple and complicated presence. So, for example, the 1862 tract *Virginia; or The Power of Grace,* which tells of an urban missionary's rescue of a wild young girl (in the first scene Genie is seen horsewhipping other street children), becomes an equally conventional "Tragic Mulatta" story when Genie turns out to be the child of a freed "Quadroon" and her southern master. In her person, and in the interweaving of these two familiar plots, Genie fuses the problems of poverty that characterized ethnically diverse northern cities with the mid–Civil War anxiety over newly freed blacks. It was so much easier when the rescued urchin could prove to have long-lost grandparents, still alive and loving, on an American farm, or even back in England.[30]

---

plaining that "in the year 1831 this tribe began to move to another part of the country" (3), but although the story centers on the conversations between a missionary to "this new settlement" and a Choctaw girl badly injured during the winter migration, not a word is said about the (governmental) causes of her life-threatening "move."

29. Homi K. Bhabha, "Interrogating Identity: The Postcolonial Prerogative," in *Anatomy of Racism,* ed. David Theo Goldberg (Minneapolis: University of Minnesota Press, 1990), 205 and 204. Bhabha is primarily concerned with the composite identities of the subjects/objects of colonial control, but his discussion remains trenchant for national identity as well.

30. Mrs. Madeline Leslie [Harriet N. W. Baker], *Virginia; or The Power of Grace* (Boston: Henry Hoyt Publishing, 1862). *Maria Cheeseman,* for example, proves to have more easily assimilated English grandparents. Despite the national desire to distinguish white Americans from the English, English ancestry is understood to offer a far more stable assurance of racial purity and seems the preferred and most frequent heritage for rehabilitated urchins.

If questions of race prove central to the formation of American national identity, they are equally pivotal for the project of Christian conversion. Missionaries may insist that the color of one's skin is irrelevant to one's spiritual salvation, but the rhetoric of religious education remains deeply mired in the language of race. The imagery of religious conversion—out of the darkness and into the light—allies religious education with racial and national norms. To remark that such imagery is conventional and pervasive does not evacuate its racial meanings.

> You have heard of Africa, I am sure; that great country from which so many poor black people, who have been stolen from their homes, their mothers and sisters, are brought to America as slaves. You have seen many of these Africans. You know that their skin is black. The hearts of these poor natives of Africa are even blacker than their skin. Very few little boys and girls who live in that land have ever heard of Christ.[31]

In this passage from a Sunday school reader on *The Heathen and their Children*, any initial criticism of American slavery as a destroyer of homes is relocated onto the blackness of the Africans' skin. Indeed, it is the color rhetoric of religious conversion that permits and enables such a moral slide, alleviating America's culpability for slavery. The Africans' pigmentation recalls and represents the hearts beneath, un-Christian hearts "even blacker than their skins." Such easy connections between skins and hearts demonstrates not only the cultural resonance (if not conscious awareness) of the racial dimensions of this religious rhetoric, but also how a racialized faith can justify national inequities. Christ constitutes, after all, the one undisputed "benefit" that American slavery bestowed upon African people.

It is interesting to recall the *Memoir of James Jackson* in this context, since Susan Paul's religious pedagogy entails lessons in racial tolerance. She ends her first chapter, for example, with a vignette that explains how "prejudice against color" is taught to children. The threat "if you don't stop, I *will certainly* give you to the *old black man*" may curb bad behavior, but in merging the traditional imagery of the devil with the real black men on Boston's streets, it also instills harmful associations—"that child will *fear* and *hate* a black man for years."[32]

31. "Abbe Gunga, The African Boy," in *Stories about the Heathen and their Children* (Boston: American Tract Society, n.d.), no. 12, 1–2. Internal evidence suggests that the collection was assembled circa 1860.

32. Susan Paul, *Memoir of James Jackson, the Attentive and Obedient Scholar, who Died in Boston, October 31, 1833, Aged Six Years and Eleven Months (1835)*, ed. Lois Brown (Cambridge: Harvard University Press, 2000), 72.

Paul had hoped that the American Sunday School Union would publish her story of the life and death of this "attentive and obedient scholar," with its conventional celebration of a child's piety, and its radical embodiment of this virtue in a free black boy. But the American Sunday School Union, interested in selling its tracts in all regions of the country, declared it a matter of policy to avoid mention of "the subject of slavery, abolition, and every other irritating topic" that might alienate southern congregations, and consequently refused to print or distribute this book.[33] Thus, the racial discourse of missionary stories must be understood in part as displacing discussions of slavery in Sunday School publications.

Susan Paul belonged to a prominent family of teachers and ministers in the free black community of Boston, and was among the first African Americans to join the Boston Female Anti-Slavery Society. Thus, she had experience with an unusually broad range of social intimates, and the multiple audiences addressed in her book attest to this diversity: seeking to "do something towards breaking down that unholy prejudice which exists against color" in her white readers, she simultaneously hopes the book will inspire "colored friends" to tend to the religious instruction of their children, and she provides lessons in Christian virtue and racial tolerance to "dear children" both white and black (67, 69). Paul's conjuring of a racially diverse audience disallows the slippage into a presumptively white Christianity so evident in other Sunday school texts. It does not presume a racial divide between its readers and those in need of salvation. James's Sunday school teacher "told the children that there were a great many thousands of their color who were not allowed to read, who had no schools, nor any books. These persons she said were slaves," and when she asks her students to pray for these slaves, James's prayers emphasize lessons of identification, not differentiation. He prays that the slaves may "be happy as I am,—and may they have good teachers to learn them to read, as I have" (88–89). We have some evidence of actual Sunday school use of Paul's *Memoir, The Liberator* having printed an exchange of letters between the clearly white students of the Union Evangelical Sabbath School of Amesbury and Salisbury, Massachusetts, and Paul's own students in Boston's African American Primary School No. 6 (Appendix, 123–27). The students from Amesbury and Salisbury echo the language of James's prayer for the slaves as they send three dollars "to your teacher for your benefit" saved from their Fourth of July "holiday pocket money" in an act of "self-

---

33. Boylan, *Sunday School,* 82. Lois Brown details Paul's efforts to publish the *Memoir* in her fine introduction; it was eventually published locally by James Loring and distributed by the Massachusetts Anti-Slavery Society. Paul, *Memoir of James Jackson,* 27–34.

denial" much like the donations urged in *Alice Wood and Her Missionary Society*. This act of charity demonstrates the liminal place of Paul's students in conventional Sunday school discourse; at once Christian and black, they are allies in "pity" for "ignorant slaves," and yet are themselves in need. "Let us all hope that not many more 'independent days' will come, before every little girl and boy, white or black, in America, will be as free and happy as we are," this letter concludes, the "we" of these Sabbath School scholars imitating James's own acts of identification as it stretches to admit the students of these two very different schools into a single national ideal (124).

Paul's book is an anomaly, but its vision of a multiracial Christianity does not stand completely alone even among texts produced by the mainstream religious press; the Sunday school story that in my reading most explicitly narrates the formation of America as a Christian nation derives both Christian salvation and national allegiance from an interracial friendship. *The Indian's Revenge* tells the story of William Sullivan, who had come to America from England to make his "home and fortune":

> He was filled with prejudices, acquired when in England, against Americans in general, and the North American Indians in particular. . . . [O]f the sweet precepts of the gospel he was as practically ignorant as if he had never heard them, and in all respects was so thoroughly an Englishman, that he looked with contempt on all who could not boast of belonging to his own favored country. The Indians he especially despised and detested as heathenish creatures.[34]

Ensconced in his American homestead William spurns an Indian who asks for food and shelter, calling him an "Indian dog," though William's wife proves more generous and secretly feeds Carcoochee. Later, when William is himself lost and wounded during a hunting expedition, Carcoochee takes his "revenge"—and repays his gratitude to the woman who aided him—by helping the wounded man home. Revealing his identity, the illiterate heathen leaves William with an unwitting paraphrase of scripture: "when hereafter you see a red man in need of kindness, do to him as you have been done by" (21). Thanks to this act of mercy the Sullivans both embrace their new homeland and "turn their hearts to God"; Carcoochee remains a friend and seated by their hearth learns to read the Bible and to love the Savior he had unknowingly imitated. The truly American Christian is thus born of contact between the godless Englishman and the heathen Indian. Rather than a mono-

34. "The Indian's Revenge," in *Morning Glory* (New York: American Tract Society, n.d. [1848?]), 5, 7–8.

lithic narrative of white superiority, of inflexible assimilation and erasure, such stories suggest that national identity and religious identity are at once complicated and propped by race.

Little Angels and Little Heathens

The stories Sunday school texts tell about the formation of national and religious identity were written for child readers. The rearing of children involves the inculcation of such identities, the reproduction of national formation within the individual child. Thus the nation's ambiguous relation to its heathen others is replayed in these texts' response to the children they would fashion into properly Christianized and Americanized citizens.[35] Much like the erotic innocence of temperance fiction, this emphatically didactic juvenile literature demonstrates the circularity of the "pedagogical" and "performative" aspects of national narrations: these texts simultaneously teach a nationalist culture and perform that culture.[36] In particular, these pedagogic stories function to reenact, and so transform, anxieties over the threat internal differences pose to national, racial, and religious identity. In practical terms the religious education of children promises to produce an ever more Christian nation. In narrative terms that education is revealed as itself a *mise-en-abîme* of cultural conversion in which stories of missionaries converting heathens work to further Americanize and Christianize children—already identified as American and Christian—by turning them into missionaries eager to convert yet more heathens. Thus the child so disciplined into Americanness performs as a model for national identity, and hence as a means of disciplining the nation. But in order to grasp this cycle fully we need to know more about how the religious education of children was imagined in nineteenth-century America.

"Where do you discover the *supreme selfishness* which is the essence and substance of all sin, if not in a little child?" queried Gardiner Spring in his 1833 *Dissertation on Native Depravity*.[37] Throughout the early decades of the

35. David Lloyd offers a stunning example of how racial identity and ego formation have been imagined in similar ways when he compares the "visual structure of racism . . . with what psychoanalysis supposes to take place in the castration complex"; in both cases difference must be recognized "as a mutilation of identity." "Race under Representation," *Oxford Literary Review* 13 (1991): 74.

36. For a discussion of the split between pedagogic and performative narratives of national identity see Homi K. Bhabha, "DissemiNation: Time, Narrative, and the Margins of the Modern Nation," in *Nation and Narration*, 297–99.

37. Gardiner Spring, *A Dissertation on Native Depravity* (New York: Jonathan Leavitt, 1833), quoted in Boylan, *Sunday School*, 145.

Republic, Calvinist belief that children are "by nature sinners . . . estranged from the womb, they go astray as soon as they be born" dominated the discourse of child-rearing, and especially of religious education, with its emphasis on the need for conversion.[38] Orthodox ideas of infant depravity were countered with increasing authority by arguments for children's essential innocence, such as Horace Bushnell's famous 1847 treatise on *Christian Nurture,* with its proposal that children need not be converted, but rather if properly reared could be true Christians from birth. Indeed, far from periods of natural depravity, Bushnell claimed that "infancy and childhood are the ages most pliant to good."[39] By 1850 more radical thinkers, the direct and indirect heirs of Rousseau, would not merely reject any notion of innate sin, but actually posit that "at birth the child is . . . but an incipient receptacle of that thought and affection, the proper protection, nourishment and exercise of which are capable of forming it into an angel; and this, indeed, is the ultimate design of its being."[40] As I elaborate in earlier chapters, between these images of the innately depraved and the incipient angel historians have noted a gradual evolution whereby Calvinist doctrines of original sin slowly gave way before the desire of an increasingly domestic and child-centered American middle class to believe that their children, at least, were innately good.[41] However clear this transition may appear from our historical vantage, the nineteenth

---

38. Rev. Allen Hyde, *Essay on the State of Infants* (New York: Cornelius Davis, 1830), quoted in Bernard Wishy, *The Child and the Republic: The Dawn of American Child Nurture* (Philadelphia: University of Pennsylvania Press, 1968), 18.

39. Horace Bushnell, *Christian Nurture* (New Haven, Conn.: Yale University Press, 1947), 14.

40. "Errors of Education," *The New Jerusalem* 23 (August 1850): 296; quoted in Wishy, *The Child and the Republic*, 23. *The New Jerusalem* is a Swedenborgian publication; in general, nonconformist thinkers were much quicker and more thorough in their rejection of the fundamental tenets of original sin and infant depravity. For an early and influential example see Bronson Alcott, *Observations on the Principles and Methods of Infant Instruction* (Boston: Carter and Hende, 1830). This fundamental reimagining of childhood as untainted potentiality has its roots in Enlightenment thought, and particularly in the educational philosophies of Rousseau and Pestalozzi.

41. The conceptual evolution from the depraved infant, through "the child redeemable" to "the child redeemer," structures Bernard Wishy's *The Child and the Republic*. Stanford Flemming ends his study of *Children and Puritanism: The Place of Children in the Life and Thought of the New England Churches, 1620–1847* (New Haven, Conn.: Yale University Press, 1933) with the publication on Bushnell's treatise, implying that after *Christian Nurture* religious education is no longer truly Calvinist. Anne M. Boylan's *Sunday School* traces the institutional implications of this transition. She cautions that "it would be erroneous to assume, however, that Christian nurture quickly displaced conversion as the main goal of Sunday School instruction. The two goals existed side by side for sometime" (149). Conversely, Philip Greven even finds signs of ambivalence over whether children are "embryo angels or infant fiends" among seventeenth- and eighteenth-century evangelicals. Greven, *The Protestant Temperament: Patterns of Child-Rearing, Religious Experience, and the Self in Early America* (New York: Knopf, 1977), 28–31.

century largely experienced childhood sin and sinlessness in a paradoxical si-multaneity of opposing views.[42] In practice American parents, Sunday school teachers, and the authors of juvenile religious fiction held an unstable double vision of children's relation to religion, seeing the child as at once naturally depraved and naturally angelic.

This double conception of the child proves especially provocative for my argument that nineteenth-century America used the religious education of its children as a site on which to enact its anxieties over national and racial iden-tity. For once understood as both depraved like the savage and angelic like the perfect missionary, the American child could fully and ambivalently per-form *all* roles in America's Christian and civilizing mission to the world. By simultaneously working to convert heathens out there and to Christianize children at home, these stories illustrate how the American child comes both to reflect and to inform American imperialism.

The very notion of child as missionary is predicated upon a racial and na-tional conception of evangelism: in arguing for the essential innocence and godliness of children, Bushnell purports that the gradual educational pro-cesses that nurture Christianity within the Christian home would supple-ment—indeed, would prove more potent than—the conversion of the hea-then for the task of evangelizing the world. In a chapter titled "Christian Stock" he depicts Christianity as an inbred trait of character and spirit, and hence a stock that can be consciously and biologically propagated.

> To be more explicit, there are two principal modes by which the kingdom of God among men may be, and is to be extended. One is by the process of conversion, and the other by that of family propagation; one by going over to the side of faith and piety, the other by the populating force of faith and piety themselves. (165)

"Civilization," he concludes, "is, in great part, an inbred civility" (172). Chris-tian nurture thus differs from the dominant discourse of mission work through its linking of race and culture—the belief that civilization can be transmitted both educationally and biologically.[43] Bushnell's notion of spreading Chris-

---

42. G. M. Goshgarian describes this paradox as "the intellectual acrobatics . . . performed in both extolling and depreciating efforts to save naturally depraved young souls with inborn affinities for the good." Goshgarian, *To Kiss the Chastening Rod: Domestic Fiction and Sexual Ideology in the American Renaissance* (Ithaca, N.Y.: Cornell University Press, 1992), 42.

43. For a discussion of Bushnell's position on the biological transmission of civilization in relation to *Uncle Tom's Cabin*, see Lynn Wardley, "Relic, Fetish, Femmage: The Aesthetics of Sentiment in the Work of Stowe," in *The Culture of Sentiment: Race, Gender, and Sentiment in Nineteenth-Century America*, ed. Shirley Samuels (New York: Oxford University Press, 1992), 210.

tianity through propagation depends, moreover, upon asserting the superior vigor of the "Christian races":

> The Christian body . . . stands among the other bodies and religions, just as any advanced race, the Saxon for example, stands among the feebler, wilder races. Like the Aborigines of our continent; having so much power of every kind that it puts them in shadow, weakens them, lives them down, rolling its over-populating tides across them, and sweeping them away, as by a kind of doom. Just so there is, in the Christian church, a grand law of increase by which it is rolling out and spreading over the world. (180)

It is chilling to find that the text so celebrated for "sweeping away" popular adherence to the Calvinist ideas of infant depravity roots its recognition of the inherent goodness of the child in the act of sweeping away the "feebler, wilder races." Bushnell's Christian child incarnates a religious advance inseparable from racial advantage. In the project of disseminating Christian civilization the child serves as the perfect and necessary conduit, since Christian nurture is the propagation that gives faith more bodies. The child thus sutures the potential gap between race and culture that constantly threatens to split open the myth of a white, Christian America. Furthermore, Bushnell's insistence on the importance of familial nurture—his contention that Christianity is best produced by Christian parentage and a Christian home—reiterates the conviction that the child at home coalesces national identity. Bushnell wrote this spiritual celebration of the nation's westward expansion, moreover, at a moment in the late 1840s when the cities of the northeastern United States were themselves being deluged by an unprecedented wave of non-Protestant immigration. Thus, Bushnell's imperialist assurances stand also as a defense; he promises middle-class, Christian parents that with proper tending neither their cities nor their children will suffer in spiritual or class terms.

Poised between savagery and salvation, the American child reveals the precariousness of this national and religious progress narrative. Stories about the conversion of heathens frequently conclude by asking their child readers: "Shall that little girl in a heathen land, be a disciple of Christ, and you, in a land of Sabbaths and Sabbath-Schools and Bibles, not give your hearts to the savior?" or "Are you doing as much as Akatangi to give the gospel to the heathen?"[44] To answer "no" to such questions would threaten the alliance be-

---

44. Dr. John Scudder, *Appeal to the Children and Youth of the United States of America in Behalf of the Heathen World* (Philadelphia: American Sunday School Union, 1846), 135–36. "Akatangi, The Island Boy," in *Stories about the Heathens and their Children*, no. 15, 8.

tween Christian nurture and Christian stock, while having to answer "yes" casts the American Sunday school student as the anxious guarantor of a national, class, and racial world order. Letters children sent to Scudder in response to his books and lectures often echo Frado's "knotty questions," a hint that his missionary rhetoric may have had unintended, depraved results. In one letter, published as an appendix to his *Tales for Little Readers* along with many other amusing epistles from pious children, the missionary's comparison of American child and savage are transmuted with a childish literalism into a quite unacceptable cultural relativism.

> O, how thankful we ought to be, that we were not born in heathen lands, O, if the poor heathen could only have such privileges as we have, how thankful they would be; and if we were born in heathen lands, I have no doubt that they would come and tell us about a savior. (170)

Domestic Savagery

The anxious doubling of the American child and Akatangi suggests that there may be two sides to the analogies Sunday school texts draw between the child and the savage. While attitudes toward religious education reflect nineteenth-century notions of America's world mission, depictions of missionary work encode anxieties about family order. If unconverted American children were often represented as heathen, missionary work was frequently cast as the project of making heathens into good little children. Colonial discourses often aver that "primitive people" are infantile—a cultural stage to be outgrown. Nicholas Thomas has compellingly argued that this formulation proves particularly potent for mission work, since the image of savage as child (unlike more ethnological models of cultural hierarchy) facilitates the understanding of conversion as a kind of growth. Thomas argues that it is this emphasis on conversion, and the consequent need to represent missionary subjects in a manner that can "at once emphasize savagery and yet signal the essential humanity of the islanders to be evangelized," that causes missionary work to employ and enact "the notions of infantilization and quasifamily hierarchy in a far more thorough way than any other colonial project."[45] Comparing Thomas's findings with my own, it becomes clear that the nineteenth-century American child and the heathen to be converted prove

---

45. Nicholas Thomas, "Colonial Conversions: Difference, Hierarchy, and History in Early Twentieth-Century Evangelical Propaganda," *Comparative Studies in Society and History* 34 (April 1992): 374, 380.

such apt and powerful metaphors for each other because *both* are viewed as ambivalent embodiments of wildness and innocence.

Sunday school stories about foreign missions depicted the heathen as depraved more on familial than on religious grounds. Without the Bible, little heathens could never learn to be proper children. This is the lesson the American Tract Society's *Stories about the Heathen and their Children* derives from a meeting between a missionary to Africa—the famed Mr. Moffat—and an elderly woman whose family, no longer able to support her, has abandoned her by the side of a mountain path: "We can not wonder that such things happen in Africa; for the same Bible tells us that 'the dark places of the earth are full of the habitations of cruelty.' If these children had learned the holy words, 'Honor thy father and mother,' they would not have left their poor old mother to die."[46] Under the racial logic that colors spiritual uplift there can be no wonder that dark things are done in dark places by dark people. Here the darkness of Africa is, however, given specific content: the rupture of what missionary, Sunday school teacher, and good American child must all recognize as the appropriate, and indeed biblically commanded, way of being a family. Heathenism may be a religious problem, requiring the religious solution of conversion, but its sign is not spiritual so much as domestic. Thus in his *Missionary Narrative of the Triumphs of Grace; As Seen in the Conversion of Kafirs, Hottentots, Fingos and Other Natives of South Africa,* Samuel Young begins by describing not religious rites but dining arrangements: "They use no tables, dishes, knives, or forks at their meals; but everyone helps himself by means of sticks, to the meat which is in the pot. For seats, they use the skulls of oxen, with the horns still attached to them."[47] Eating straight from the pot, seated upon the still horned trophies of the kill, the Kafirs scorn the divisions and distinctions characteristic of the well-kept nineteenth-century American home, thereby inviting Young's and his reader's scorn for the Kafir.

Theories of colonialism have often noted how Western assertions of cultural superiority have rested on the comparison of domestic norms.[48] Ac-

---

46. "Lying Charts," in *Stories about the Heathen and their Children*, no. 13, 3.

47. Samuel Young, *Missionary Narrative of the Triumphs of Grace; As Seen in the Conversion of Kafirs, Hottentots, Fingos and Other Natives of South Africa* (New York, 1843), 5–6.

48. Sherry B. Ortner's paradigmatic essay, "Is Female to Male as Nature Is to Culture?" in *Woman, Culture, and Society*, ed. Michelle Rosaldo and Louise Lamphere (Stanford, Calif.: Stanford University Press, 1974), 67–87, suggests the extent to which women function as signs of culture. For a salient historical example see Meredith Borthwiel's account in *The Changing Role of Women in Bengal, 1849–1905* (Princeton, N.J.: Princeton University Press, 1984) of how the question of the "condition of women" informed imperialist evaluations of the region's claims to "civilization" and justified assaults on Hindu domestic life. Interestingly, in "Woman Skin Deep: Feminism and the Postcolonial Condition," *Critical Inquiry* 18 (summer 1992): 756–69, Sara Su-

counts of heathen savagery work to justify imperial expansion, and such barbarism is best indexed by the condition of those whom the West recognizes as most vulnerable—that is, by women and children. Thus the household, the appropriate locus for woman and child, imagined within Western society as removed from the sites of cultural conflict and cultural power, becomes the essential index of social order. Imputations of domestic dysfunction can then be used to justify redressive external intervention. The cultural import missionary discourse ascribed to the American home in no way contradicts its depiction as a "separate sphere" excluded from political, economic, and artistic power. To represent the bourgeois home with its properly privatized housekeeping and its properly affectionate family as the guarantor of American cultural superiority only confirms the vicarious role of the domestic woman and child as markers rather than producers or possessors of status.

Western colonialism's generalized conviction that domesticity is the antithesis of heathenism gains quite specific and provocative meanings, however, once aimed at a juvenile readership. Sunday school writings about missionary work focus obsessively on familial behaviors. Such a focus undoubtedly had pedagogic intentions, making the "cruelty" and disorder of heathen ways recognizable by casting them in familiar—that is, family—terms. The didactic intentions of these stories remain, moreover, explicitly double, seeking both to enlist American children in the support of mission work and to further their individual spiritual development. The failure of African children to properly honor "their poor old mother" both illustrates the difference of the Africans' darkness and suggests that American children who do not honor their parents are likewise savage and black. The Kafir seated on their ox skulls serve as exotic reminders that civilization rests upon that childhood nemesis, good table manners.

The Christian child, moreover, should not merely conform to proper domestic norms, but even becomes responsible for the familial perpetuation of these norms. Thus the first lesson in honoring father and mother lies in ensuring that they behave as Christian parents ought. This is clearly true for foreign heathen like the newly christened "Bathsheba": when she became a

---

leri's critique of the contemporary "coalition between postcolonial and feminist theories, in which each term serves to reify the potential pietism of the other" (759), ends with the evocation of a far less pietistic alliance between postcolonial and female experience: the horrifying curtailment of women's rights that accompanies the Islamization of Pakistan. To note that Suleri's tactics here recapitulate those of the nineteenth-century British colonialists described by Borthwiel only intensifies the validity of her critique: the difficulty of an alliance between postcolonial and feminist theories stems precisely from the fact that concern with the "condition of women"—at least as understood by the West, but even in many instances as adduced by a multiculturally sensitive "harm principle"—often conflicts with concerns for cultural sovereignty.

Christian her mother attempted to reclaim her for Hinduism by "beating her and spitting upon her," but "she behaved as a Christian daughter should do, and spoke none but words of kindness to her poor old heathen mother" until "at last [the Hindoo mother] saw that this was a better religion than her own." Thus by behaving "as a Christian daughter should do," Bathsheba converts her mother both from her savage faith and from her savagely violent modes of child-rearing. The tract concludes by insisting on the relevance of this pattern of disciplining one's parents for American families when it asks its readers, "have you a mother or father, brothers or sisters who are not yet believers in Jesus? If so try by conduct like Bathsheba's to make them love the gospel."[49] Indeed, even a story about Sunday school students from middle-class American homes (where the great trauma of the plot lies in the news that a beloved Sunday school teacher will be leaving her class) advises that if you behave like a "gentle, loving daughter and sister" "Christ will make you the preacher to bring your father and mother and brothers and sisters to him."[50] The task of disciplining one's parents, of producing the Christian and domestic order of the family, epitomizes the double bind of the child in didactic fiction: however much these children may appear as disciplinary agents, they themselves remain without agency. Dependent, it is never up to Bathsheba, or even the American Sunday school student, to define what a Christian child should do.

Only by working to save the heathens—including the unbelievers in their own homes—can American children secure their own spiritual and domestic welfare. Dr. John Scudder's many books and pamphlets for children offer particularly adamant, and indeed sadistic, examples of this argument. He concludes, for instance, a discussion of the lives of girls in China with this call for American girls to support missionary work:

> Did you ever, my dear girls, think why it is that your parents love you, and educate you—why it is that they try to make you happy, instead of cramping your feet, shutting you up, and perhaps, at last selling you? It is because they have the Bible. Then, how anxious should you be to save what money you can to buy Bibles to send to those poor heathen.[51]

How anxious indeed, when the failure to provide Bibles threatens to deprive not only the girls of China but also Scudder's "dear girls" of love, education, happiness, and the kind of parents who provide these blessings. That the ul-

---

49. *Old Jesse the Hindoo Mother* (Philadelphia, n.d. [1857?]), 9, 11, 13, 15–16.
50. Caroline E. Kelly Davis, "Friday Lowe," *Sunday School Times* (February 12, 1870): 101.
51. Scudder, *Dr. Scudder's Tales for Little Readers*, 154.

timate foreign horror—the sale of daughters—can only be warded off by the American girl's accumulation of pennies neatly illustrates the imagined congruence between Christian civilization and the bourgeois compulsion to "be economical" celebrated on one Sunday school girl's red leather purse. Instead of Chinese parents converting their children into money, this passage urges American children to invest their money in the conversion of such cruel adults into good Christian parents.

The horrors of domestic savagery narrated in these tracts focus on the cruelty of heathen parents, and especially of delinquent, non-Christian mothers. Such a focus emphasizes the vulnerability of children, and so emphasizes the threat to their own happiness and indeed survival should the project of Christianization fail. This structure reflects not only children's dependence on their parents, and particularly their mothers, but also the equation of parental nurture with Christianity. After all, given the pious status of motherhood in Victorian America, a non-Christian mother appears as a contradiction in terms. The pathos of Little Ben's plight in the Five Points district of New York is epitomized in his efforts to apologize for his cruelly selfish mother: "Please, sir, if my mother is tipsy and cross with me, don't mind; she loves me *sometimes.*" True mothers, of course, love their children all the time; they also serve as moral models, eschewing alcohol and anger. Thus it is with an italicized sense of outrage that Aunt Fanny reports how "one of the miserable children stole the old gentleman's red silk pocket handkerchief. A little girl stole it, and *her own mother* had taught her."[52]

Heathen mothers abroad not only frequently fail to conform to these bourgeois idealizations of motherhood, but exhibit deviance that takes even more dramatic and terrifying forms. Instead of loving their children—even "sometimes"—they feed their babies to fish and alligators (the most often repeated image of heathen maternal depravity).

> You see how a mother loves her babe, how she carries it in her arms, how tenderly she nourishes it, if it is sick, how she nurses it night and day with pitying love, if it dies, how she weeps for its loss. But the heathen mother, tears her infant from her breast, and casts it into the river for the fishes to devour.[53]

Lydia Sigourney's comparison of two emblematic mothers reveals how much the power of depictions of maternal violence depends upon the idealization of maternal nurture. Conversely, evocations of cruel heathen mothering work

---

52. Barrow, "Little Ben," in *All Sorts of Pop-guns*, 151, 150.
53. Sigourney, *How to be Happy*, 56–57.

to shore up the appeal of maternal Christian virtue. There is no greater threat to Victorian cultural norms than the possibility that the "maternal hand" could find itself in league with "frightful monsters":

"See that heathen mother stand
    Where the sacred currents flow;
With her own maternal hand,
    Mid the waves her infant throw.

"Hark! I hear the piteous scream,
    Frightful monsters seize their prey,
Or the dark and bloody stream
    Bears the struggling child away.

"Fainter, now, and fainter still,
    Breaks the ring upon the ear;
But the mother's heart is steel,—
    She, unmoved, that cry can hear.

"Send, O send the Bible there,—
    Let its precepts reach the heart!
She may then her children spare,
    Act the mother's tender part."

This hymn appears within the story of a boy who, motivated by its tuneful plea, works and saves in order to purchase Bibles that he may "send, O send" to India.[54] Hymn and story suggest that children's missionary zeal can actually produce "the mother's tender part"—can make steel-hearted heathens into proper mothers. Since such perceived maternal dysfunctions and the social disorder they symbolize validate British colonial control as well as American missionary action in India, imperial power once again rests upon a domestic ethos, and the culture of domesticity comes to serve imperialist ends.

Harriette G. Brittan was sent to Calcutta by the Woman's Union Missionary Society in the 1860s—among the first group of single American women

54. Scudder, *Appeal*, 122. Scudder further suggests the efficacy of this image for recruiting child missionaries with the story of a child whose "attention was first directed to the miseries of the heathen, when she was eighteen months old," by seeing a picture of "a heathen mother throwing her child into the mouth of a crocodile" (150–51). Such imagery promises to make even extremely young children into missionaries by representing heathenism as a direct threat to children and, as usual, blaming the mothers.

to engage in foreign mission work. There she wrote *Kardoo, the Hindoo Girl,* a story (told in the voice of young Kardoo) that recasts these familiar tropes of heathen domestic disorder from a more feminist perspective that discloses some of their cultural assumptions.[55] While Kardoo describes her mother as all "love and tenderness" (10), she is highly critical of the distant (anti-domestic) parenting proffered by Indian fathers: she complains about the division of the house into male rooms and those permitted to women and children and argues that such distinctions prevent them from eating together as a family (they do not eat as "father and mother with their children sitting down around a table spread with clean cloth" [31]); most poignant of all, she confides to her child readers, her father "never took me up in his arms and kissed me; he never set me on his knee and showed me pictures, or told me pretty stories as your father does" (9). It is within this context of paternal absence and patriarchal power that Kardoo tells the story of the vow that bound her mother to cast her baby boy into the Ganges "with her own hands" (116):

> I had not once seen her kiss or embrace her darling. No tear was in her eye when she looked at him. . . . She seemed petrified to stone. Her every movement seemed as though it were, by some means, independent of her will. (120)

When the time for the sacrifice comes, the nursemaid's narration endows the familiar scene with unfamiliar affect:

> She walked quickly down to the river's brink and without pausing an instant flung her babe from her as far as she could into the water. He sunk, rose again instantly, and as instantly the immense head and open jaws of an alligator appeared beside him, the next moment the headless trunk of the babe floated before us, dyeing the water with its blood. Your mother uttered a wild cry and would have flung herself after the child, had I not held her back. (123–24)

Here the mother's stoniness, her refusal to fondle her child, the quickness of her throw—all the marks other versions have taken to signify her unnaturally steely heart—stand instead as signs of her maternal love, of how much self must be turned to stone for the required sacrifice to become possible. The religious vow

---

55. Harriette G. Brittan, *Kardoo, the Hindoo Girl* (New York: William B. Bodge, 1869). Patricia R. Hill, in *The World Their Household: The American Woman's Foreign Mission Movement and Cultural Transformation, 1870–1920* (Ann Arbor: University of Michigan Press, 1985), recounts both the reluctance of traditional mission boards to send single women overseas, and the consequent development of female boards. The interdenominational Woman's Union Missionary Society, founded in 1860, was the first mission board devoted to sending single women overseas (44–46).

that ends in this baby's gruesome death was taken by Kardoo's father, and it is thus his will and his non-Christian faith that abuse and torture this beloved and loving mother. Brittan's reimagining of this scene unmasks the extent to which missionary fantasies of heathen domestic disorder generally work to construct an image of a happy, American domesticity dependent not only on Christian faith, but also on patriarchal gender arrangements: the cult of domesticity's penchant for idealizing and blaming the comparatively powerless mother.

Hinduism fascinates and appalls American readers precisely because of the ways it is seen to ritualize forms of patriarchal violence, present but disavowed in American society. The practice of *suttee* may thus be oddly directed in Sunday school fiction not at wives, the patriarchal victims, but at little boys, the heirs to patriarchal power:

> My dear little boys, would you like to see your mother sacrificed in this way?—
> Those mothers who nursed you when you were infants; who used to sit by your
> cradles and rock you to sleep when you cried; and who used to watch you by
> day and by night, when you were sick? No! you would not like to see such
> mothers burned as a sacrifice to idols—but if you had been born in some parts
> of India, you would, with your own hands, kindle the fire to burn them. O how
> thankful you ought to be that you were born in a Christian land,—a land where
> you have the Bible, which teaches you not to do such dreadful things.[56]

John Scudder goes on to describe this "dreadful thing" in great detail for six pages and includes a "beautiful" illustration representing "the burning of one of these wretched women." In these pages the patriarchal marital rights protected by *suttee* go unmentioned. The passage concerns only mother-love and the love of mothers; thus even as it denounces heathen savagery, Scudder's narration absorbs the image of marriage and maternity as a socially sanctioned, even compulsory self-immolation.[57] Addressed to boys, Scudder's discussion of *suttee* offers a disquietingly double threat to its girl readers. With his long description of the good (American) mother he provides a model of feminine behavior such readers should follow, suggesting, indeed,

---

56. Scudder, *Appeal*, 23–24.

57. Among nineteenth-century domestic writers *suttee* became a fairly conventional image for the self-abnegation demanded by marriage. See for example Lydia Sigourney's early poem "The Suttee" (1827). The poem is unusual among her generally pious *oeuvre* in that its outrage at this barbaric custom does not include a missionary appeal to convert and so rescue Hindu women; rather, it seems to suggest that, like the victim in the poem, the American wife is often "bound . . . fast down to her loathsome partner." Paula Bernat Bennett, *Nineteenth-Century American Women Poets, an Anthology* (Oxford: Blackwell, 1998), 5–6.

that if Indian mothers were more like these nurturing American mothers, sons wouldn't or couldn't burn them. And yet within the son's imagined pain at his potential loss, there may lurk another feeling, the titillating and submerged desire to "with your own hands, kindle the fire to burn" that omnipresent American mother with her pitying and controlling love. Indeed, in Scudder's detailed elaboration of this ritual immolation there are marks of taking pleasure in female suffering and self-abnegation that reinforce this doublebind. These stories of violence by and against heathen women make it clear that while linking domesticity and empire may suggest the porosity of these putatively separate spheres, it also provides new trajectories for domination.

The Missionary at Home

The goal of missionary work is quite literally the multiplication of the American Christian family unit, and especially the organization of gender and idealization of motherhood that characterizes it. The anxiety remains, however, that contact with heathens may in fact produce the opposite result—fostering the latent savagery and familial disorder that may yet lurk in American children and American homes. Or less obliquely, in this period of resistance to employing single women as foreign missionaries, there is the fear that missionary activity may destabilize familial and especially feminine roles, and thus put at risk the very domesticity missionaries were called to spread. Of all the children invited to *Arthur's Birthday Party* to hear "a talk about China," only little Hatty exclaims that "I should like to be a missionary too," and in the summary of happy and successful life forecasts that concludes the book it is only "dear Hatty Fuller" who no longer "lives upon the earth, but with the angels and our dear Savior in Heaven. And though she will never be a missionary to the poor heathen as she wished, we may be sure that there will be others found."[58] Such a conclusion suggests that the missionary calling is most desirable, productive, and safe when it remains a childhood wish. Why, we may ask, would a Sunday school story choose to kill off the one little girl who seeks to follow this evangelical call?

Sunday school literature about missions thus remains at best ambivalent about actual contact with otherness. Better to stay home and send Bibles. Surely there is a double message in the Anniversary Missionary Meeting of a Presbyterian church rewarding Sunday school students for their dedication to mission work by giving each child "the beautiful little paper, 'The Child

58. *Arthur's Birthday Party: or, A Talk about China* (Boston: Massachusetts Sabbath School Society Depository, 1856?), 41, 52.

at Home.'"[59] With similar ambivalence *Harriet Fisher: or The Missionary at Home*—a juvenile biography of a woman who founded a successful urban mission—tells of young Harriet's desire to be a missionary, and of how that desire must be constantly deferred by the needs of her elderly father, her own community, and what the book calls her "every-day duties." When finally her father's death frees her to do missionary work her desire to go to foreign lands is displaced onto needs closer to home:

> I know a place that will just suit you, if you wish to go among the heathen! For a more heathenish place I do not believe you can find in Hindostan, than in one part of the town of S___, not more than thirty miles from where we stand.[60]

Ultimately *The Missionary at Home* chooses home as the best mission and actively warns against the self-aggrandizing allures of missions abroad. Much like Brace's Children's Aid Society, the asylum Harriet founds presents itself as a happily Christian and domestic home for "ragged and filthy" (75) children who "must be separated from the evil influences of their homes, or little hope of their reformation could be cherished" (76). Harriet's skill in creating such a home for her asylum "family" compensates only uneasily in this narrative for her own lack of a more conventional family structure. Having her wards call her "mother" is not enough, and so this book, apparently written to celebrate Harriet's work with urban children, finds the asylum of less interest than the daily responsibilities and relationships that impede her missionary zeal. What finally makes Harriet a good missionary, and a good model for Sunday school scholars, is in fact her very lack of zeal: "imagination—she had none! I could never discover anything like romance in her views" (9), the narrator exclaims in praise; rather, "her life is full of the lesson that one need not be great to be useful" (11). Thus, this biography of a young missionary strives to eliminate all the attractions and adventures of a missionary calling—including the calling itself. The book closes by urging its readers to be "true messengers of [God's] kindness and mercy to all whom they meet beside the paths of every-day life. TO DO THIS IS TO BE A MISSIONARY" (105). To imagine more may actually disrupt the sanctified domestic contours of the American home, especially if you are a girl.

The anxieties about missionary work evident in such stories are not simply gratuitous; rather, they parallel what Jane Hunter calls "the paradox of

---

59. Barrow, *All Sorts of Pop-guns*, 97.

60. *Harriet Fisher: or, The Missionary at Home* (Philadelphia: American Sunday School Union, 1843), 37.

the missionary experience": how, in practice, missionary work afforded white American women power, independence, and authority well beyond the possibilities of normative domestic roles, without requiring them to repudiate— as did more politically or professionally active women of these generations— the traditional genteel and self-abnegating image of proper femininity. Rather, inverting these stories that at once praise missionary work and recoil from its unfeminine ramifications, missionary women "extolled the virtues of the evangelical woman's sphere at the same time that their lives were celebrating their surprising and abundant liberation from its bonds" (265).

Such textual resistance demonstrates, moreover, that while the Christian education of American children may offer a benign model for expressing America's world-civilizing goals, the mirroring of home and empire may yet prove disquieting on both fronts. The contiguity between the religious education of children and imperial cultural expansion seem as threatening to the American home as they are infantilizing to the others—home and abroad— they would evangelize. What I find most important about these stories is precisely the excessive and circular nature of the cultural anxieties they betray. The sanctity of the home and of the gender roles that define it, the purity (or even existence) of racial or national identity in an ever more diverse America, may prop each other, but in their interdependence they must also threaten to reveal each other's insufficiencies. These stories of America's global mission to convert the heathen thus display, however unintentionally, all the ways in which America and the idealized American home are themselves ever in need of conversion. In one story intended to teach the Sunday lesson "honor thy mother and father," Tiny, allured by fantasies of Indian life, tracks an Indian girl to her tent in the woods only to find not charm but dirt and disorder. Afraid that she will be scalped—itself a falsely romantic view—she is only robbed:

> Tiny waited and wondered and thought of home and her father and mother and the baby, as she used to think about fairs, and Europe, and Heaven, as if it were something that she should never see; or as if she had been an Indian all her life and dreamed it all, and just woke up.[61]

Or as if she understood the strange self-reflective manner in which the American home, family, celebrations of national community, sense of the world outside, and even religious faith all dream themselves through the never fully autonomous, never fully civilized figure of the child.

---

61. Elizabeth Stuart Phelps [Ward], "Tiny Wants to Be an Indian," in *Tiny's Sunday Nights* (Boston: Massachusetts Sunday School Society, 1866), 100.

Of Children and Flags

Dreaming America through his child, Marcus Aurelius Root made a daguerreotype portrait of his son, "Albert Pritchard Root, asleep by the flag" (fig. 6.1). With plump limbs pliable and limp, face flushed, hair damp and disheveled, the sleeping Albert offers an extraordinarily natural appearance, even though the elegant carpet arranged over a studio box and the flag hung behind announce this as highly contrived space.[1] The commercial arena of the photographer's studio juxtaposes the domestic and the national as Root builds the set for this image from materials that clearly belong to these distinct spheres. Fabric splits the location and meaning of this scene, ground set against sky; the carpet of a familial middle-class parlor clashes with the symbolic and public context evoked by the flag. So framed, Albert appears both as a unique, highly individual child, singled out and cherished by his father's camera, and as an emblematic figure, "the child" set beside "the flag." Locating his son simultaneously inside the family and within the nation, Root proposes a sort of symmetry between them, as sites of responsibility, care, and trust. This

1. Such arrangements of carpets and boxes are a trade standard. In a column of advice to other daguerreotypists, the Rochester photographer Edward Tompkins Whitney suggests that "when a picture is to be made to represent the child reclining on the carpet," the photographer should "have some boxes, assorted sizes, covered with carpet; use one the proper size for it to lean on." "On Taking Daguerreotypes of Children," *The Photographic and Fine Art Journal* 8 (March 1855): 76.

Fig. 6.1. "Portrait of Albert Pritchard Root Asleep by the Flag." Daguerreotype by Marcus Aurelius Root, ca. 1850. Courtesy George Eastman House.

image thus encapsulates the tensions and contradictions that animate my project of recognizing childhood's part in the making of social order, for both the household and the state. In its taut union of individual child with public symbol this image remains resistant to any single interpretation. Does the flag protect the child, casting the nation as parent, another set of secure and loving arms that promise safety? Or does this image ally the innocence and vulnerability of child and nation? The prone figure of this sleeping child closely resembles the dead children preserved in postmortem portraits, and so may evoke for a swiftly growing and changing country the ambivalent knowledge that such growth is precarious and laced with longing and bereavement.

Root made this daguerreotype in the early 1850s, but in the next decade, with the coming of the Civil War, the pairing of child and flag became increasingly common. The dyad of child and flag promised futurity: that the child would remain loyal to the nation, that the nation would defend its innocents. Of course all such promises carry a hint of desperation, but the suggestions of vulnerability that childhood bears must have felt particularly intense during this period of national fragmentation. Secession, after all, literally threatened to deface the flag, removing the stars of Southern states. Yet children were frequently called upon to assuage this threatened rupture. At a Grand National Union Concert in Newton, Massachusetts, July 4, 1862, bands of Sabbath and Public School choirs optimistically sang "The Flag of Our Union":

> A song for our banner! . . .
> The union of states none can sever
> The union of hearts—the union of hands,
> And the flag of our union forever.

A Fourth of July broadside from the previous year insists "deep is the blue with its stars spangled o'er— / they cluster there yet—they are still thirty-four," the voices of children's choirs used to affirm the inviolability of the flag.[2] Presumably the very youth of these singers, the purity and fragility of their voices, served to strengthen the guarantee these verses offer of what at this point in the war could only be anxious and precarious assertions of wholeness. Like the redemptive embraces of a drunkard's child, or the sense of family produced by a child's death, vulnerability itself rises as the most potent answer to danger and loss. The cultural ambivalence of childhood I trace in these pages—childhood as powerful and powerless, as promise and risk, as innocence and desire, as play and responsibility, as angelic and barbaric, as free and dependent—proves so tenacious and incisive because it bespeaks not just the personal complexities of growing up, but more the collective experience of social belonging and of citizenship itself. How often is identity built not out of strength, but through weakness?

The contradictions that hone the dependent state of childhood emerge in most occasions of civic belonging, however well they may be disguised by the conventional language of enfranchisement and agency. Attention to childhood makes visible notions of protection and care, of rights to dependency that match the right to independence, of modes of voice and agency that promise only a partial authority. When the boys in *McGuffey's First Eclectic Reader*

---

2. *Grand National Union Concert,* July 4, 1862, by the Sabbath and Public Schools of Newton and the surrounding towns. This broadside holds eleven songs. This second song, also titled "Flag of Our Union," comes from a broadside collection of songs sung by J. M. Dunbar (July 4, 1861). See also the song "Rally Round the Flag," which tells of secession in the idiom of schoolyard taunts: "Their flag is but a rag—ours is the true one; / Up with the stars and stripes, down with the new one" (Boston: Horace and Partridge, 1862). All three broadsides are in the collection of the American Antiquarian Society.

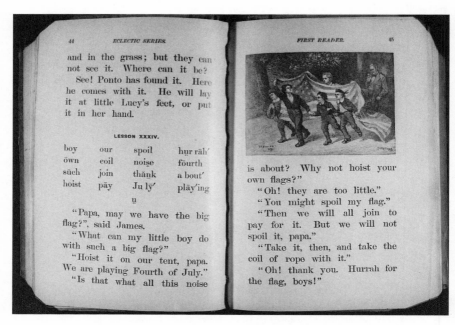

Fig. 6.2. Lesson 34 from *McGuffey's First Eclectic Reader* (New York, 1879).

(fig. 6.2) run off with their father's "big flag," scorning their own "little" ones, they may impersonate adult agency and responsibility, and even be willing to tax themselves for possible damages, yet their play at autonomy remains securely held by their father's eye. "Playing the Fourth of July" they do not rebel, they plead for permission to usurp. The boys run through woods imagining revolutionary battles, but they do not escape the stability and guardianship of their father's gaze as he sits, leaning back in an elegant chair to smoke his pipe. This gaze may be understood as the perspective of the primer, teaching its young readers to claim independence through a reliance upon its supervisory protection. Such negotiations between daring and deference demonstrate a psychic, imaginative link made possible by affection. The boy does not forget his father in his play; the father, like the primer itself, creates and contains the child's autonomy, and endows it, carefully, incrementally—"take the coil of rope"—with his authority. As in Root's daguerreotype, childhood is thus scripted as the cusp between family and nation, and as an expression of the emotional ties and responsibilities of both.

Thomas Wentworth Higginson's memoir of the "Baby of the Regiment" literalizes the mingling of familial and public space proposed by these images, as it describes the effect of baby Annie—domesticating the regiment or militarizing babyhood—as she and her mother come to live in the Civil War camp with her sergeant father. Higginson, of course, served as the white commander of the first black regiment to fight in the Civil War, his unit itself a marching symbol. "I looked with so much interest for her small person," Higginson writes, "that instead of saying at the proper time 'Attention, Battalion! Shoulder arms!' it is a wonder that I did not say 'shoulder babies!'" But he did not, and far from a threat to military training, Annie's presence among the troops becomes a source of patriotic inspiration. "Sometimes the Sergeant-major would wrap her in the great folds of the flag and she would peep out very prettily from amidst the stars and stripes, like a new born Goddess of Liberty" (fig. 6.3).[3] Symbolic adult women have been a staple of American iconography since colonial times, whether as Goddess or as victim, and feminist scholarship has richly articulated the relations between the role of "woman" as a political icon and women's active exclusion from the political process.[4] One of the most influential accounts of this dynamic has been the concept of "Republican Motherhood" and its promise that women could assert their own political importance and efficacy through, as Linda Kerber puts it, "the raising of a patriotic child."[5] Annie, swaddled in the flag, poses as just such a patriotic child, but in doing so she raises similar iconographic questions about the stakes of expressing national aspirations and identity through this "new born" figure. The patriotic child enacted by Annie has little agency or intention of her own as she peeps and charms, and yet much of Higginson's play and pleasure in this story derives from his assertions of Annie's regimental power as she "inspected" the troops, gave "her orders" (28), and performed "her duties" (33). More seriously, she serves for him as a token of his anti-racist ideals, for Annie, "very impartial . . . distributed her kind looks to everybody. She had not the slightest prejudice against color and did not care whether her particular friends were black or white" (29–30). Thus while Annie may be wrapped in the flag, she herself wraps and enraptures the regiment, becoming a repository of its best hopes and possibilities for the nation. Annie's racial impartiality shows up Higginson's own lapses as he makes fun of her black nurse, or describes life in camp in a manner that betrays how

3. Thomas Wentworth Higginson, "The Baby of the Regiment," in *Child Life in Prose*, ed. John Greenleaf Whittier (Boston: James R. Osgood, 1874), 29, 30. This story is an excerpt from Higginson's *Army Life in a Black Regiment* (Boston: Beacon Press, 1962).

4. For a splendid reading of colonial and revolutionary images of a female America, see Shirley Samuels, *Romances of the Republic: Women, the Family, and Violence in the Literature of the Early American Nation* (New York: Oxford University Press, 1996), 3–14.

5. Linda Kerber, *Women of the Republic: Intellect and Ideology in Revolutionary America* (New York: Norton, 1986), 238.

beat for dinner she liked to see the long row of men in each company march up to the cook-house, in single file, each with tin cup and plate.

During the day, in pleasant weather, she might be seen in her nurse's arms, about the company streets, the centre of an admiring circle, her scarlet costume looking very pretty amidst the shining black cheeks and neat blue uniforms of the soldiers. At "dress-parade," just before sunset, she was always an attendant. As I stood before the regiment, I could see the little spot of red, out of the corner of my eye, at one end of the long line of men · and I looked with so much

interest for her small person, that, instead of saying at the proper time, "Attention, Battalion! Shoulder arms!" it is a wonder that I did not say, "Shoulder babies!"

Our little lady was very impartial, and distributed her kind looks

Fig. 6.3. Annie reviewing the regiment. An illustration for Thomas Wentworth Higginson's "The Baby of the Regiment," in *Child Life in Prose,* ed. John Greenleaf Whittier (Boston: James R. Osgood and Co., 1874), 29.

much this white baby's position as the darling of a black regiment in a "pleasant southern home" full of "mocking-birds" and "magnolias" mimics the plantation dynamics these soldiers are fighting to abolish (36). Given the light, witty tone of this piece, its final paragraph comes as something of a shock. Like so many emblematic nineteenth-century babies, Annie dies. But Higginson remains clear that his "Goddess of Liberty" is not a figure of the frailty of the Union, or the ephemeral nature of anti-slavery ideals, but rather in that familiar and troubling paradox: even her death empowers and reforms, "holding us by unsuspected ties to whatsoever things were pure" (37).

Another Northern officer, Colonel George Hanks, also enlisted images of children and flags in his efforts to energize the Union cause. In the winter of 1863–64 he brought a group of eight freed slaves north from New Orleans and had *cartes de visite* made of "the separate figures" and especially of the three whitest children—their sale "at the rooms of the national Freedmen's Relief Association" would raise funds to support Freedman schools in Louisiana and would fuel Northern anxiety and disgust at a system that could enslave such pale and pretty children.[6] Most of these popular images present the children in appealingly affluent clothes and poses, often haloed in the ethereal mist of vignette portraiture, the only mark of their history being the words printed below their pale faces: "A Slave Girl from New Orleans" (fig. 6.4). Two photographs in the series, however, literally surround these freed slaves with the Stars and Stripes. Mary Mitchell notes that these two photographs "were far less subtle than the vignette portraits"; in their parading of the American flag they make "explicit the threat slavery (and not emancipation) poses to the liberties of white people . . . representing the Union as a refuge for white-looking children from the evils of slavery."[7] "Oh! How I Love the Old Flag" reads a caption below an image of Rebecca sitting on the stripes and looking prayerfully up at the stars (fig. 6.5). Her "love" for the flag, suffused with supplication, cannot risk Albert's sleep or Annie's charming glee.

6. "White and Colored Slaves," *Harper's Weekly* 8 (January 30, 1864): 71. Mary Niall Mitchell's splendid essay, "'Rosebloom and Pure White,'or So It Seemed," *American Quarterly* 54 (September 2002): 369–410, explores the racial dynamics of these images for northern viewers who are pressed by them to imagine the enslavement of their own children. Kathleen Collins provides a detailed history of this photographic tour, noting that while she has been able to locate only three images of the darkest-skinned little boy, she has found a dozen different images of the lightest girls. "Portraits of Slave Children," *History of Photography* 9 (July–September 1985): 189. The Garrison papers in the Sophia Smith Collection at Smith College contain a good selection of these images, including *cartes de visite* made in two different New York photographic studios, nine in all. The Garrison family, not surprisingly, possessed a large number of anti-slavery images, but the collection holds more pictures of these children than of any other single abolitionist subject—one marker of the images' popularity in abolitionist and Union circles.

7. Mitchell, "'Rosebloom and Pure White,'" 398.

Fig. 6.4. Portrait of Rebecca Hugar, *carte de visite*, 1863. Garrison Papers. Courtesy of the Sophia Smith Collection, Smith College.

Still, that Rebecca has been posed actually sitting on the flag suggests a certain level of secure arrival, and her pious bearing and somber dress promise that her inclusion will not threaten the nation. The other flag *carte de visite* is far more disconcerting (fig. 6.6). This image was clearly taken the same day: Rebecca's hair is in the same snood and the collar and ribbon of the same dress show. But all pretense of a conventional scene has been stripped

"OH! HOW I LOVE THE OLD FLAG."

REBECCA,

A Slave Girl from New Orleans.

Fig. 6.5. "Oh! How I Love the Old Flag." Garrison Papers. Courtesy of the Sophia Smith Collection, Smith College.

OUR PROTECTION.

ROSA, CHARLEY, REBECCA.

Slave Children from New Orleans.

Fig. 6.6. "Our Protection." Garrison Papers. Courtesy of the Sophia Smith Collection, Smith College.

away. Instead each child appears wrapped in a flag—Rosa wearing the Stars, and Charley and Rebecca in the Stripes—so that standing together the three of them approximate a single banner.[8] The picture is captioned "Our Protection," although as Caroline Levander points out, in highlighting the children's vulnerability to enslavement "the American flag here symbolizes the contingency . . . of freedom."[9] The knowledge that the flag endangers rather than protects American slaves had long been a staple of anti-slavery speeches. "Wherever the stars and stripes are seen flying upon American soil, I can receive no protection; I am a slave," William Wells Brown explained, going on to ridicule the image of being wrapped in the flag for safety: "I might climb to the very top of your liberty-pole, I might cut the cord that held your stars and stripes and bind myself with it as closely as I could to your liberty-pole," but the flag would not prevent recapture.[10] The Emancipation Proclamation, of course, only freed those slaves living in Confederate states—it did not affect the status of any slaves held under the Stars and Stripes.

In all of the other couplings of child and flag I have found, this pairing has expressed the relation between the domestic and the national. But in this image there are no markers of any recognizable setting, clothes, or props. There is nothing but the bodies of children swaddled in flags, so bundled that only their faces show, the space in which they stand not even recognizable as a room. None of the pictures of these slave children give us much vantage onto their experiences with the making of these photographs, nor do they tell us much about how they understood themselves and their condition. But in this image, the three standing in a void, their bodies only bulk to wrap the flag around, they have no personal identities, no lives, no agency, they are only what they symbolize. This barrenness no doubt bespeaks the period's great uncertainty as to what it would mean to incorporate such children into the nation: the doubtfulness of race and emancipation. It vividly presents the future of such children as the responsibility and promise of the nation. In so doing, it serves to monumentalize and generalize the pairing of child and

8. The gendered arrangement of the group, with Charley standing tall in the center, has been contrived by the photographer. Other images of the group, in which they stand in regular clothes, show Charley and Rebecca to be nearly the same height, with Rosa a good head shorter. The flags obscure their poses in this picture, but Rebecca and Rosa must be kneeling or squatting so as to appear symmetrical, and Charley may even be standing on a studio box.

9. Caroline Levander, "'Letting Her White Progeny Offset Her Dark One': The Child and the Racial Politics of Nation Making," *American Literature* 76 (June 2004): 221.

10. William Wells Brown, "A Lecture Delivered before the Female Anti-Slavery Society of Salem," Lyceum Hall, November 14, 1847 (Boston: Anti-Slavery Society, 1847), 15.

flag, to grant this pair an iconic status that evades the particularities of context and interpretation. In its starkness the photograph brings us face to face with the questions of this book. How do children carry and express the nation's story? Who are they? How do we use them? What sort of symbols do children make? What sort of agency can children have? How are we to understand these dependent states?

BIBLIOGRAPHY

Abbott, Jacob. *Gentle Measures in the Management of the Young.* New York: Harper and Brothers, 1872.

———. *Rollo Learning to Read.* 1835. Reprint. Boston: Phillips Sampson and Co., 1855.

———. *The Little Scholar Learning to Talk: A Picture Book for Rollo.* Boston: John Allen and Co., 1835.

———. *Rollo at School.* Boston: Weeks, Hordan and Co., 1839.

———. *Rollo at Work.* Boston: T. H. Carter, 1838.

Abbott, John S. C. *The Child at Home; or the Principles of Filial Duty Familiarly Illustrated.* New York: American Tract Society, 1833.

———. *The Mother at Home.* 1833. Reprint. Sterling, Va.: G A M Publishers, 1989.

———. *The School Boy; or a Guide for Youth to Truth and Duty.* Boston: Crocker and Brewster, 1839.

Alcott, Amos Bronson. *Essays on Education, 1830–1862.* Gainesville, Fla.: Scholars Facsimiles and Reprints, 1960.

———. *Observations on the Principles and Methods of Infant Instruction.* Boston: Carter and Hendee, 1830.

Alcott, Louisa May. *The Journals of Louisa May Alcott.* Edited by Joel Myerson, Daniel Shealy, and Madeline B. Stern. Boston: Little, Brown and Co., 1989.

———. "Our Little Newsboy." In *Aunt Jo's Scrap Bag.* Boston: Robert Brothers, 1872.

Alger, Horatio. *Fame and Fortune.* Boston: A. K. Loring, 1868.

———. *Ragged Dick.* 1867. Reprint. New York: Collier Books, 1962.

———. *Rough and Ready.* 1896. Reprint. Philadelphia: Porter and Coates, n.d.

———. *Struggling Upwards.* 1890. Reprint. New York: Hurst, n.d.

———. *The Young Outlaw.* Boston: A. K. Loring, 1875.

Allen, Mary Ware. Diary. American Antiquarian Society.

Anderson, Benedict. *Imagined Communities: Reflections on the Origins and Spread of Nationalism*. New York: Verso, 1991.

Andrews, William L. "The Novelization of Voice in Early African American Narrative." *PMLA* 105 (1990).

Anonymous. Diary for 1833–34. New York Public Library.

Appleton, Harriet. Blank Book and School Compositions. Curtis Family Papers. Massachusetts Historical Society.

Ariés, Philippe. *Centuries of Childhood: A Social History of Family Life*. Translated by Robert Baldick. New York: Alfred A. Knopf, 1962.

———. *Western Attitudes toward Death: From the Middle Ages to the Present*. Translated by Helen Weaver. New York: Alfred A. Knopf, 1981.

Arthur, Timothy Shay. *The Pitcher of Cool Water and Other Stories*. New York: National Temperance Society and Publication House, 1873.

———. *Ten Nights in a Bar-Room, and What I Saw There*. 1854. Reprint. Cambridge: Belknap Press, 1964.

Arthur's Birthday Party: or, A Talk about China. Boston: Massachusetts Sabbath School Society Depository, n.d. (1856?).

Ashby, Leroy. *Endangered Children: Dependency, Neglect and Abuse in America*. New York: Twayne Publishers, 1997.

Association for the Improvement of Juvenile Books. *First Reading Lessons for Children*. Philadelphia: Grigg and Elliot, 1830.

"At Our Desk." *Student and Schoolmate* 24 (November 1869): 530.

Augst, Thomas. *The Clerk's Tale: Young Men and Moral Life in Nineteenth-Century America*. Chicago: University of Chicago Press, 2003.

Avery, Gillian. "Origins of the *New England Primer*." *Proceeding of the American Antiquarian Society* 113, part 1 (1999): 33–61.

———. *Behold the Child: American Children and Their Books 1621–1922*. Baltimore: Johns Hopkins University Press, 1994.

[Baker, Harriet N. W.] Mrs. Madeline Leslie. *Virginia; or The Power of Grace*. Boston: Henry Hoyt Publishing, 1862.

[Barrow, Frances Elizabeth Mease] Aunt Fanny. *All Sorts of Pop-guns*. New York: Sheldon and Co., 1864.

Baldwin, James. *The Price of the Ticket: Collected Non-Fiction, 1948–1985*. New York: St. Martin's Press, 1985.

Balibar, Etienne. "Paradoxes of Universality." Translated by Michael Edwards. In *Nation and Narration*, ed. Homi K. Bhabha. New York: Routledge, 1990.

———. "Racism as Universalism." In *New Political Science* 16 (fall/winter 1989): 9–22.

Barnes, Elizabeth. *States of Sympathy: Seduction and Democracy in the American Novel*. New York: Columbia University Press, 1997.

Barthes, Roland. *Camera Lucida: Reflections on Photography*. Translated by Richard Howard. New York: Hill and Wang, 1981.

Bassard, Katherine Clay. "'Beyond Mortal Vision': Harriet E. Wilson's *Our Nig* and the American Racial Dream Text." In *Female Subjects in Black and White: Race, Psychoanalysis, Feminism*, ed. Elizabeth Abel, Barbara Christian, and Helen Moglen. Berkeley: University of California Press, 1997.

Baym, Nina. "Hawthorne's Myths for Children: The Author Versus His Audience." *Studies in Short Fiction* 10 (1973): 35–46.

———. *Novels, Readers and Reviewers: Responses to Fiction in Antebellum America.* Ithaca, N.Y.: Cornell University Press, 1984.

Beauchamp, Virginia Walcott, ed. *A Private War: Letters and Diaries of Madge Preston, 1862–1867.* New Brunswick, N.J.: Rutgers University Press, 1987.

Beecher, Catharine. *Treatise on Domestic Economy: For the Use of Young Ladies at Home and at School.* Boston: Marsh, Capen, Lyon, and Webb, 1841.

Beecher, Catharine, and Harriet Beecher Stowe. *The American Woman's Home: or, Principles of Domestic Science; Being a Guide to the Formation and Maintenance of Economical, Healthful, Beautiful, and Christian Homes.* New York: J. B. Ford and Co., 1869.

Beecher, Henry Warner. *American Indians and Christian Missions: Studies in Cultural Conflict.* Chicago: University of Chicago Press, 1981.

Benjamin, Walter. *Illuminations.* Edited by Hannah Arendt. Translated by Harry Zohn. New York: Schocken Books, 1969.

———. *The Origins of German Tragic Drama.* Translated by John Osborne. London: Verso, 1977.

Bennett, Paula Bernat. *Nineteenth-Century American Women Poets, an Anthology.* Oxford: Blackwell, 1998.

Bentley, Rensselaer. *Pictorial Primer.* New York: Cooledge, 1842.

Bercovitch, Sacvan. *The Office of the Scarlet Letter.* Baltimore: Johns Hopkins University Press, 1991.

Berger, John. *About Looking.* New York: Pantheon Books, 1980.

Berlant, Lauren. *The Anatomy of National Fantasy: Hawthorne, Utopia, and Everyday Life.* Chicago: University of Chicago Press, 1991.

Berrol, Selma Cantor. *Growing Up American: Immigrant Children in America Then and Now.* New York: Twayne Publishers, 1995.

Bhabha, Homi K. "Interrogating Identity: The Postcolonial Prerogative." In *Anatomy of Racism,* ed. David Theo Goldberg. Minneapolis: University of Minnesota Press, 1990.

———. *The Location of Culture.* New York: Routledge, 1994.

Bhabha, Homi K., ed. *Nation and Narration.* New York: Routledge, 1990.

Bigelow, Samuel A. Diaries. Bigelow Papers. Massachusetts Historical Society.

The Biography of a Bottle, By a Friend of Temperance. Boston: Perkins, Marvin and Co., 1835.

Black, James. "National Temperance and Tract Publication House." In *Proceedings of the Fifth National Temperance Convention, Saratoga Springs, New York, August 1,2 and 3, 1865.* New York: National Temperance Society and Publication House, 1865.

Blanchot, Maurice. *The Writing of the Disaster.* Translated by Ann Smock. Lincoln: University of Nebraska Press, 1986.

Blum, Virginia L. *Hide and Seek: The Child between Psychoanalysis and Fiction.* Urbana: University of Illinois Press, 1995.

Bordin, Ruth. *Woman and Temperance: The Quest for Power and Liberty, 1873–1900.* Philadelphia: Temple University Press, 1981.

Borthwiel, Meredith. *The Changing Role of Women in Bengal, 1849–1905.* Princeton, N.J.: Princeton University Press, 1984.

Boyd, Robert. *Wee Willie; or Truth Sought and Found.* Chicago: Henry A. Sumner, 1870.

Boylan, Anne M. *Sunday School: The Formation of an American Institution, 1790–1880.* New Haven, Conn.: Yale University Press.

The Boys of Gotham. New York, (1876).

The Boys' Own Weekly. New York (1877).

Brace, Charles Loring, ed. *Annual Reports of the Children's Aid Society: Nos. 1–10, February 1854–1863.* Reprint. New York: Arno Press, 1971.

———. *The Dangerous Classes of New York, and Twenty Years' Work among Them.* New York: Wynkoop and Hallenbeck, 1872.

Brittan, Harriette G. *Kardoo, the Hindoo Girl.* New York: William B. Bodge, 1869.

Brodhead, Richard H. *Cultures of Letters: Scenes of Reading and Writing in Nineteenth-Century America.* Chicago: University of Chicago Press, 1993.

———. *The School of Hawthorne.* New York: Oxford University Press, 1986.

———. "Sparing the Rod: Discipline and Fiction in Antebellum America." *Representations* 21 (winter 1988): 67–96.

Brown, Bill. *The Material Unconscious: American Amusement, Stephen Crane, and the Economics of Play.* Cambridge: Harvard University Press, 1996.

Brown, Gillian. "Child's Play." *Differences* 11 (fall 1999): 76–106.

———. *Domestic Individualism: Imagining Self in Nineteenth-Century America.* Berkeley: University of California Press, 1990.

Brown, Herbert Ross. *The Sentimental Novel in America, 1789–1860.* Durham, N.C.: Duke University Press, 1940.

Brown, William Wells. "A Lecture Delivered before the Female Anti-Slavery Society of Salem," Lyceum Hall, November 14, 1847. Boston: Anti-Slavery Society, 1847.

Buell, Lawrence. *New England Literary Culture: From Revolution through Renaissance.* New York: Cambridge University Press, 1986.

Bull, Lucy Catlin. *A Child's Poems from October to October, 1870–1871.* Hartford, Conn.: Case, Lockwood and Brainard, 1872.

Bunkers, Suzanne L., and Cynthia A. Huff., eds. *Inscribing the Daily: Critical Essays on Women's Diaries.* Amherst: University of Massachusetts Press, 1996.

Bushnell, Horace. *Christian Nurture.* New Haven, Conn.: Yale University Press, 1947.

Calvert, Karin. *Children in the House: The Material Culture of Early Childhood 1600–1900.* Boston: Northeastern University Press, 1992.

Cameron, Sharon. "Representing Grief: Emerson's 'Experience.'" In *The New American Studies: Essays from Representations,* ed. Philip Fisher. Berkeley: University of California Press, 1991.

Cavell, Stanley. *This New Yet Unapproachable America: Lectures after Emerson and Wittgenstein.* Albuquerque, N.M.: Living Batch Press, 1989.

Cayton, Mary Kupiec. "The Making of an American Prophet: Emerson, His Audiences, and the Rise of the Culture Industry in Nineteenth-Century America." *The American Historical Review* 92 (June 1987): 597–620.

Chapman, Mary, and Glenn Hendler, eds. *Sentimental Men: Masculinity and the Politics of Affect in American Culture.* Berkeley: University of California Press, 1999.

Child, Lydia Maria. *Letters from New York.* New York: Charles S. Francis and Co., 1843.

———. *The Mother's Book.* Boston: Carter and Hendee, 1831.

"Children's Books of the Year." *North American Review 102* (January 1866): 236–49.

Chipman, Samuel. *The Temperance Lecturer.* Albany, N.Y.: n.p., 1834.

The Choctaw Girl. Philadelphia: American Sunday School Union, 1835.

Chudacoff, Howard P. *How Old Are You? Age Consciousness in American Culture.* Princeton, N.J.: Princeton University Press, 1989.

Clement, Priscilla Ferguson. *Growing Pains: Children in the Industrial Age, 1850–1890.* New York: Twayne Publishers, 1997.

Coleman, Michael C. "Not Race, but Grace: Presbyterian Missionaries and American Indians, 1837–1893." *Journal of American History* 67 (June 1980): 41–60.

Collins, Kathleen. "Portraits of Slave Children." *History of Photography* 9 (July–September 1985): 187–210.

Cox, James. "Ralph Waldo Emerson: The Circle of the Eye." In *Emerson: Prophecy, Metamorphosis and Influence,* ed. David Levin. New York: Columbia University Press, 1975.

Crain, Patricia. "Childhood as Spectacle." *American Literary History* 11 (fall 1999): 545–53.

———. *The Story of A: The Alphabetization of America from* The New England Primer *to* The Scarlet Letter. Palo Alto, Calif.: Stanford University Press, 2000.

Cross, Gary. *Kids' Stuff: Toys and the Changing World of American Childhood.* Cambridge: Harvard University Press, 1997.

Crummell, Alexander. *The Future of Africa: Being Addresses, Sermons, etc., etc., Delivered in the Republic of Liberia.* New York: Scribner, 1862.

Cummins, Maria S. *The Lamplighter.* 1854. Reprint. New Brunswick, N.J:. Rutgers University Press.

Curtis, Greely Stevenson. Diary. Curtis Family Papers. Massachusetts Historical Society.

Dannenbaum, Jed. *Drink and Disorder: Temperance Reform in Cincinnati from the Washingtonian Revival to the WCTU.* Urbana: University of Illinois Press, 1984.

———. "The Social History of Alcohol." *Drinking and Drug Practices Surveyor* 19 (1984).

Das, Veena. "Language and Body: Transactions in the Construction of Pain." *Daedalus* 125 (winter 1996): 67–98.

Davidson, Cathy N., ed. *No More Separate Spheres!* Special Issue, *American Literature* 70 (September 1998).

———. *Revolution and the Word: The Rise of the Novel in America.* New York: Oxford University Press, 1986.

Davis, Caroline E. Kelly. "Friday Lowe." *The Sunday School Times,* February 12, 1870.

de Certeau, Michel. *The Practices of Everyday Life.* Berkeley: University of California Press, 1984.

Denning, Michael. *Mechanic Accents: Dime Novels and Working Class Culture in America.* London: Verso, 1987.

"Devouring Books." *The American Annals of Education* 5 (January 1835): 30–32.

DiGirolamo, Vincent. "Newsboy Funerals: Tales of Sorrow and Solidarity in Urban America." *Journal of Social History* 36 (fall 2002): 5–30.

Dilworth, Leah, ed. *Acts of Possession: Collecting in America.* New Brunswick, N.J.: Rutgers University Press, 2003.

Dimock, Wai Chee. "Class, Gender and a History of Metonymy." In *Rethinking Class: Literary Studies and Social Formations,* ed. Wai Chee Dimock and Michael T. Gilmore. New York: Columbia University Press, 1994.

———. "Scarcity, Subjectivity and Emerson." *Boundary 2.* 17 (Spring 1990): 83–99.

Dimock, Wai Chee, and Michael T. Gilmore, eds. *Rethinking Class: Literary Studies and Social Formations.* New York: Columbia University Press, 1994.

Dodd, Jill Seigel. "The Working Classes and the Temperance Movement in Ante-Bellum Boston." *Labor History* 19 (fall 1978): 510–31.

Donzelot, Jacques. *The Policing of Families.* Translated by Robert Hurley. Baltimore: Johns Hopkins University Press, 1997.

Douglas, Anne. *The Feminization of American Culture.* New York: Avon, 1977.

The Drinking Fountain Stories. New York: National Temperance Society and Publication House, 1873.

Duane, Anna Mae. *Suffering Childhood in Early America: Race, Nation and the Disciplined Body.* Ph.D. dissertation, Fordham University, 2004.

Dulles, Foster Rhea. *America Learns to Play: A History of Popular Recreation 1607–1940.* New York: Peter Smith, 1952.

Dunbar, J. M. Broadside. July 4, 1861. Collection of the American Antiquarian Society.

Edmundson, Mark. "Emerson and the Work of Melancholia." *Raritan* 6 (spring 1987): 120–36.

Ellison, Julie. *Cato's Tears and the Making of Anglo-American Emotion.* Chicago: University of Chicago Press, 1999.

Elson, Ruth Miller. *Guardians of Tradition: American Schoolbooks of the Nineteenth Century.* Lincoln: University of Nebraska Press, 1964.

Emerson, Ralph Waldo. *Essays and Lectures.* New York: The Library of America, 1983.

———. *The Journals and Miscellaneous Notebooks of Ralph Waldo Emerson.* Edited by William H. Gilman and J. E. Parsons. 16 vols. Cambridge: Harvard University Press, 1960–1982.

———. *The Letters of Ralph Waldo Emerson.* Edited by Ralph Rusk. 6 vols. New York: Columbia University Press, 1939.

Eng, David L., and David Kazanjian, eds. *Loss.* Berkeley: University of California Press, 2003.

Epstein, Barbara Leslie. *The Politics of Domesticity: Women, Evangelism, and Temperance in Nineteenth-Century America.* Middletown, Conn.: Wesleyan University Press, 1981.

Fanon, Frantz. *Black Skin, White Masks.* New York: Grove Press, 1967.

Fass, Paula S., and Mary Ann Mason, eds. *Childhood and America.* New York: New York University Press, 2000.

Fern, Fanny [Sara Parton]. *Fern Leaves from Fanny's Port-folio.* Buffalo, N.Y.: Miller, Orton, and Mulligan, 1854.

Fernando, Jude, ed. *Children's Rights.* Thousand Oaks, Calif.: Sage, 2001.

Finkelstein, Barbara. *Regulated Children / Liberated Children: Education in Psychohistorical Perspective.* New York: Psycho-history Press, 1979.

Fleming, Marjory. *The Complete Marjory Fleming: Her Journals, Letters and Verses.* London: Sidgwick and Jackson, 1934.

Flemming, Stanford. *Children and Puritanism: The Place of Children in the Life and Thought of the New England Churches, 1620–1847.* New Haven, Conn.: Yale University Press, 1933.

Ford, Leicester, ed. *The New England Primer: A History of Its Origin and Development.* New York: Dodd, Mead, 1897.

Foreman, Gabrielle P. "The Spoken and the Silences in *Incidents in the Life of a Slave Girl* and *Our Nig.*" *Callaloo* 13 (spring 1990): 313–24.

Foresta, Merry A., and John Wood. *Secrets of the Dark Chamber: The Art of the American Daguerreotype.* Washington, D.C.: Smithsonian Institution Press, 1995.

Foster, Frances. *Written by Herself: Literary Production by African American Women, 1746–1892.* Bloomington: Indiana University Press, 1993.

Foster, George G. *New York by Gas-Light and Other Urban Sketches.* Berkeley: University of California Press, 1990.

Foucault, Michel. *The History of Sexuality, Volume I: An Introduction.* New York: Vintage Books, 1978.

Fraser, Nancy, and Linda Gordon. "A Genealogy of Dependency: Tracing a Keyword of the U.S. Welfare State." *Signs* 19 (1994): 309–36.

Freeman, Elizabeth. "Honeymoon with a Stranger: Pedophiliac Picaresque from Poe to Nabokov." *American Literature* 70 (December 1998): 863–97.

Freud, Sigmund. "Mourning and Melancholia." In *The Standard Edition of the Complete Psychological Works of Sigmund Freud,* Trans. and ed. James Stratchey, vol. 14 (1914–1916). London: Hogarth Press, 1957.

Fuss, Diana, ed. *Human, All Too Human.* New York: Routledge, 1996.

Gardner, Eric. "'This Attempt of Their Sister': Harriet Wilson's *Our Nig* from Printer to Readers." *New England Quarterly* 66 (June 1993): 226–46.

Garlitz, Barbara. "Pearl: 1850–1955." *PMLA* 72 (September 1957): 689–99.

Genovese, Elizabeth Fox. "'To Weave It into the Literature of the Country': Epic and the Fictions of African American Women." In *Poetics of the Americas: Race, Founding, and Textuality,* ed. Bainard Cowan and Jefferson Humphries. Baton Rouge: Louisiana State University Press, 1997.

Giles, Henry. *Illustrations of Genius.* Boston: Ticknor and Fields, 1854.

Gilmore, Michael T. "Hawthorne and the Making of the Middle Class." In *Rethinking Class: Literary Studies and Social Formations,* ed. Wai Chee Dimock and Michael T. Gilmore. New York: Columbia University Press, 1994.

Gilmore, William J. *Reading Becomes a Necessity of Life: Material Cultural Life in Rural New England, 1780–1835.* Knoxville: University of Tennessee Press, 1989.

Gilroy, Paul. *There Ain't No Black in the Union Jack.* London: Hutchinson, 1987.

Ginzberg, Lori D. *Women and the Work of Benevolence: Morality, Politics and Class in the Nineteenth-Century United States.* New Haven, Conn.: Yale University Press, 1990.

Gleason, William A. *The Leisure Ethic: Work and Play in American Literature 1840–1940.* Stanford, Calif.: Stanford University Press, 1999.

The Good Boy's and Girl's Alphabet. Philadelphia: B. Bramell, 1841.

Goodenough, Elizabeth, Mark Heberle, and Naomi Sokoloff. *Infant Tongues: The Voice of the Child in Literature.* Detroit, Mich.: Wayne State University Press, 1994.

[Goodrich, Samuel]. *Peter Parley's Primer.* Philadelphia: Henry Anners, 1835.

Gordon, Linda. *Heroes of Their Own Lives: The Politics and History of Family Violence, Boston 1880–1960.* New York: Viking, 1988.

Gordon, Linda, and Paul O'Keefe. "Incest as a Form of Family Violence: Evidence from Historical Case Records." *Journal of Marriage and the Family* 46 (February 1984): 27–34.

Goshgarian, G. M. *To Kiss the Chastening Rod: Domestic Fiction and Sexual Ideology in the American Renaissance.* Ithaca, N.Y.: Cornell University Press, 1992.

Gossett, Thomas. *Race: The History of an Idea in America.* Dallas, Tex.: Southern Methodist University Press, 1963.

Grand National Union Concert. Broadside. July 4, 1862. Collection of the American Antiquarian Society.

Gratacap, Louis Pope. Diary. New York Public Library.

Greven, Philip. *The Protestant Temperament: Patterns of Child-Rearing, Religious Experience, and the Self in Early America.* New York: Knopf, 1977.

Grover, Kathryn. *Hard at Play: Leisure in America 1840–1940.* Amherst: University of Massachusetts Press, 1992.

Hale Family Papers. Sophia Smith Collection, Smith College.

Haller, John S. Jr. *Outcasts from Evolution: Scientific Attitudes of Racial Inferiority, 1859–1900.* Urbana: University of Illinois Press, 1971.

Halttunen, Karen. *Confidence Men and Painted Women: A Study of Middle-Class Culture in America 1830–1870.* New Haven, Conn.: Yale University Press, 1982.

Hancock, Mrs. L. B. *A Mother's Scrap-Book Only.* Cincinnati: Hitchcock and Walden, 1878.

———. *Heart's-ease: A Mother's Offering.* Cincinnati: Curtis and Jennings, 1899.

Handy, Robert. *A Christian America: Protestant Hopes and Historical Realities.* New York: Oxford University Press, 1984.

Harriet Fisher; or, The Missionary at Home. Philadelphia: American Sunday School Union, 1843.

Harrison, Eli Lee. Copybook facsimile pages. c. 1850. Private Collection of Pat Pfliegler. www.merrycoz.org/lee/Lee.HTML.

Harrison, Gabriel. "Lights and Shadows of Daguerrean Life." *The Photographic Art-Journal* 1 (March 1851): 179–181.

Hawthorne, Nathaniel. *The Centenary Edition of the Works of Nathaniel Hawthorne.* Edited by William Charvat et al. 20 vols. Columbus: Ohio State University Press, 1963–1997.

———. *Peter Parley's Universal History, on the Basis of Geography, for the Use of Families.* 2 vols. New York: S. Coleman, 1839.

———. *Twenty Days with Julian & Little Bunny by Papa.* New York: New York Review of Books, 2003.

Hedrick, Joan D. *Harriet Beecher Stowe: A Life.* New York: Oxford University Press, 1994.

Heininger, Mary Lynn Stevens, et al. *A Century of Childhood: 1820–1920.* Rochester, N.Y.: The Margaret Woodbury Strong Museum, 1984.

Henkin, David M. *City Reading: Written Words and Public Spaces in Antebellum New York.* New York: Columbia University Press.

Herbert, T. Walter. *Dearest Beloved: The Hawthornes and the Making of the Middle-Class Family.* Berkeley: University of California Press, 1993.

———. "Nathaniel Hawthorne, Una Hawthorne, and *The Scarlet Letter:* Interactive Selfhoods and the Cultural Construction of Gender." *PMLA* 103 (May 1988): 285–97.

Herman, Judith Lewis. *Trauma and Recovery.* New York: Basic Books, 1992.

Higginson, Thomas Wentworth. *Army Life in a Black Regiment.* Boston: Beacon Press, 1962.

———. "The Baby of the Regiment." In *Child Life in Prose,* ed. John Greenleaf Whittier. Boston: James R. Osgood, 1874.

Hill, Patricia R. *The World Their Household: The American Woman's Foreign Mission Movement and Cultural Transformation, 1870–1920.* Ann Arbor: University of Michigan Press, 1985.

Hobbs, Catherine, ed. *Nineteenth-Century Women Learn to Write.* Charlottesville: University Press of Virginia, 1995.

Hogan, Rebecca. "Engendered Autobiographies: The Diary as a Feminine Form." In *Autobiography and Questions of Gender,* ed. Shirley Neuman. London: F. Cass, 1992.

Holmes, Oliver Wendell. "Doings of the Sunbeam." *The Atlantic Monthly* 12 (12 July 1863): 1–16.

Holt, Marilyn Irvin. *The Orphan Trains: Placing Out in America.* Lincoln: University of Nebraska Press, 1992.

Homberger, Eric. *Scenes from the Life of a City: Corruption and Conscience in Old New York.* New Haven, Conn.: Yale University Press, 1994.

Howard, June. "What is Sentimentality?" *American Literary History* 11 (spring 1999): 63–81.

Hull, David Stuart. *James Henry Cafferty, N. A. (1819–1869).* New York: New York Historical Society, 1986.

Hunt, Peter. *An Introduction to Children's Literature.* New York: Oxford University Press, 1994.

Hunter, Jane. *The Gospel of Gentility: American Women Missionaries in Turn-of-the-Century China.* New Haven, Conn.: Yale University Press, 1984.

Huizinga, Johan. *Homo Ludens: A Study of the Play Element in Culture.* Boston: Beacon Press, 1950.

Hyde, Rev. Allen. *Essay on the State of Infants.* New York: Cornelius Davis, 1830.

Ingraham, Joseph Holt. *Jemmy Daily: or, the Little News Vendor a Tale of Youthful Struggles, and the triumph of truth and virtue over vice and falsehood.* New York: Sun Office, 1843.

Jackson, Charles O., ed. *Passing: The Vision of Death in America.* Westport, Conn.: Greenwood Press, 1977.

Jameson, Fredric. *Signatures of the Visible.* New York: Routledge, 1990.

Jay, Bill. "Infantry Tactics." In Sue Packer, *The Babies.* Manchester, Mich.: Cornerhouse, 1989.

Jenkins, Henry, ed. *The Children's Culture Reader.* New York: New York University Press, 1998.

Jewett, Charles. *Forty Years Fight with the Drink Demon; or a History of the Temperance Reform as I Have Seen It and of My Labor in Connection Therewith.* New York: National Temperance Society and Publishing House, 1872.

Johannsen, Albert. *The House of Beadle and Adams and Its Dime and Nickel Novels: A Study of Vanished Literature.* Norman: University of Oklahoma Press, 1950.

Johnson, Alexandra. "The Drama of Imagination: Marjory Fleming and Her Diaries." In *Infant Tongues: The Voice of the Child in Literature,* ed. Elizabeth Goodenough, Mark Heberle, and Naomi Sokoloff. Detroit, Mich.: Wayne State University Press, 1994.

Johnson, Paul E. *A Shopkeeper's Millennium: Society and Revivals in Rochester, New York, 1815–1837.* New York: Hill and Wang, 1978.

Juvenile Key or Child's Newspaper. Brunswick, Maine, 1850.

Kagle, Steven E. *Early Nineteenth-Century American Diary Literature.* Boston: Twayne Publishers, 1986.

Kaplan, Amy. *The Anarchy of Empire in the Making of U.S. Culture.* Cambridge: Harvard University Press, 2002.

Kaplan, Amy, and Donald Pease, eds. *The Cultures of United States Imperialism.* Durham, N.C.: Duke University Press, 1993.

Kerber, Linda. *Women of the Republic: Intellect and Ideology in Revolutionary America.* New York: W. W. Norton, 1986.

Kincaid, James R. *Child-Loving: The Erotic Child and Victorian Culture.* New York: Routledge, 1992.

[Knight, Helen Cross]. *The Missionary Cabinet.* Boston: Massachusetts Sabbath School Repository, 1847.

Knoepflmacher, U. C. *Ventures into Childland: Victorians, Fairy Tales, and Femininity.* Chicago: University of Chicago Press, 1998.

Kohn, Melvin L. *Class and Conformity: A Study in Values, with a Reassessment, 1977.* Chicago: University of Chicago Press, 1977.

Kopacz, Paula. "The School Journal of Hannah (Anna) Gale." In *Studies in the American Renaissance,* ed. Joel Myerson. Charlottesville: University Press of Virginia, 1996.

Laffrado, Laura. *Hawthorne's Literature for Children.* Athens: University of Georgia Press, 1992.

Langsam, Miriam Z. *Children West: A History of the Placing-Out System of the New York Children's Aid Society, 1853–1890.* Madison: State Historical Society of Wisconsin, 1964.

Laurie, Bruce. *Working People of Philadelphia, 1800–1850.* Philadelphia: Temple University Press, 1980.

Laurie, Dennis R. "Amateur Journalism." *Collectible Newspapers: Official Journal of the NCSA* (April 1989).

Lawson, A. G. "Temperance Literature." In *Proceedings of the Seventh National Temperance Convention, Saratoga Springs, New York, August 26 and 27, 1873.* New York: National Temperance Society and Publication House, 1873.

Layne, Linda. "Of Fetuses and Angels: Fragmentation and Integration in Narratives of Pregnancy Loss." *Knowledge and Society: The Anthropology of Science and Technology* 9 (1992): 29–58.

Leigh, Edwin. *McGuffey's New Primary Reader.* New York: Wilson Hinkle and Co., 1864.

Lejeune, Philippe. "The 'Journal de Jeune Fille' in Nineteenth-Century France." Translated by Martine Breillac. In *Inscribing the Daily: Critical Essays on Women's Diaries,* ed. Suzanne L. Bunkers and Cynthia A. Huff. Amherst: University of Massachusetts Press, 1996.

Lesnik-Oberstein, Karín. *Children in Culture: Approaches to Childhood.* New York: St. Martin's Press, 1998.

Levander, Caroline. "'Letting her White Progeny Offset Her Dark One': The Child and the Racial Politics of Nation Making." *American Literature* 76 (June 2004).

Levander, Caroline, and Carol Singly, eds. *The American Child: A Cultural Studies Reader.* New Brunswick, N.J.: Rutgers University Press, 2003.

Livingston, Myra Cohen. *The Child as Poet: Myth or Reality?* Boston: Horn Book Inc., 1984.

Lloyd, David. "Race Under Representation." *Oxford Literary Review* 13 (1991): 62–94.

Lopez, Michael. *Emerson and Power: Creative Antagonism in the Nineteenth Century.* DeKalb: Northern Illinois University Press, 1996.

Loring, George P. "Hawthorne's *Scarlet Letter.*" *Massachusetts Quarterly Review* 3 (September 1850): 484–500.

Lovechild, Mrs. "The Missionary." In *The Christmas Tree and Other Stories for the Young.* Boston: William H. Hill Jr., 1863.

MacLeod, Anne Scott. *American Childhood: Essays on Children's Literature of the Nineteenth and Twentieth Centuries.* Athens: University of Georgia Press, 1994.

Manzo, Kate. *Racial Nationalism and the Politics of Exclusion.* Boulder, Colo.: Lynne Rienner, 1994.

Maria Cheeseman or the Candy Girl. Philadelphia: American Sunday School Union, 1855.

Marryat, Captain Frederick. *The Mission: or Scenes in Africa Written for Young People.* 2 vols. New York: Geo. S. Appleton, 1845.

Marsh, Rev. John. *Hannah Hawkins: The Reformed Drunkard's Daughter.* New York: American Temperance Union, 1848.

Marshall, David. *The Surprising Effects of Sympathy: Marivaux, Diderot, Rousseau, and Mary Shelley.* Chicago: University of Chicago Press, 1988.

Marx, Karl. *Capital: A Critique of Political Economy.* 1867. Reprint. New York: Modern Library, 1936.

Mavor, Carol. *Pleasures Taken: Performances of Sexuality and Loss in Victorian Photographs.* Durham, N.C.: Duke University Press, 1995.

McGill, Meredith L. *American Literature and the Culture of Reprinting, 1834–1853.* Philadelphia: University of Pennsylvania Press, 2003.

———. "The Duplicity of the Pen." In *Language Machines: Technologies of Literacy and Cultural Production,* ed. Jeffrey Masten, Peter Stallybrass, and Nancy Vickers. New York: Routledge, 1997.

McHugh, Kathleen. *American Domesticity: From How-To Manual to Hollywood Melodrama.* New York: Oxford University Press, 1999.

McLoughlin, William G. *Cherokees and Missionaries, 1789–1839.* New Haven, Conn.: Yale University Press, 1984.

"Missionary Collections in the Sunday Schools." *Sunday School Times* 12 (October 8, 1870): 648.

Millington, Richard H. *Practicing Romance: Narrative Form and Cultural Engagement in Hawthorne's Fiction.* Princeton, N.J.: Princeton University Press, 1992.

Mintz, Steven. *A Prison of Expectations: The Family in Victorian Culture.* New York: New York University Press, 1983.

Mitchell, Mary Niall. "'Rosebloom and Pure White,' or So It Seemed." *American Quarterly* 54 (September 2002): 369–410.

Monaghen, E. Jennifer. *A Common Heritage: Noah Webster Blue-Back Speller.* Hamden, Conn.: Archon Books, 1983.

Moon, Michael. "'The Gentle Boy from the Dangerous Classes': Pederasty, Domesticity and Capitalism in Horatio Alger." *Representations* 19 (summer 1987): 87–110.

———. *Disseminating Whitman: Revision and Corporeality in* Leaves of Grass. Cambridge: Harvard University Press, 1991.

Moore, R. Laurence. "Religion, Secularization, and the Shaping of the Culture Industry in Antebellum America." *American Quarterly* 41 (June 1989): 216–42.

Moorhead, James H. *American Apocalypse: Yankee Protestants and the Civil War, 1860–1869.* New Haven, Conn.: Yale University Press, 1978.

Morning Glory. New York: American Tract Society, n.d. (1848?).

Morrow, John. *A Voice from the Newsboys.* New York?: Published for the author, 1860.

Murray, Gail Schmunk, *American Children's Literature and the Construction of Childhood.* New York: Twayne Publishers, 1998.

Murray, Joan. "Rags to Riches: The Newsboy in Nineteenth-Century American Art." *Canadian Collector: A Journal of Antiques and Fine Arts* 17 (September/October 1982): 26–31.

Nackenoff, Carol. *The Fictional Republic: Horatio Alger and American Political Discourse.* New York: Oxford University Press, 1994.

Nasaw, David. *Children of the City at Work and Play.* New York: Oxford University Press, 1985.

———. *Going Out: The Rise and Fall of Public Amusements.* New York: Basic Books, 1993.

Neu, Jerome. "A Tear Is an Intellectual Thing." *Representations* 19 (summer 1987): 35–61. *New England Journal of Education* 17 (1883).

The New England Primer Enlarged for More Easy Attaining the True Reading of English. To Which Is Added, the Assembly of Divines Catechism. Boston: S. Kneeland and T. Green, 1727.

Newell, William Wells. *Games and Songs of American Children.* 1883. Reprint. New York: Harper and Brothers, 1903.

Newfield, Christopher. *The Emerson Effect: Individualism and Submission in America.* Chicago: University of Chicago Press, 1996.

Newhall, Beaumont. *The Daguerreotype in America.* New York: Duell, Sloan and Pearce, 1961.

Newhall, Beaumont, ed. *Photography: Essays and Images, Illustrated Readings in the History of Photography.* New York: Museum of Modern Art, 1980.

Noble, Marianne. *The Masochistic Pleasures of Sentimental Literature.* Princeton, N.J.: Princeton University Press, 2000.

Norcross, Grenville H. Diary. American Antiquarian Society.

Nudelman, Franny. "'Emblem and Product of Sin': The Poisoned Child in *The Scarlet Letter* and Domestic Advice Literature." *Yale Journal of Criticism* 10 (spring 1997).

Old Jesse the Hindoo Mother. Philadelphia: n.d. (1857?).

Opie, Iona, and Peter Opie, eds. *The Oxford Dictionary of Nursery Rhymes.* New York: Oxford University Press, 1951.

Ortner, Sherry B. "Is Female to Male as Nature Is to Culture?" In *Woman, Culture, and Society,* ed. Michelle Rosaldo and Louise Lamphere. Stanford, Calif.: Stanford University Press, 1974.

Ours. New York. 1873.

Paoletti, Jo B., and Carol L. Kregloh. "The Children's Department." In *Men and Women: Dressing the Part,* ed. Claudia Brush Kidwell and Valerie Steel. Washington, D.C.: Smithsonian Institution Press, 1989. 22–41.

Parker, Jenny Marsh. *The Story of a Story-Book.* New York: General Protestant Episcopal Sunday School Union, and Church Book Society, 1858.

Pascoe, Peggy. *Relations of Rescue: The Search for Female Moral Authority in the American West, 1874–1939.* New York: Oxford University Press, 1990.

Paul, Susan. *Memoir of James Jackson, the Attentive and Obedient Scholar, who Died in Boston, October 31, 1833, Aged Six Years and Eleven Months (1835).* Edited by Lois Brown. Cambridge: Harvard University Press, 2000.

Peabody, Elizabeth. *Record of a School: Exemplifying the General Principles of Spiritual Culture.* Boston: J. Munroe, 1835.

Peterson, Carla. "Capitalism, Black (Under)development, and the Production of the African-American Novel in the 1850s." *American Literary History* 4 (1992): 559–83.

Petrino, Elizabeth A. "Feet so Precious Charged: Dickinson, Sigourney and the Child Elegy." *Tulsa Studies in Women's Literature* 13 (fall 1994): 317–38.

Phelps, Elizabeth Stuart [Ward]. *Tiny's Sunday Nights.* Boston: Massachusetts Sunday School Society, 1866.

Phillips, Adam. *The Beast in the Nursery.* New York: Pantheon Books, 1998.

———. *Winnicott.* Cambridge: Harvard University Press, 1988.

Pleck, Elizabeth. *Domestic Tyranny: The Making of Social Policy against Family Violence from Colonial Times to the Present.* New York: Oxford University Press, 1987.

Poirier, Richard. *The Renewal of Literature: Emersonian Reflections.* New York: Random House, 1987.

Poovey, Mary. *Uneven Developments: The Ideological Work of Gender in Mid-Victorian England.* Chicago: University of Chicago Press, 1988.

Potter, William Henry. Diary. New York Public Library.

Pratofiorito, Ellen. "'To Demand Your Sympathy and Aid': *Our Nig* and the Problem of No Audience." *Journal of American and Comparative Cultures* 24 (spring–summer 2001): 31–48.

Prentiss, Elizabeth, ed. *The Old Brown Pitcher and Other Tales.* New York: National Temperance Union and Publication House, 1863.

Prine, S. Irenaues D. D. et al., eds. *The Smitten Household; or Thoughts for the Afflicted.* New York: Anson D. F. Randolph, 1860.

Pufall, Peter, and Richard Unsworth, eds. *Rethinking Childhood.* New Brunswick, N.J.: Rutgers University Press, 2004.

Purdy, Laura. *In Their Best Interest? The Case against Equal Rights for Children.* Ithaca, N.Y.: Cornell University Press, 1992.

Quincy, P. *Public Libraries in the United States of America: Their History, Condition, and Management.* Washington, D.C.: Government Printing Office, 1876.

The Ragged Scholars, Perils in the Desert, and *The Avenger Stayed.* Philadelphia: Presbyterian Board of Publications, n.d. (1850–57?).

"Rally Round the Flag." Broadside. Boston: Horace and Partridge, 1862. American Antiquarian Society.

The Red Brothers. Philadelphia: American Sunday School Union, 1846.

Reinier, Jacqueline S. *From Virtue to Character: American Childhood 1775–1850.* New York: Twayne Publishers, 1996.

Reynolds, David S. *Beneath the American Renaissance: The Subversive Imagination on the Age of Emerson and Melville.* New York: Alfred Knopf, 1988.

Reynolds, David S., and Debra J. Rosenthal, eds. *The Serpent in the Cup: Temperance in American Literature.* Amherst: University of Massachusetts Press, 1997.

Rickard, Truman, and Hiram Orcutt. *Class Book of Prose and Poetry: Consisting of Selections from the Best English and American Authors Designed as Exercises in Parsing; for the Use of Common Schools and Academies.* Boston: Roberts S. Davis & Co., 1863.

Roberts, Daniel T. "Socializing Middle-Class Children: Institutions, Fables, and Work Values in Nineteenth-Century America." *Journal of Social History* 13 (spring 1980): 354–67.

Robbins, Sarah. *Managing Literacy, Mothering America: Women's Narratives on Reading and Writing in the Nineteenth Century.* Pittsburgh: University of Pittsburgh Press, 2004.

Robinson, Joyce Henri. "'And a Little Child Shall Lead Them': American Children's Cabinets of Curiosities." In *Acts of Possession: Collecting in America,* ed. Leah Dilworth. New Brunswick, N.J.: Rutgers University Press, 2003.

Rockwood, George G. *Rockwood's Photographic Art-illery Manual and Infantry Tactics.* New York: H. S. Zucker, 1874.

Rogin, Michael Paul. *Fathers and Children: Andrew Jackson and the Subjugation of the American Indian.* New York: Knopf, 1975.

Romero, Lora. *Home Fronts: Domesticity and Its Critics in the Antebellum United States.* Durham, N.C.: Duke University Press, 1997.

———. "Vanishing Americans: Gender, Empire, and New Historicism." In *The Culture of Sentiment: Race, Gender, and Sentiment in Nineteenth-Century America,* ed. Shirley Samuels. New York: Oxford University Press, 1992.

Rose, Jacqueline. *The Case of Peter Pan: The Impossibility of Children's Fiction.* London: Macmillan, 1984.

Rosenzweig, Roy. *Eight Hours for What We Will: Workers and Leisure in an Industrial City, 1870–1920.* New York: Cambridge University Press, 1983.

Ruby, Jay. *Secure the Shadow: Death and Photography in America.* Cambridge: MIT Press, 1995.

Rudisill, Richard. *Mirror Image: The Influence of the Daguerreotype on American Society.* Albuquerque, N.M.: University of New Mexico Press, 1971.

Ryan, Mary. *Cradle of the Middle Class: The Family in Oneida County, New York, 1790–1865.* New York: Cambridge University Press, 1981.

———. *The Empire of the Mother: American Writing about Domesticity, 1830–1860.* New York: Harrington Park Press, 1985.

Ryan, Susan M. *The Grammar of Good Intentions: Race and the Antebellum Culture of Benevolence.* Ithaca, N.Y.: Cornell University Press, 2003.

Samuels, Shirley, ed. *The Culture of Sentiment: Race, Gender, and Sentiment in Nineteenth-Century America.* New York: Oxford University Press, 1992.

———. *Romances of the Republic: Women, the Family, and Violence in the Literature of the Early American Nation.* New York: Oxford University Press, 1996.

Sanders, Charles W. *Sanders's Pictorial Primer.* New York: Ivison, Phinney and Co., 1860.

———. *Sanders's Second Reader.* New York: Ivison, Phinney and Co., 1853.

———. *Sanders's Union Speller.* New York: Ivison, Blakeman, Taylor, and Co., 1871.

Sargent, Lucius Manlius. *My Mother's Gold Ring; Founded on Fact.* Boston: Ford and Damrell, 1833.

Sargent, Lucius. *Temperance Tales*. Boston: American Tract Society, 1863.

Saxton, Alexander. *The Rise and Fall of the White Republic: Class, Politics and Mass Culture in Nineteenth-Century America*. New York: Verso, 1990.

Scenes in the Wilderness. Philadelphia: American Sunday School Union, 1846.

Scheper-Hughes, Nancy, and Carolyn Sargent, eds. *Small Wars: The Cultural Politics of Childhood*. Berkeley: University of California Press, 1998.

Schor, Esther. *Bearing the Dead: The British Culture of Mourning from the Enlightenment to Victoria*. Princeton N.J.: Princeton University Press, 1994.

Schudson, Michael. *Discovering the News: A Social History of American Newspapers*. New York: Basic Books, 1978.

Scudder, Dr. John. *Appeal to the Children and Youth of the United States of America in Behalf of the Heathen World*. Philadelphia: American Sunday School Union, 1846.

———. *Dr. Scudder's Tales for Little Readers, about the Heathen*. New York: American Tract Society, 1849.

Sedgwick, Catherine. *Home*. Boston: James Munroe and Company, 1845.

The Sedley Family; or, The Effect of the Maine Liquor Law. Boston: T. O. Walker, 1853.

Seiter, Ellen. *Sold Separately: Children and Parents in Consumer Cultures*. New Brunswick, N.J.: Rutgers University Press, 1993.

Self-Denial; or Alice Wood and Her Missionary Society. [Philadelphia?: American Sunday School Union?, n.d., 1846?]

Sewall, Edmund Quincy. Diary. The American Antiquarian Society.

Shealy, Daniel. "Margaret Fuller and her 'Maiden': Evelina Metcalf's 1838 School Journal." In *Studies in the American Renaissance*, ed. Joel Myerson. Charlottesville: University Press of Virginia, 1996.

Sherman, Stuart. *Telling Time: Clocks, Diaries, and English Diurnal Form, 1660–1875*. Chicago: University of Chicago Press, 1996.

Shesgreen, Sean. *Images of the Outcast: The Urban Poor in the Cries of London*. New Brunswick, N.J.: Rutgers University Press, 2002.

Sheumaker, Helen. *"A Token that Love Entwines": Nineteenth-Century Human Hair Work and the American White Middle Class*. Ph.D. dissertation, University of Kansas, 1999.

Siegel, Adrienne. *The Image of the American City in Popular Literature, 1820–1870*. Port Washington, N.Y.: Kinnikat Press, 1981.

Sigourney, Lydia H. *A Book for Girls in Prose and Poetry*. New York, 1843.

———. *How to Be Happy. Written for the Children of Some Dear Friends. By a Lady*. Hartford, Conn., 1833.

———. *Water Drops*. New York: R. Carter, 1850.

Silverman, Joan. *"I'll Never Touch Another Drop": Images of Alcoholism and Temperance in American Popular Culture, 1874–1918*. Ph.D. dissertation, New York University, 1979.

Simonds, Wendy, and Barbara Katz Rothman. *Centuries of Solace: Expressions of Maternal Grief in Popular Literature*. Philadelphia: Temple University Press, 1992.

Smith, Elizabeth Oakes. *The Newsboy*. New York: J. C. Derby, 1854.

Smith, Valerie. *Self-discovery and Authority in Afro-American Narrative*. Cambridge: Harvard University Press, 1987.

Snelling, Anna L. *The Photographic Art-Journal* 1 (February 1851): 126.

Soltow, Lee, and Edward Stevens. *The Rise of Literacy and the Common School in the United States: A Socioeconomic Analysis to 1870.* Chicago: University of Chicago Press, 1981.

Sontag, Susan. *On Photography.* New York: Penguin, 1978.

Southworth, E. D. E. N. *The Hidden Hand.* 1859. Reprint. New Brunswick, N.J.: Rutgers University Press.

Spigel, Lynn. "Television and the Family Circle: The Popular Reception of a New Medium." In *Logics of Television: Essays in Cultural Criticism,* ed. Patricia Mellencamp. Bloomington: Indiana University Press, 1990.

Spring, Gardiner. *A Dissertation on Native Depravity.* New York: Jonathan Leavitt, 1833.

[Starr, F. Ratchford]. *John Ellard: The Newsboy.* Philadelphia: William S. and Alfred Martien, 1860.

Stannard, David E., ed. *Death in America.* Philadelphia: University of Pennsylvania Press, 1975.

Stansell, Christine. *City of Women: Sex and Class in New York, 1789–1860.* New York: Alfred A. Knopf, 1986.

[Stanton, Elizabeth Cady], S. F. *The Lily* 2 (April 1850): 31.

———. *The Una* 2 (May 1854): 260.

Stanton,William. *The Leopard's Spots: Scientific Attitudes toward Race in America, 1815–1859.* Chicago: University of Chicago Press, 1960.

Stearns, J. N., ed. *The Temperance Speaker: A Collection of Original and Selected Dialogues, Addresses and Recitations, for the Use of Temperance Organizations, Schools, Bands of Hope, Anniversaries, etc.* New York: National Temperance Society and Publication House, 1873.

Stebbins, Jane E. *Fifty Years History of the Temperance Cause,* published in the same volume with T. A. H. Brown. *A Full Description of the Origin and Progress of the New Plan of Labor by the Women Up to the Present Time.* Hartford, Conn.: L. Stebbins, 1876.

Steedman, Carolyn Kay. *Landscape for a Good Woman: A Story of Two Lives.* New Brunswick, N.J.: Rutgers University Press, 1987.

———. *Strange Dislocations: Childhood and the Idea of Human Interiority, 1780–1930.* Cambridge: Harvard University Press, 1995.

———. "The Tidy House." In *The Children's Culture Reader,* ed. Henry Jenkins. New York: New York University Press, 1998.

Stephens, Sharon, ed. *Children and the Politics of Culture.* Princeton, N.J.: Princeton University Press, 1995.

Stern, Julia. "Excavating Genre in *Our Nig.*" *American Literature* 67 (September 1995): 439–66.

———. *The Plight of Feeling: Sympathy and Dissent in the Early American Novel.* Chicago: University of Chicago Press, 1997.

Stewart, Susan. *On Longing: Narratives of the Miniature, the Gigantic, the Souvenir, the Collection.* Durham, N.C.: Duke University Press, 1993.

Stocking, George W. Jr. *Race, Culture and Evolution: Essays in the History of Anthropology.* New York: Free Press, 1968.

Stories about the Heathen and Their Children. Boston: American Tract Society, n.d. (1860?).

Stowe, Harriet Beecher. *Uncle Tom's Cabin; or, Life among the Lowly.* New York: Penguin, 1981.

Stowe, Charles Edward. *The Life of Harriet Beecher Stowe Compiled from Her Letters and Journals.* Boston: Houghton and Mifflin, 1889.

Strong, Bryan. "Toward a History of the Experiential Family: Sex and Incest in the Nineteenth-Century Family." *Journal of Marriage and the Family* 35 (August 1973): 457–66.

Suleri, Sara. "Woman Skin Deep: Feminism and the Postcolonial Condition." *Critical Inquiry* 18 (summer 1992): 756–69.

Syper, J. R. "Temperance Literature." In *Proceedings of the Sixth National Temperance Convention, Cleveland, Ohio, July 29, 1868.* New York: National Temperance Society and Publication House, 1868.

Tagg, John. *The Burden of Representation: Essays on Photographies and Histories.* Minneapolis: University of Minnesota Press, 1899.

Takaki, Ronald T. *Iron Cages: Race and Culture in Nineteenth-Century America.* Seattle: University of Washington Press, 1979.

Tate, Claudia. *Domestic Allegories of Political Desire: The Black Heroine's Text at the Turn of the Century.* New York: Oxford University Press, 1992.

Taves, Ann, ed. *Religion and Domestic Violence in Early New England: The Memoirs of Abigail Abbot Bailey.* Bloomington: Indiana University Press, 1989.

Teichgraeber, Richard F. *Sublime Thoughts / Penny Wisdom: Situating Emerson and Thoreau in the American Market.* Baltimore: Johns Hopkins University Press, 1995.

Ten Books Beautifully Illustrated for Children. New York: Protestant Episcopal Society for the Promotion of Evangelical Knowledge, 1861.

Thomas, Nicholas. "Colonial Conversions: Difference, Hierarchy, and History in Early Twentieth-Century Evangelical Propaganda." *Comparative Studies in Society and History* 34 (April 1992): 366–89.

Tompkins, Jane. *Sensational Designs: The Cultural Work of American Fiction, 1790–1860.* New York: Oxford University Press, 1985.

[Thompson, George], The Greenhorn. *Life and Exploits of the Noted Criminal Bristol Bill.* New York: M. J. Ivers, 1851.

Trachtenberg, Alan. *Reading American Photographs: Images as History, Matthew Brady to Walker Evans.* New York: Hill and Wang, 1989.

Trachtman, Paula, ed. *Out of Season: An Anthology of Work By and about Young People who Died.* Amagansett, N.Y.: Amagansett Press, 1993.

Trumbull, Louisa Jane. Diaries. Trumbull Family Papers. American Antiquarian Society.

United Nations Convention on the Rights of the Child. Geneva: United Nations, 1989.

United States School Primer. New York: G. F. Cooledge and Brother, 1839.

Valenti, Patricia Dunlavy. "Sophia Peabody Hawthorne's American Notebook." In *Studies in the American Renaissance,* ed. Joel Myerson. Charlottesville: University Press of Virginia, 1996.

Van Wart, Irving. Diary. New York Public Library.

Wald, Priscilla. "Terms of Assimilation: Legislating Subjectivity in the Emerging Nation." *Boundary* 2, no. 19 (fall 1992): 77–104.

Walt Whitman: The Early Poems and Fiction. Edited by Thomas L. Brasher. New York: New York University Press, 1963.

Wardley, Lynn. "Relic, Fetish, Femmage: The Aesthetics of Sentiment in the Work of Stowe." In *The Culture of Sentiment: Race, Gender, and Sentiment in Nineteenth-Century America,* ed. Shirley Samuels. New York: Oxford University Press, 1992.

Warner, Susan. *The Wide, Wide World.* 1850. Reprint. New York: Feminist Press at CUNY, 1987.

Webster, Noah. *The American Spelling Book.* Boston: Thomas and Andrews, 1798.

———. *The Elementary Spelling Book.* New York: G. F. Cooledge and Brother, 1829.

———. *Essays on Education in the Early Republic.* Edited by Frederick Rudolph. Cambridge: Harvard University Press, 1965.

West, Elliott, and Paula Petrik, eds. *Small Worlds: Children and Adolescents in America, 1850–1950.* Lawrence: University of Kansas Press, 1992.

Wexler, Laura. *Tender Violence: Domestic Visions in an Age of U.S. Imperialism.* Chapel Hill: University of North Carolina Press, 2000.

"White and Colored Slaves." *Harper's Weekly* 8 (January 30, 1864): 71.

Whicher, Stephen. *Freedom and Fate: An Inner Life of Ralph Waldo Emerson.* Philadelphia: University of Pennsylvania Press, 1971.

Whisnant, David E. "Selling the Gospel News, or: The Strange Career of Jimmy Brown the Newsboy." *Journal of Social History* 5 (spring 1972): 269–309.

White, Barbara. "*Our Nig* and the She-Devil: New Information about Harriet Wilson and the 'Bellmont' Family." *American Literature* 65 (March 1993): 21–25.

Whitman,Walt. *Poetry and Prose.* New York: The Library of America, 1996.

Whitney, Edward Tompkins. "On Taking Daguerreotypes of Children." *The Photographic and Fine Art Journal* 8 (March 1855).

Whittier, John Greenleaf, ed. *Child Life in Prose.* Boston: James R. Osgood and Co., 1874.

Wiggin, Charles H. Diary. American Antiquarian Society.

Williams, Raymond. *Keywords: A Vocabulary of Culture and Society.* New York: Oxford University Press, 1976.

Wilson, Harriet E. *Our Nig; or, Sketches from the Life of a Free Black, in a Two-Story White House, North. Showing that Slavery's Shadows Fall Even There.* New York: Vintage Books, 1983.

Winnicott, D. W. *Playing and Reality.* New York: Routledge, 1989.

Wishy, Bernard. *The Child and the Republic: The Dawn of American Child Nurture.* Philadelphia: University of Pennsylvania Press, 1968.

Wright, Julia McNair. *A Million Too Much, A Temperance Tale.* Philadelphia: Porter and Coates, 1871.

Young, Samuel. *Missionary Narrative of the Triumphs of Grace; As Seen in the Conversion of Kafirs, Hottentots, Fingos and Other Natives of South Africa.* New York, 1843.

Zboray, Ronald. *A Fictive People: Antebellum Economic Development and the Reading Public.* New York: Oxford University Press, 1993.

Zelizer, Viviana A. *Pricing the Priceless Child: The Changing Social Value of Children.* New York: Basic Books, 1985.

INDEX

Abbott, Jacob, 3–4, 10, 14
Abbott, John S. C., 10, 14n27
African Americans: anti-slavery movement, 204, 227–31; Christianity and, 200–202, 203, 205–6, 208, 209–10; contingency of freedom, 231; exploration of black self-hood (see *Our Nig*); first woman-published novel, 41; meaning of being a black man, 43, 44; racial framing, 44–45, 211; racial identity and, 42–44; racialized faith, 203; racial prejudice and, 203–4; reading, 8–9; scientific racialism, 199
Akatangi, 209, 210
alcoholism: argument for stronger divorce laws, 77–78; correlation with domestic violence, 77; fiction used for moral suasion (*see* temperance fiction); prohibition movement, 72–73, 75
Alcott, Bronson, 19n32, 152, 153, 207n40
Alcott, Louisa May, 164
Alger, Horatio, 166, 167, 170, 171
Allen, Mary Ware, xiii–xiv, xxviii, 39
American Colonization Society, 202
American Home, 197
American imperialism: internationalizing of U.S. domestic empire, 187–88; in missionary stories, 208; missionary's condemnation of, 201; nature of missionary sentiments, 188–89; rejection of domesticity, 187. *See also* national identity

American Indian, 201, 202, 220
American Spelling Book, 6
American Sunday School Union, 200, 204
American Temperance Union, 70n2
American Tract Society, 211
American Woman's Home, The (Tompkins), 189
Anderson, Benedict, 156, 196
Anderson, Max, 132, 134f
Annual Report of Children's Aid Society, 172, 175n49, 176, 181, 183, 184
Appleton, Harriet, 19n32, 30, 35
Archer, Frederick Scott, 143
Ariés, Philippe, xviii
Augst, Thomas, 20n33, 31
Aunt Fanny's *Pop-gun* anthologies, 192, 193f
Avery, Gillian, 7

"Baby in the Brown Cottage, The," 95–96
"Baby in the Regiment, The" (Higginson), 224–27
"Baby's Drawer, The," 109, 110–12
Baldwin, James, 43
Balibar, Etienne, 199n23, 200
Barclay, William, 29
Barthes, Roland, 109, 112
Baym, Nina, 9n14
Beecher, Catharine, 188, 189
Beecher, Henry Warner, 201n28
Benjamin, Walter, 136, 145
Berger, John, 131
Bhabha, Homi, 176, 177, 202

231; missionaries' goal of converting black Americans, 198–200; morality presented in a racial framing, 211; racialized faith used to justify national inequities, 203; racial prejudice and, 201, 203–4; reading and racial equality, 8–9; scientific racialism, 199; white children taught to pity black children, 169–71. *See also* national identity in racial terms

Ragged Dick Series (Alger), 171

reading. *See* children and reading

Red Brothers, The, 200–201

"Red Frock, The," 75–76

Reynolds, David S., 71n4

Robbins, Sarah, 6n3

Roberts, Daniel T., 153n7

Rockwood, George, 116

Rollo books by Abbott, 3–4

"Romance" (Hawthorne), 55, 62, 63

Root, Marcus Aurelius, 135, 221

Rosaldo, Michelle, 211n48

Rose, Jacqueline, xvi, 65

Rosenzweig, Roy, 91n44

Rothman, Barbara Katz, 145n70

Ryan, Mary, 13n24

Sander's Second Reader, 11

Sargent, Carolyn, xix

Sargent, Lucius Manlius, 83–84, 93, 95

Scarlet Letter, The (Hawthorne), 53–54, 59, 60, 62

Scenes in the Wilderness, 194

Scheper-Hughes, Nancy, xix

School Boy, The (Abbott), 11

Schor, Esther, 102

scientific racialism, 199

Scudder, John, 188, 189, 210, 213, 215n54, 217

Sedgwick, Catherine, 28–29

Sedley Family, The, 75

Self-Denial; or Alice Wood and Her Missionary Society, 190

Sheumaker, Helen, 129n44

Sigourney, Lydia, 73, 94, 191, 214, 217n57

Simonds, Wendy, 145n70

Smith, Elizabeth Oakes, 162n25, 163

Snelling, Anna L., 114

social history of children: age consciousness, xxi; changes in the status of children, xvi–xviii; child-labor laws, xviii; children as consumers and commodities, xviii; child's relation to childhood, xxvi; expansion of the state and, xix; myth of child-centeredness, xix–xx; view of children with respect to culture, xv–xvi

Southworth, Albert S., 104n4

Spencer, F. R., 158, 161f

Spring, Gardiner, 206

Stanton, Elizabeth Cady, 77–78

Starr, Frederick Ratchford, 156, 172, 174, 175n49

states and children. *See various national identity headings*

Stebbins, Jane E., 99f

Steedman, Carolyn, xxiii, xxvi, 39, 145n70

Stern, Julia, 45, 47

Stewart, Susan, 129

Stocking, George W., 199

Stories about the Heathen and Their Children, 211

Stowe, Harriet Beecher, 188, 189; daguerreotype of her son, 109, 110f; depiction of family's capacity to mourn, 106–8; treatment of sentimental identification, 108–9; *Uncle Tom's Cabin,* 13, 106–9

Sturgis, Caroline, 123

Suleri, Sara, 211–12n48

Sullivan, William, 205

Sunday School (Boylan), 207n41

Sunday school texts: British tales of missionary work, 196; children called by missions to give money, 189–91, 214; city children presented as half-civilized, 197; conversion of heathens and, 209–10; domestic order related to international order, 189; focus on virtues, 7n6; heathens depicted as familially depraved, 211; maternal tenderness related to missionary zeal, 215; national anxieties indicated in stories, 186–87; national identity taught to children through, 206; promise of bringing Christian order to a heterogeneous nation, 196–97, 198; refusal to discuss slavery, 204; relation between domesticity and the adventurous in, 192–93; religious conversion related in racial terms, 203; sentimental nature of sto-

Sunday school texts (*continued*)
ries, 188–89; vision of a multiracial
Christianity, 205–6
suttee, 217
Swiss Family Robinson, The, 26

Takaki, Ronald T., 201n28
Tales for Little Readers (Scudder), 188, 210
Tate, Claudia, 49
Teichgraeber, Richard F., 128n41
temperance fiction: attempts to reach
drunkards through their children, 70–
71, 72, 77, 78, 82–85; celebration of female submissiveness, 92–93; concern
with creation of effeminate men, 93–
95, 96–98; difficulty in reaching drunkards, 82–83; disciplinary intimacy and,
83–84, 86–88; distribution means, 81–
82; domesticity in the middle class
and, 88; domestic violence correlated
with inebriation, 77–78; emotional
persuasion as a plot device, 75–76; formula of conversion, 70–71; gendered
nature of redemption stories, 92; incest
depicted in, 78–79, 80, 95; male violence reimagined as domestic love, 81;
monetary impact of drinking, 89–90;
moral suasion, 72–73, 76; new disciplinary intimacy, 74; readership, 81; reorganization of patriarchal norms, 100;
restraint reconciled with indulgence,
91; romanticization of childhood vulnerability, 74–75; sensuality implied
by the redemption plot, 71; stories
calling for legal and social reforms, 75;
vulnerability as power in, 95
Temperance Speaker, The, 94
Temperance Tales, 83–84
*Ten Books Beautifully Illustrated for Chil-
dren,* 196
Ten Nights in a Bar-room, 90–91
Thomas, Nicholas, 210
Thoreau, Henry David, 19n32
Thorn, Margaretta, 47
Tompkins, Jane, 189
Trumbull, Louisa Jane (Jenny), 20, 22–23,
24f, 26, 31, 35, 141

Uncle Tom's Cabin (Stowe), 13, 106–9
Union Speller, 25

*United Nations Convention on the Rights of
the Child,* xxiv n21
Universal History. See *Peter Parley's Universal History*

Van Wart, Irving and Ames, 29
Virginia: or The Power of Grace, 202
virtues. *See* morality

Wald, Priscilla, 201n28
Washingtonians, 73n7
WCTU (Woman's Christian Temperance
Union), 73n8
Webster, Noah, 6
Wexler, Laura, 188n4
Whicher, Stephen, 126n37
Whitman, Walt, xiv, xix, xxvii, 97–98
Whitney, Edward Tompkins, 116, 221n1
Whittier, John Greenleaf, 15
Wiggin, Charles, 170, 171n40
Wilson, George Mason, 41
Wilson, Harriet: ideas of childhood, 42, 44;
literary goals, 41–42, 46, 51; mother-
hood, 42, 50, 51; verification of iden-
tity 40–41. See also *Our Nig*
Winnicott, D. W., 18, 63
Wishy, Bernard, 13n24, 207n41
Woman's Christian Temperance Union
(WCTU), 73n8
Woman's Union Missionary Society,
216n55
women: circumvented in temperance
fiction, 95; moral suasion seen as
women's work, 72–73; role in mis-
sionary work, 216n55, 220; as a sym-
bol of America, 225
Wonder Book, The (Hawthorne), 63–64
Wood, Alice, 190
Woods, Benjamin, 169
Worcester vs. Georgia, 201n28
Wright, Julia McNair, 93n47
writing for children. *See* childhood and
writing

Young, Samuel, 211
Youth's Keepsake (Hawthorne), 56
Youth's Temperance Banner, The, 83–84

Zboray, Ronald, 7
Zeisberger, 194